AF594150

HOME *Sweet* HOME ALABAMA

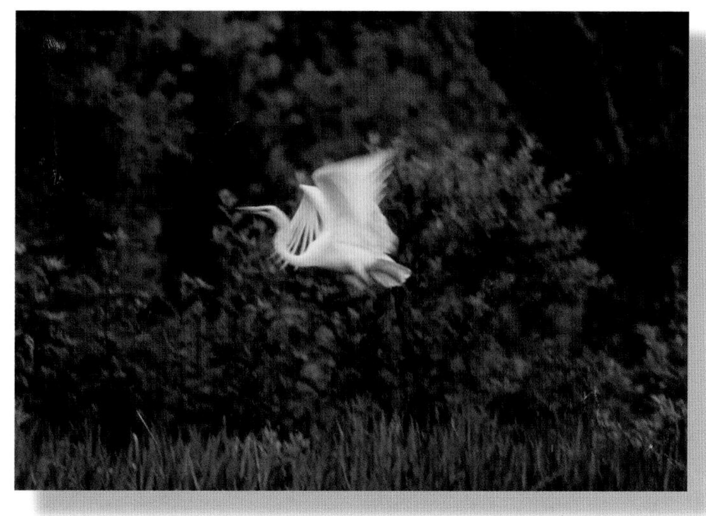

This book would not have been possible if it were not for my three children: Zade, Dury, and Demi. Their love and support have not only enabled me to do the travel necessary to produce this book, but have given me the time and strength needed to follow through with days and days of editing. I would also like to thank Ellen Sullivan, whose amazing ingenuity kept my inspiration alive through the ups and downs of putting the book together. Also, many thanks to Scott Fuller, whose beautiful design enabled my photographs to shine. Many thanks as well go to all the people featured in this book; they are what make Alabama feel so much like home. Finally, a thank-you goes to my studio manager, Hannah Slamen, who beautifully handled all the logistics and details throughout the planning and shooting phases.

SWEETWATER
PRESS

Home Sweet Home Alabama

Produced by Cliff Road Books

ISBN-13: 978-1-58173-493-5
ISBN-10: 1-58173-493-X

Design by Scott Fuller

Cover Photo: Dreamweaver Stables, Leeds, AL, owner Paula Padelford

Printed in China

HOME *Sweet* HOME ALABAMA

Karim Shamsi-Basha

Foreword by Steve Chiotakis

SWEETWATER
PRESS

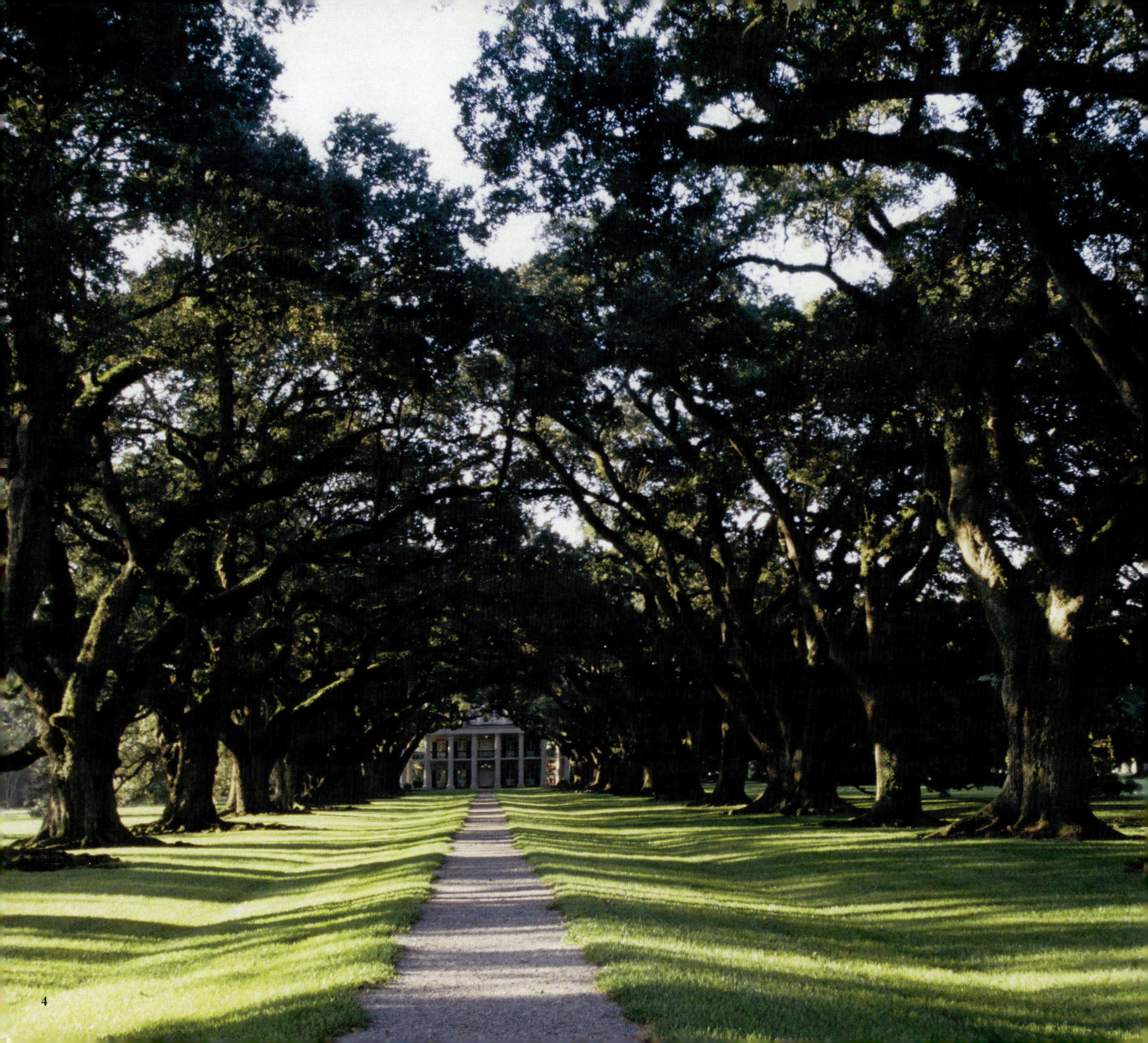

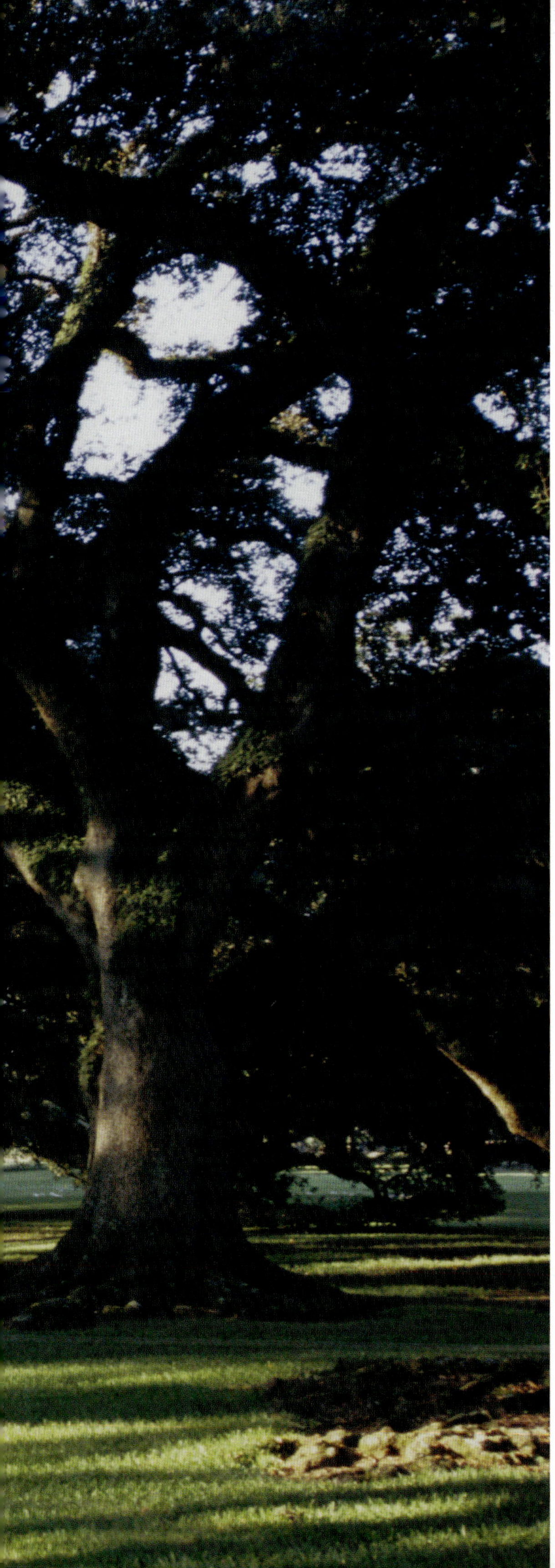

Foreword

STEVE CHIOTAKIS

Adorned with geographic and characteristic beauty, Alabama is kissed with the essentials of a near-perfect existence. Peppered with confidence and zeal, the people of this place have blessings that only those who live here – or have been here – can identify. Truly, Alabama is home to some of the finest people on Earth. Some of their faces you'll see in this book; others you'll have to see for yourself. No matter, it won't be hard to find the special people and places that make up this state.

I came to Alabama as a kid, rife with the memories of a northern steel town, which I thought would translate to this southern industrial powerhouse. But Birmingham is gentle and polished. Colors have changed from black and white to hues of blues and greens and reds. Skies have cleared, trees have been preserved, and mountains have been cut to the core to allow progress and beauty all at the same time. This place magically turns on a whim one way, then another and another, as her people collide and meld, and see the future together. People who come here, stay, and see, and evolve like their host.

I must admit, I wasn't thrilled about Alabama when I first arrived in 1978. But I had no choice about being here; my parents had plucked me from the confines of my comfort zone to this place that no one knew. "Where's Alabama?" I recall being asked. Or, "Why are you going *there*?" Indeed, all of my friends and memories, and my way of life were in Indiana. I remember thinking how funny people talked down here, and how everything was about football (and not White Sox or Cubs baseball). I had questions of my own: Where'd all the snow go? Or, How could I use my toboggan to careen down the big hill if snow only fell once every ten years? The most important question: Why are they calling a winter cap a toboggan? The idea of Alabama was insane to me. I was determined to move back one way or another.

Ah, but Alabama is contagious; it never gave me the chance to pull away.

[SPRING HILL COLLEGE, MOBILE]

And for nearly two decades, as broadcaster and reporter, I've had the opportunity to see much of this state as a spectator and witness to its wonder. I know a lot of people who believe it to be a welcome respite from some of the harsh environs elsewhere. We are small town and slow-paced – or big town and slow-paced. Our lives intermingled are more important than the rush to be homogenous. We are cultures from afar and values from around that evade the train wreck of happenstance that occurs in other metropolises. The ties are historical, mental, and ethereal.

As Alabamians, think of what's in our midst.

On a given evening in the Wiregrass, one old schoolhouse serves some mean northern beans and relish (yes, the irony), and the town folk talk about it and everything else. In Guntersville, a stroll past a fishing pier exhibits the intersection of perseverance and soul. The catch of the day is tradition, and coming back when the getting can only get better. In Bibb County, small churches that smolder find forgiveness in their foundations. What do the folks in Vance and Lincoln and Hope Hull have in common? They're driven to succeed. How do you get to Dauphin Island? By being very quiet.

I've logged many a quiet mile in Alabama.

One of my favorite drives starts in Montgomery and ends in Selma, and meanders around Fort Deposit and Hayneville – sleepy enclaves now that at one time boiled with hostility. But the elasticity of time and change – and, of course, forgiveness – permeates the soul like a dash of salt on some vine-ripened summer tomatoes. Easy for me, a Greek man who never experienced the painful – and, to some, the incomplete – road to equality. The tracing of those steps taken decades before me doesn't do the movement justice — justice being the goal – but it reminds me time and again that history is still drawing up its plans for Alabama.

There are other, shorter drives that have sustained me in my Alabama life. For many years, one of my favorite rituals was an early Sunday morning drive to church. On a dew-dropped spring morning, there's nothing like the natural sermon of Little River Canyon, where the finger of God Himself carved a path to my redemption. Rocky edges and waterfalls show us its age and maturation. Listen carefully...do you hear it? It's the sound of the white tops of hydroelectricity, the rapids of slow evolution. But the only power generated is within. It's easy to get lost in the bite of nature Alabama style. People are few, sunlight is rich, and ideas are limitless. The news is good if you're listening. The views are better if you look, everywhere.

Ascending Cheaha, the mind disappears into thin air. The breeze guides from one crest to another, and you awake to find yourself high above anything else. The smell of honeysuckle and wild privet and kudzu slaps you in the face, and you know the fragrance is home. The crunch of needles signifies what was, and the pines overhead, what is. You're brazen to endure the path, but this is Alabama, and exploration is what you do.

It's easy to do here.

When I frequently see the beaches of Gulf Shores, Orange Beach, and Fort Morgan, I know they are engrained in the very soul of our state. The sun pierces the morning sky like a flashlight to what is real, overseeing the smooth, ritualistic transition from sea to sand. It is nowhere close to the other end of the state, lest it hum the same tune as the places within the natural and unnatural boundaries. That's right, commonality keeps us whole. Offshore, seagulls deliberate between fish and bread. Onshore, the spectators marvel at their humility and the rise of the great wall of progress (or excess) that separates the masses. Fishermen and fish eaters make their way to the joint with the best catch, the best grill, and the sweetest smile. It's hard to be sad in a place where the earth, the sea, and the sky form the triumvirate of eloquence and purpose.

Yes, Alabama is near-perfect. Not content with complacency, not intent on changing too quickly. And certainly not without its problems. But we rise above the things we think separate us and focus on the ideals and the bonds that keep us within these lines, in each other's thoughts. The people I've come to know, come to befriend, in Birmingham or Huntsville, Aliceville or Enterprise, are as much in my heart as if they moved here with me from Indiana so many years ago.

You know what, scratch that. Where's Indiana?

[GULF SHORES]

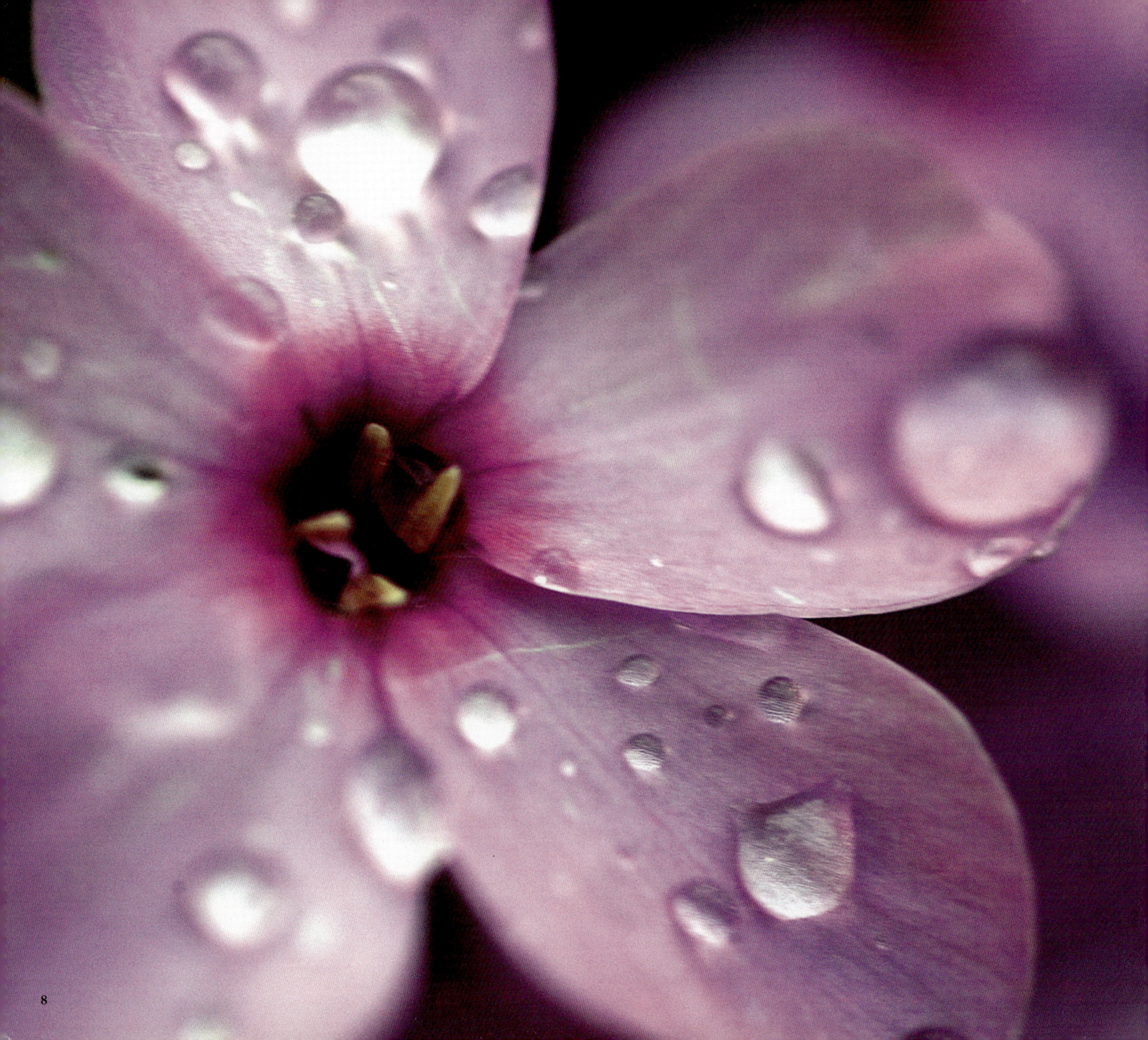

Alabamian at Heart

KARIM SHAMSI-BASHA

Alabama…a place where the sun rises every day to cover dewy fields, skyscrapers, and freckled-face kids on their way to school singing "You are my sunshine."

I have called Alabama home for the last seventeen years of my life, and it has been a period of discovering, achieving, and growing. I have spent better than half of my life in this country, after coming from Damascus, Syria, to Knoxville, Tennessee, to study engineering. Some days I think of myself as an Arab-American; others, an American-Arab. I do not lean towards one term more than the other; I just enjoy the mixture of cultures that interweaves into my being. When I think of Alabama, I think of a million little pieces of a beautiful puzzle fitting together to form a canvas. This book you are holding attempts to show off the many colors of this life-canvas, including the people and places of Alabama. My hope is that you will leave this painting assured that Alabama, for reasons too many to count, is also a sweet home to have.

Alabama is a place where the old South met and fell in love with the new. A place that hung on to its traditions while merging into the fast lane of hip trends. And a place where an Indian can grow up next to a Scandinavian and know that the differences between them are not as important as the similarities.

I moved to Birmingham in 1989 to work as a photojournalist for the *Birmingham Post-Herald*. What I found was diversity that defied the way non-Southerners think of this place. I delved into what Birmingham has to offer: superb education, excellent business opportunities, sophisticated culture in music and the arts, as well as sports and the outdoors. Young generations marry their allegiance to societal traditions with contemporary ways of thinking. This new South concept has resulted in tolerance and acceptance ranking high with the people of a state that had to redefine itself after the civil rights struggles of the sixties.

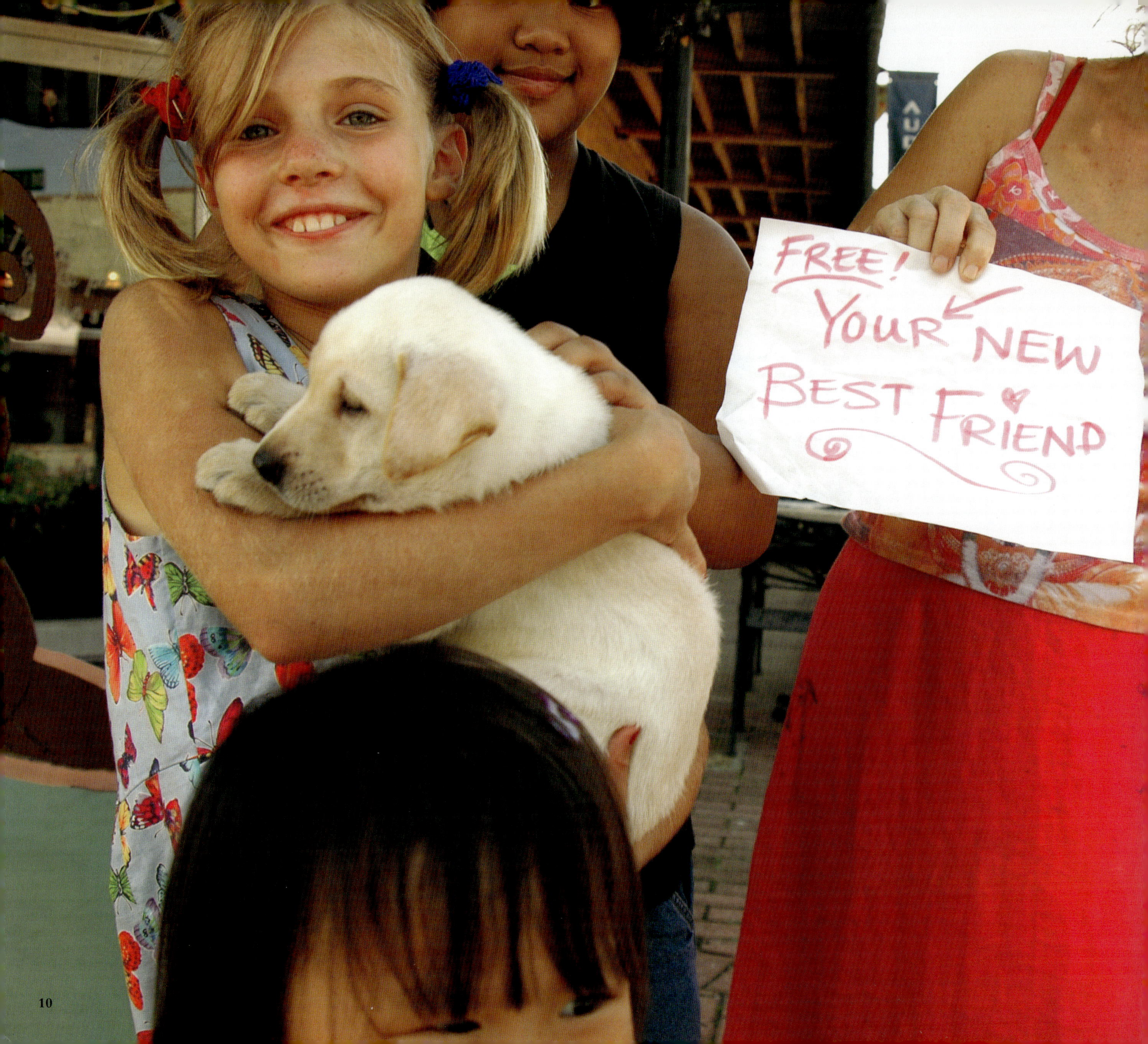
FREE!
YOUR NEW
BEST FRIEND

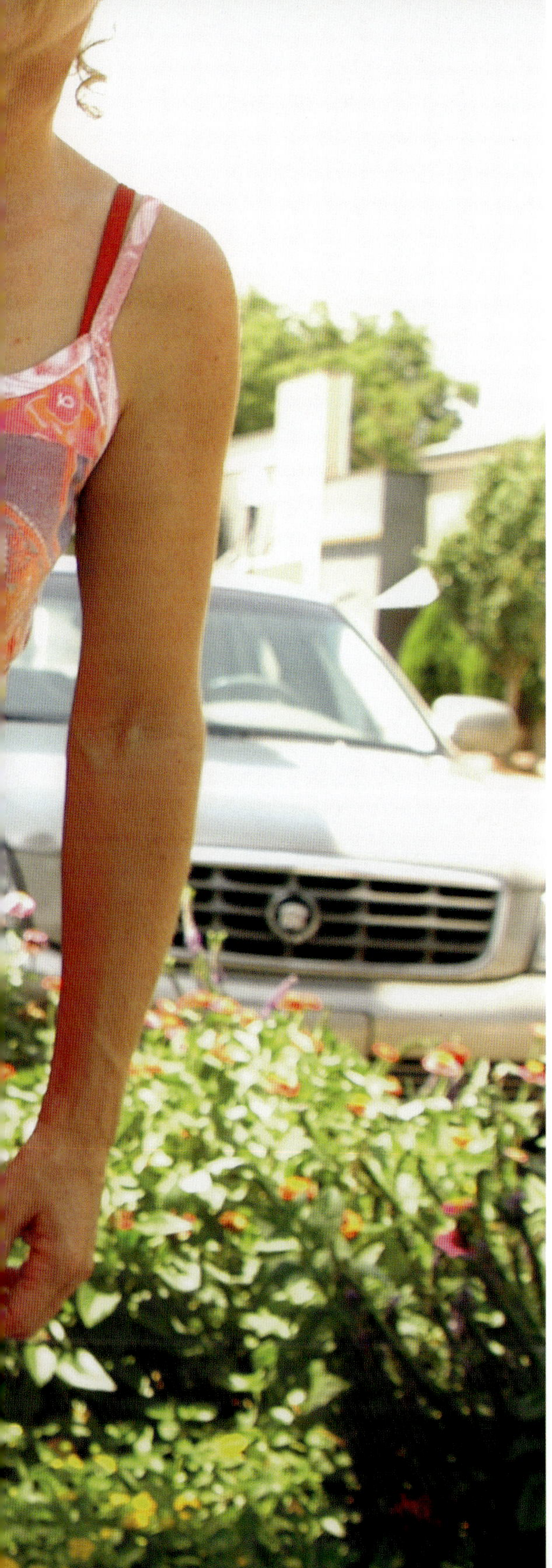

Alabama is a place where young children say "yes ma'am" and "no sir," and where freckles just mean you played where the sun shone for days and days and days.

My five years at the *Birmingham Post-Herald* were packed with stories chronicling life in this state. I covered political issues and football games, as well as stories on heroes and tragedies. I photographed farmers, lawyers, families, lakes, beaches, mountains, and much more. I will never forget the first time I received a "yes sir" from a six year-old. I looked at his mother with wonder in my eyes. She looked back and said, "You are not from around here, are you?"

Alabama is a place where secrets are kept, where a smile invites, and where the word "hospitality" finds a home other than in a dictionary.

When I came to the South from Damascus, I noticed everyone smiling at me the entire time. People I did not know were smiling as they passed by. The only explanation I had was this: I must be an extremely handsome fellow. It was not until about six months later that my roommate broke it to me: "We are just too friendly down here." I have been welcomed into the homes of just about everyone I have met to photograph. It is true that Alabamians "do not know a stranger."

Alabama is a place that introduced the phrase "Y'all come back now...hear?" to the English language, and where "down yonder" means "over there."

My coworkers at the newspaper would have fun with what were dubbed "Karimisms," my mistakes in the English language, and more importantly, in the Southern English language. They would ask me how I liked it in Alabama so far; my answer was "Yes, it is very far...(from Syria!)." I looked for words like "ain't" and "y'all" in the dictionary to no avail. Seventeen years later, the rate of making mistakes has slowed down, but I still cause a stir and a laugh among my friends every once in a while. Character of a place is marked by, among other things, how the locals define themselves. Alabamians have a plethora, or should I say bunches, of original words that define the language of this state; one of my favorites is the greeting early in the day: "mo'nin."

Alabama is a place where "Southern" is not a geographical term...it just means "charming," where the "belles" are stunning, and where opening the door for a lady is still gentlemanly.

I love all the traditions we adhere to down South...especially in Alabama. My father always taught me to be a gentleman and give my seat up in the bus for a lady, or rise

[FAIRHOPE]

when my date returns to the table, or hold the door open for the woman behind me. It was pleasant to find those customs practiced here just as they are in Syria. This is just one of the many reasons why Alabama feels so much like home.

Alabama is a place where grits, collards, and fried chicken are no less an offering than Brie cheese and a glass of Bordeaux. Where desserts range from chess and apple pie, to pot de creme and Baklava. Where football is loved as much as ballet, and where melody is curried with nuances of sound, rhythm, and Southern hymns.

My mother, Laila, was worried about the cuisine I was going to encounter in Alabama. "I will send you packages of food…regularly," she would say in my early years. Quickly I realized that there was no need for those care packages. Fusion of foods and the melting pot of cultures they come from have taken hold of this place. Delectable Southern favorites are mixed with exotic and international flavors to result in a taste unique to this area of the world. Just like food, the arts are alive and well in Alabama. From world-class dancers and musicians to renowned writers, singers, and actors, Alabama is home for many well-known names like Hank Williams, Fanny Flagg, and Courteney Cox.

Alabama…a place where the Tide defends its territory, and Tigers roam the plains.

You hear phrases like: "Football is religion down South," without knowing what it means until you attend a football game at Alabama or Auburn, and then it all becomes clear. Alabamians take football seriously. It is more than a sport…it is a way of life for many. The state has graduated some of the finest players in the country from Bart Starr to Bo Jackson. Attending a football game in Tuscaloosa or Auburn is a proud declaration of belonging…of being an Alabamian. Other sports are thriving as well, from soccer and lacrosse to track and recently, Olympic snow-sledding.

Alabama is a place where "yongens" respect their Ma's and Pa's, and where traditions are passed down from old to young like an unstoppable river raging on top but flowing calmly down below. It's a place where family can mean grandmotherly love, brotherly bickering, and reunions with so many people you have to wear a nametag. Trees are cherished in genealogy here as much as they are in the deep woods.

I fell in love with family bonds in the South. The strength of those bonds kindles feelings of closeness and intimacy. Sunday dinners, a term meaning Sunday noon meal, is still a constant event in the lives of most families. Alabama in particular, and the South in general, could be the model place to define what family should mean. It means more than

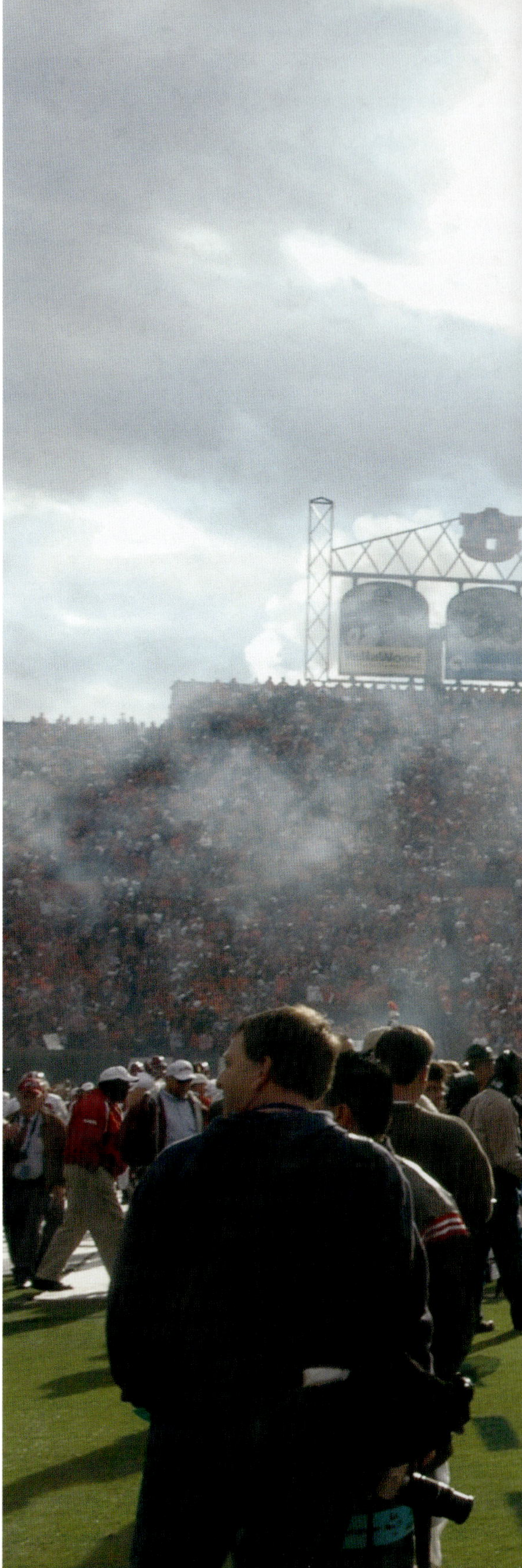

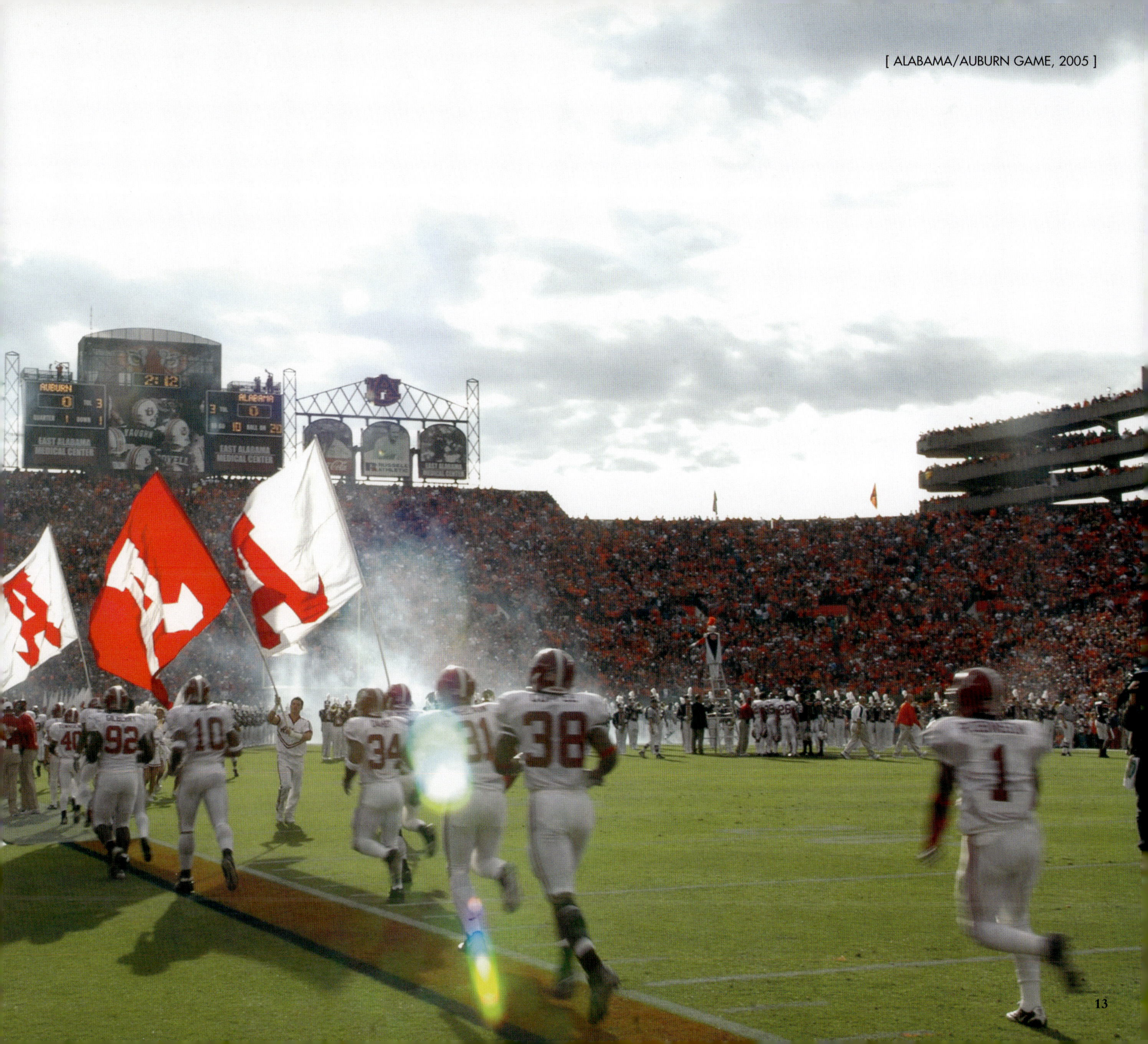
AUBURN
ALABAMA
2:12
EAST ALABAMA MEDICAL CENTER
EAST ALABAMA MEDICAL CENTER

blood…it means life with its ups and downs. People in this state have figured out it's easier to ride the roller coaster of life with your loved ones than to ride alone. Family was a huge part of my upbringing thousands of miles away from this place. It brings tears to my eyes when I see the same happening here.

Alabama is a place where cities hustle and bustle, and lazy small towns defy busyness to smell the gardenias.

I live in Homewood, a suburb of Birmingham that is a cross between Mayberry and San Francisco. Everyone knows everyone else. Your neighbors will pick up your mail when you are away, they will make you dinner if you are sick, and they will wave and holler your name when you drive by. At the same time, there is a degree of sophistication, which earmarks the high education level in this city. Shops and schools rank with the best in the country.

A place where Mercedes and Honda are building cars, and NASA is reaching for the moon.

Alabama plants turn out everything from cars and manufactured homes to small appliances and parts for the space shuttle. Huntsville is the home to the US Space and Rocket Center, one of the top space research facilities in the world. Birmingham is considered a phenomenal banking center, and is home to UAB, one of the country's most advanced medical schools. From Florence to Montgomery and Mobile, and from Dothan to Decatur and Anniston, Alabama is home to some of the world's finest medical, industrial, agricultural, and educational facilities.

A place where churches abound next to mosques and synagogues, and where a Buddhist monk can find a home.

The place that coined the term "Bible Belt" is also home to Muslim mosques, Jewish synagogues, Buddhist temples, Quaker communities, and just about every denomination on earth. Religion plays an integral part in the lives of those who practice it. As a photojournalist, I have had the pleasure of being an observer of most of these religions. While they differ in principle, they all have a common thread. The people that practice these different religions all share the same basic need for a higher power in their lives as they pursue peace. This noble quest is exemplified beautifully in this state.

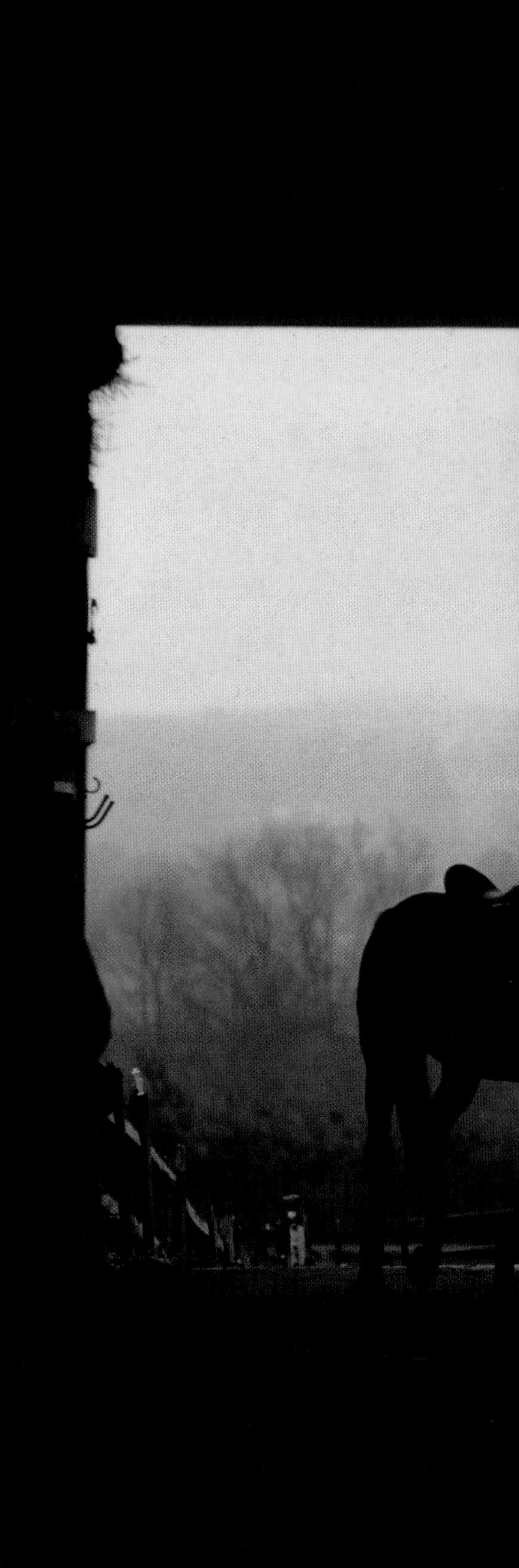

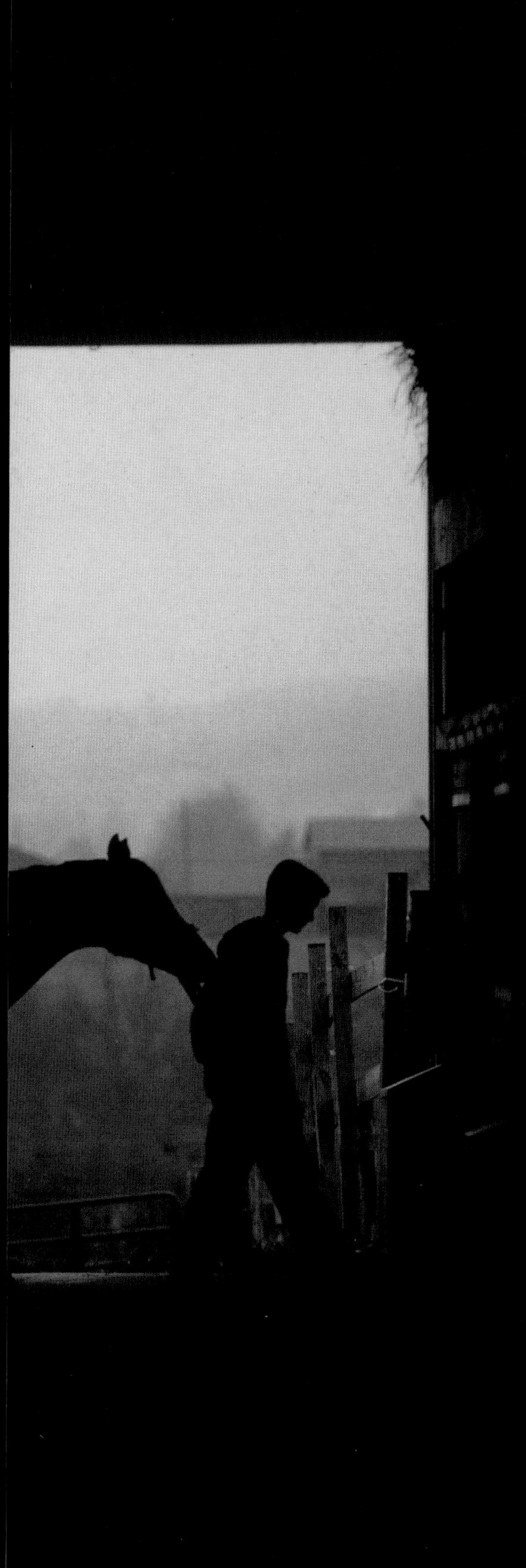

A place where the crickets can keep you up at night, and where the peepers and swamp frogs are louder than a rock 'n' roll band.

Alabama prides itself on the outdoor life it offers. Through years of photographing this stunning place, I have come to discover why Alabama is a hidden secret: because the locals want it to stay that way. Not that Alabamians do not welcome visitors — they are just aware of all the conservation efforts that take place to keep and restore the natural beauty of this state. Treasures like the Cahaba River, Little River Canyon, Mentone, the beaches, the Tennessee Valley, and the Sipsey wilderness are just a few of hundreds of areas tourists flock to every year. When you visit Alabama, you fall in love with its beauty. When you live in Alabama, you fall in love with its beauty every day of your life.

Alabama is a place where history was written so some chapters are coveted for a repeat, and some are learned from.

Alabama has had its struggles with civil rights, but with places like the Civil Rights Institute in Birmingham and numerous others around the state celebrating varied cultures, Alabama prides itself on understanding and tolerance. My testimony as an Arab-American living in Alabama is this: despite all of the events that could cloud the reputation of an Arab-American, like 9/11, the war in Iraq, and the Palestinian-Israeli conflict, I have lived a life full of friendship, loyalty, acceptance, tolerance, and positive attitude. With respect to prejudice, we may not yet be where we need to be, but we have made great strides. I know that my children will not struggle just because they have an Arabic heritage. Their life will be just as respected, cherished, and loved as mine.

In this book, you will meet some of Alabama's finest people. Some names you will recognize; others, you will be glad to meet. From farmers and doctors to athletes and judges, they all have one thing in common: They all love Alabama, and they all are proud to tell you why they call this state home.

Alabama is "home" to me...a place where my children will grow up and reach the stars...a place where the sun shines...a place that is dear to me. It's a place where the sun sets every night over the dewy fields and the skyscrapers, and where the freckled-face kids go to sleep listening to the sound of "Amazing Grace" with smiles on their faces.

[BIRMINGHAM]

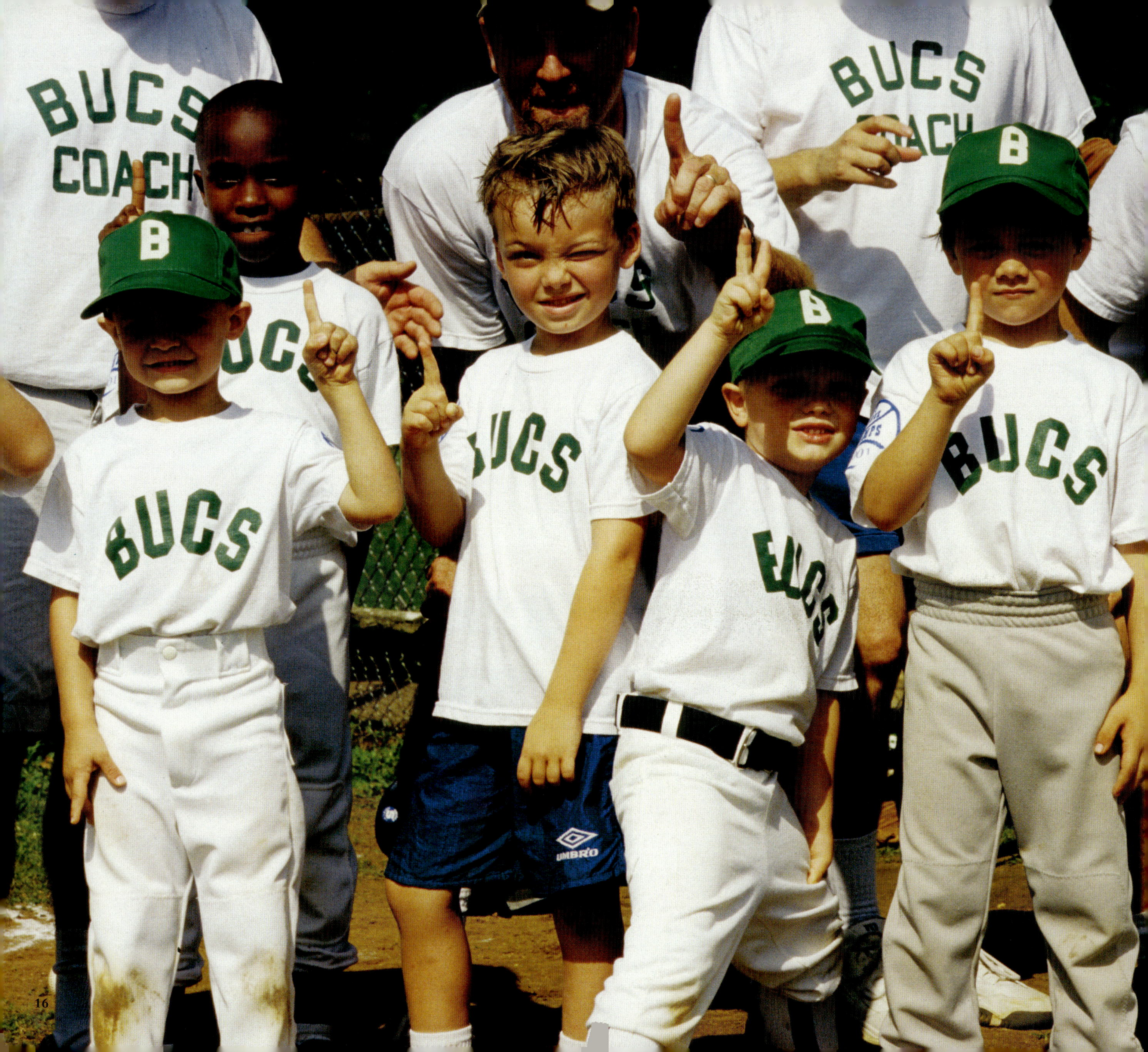
BUCS
COACH
BUCS
COACH
B
BUCS
BUCS
BUCS
BUCS
BUCS
UMBRO

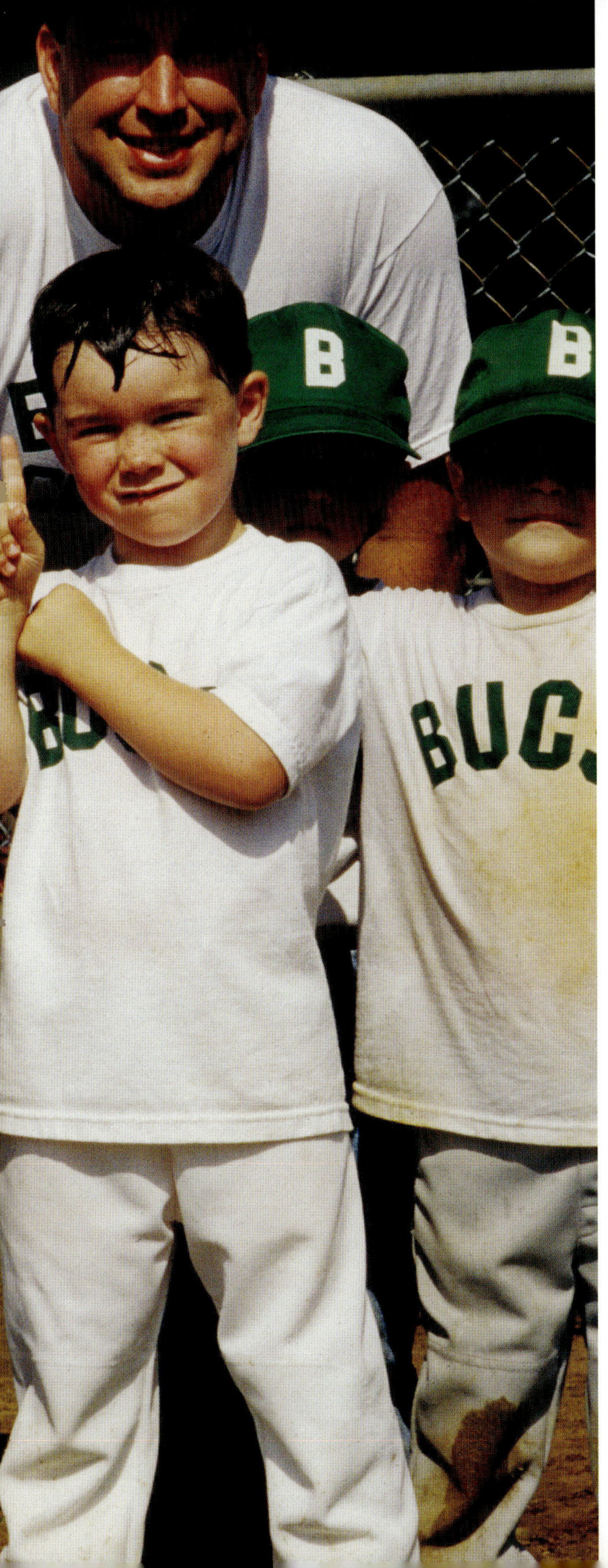

Who We Are

We are a people so real, some say we're eccentric. But we know who we are. We keep changing, but we keep the important things the same. We are all different, and we respect that. We say hello to neighbors and hold the door open for strangers. We play fair. We are moving fast. But we never lose our vision.

[HOMEWOOD BUCS, JOY LEAGUE T-BALL]

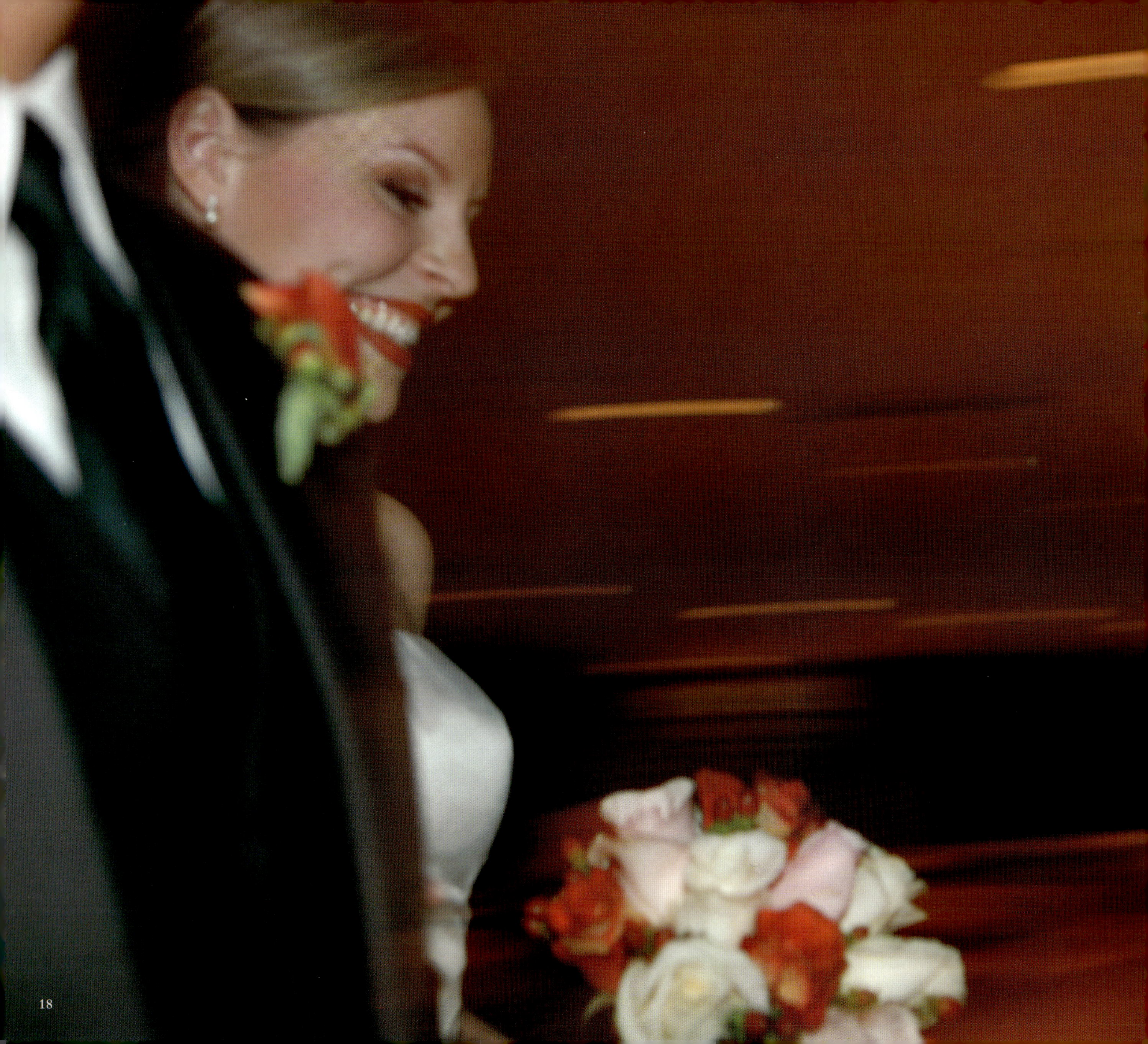

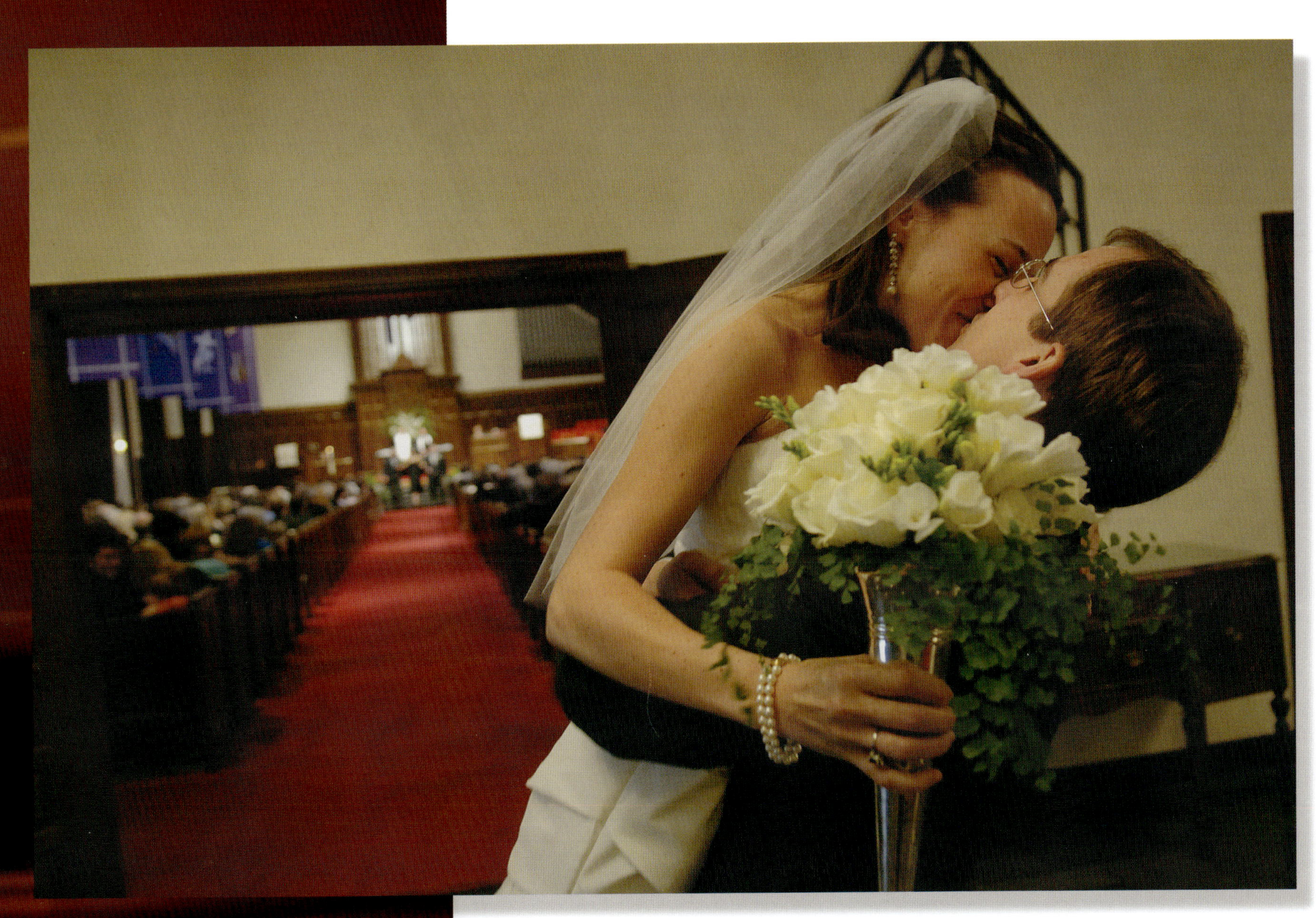

We love each other.

[COURTNEY, *LEFT*; WADE & JULIA, *ABOVE*]

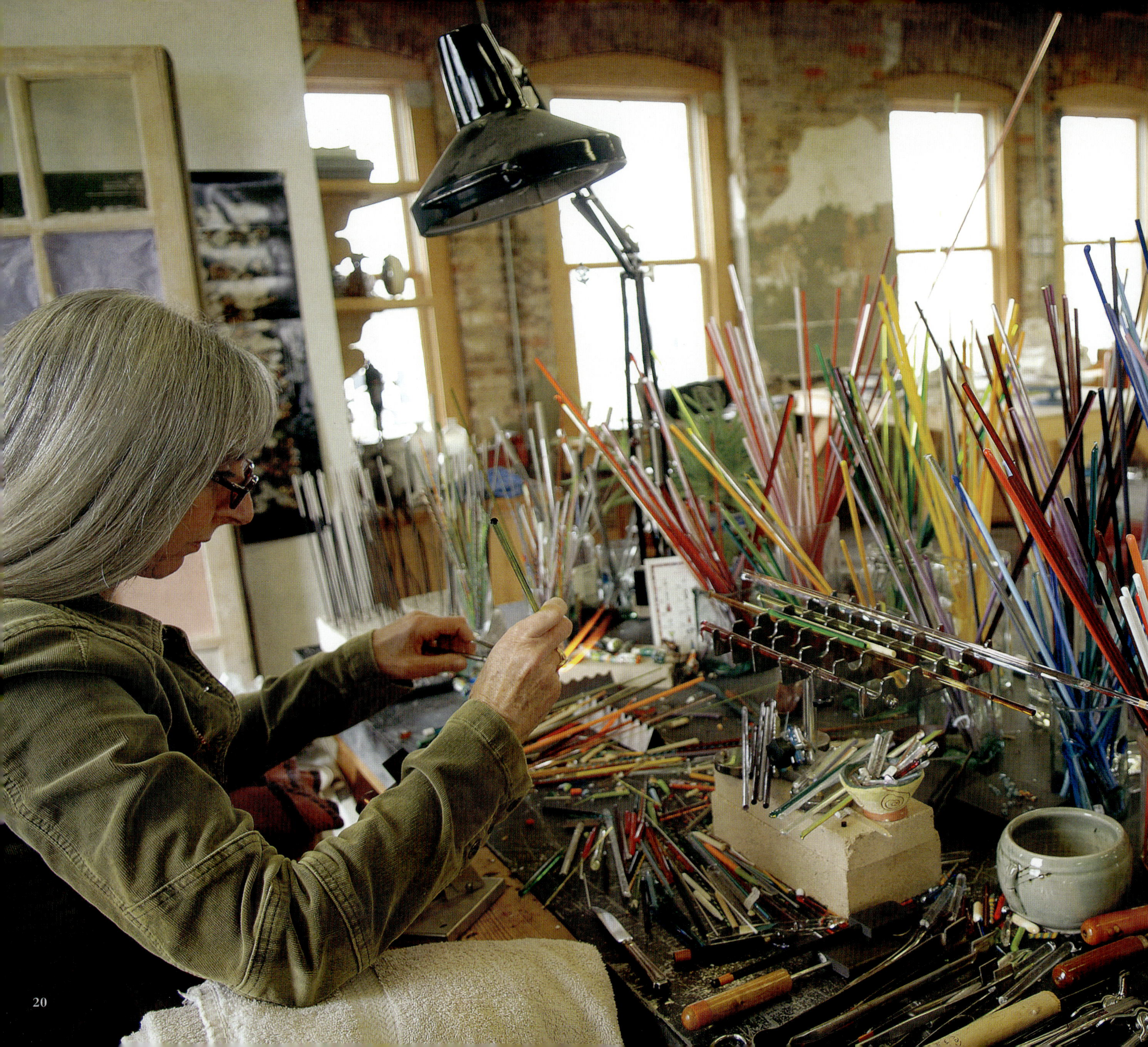

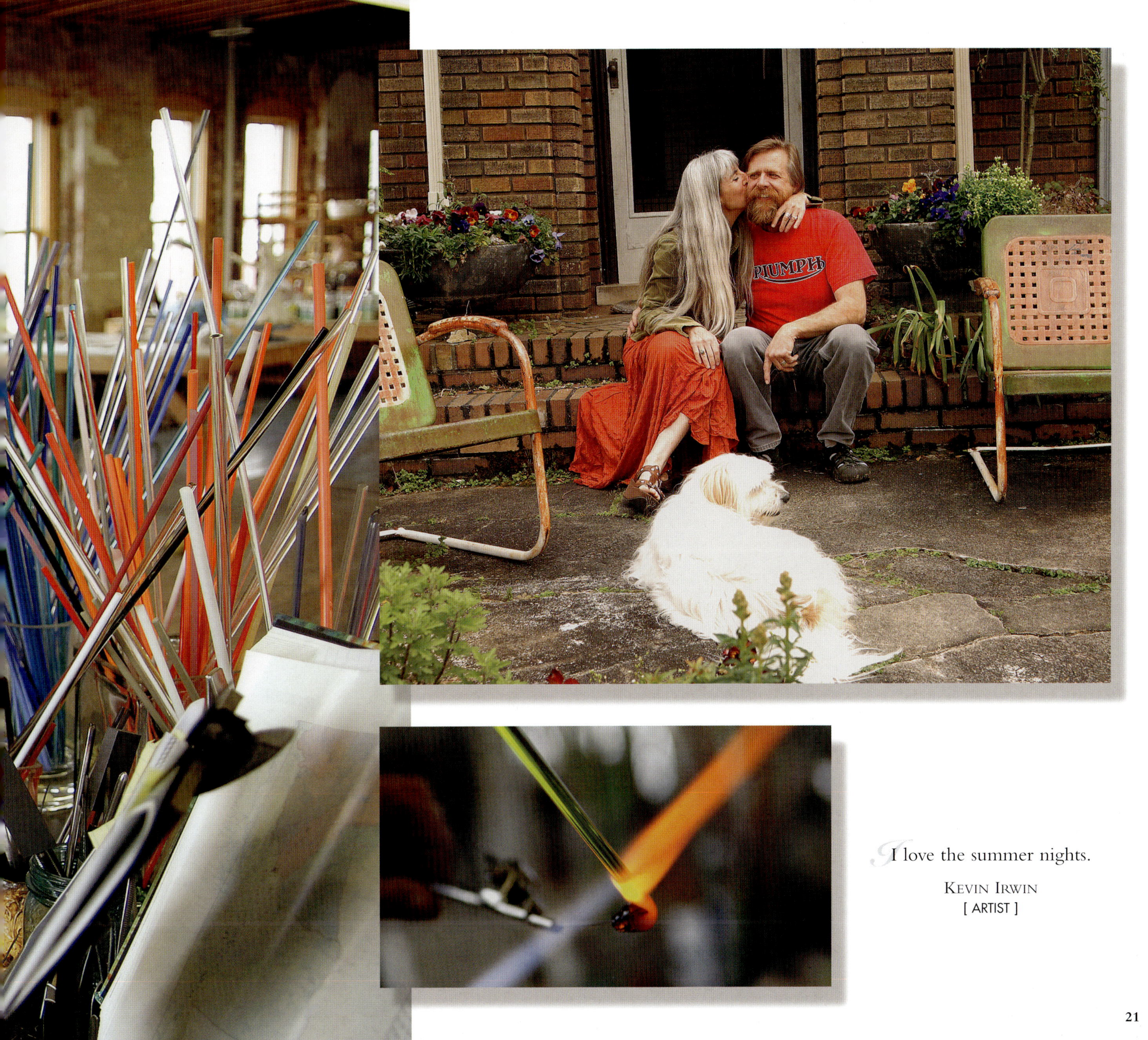

I love the summer nights.

Kevin Irwin
[ARTIST]

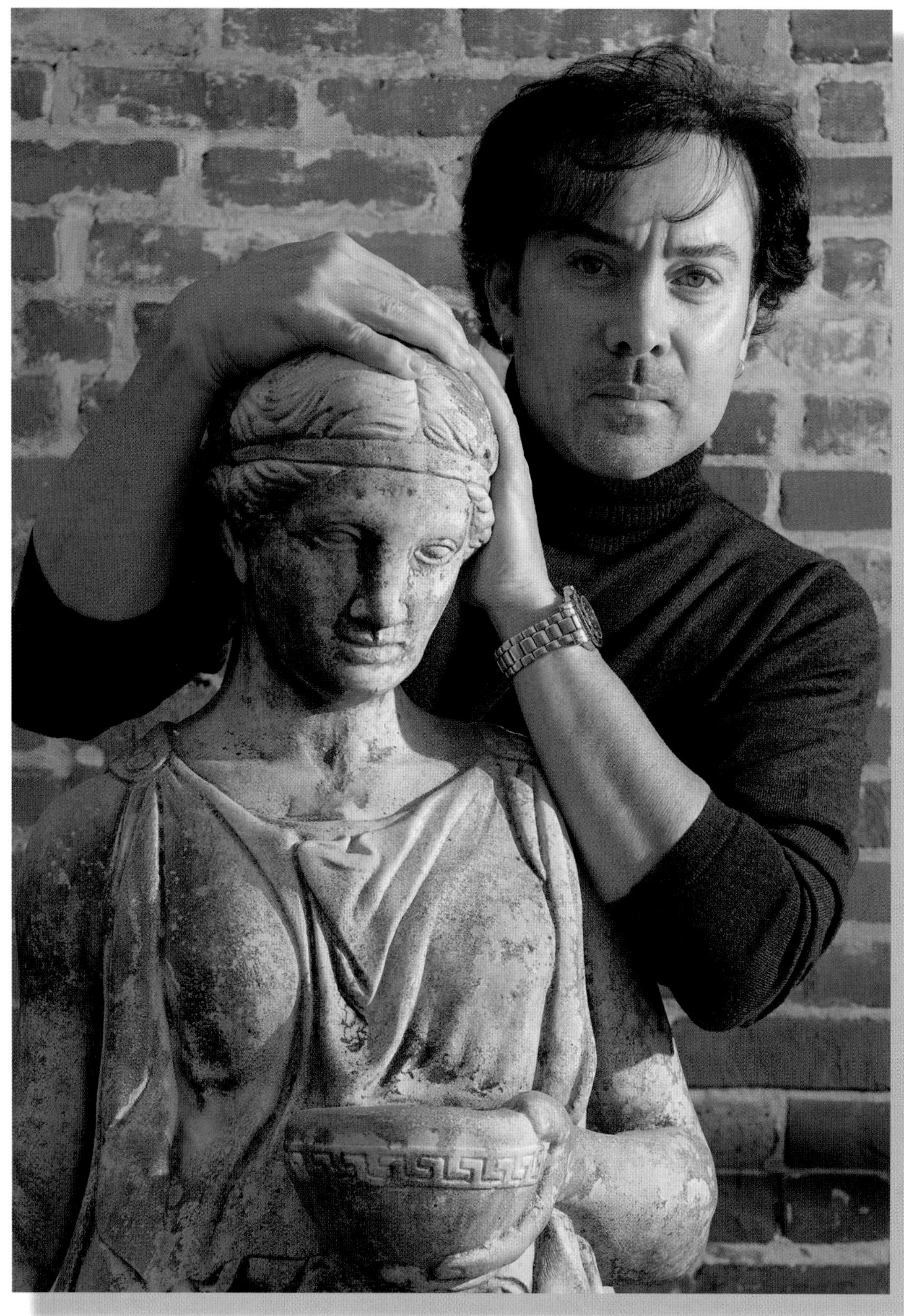

After living in New York for fourteen years, I can appreciate Alabama's open space and fresh air. The fact is, Alabama has a serene way of living that calms my soul!

DELOAIN BURGESS
[HAIRSTYLIST]

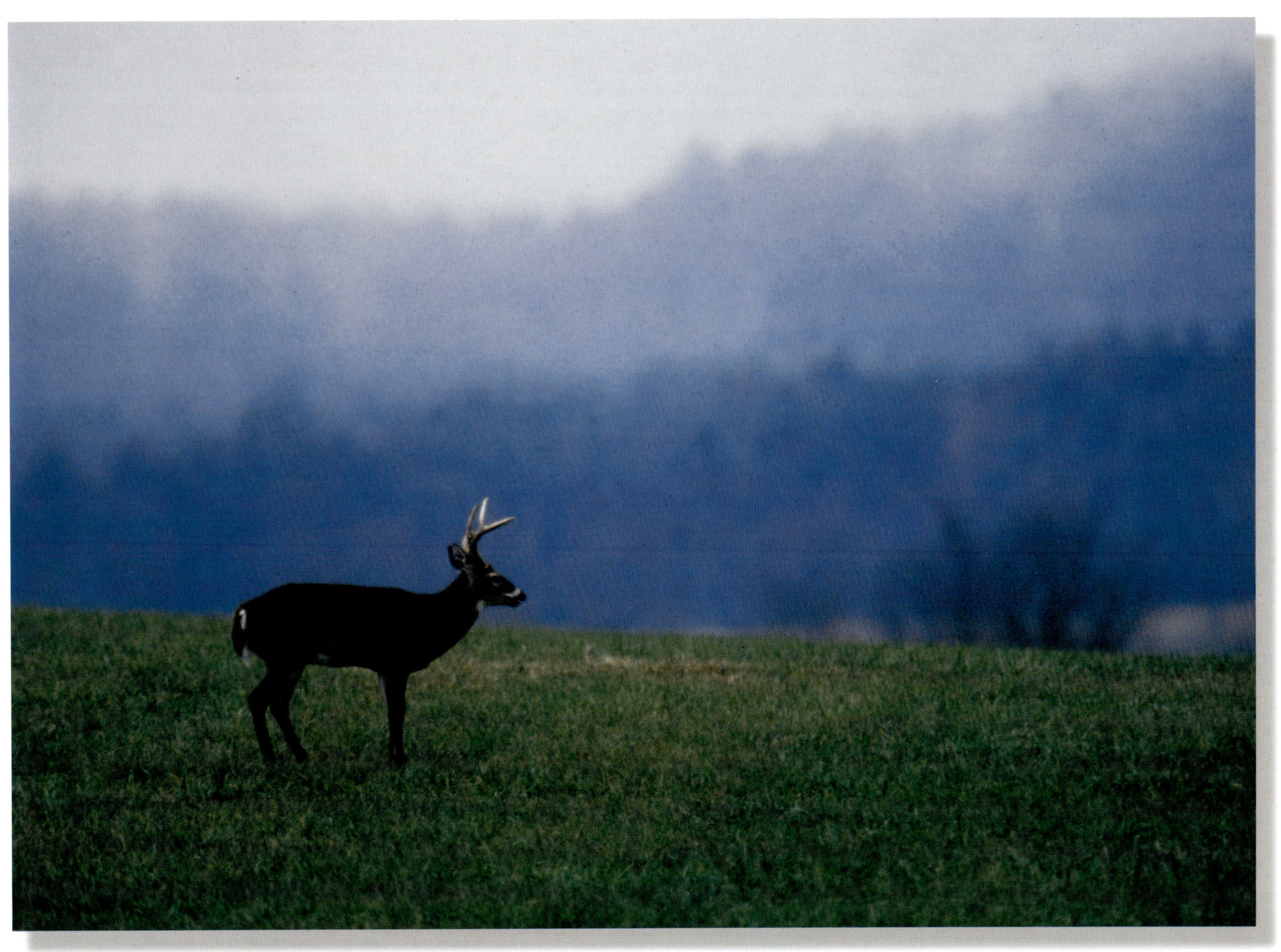

[MENTONE]

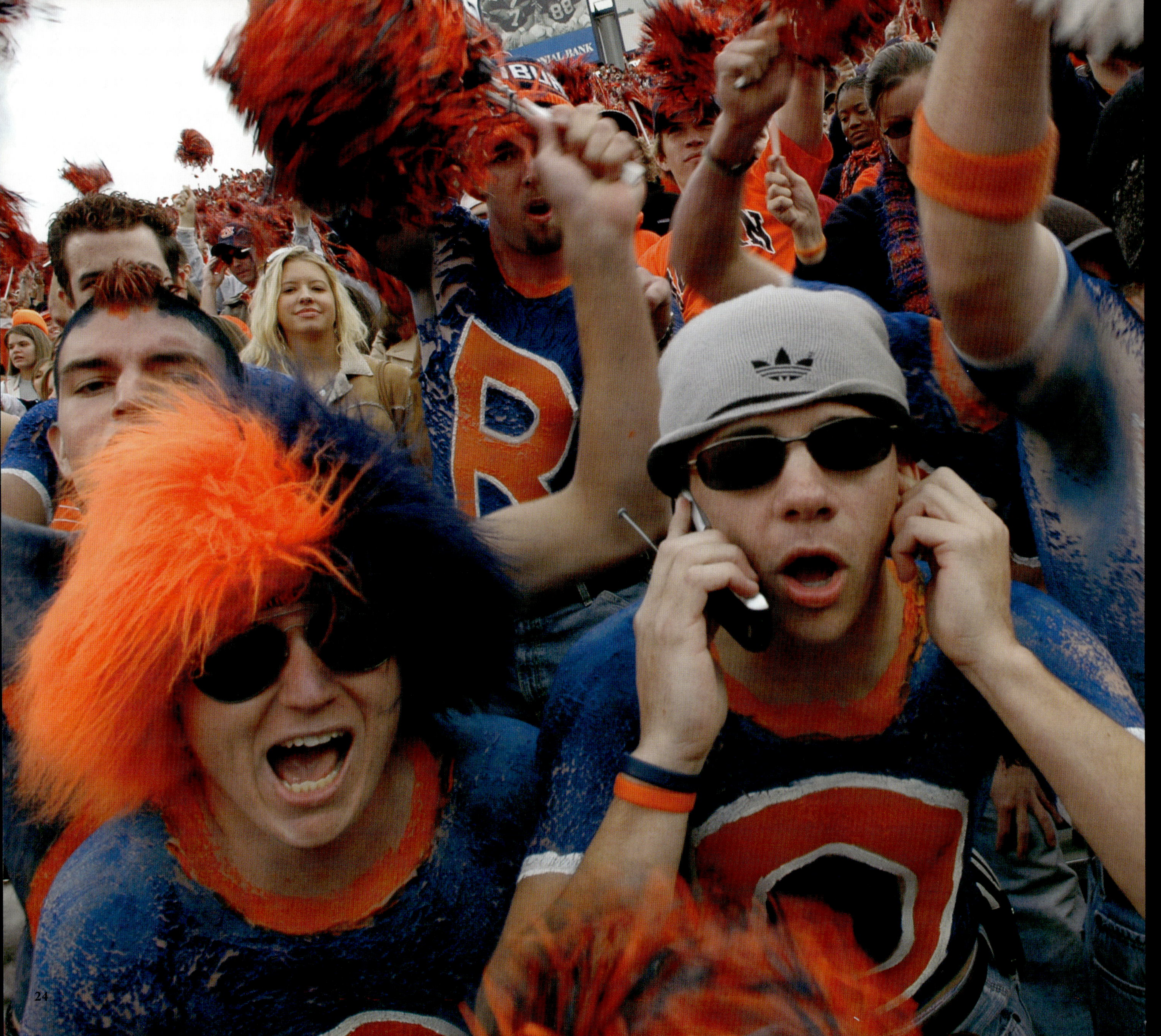

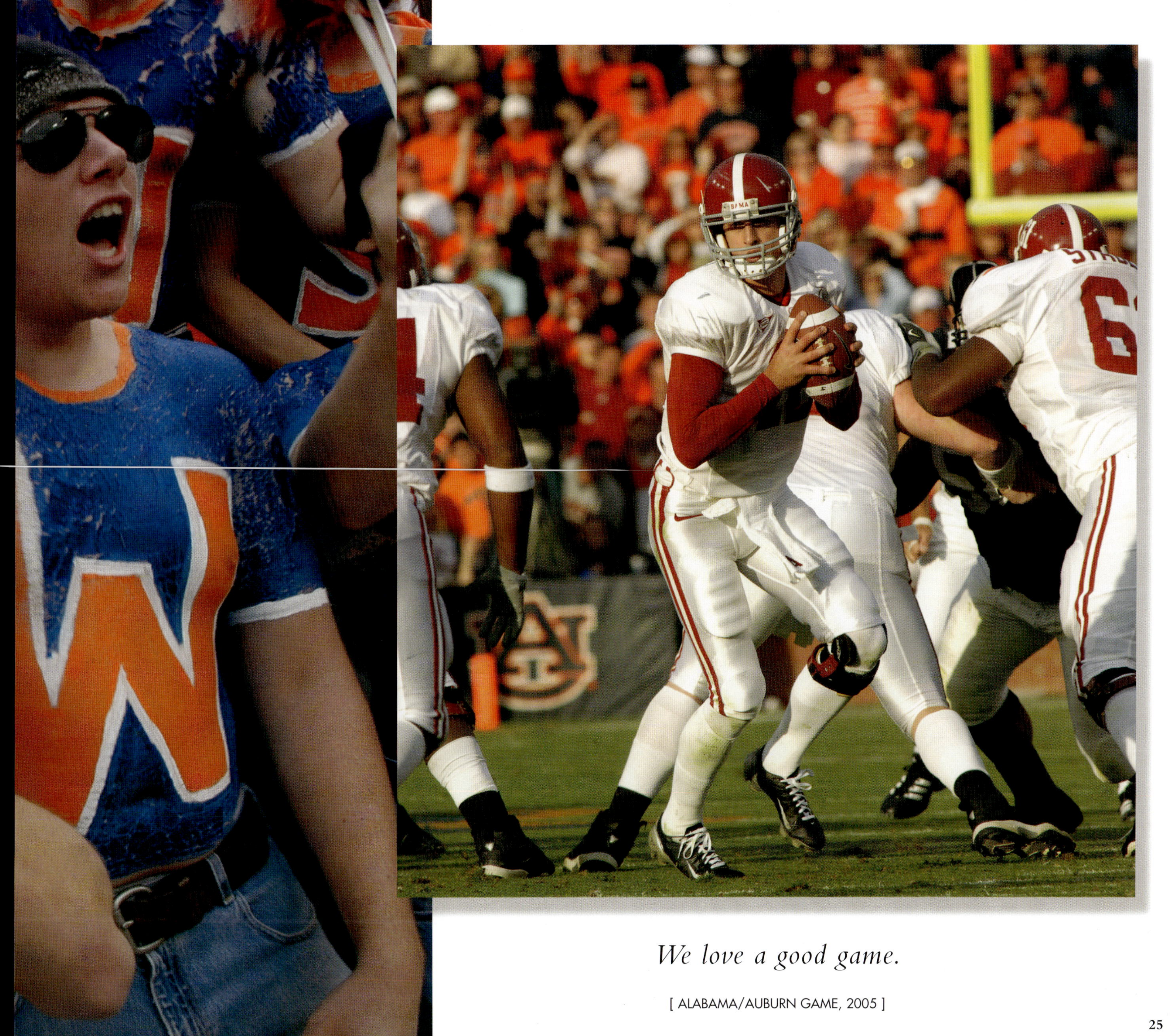

We love a good game.

[ALABAMA/AUBURN GAME, 2005]

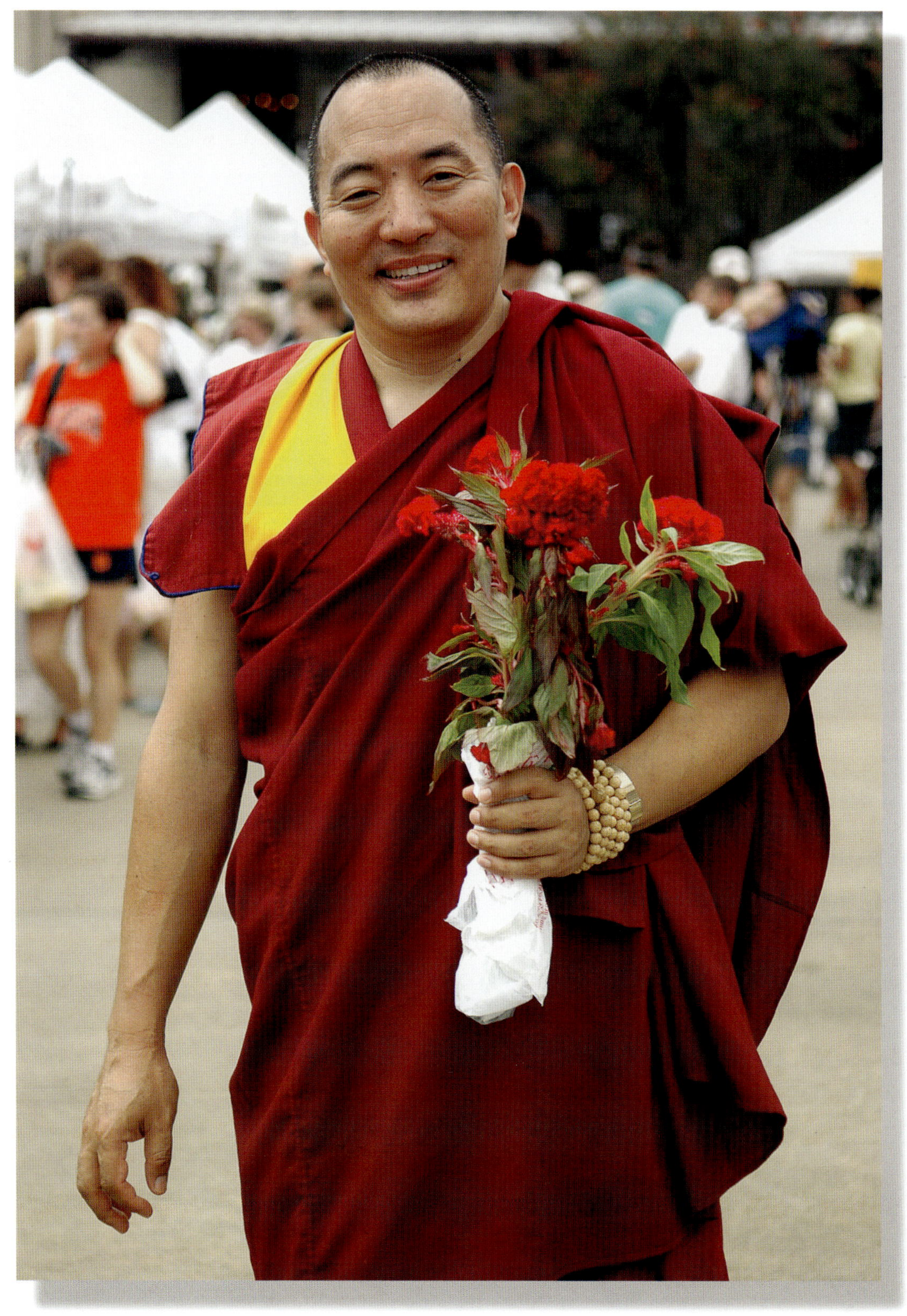

Why do I love Alabama? Oh, there are more reasons than I could tell you if we talked all night. I love the beauty of Alabama's mountains and rivers and forests, of her wildflowers, and of her carefully groomed gardens. But the most beautiful of all the things I've found in Alabama is the warmth and kindness in the hearts of her people. It is because of that kindness that I have found a home in Alabama after more than thirty years as a refugee.

How did that happen? When I was very small, Communist China invaded my country, Tibet. We Tibetans are very religious people, and when the Communists prevented us from practicing our religion, my family had no choice but to follow our religious and secular leader, His Holiness the Dali Lama, into exile by fleeing across the Himalayas into India. India has very kindly admitted more than 130 thousand Tibetans escaping from their own troubled land. It was there that my parents lived out their days and passed away. It was there that I joined Namgyal Monastery and studied Buddhist philosophy. But there, like each of my fellow Tibetans, I was always a refugee with all the uncertainty that goes with that condition.

After I completed my education at the monastery, I served in many places, both in India and other countries. Then I was invited to come and teach in Birmingham. I thought that it was right to accept because there was no lama here to teach the Buddhadharma. When I arrived, a wonderful thing happened. The people of Alabama – who well-meaning, but ignorant, friends had warned me might be prejudiced and unkind – met me with open hearts and came to my aid at every turn. As a result of their kindness, I have now become a permanent United States resident with hopes of soon becoming a citizen, and I know that I will never again face the uncertain world as a refugee.

So now you know both how Alabama came to be my home and why I love it as only someone who has once lost their home ever could. It was in the hills and hearts of Alabama that finally I found comfort for the pangs of longing for the snowy mountains of my homeland that have followed me all my life.

TENZIN DESHEK
[BUDDHIST MONK]

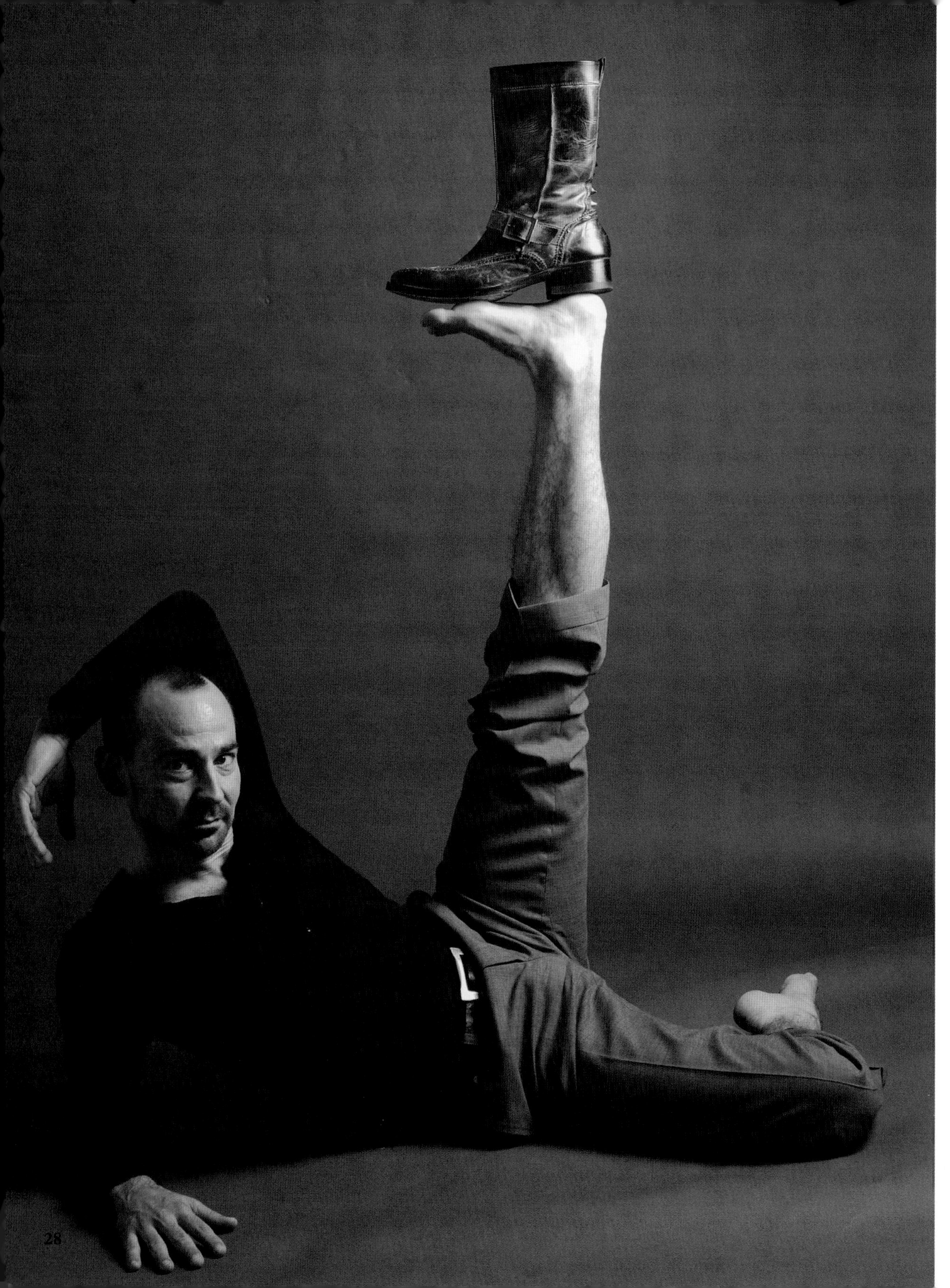

Alabama is a magical place; it's allowed me to realize a dream and to create the fine art of dance, through the Alabama Ballet.

WES CHAPMAN
[DIRECTOR, ALABAMA BALLET]

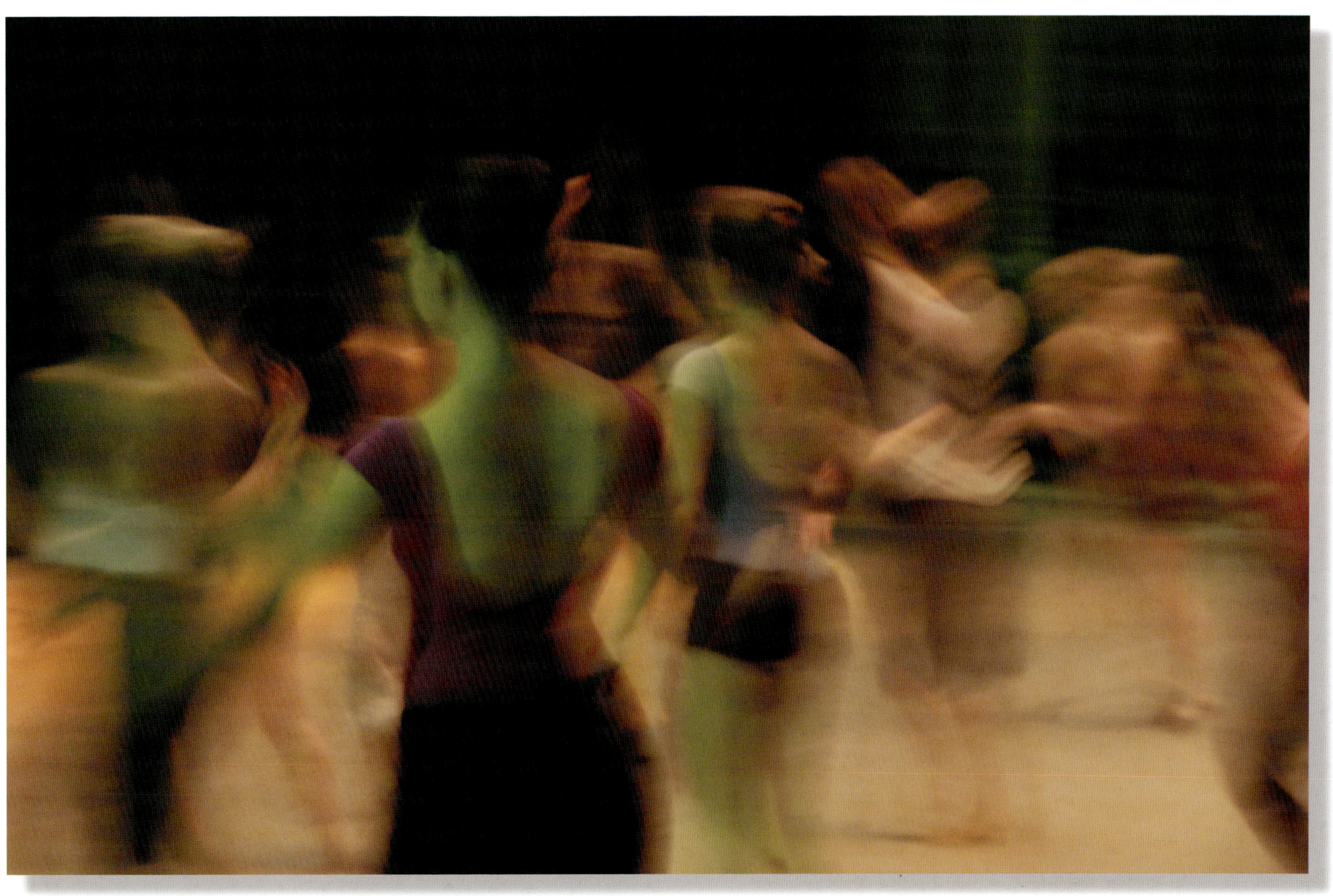

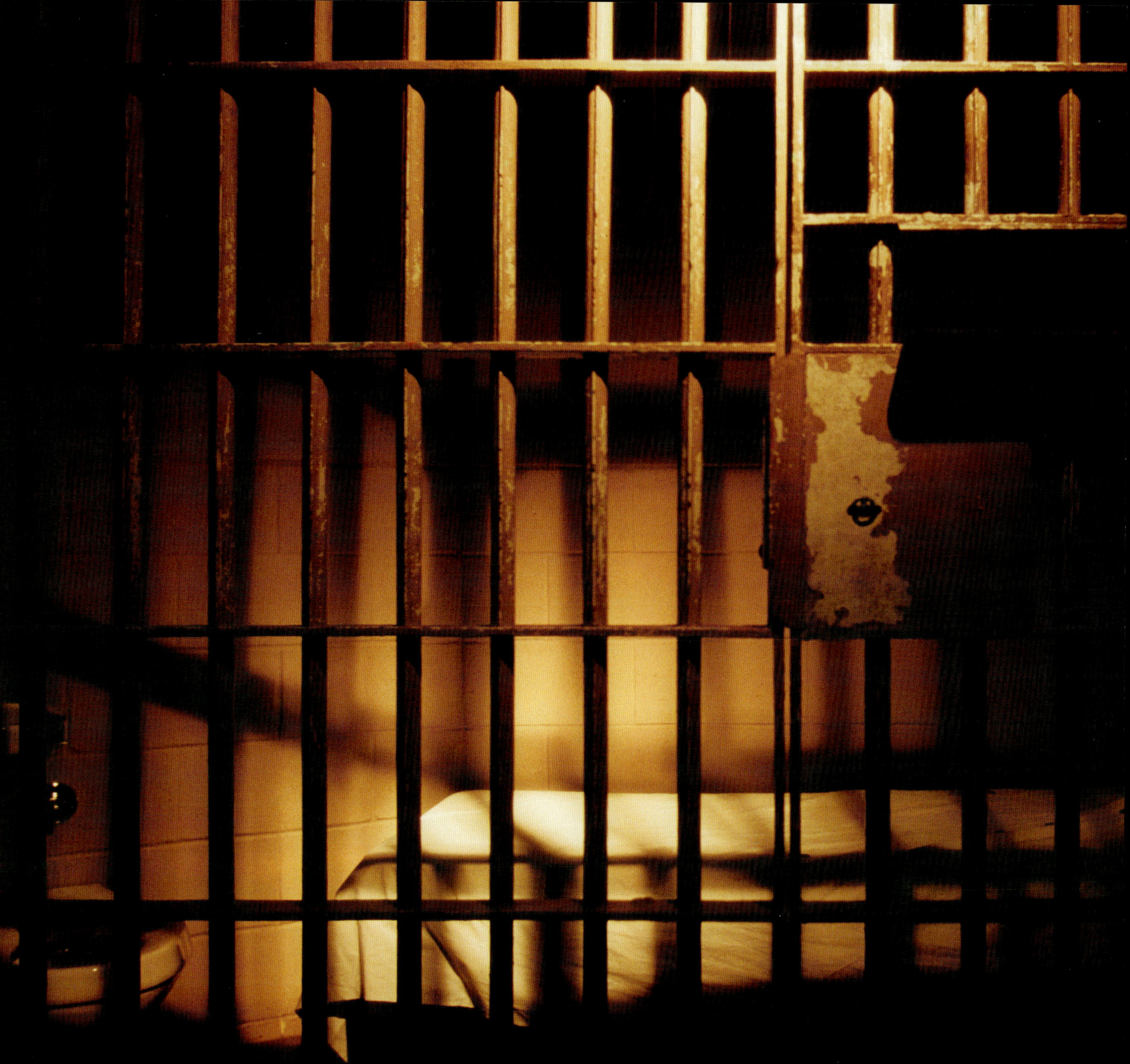

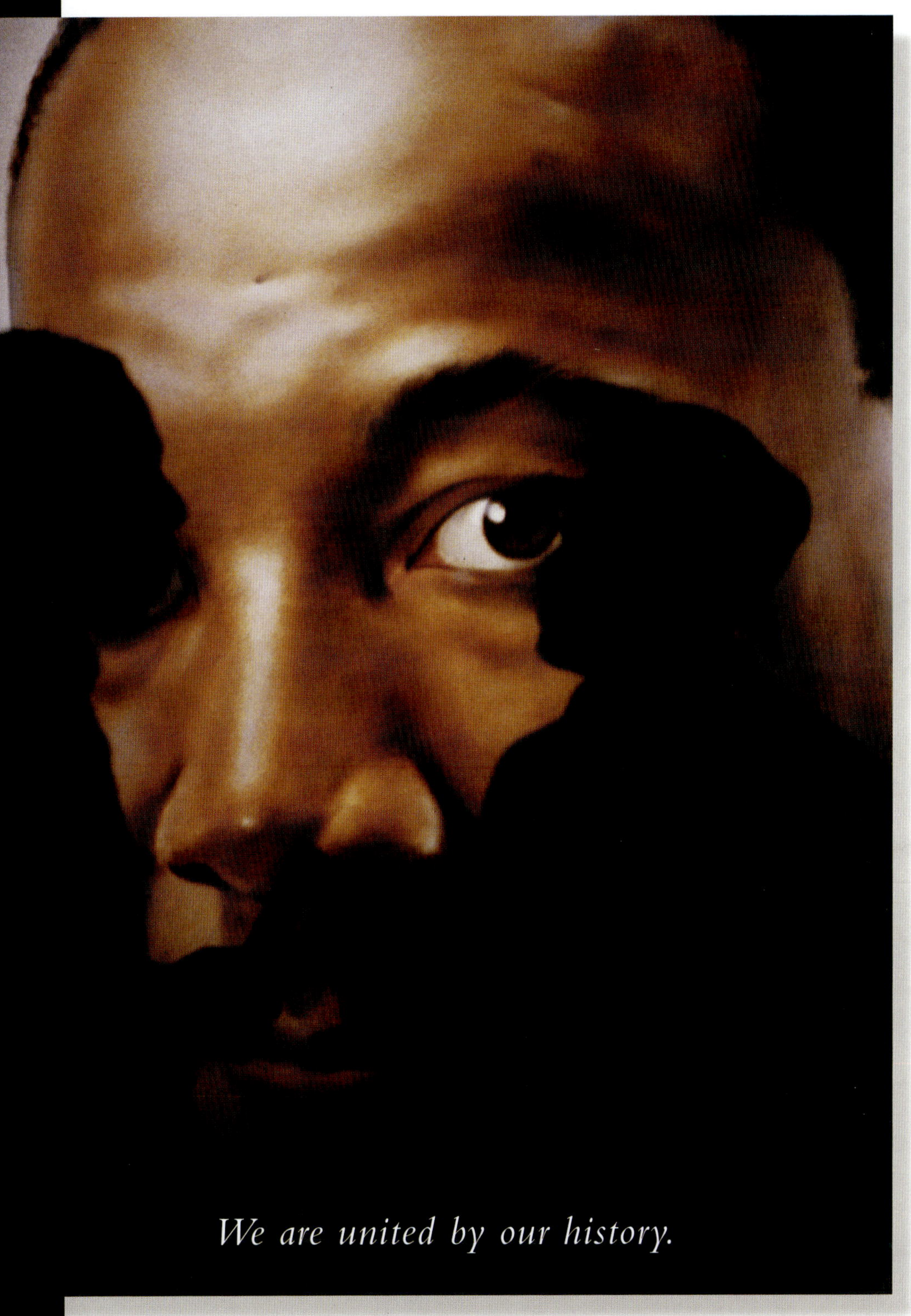

[BIRMINGHAM CIVIL RIGHTS INSTITUTE]

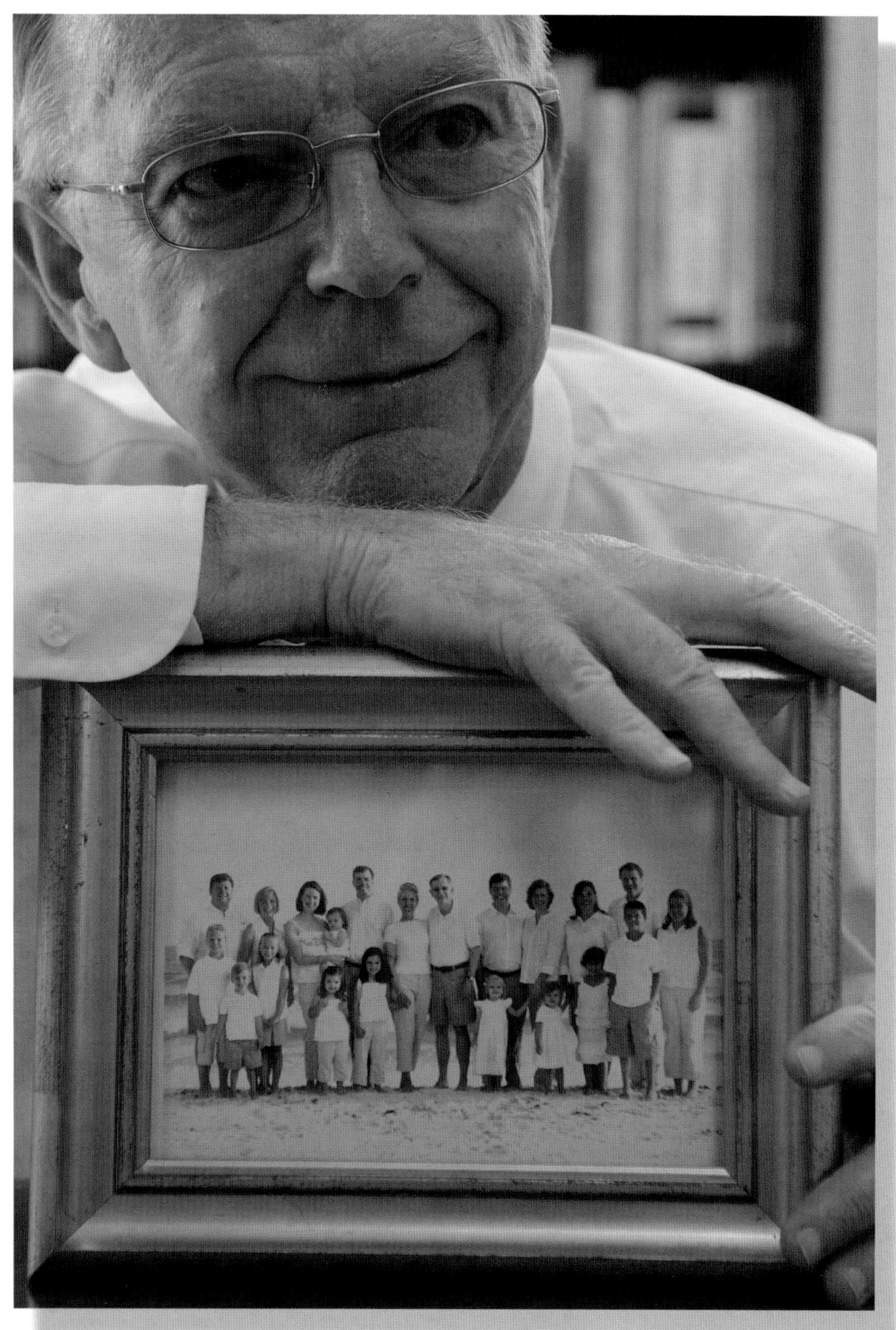

We count it a privilege to have lived in Alabama the last thirty-six years. The friendliness of the people, the beauty of the entire state, plus the civic spirit that represents the best of what volunteerism is all about in responding to so many good causes come together to make this a very special place.

NEAL R. BERTE
[PAST PRESIDENT, BIRMINGHAM-SOUTHERN COLLEGE]

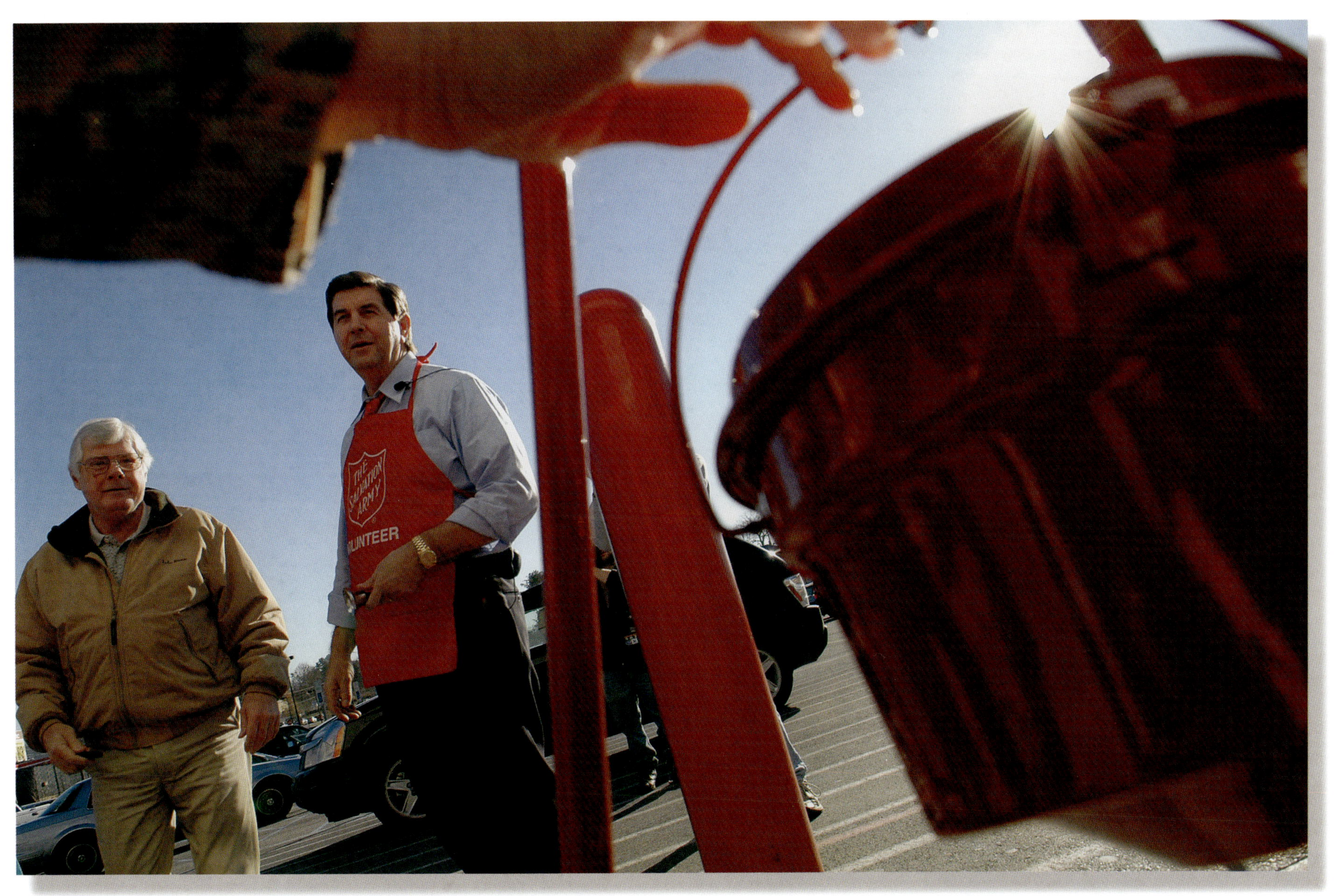

[GOVERNOR BOB RILEY RAISES FUNDS FOR THE SALVATION ARMY]

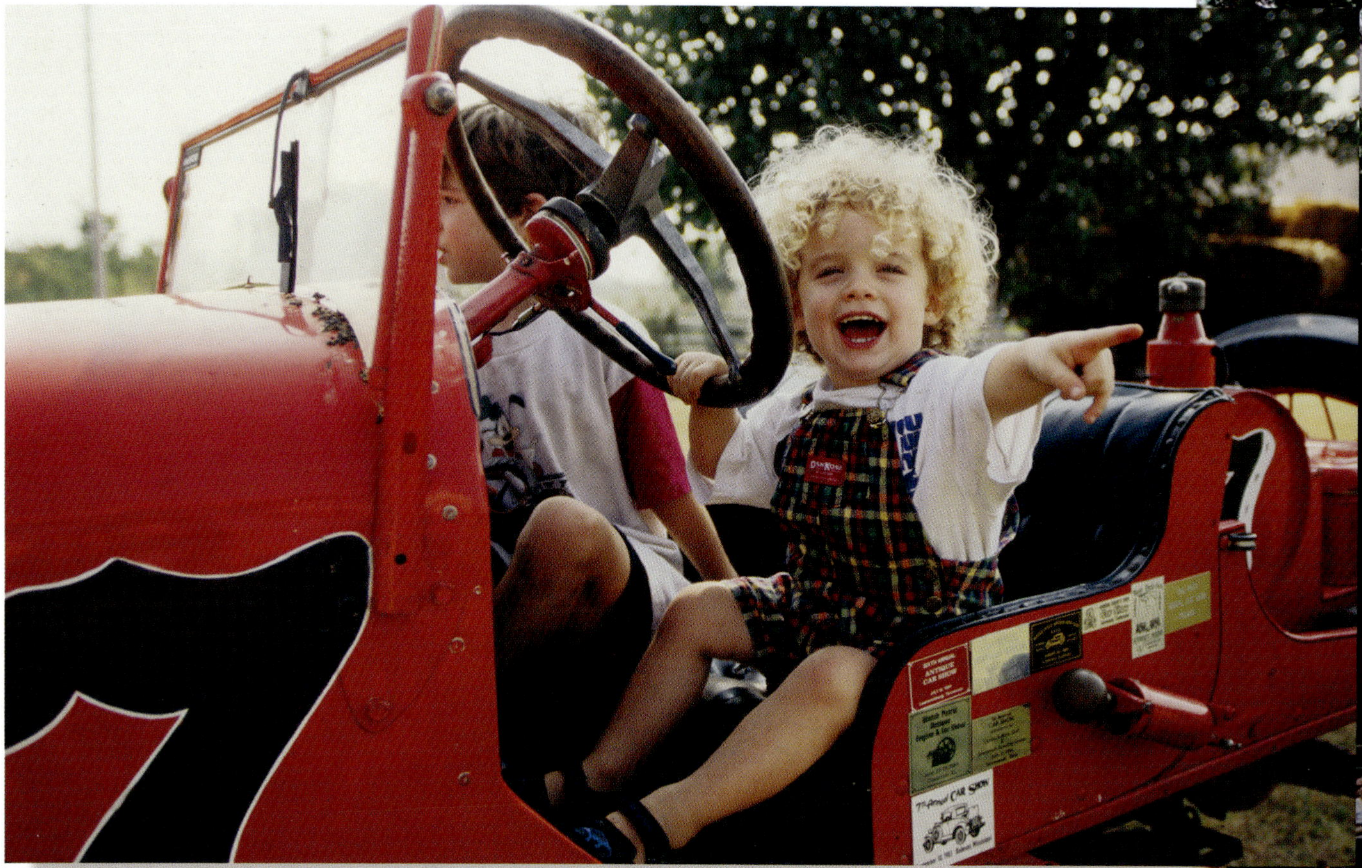

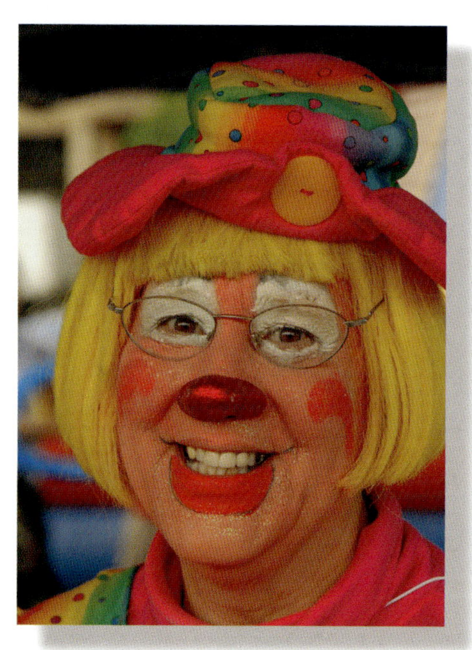

We really love a parade.

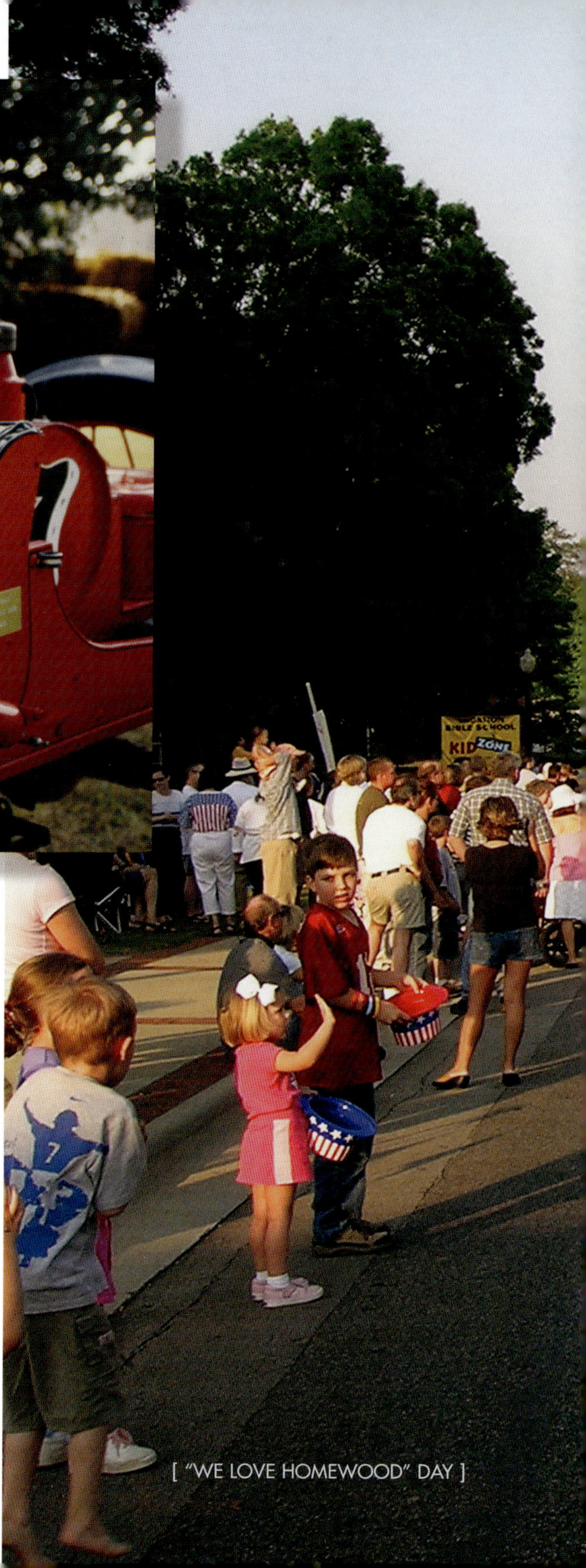

["WE LOVE HOMEWOOD" DAY]

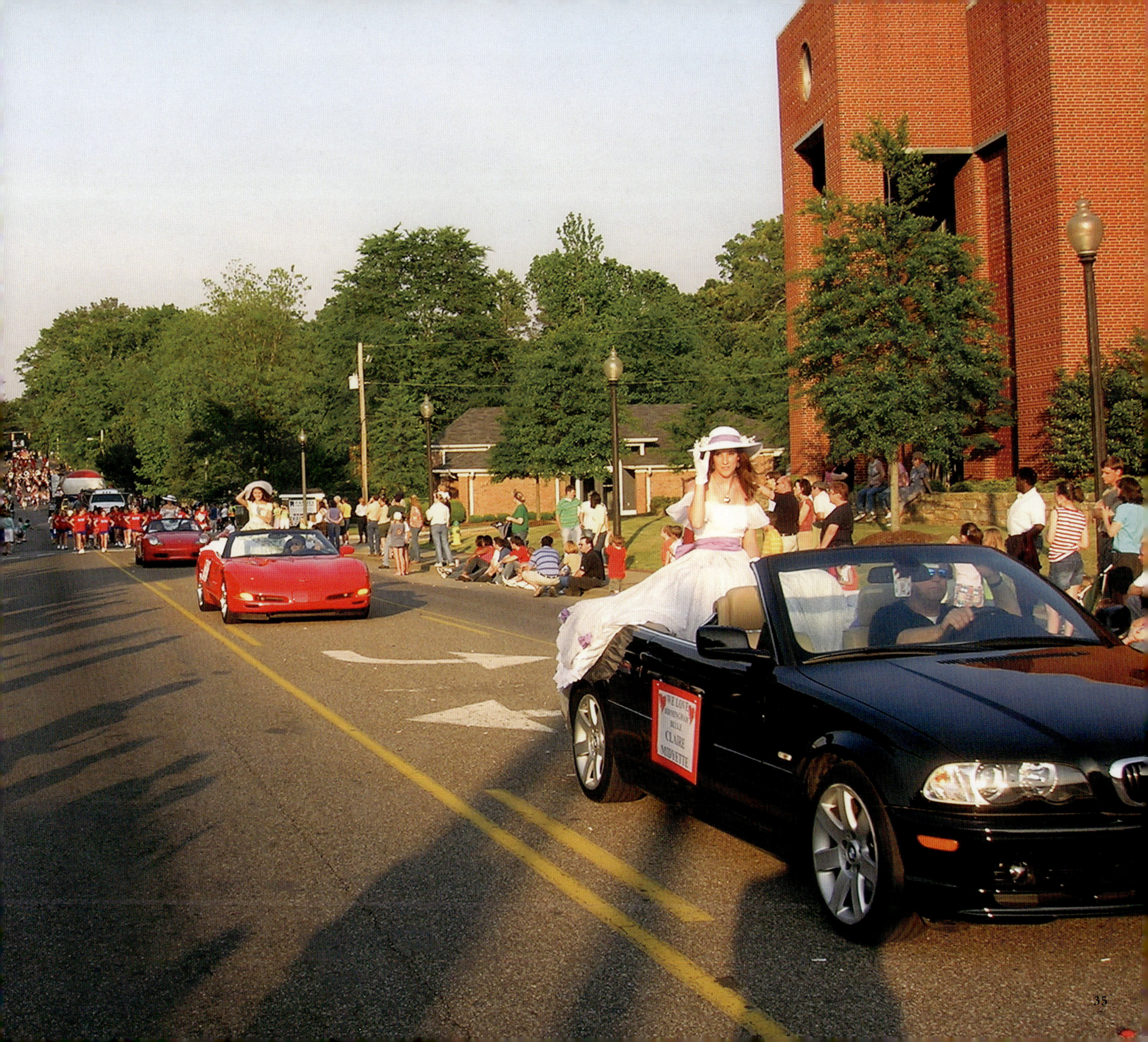
CLAIRE

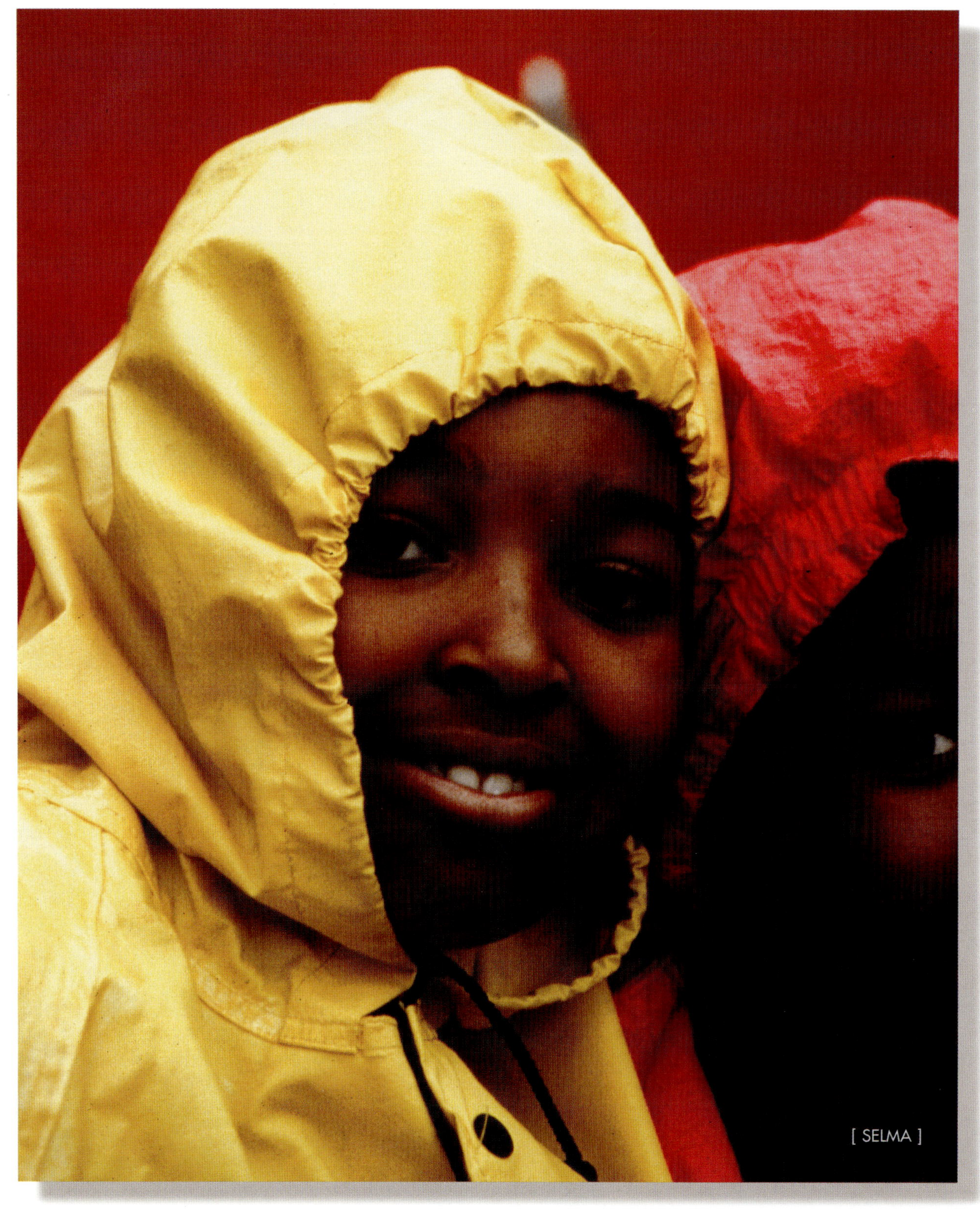

[SELMA]

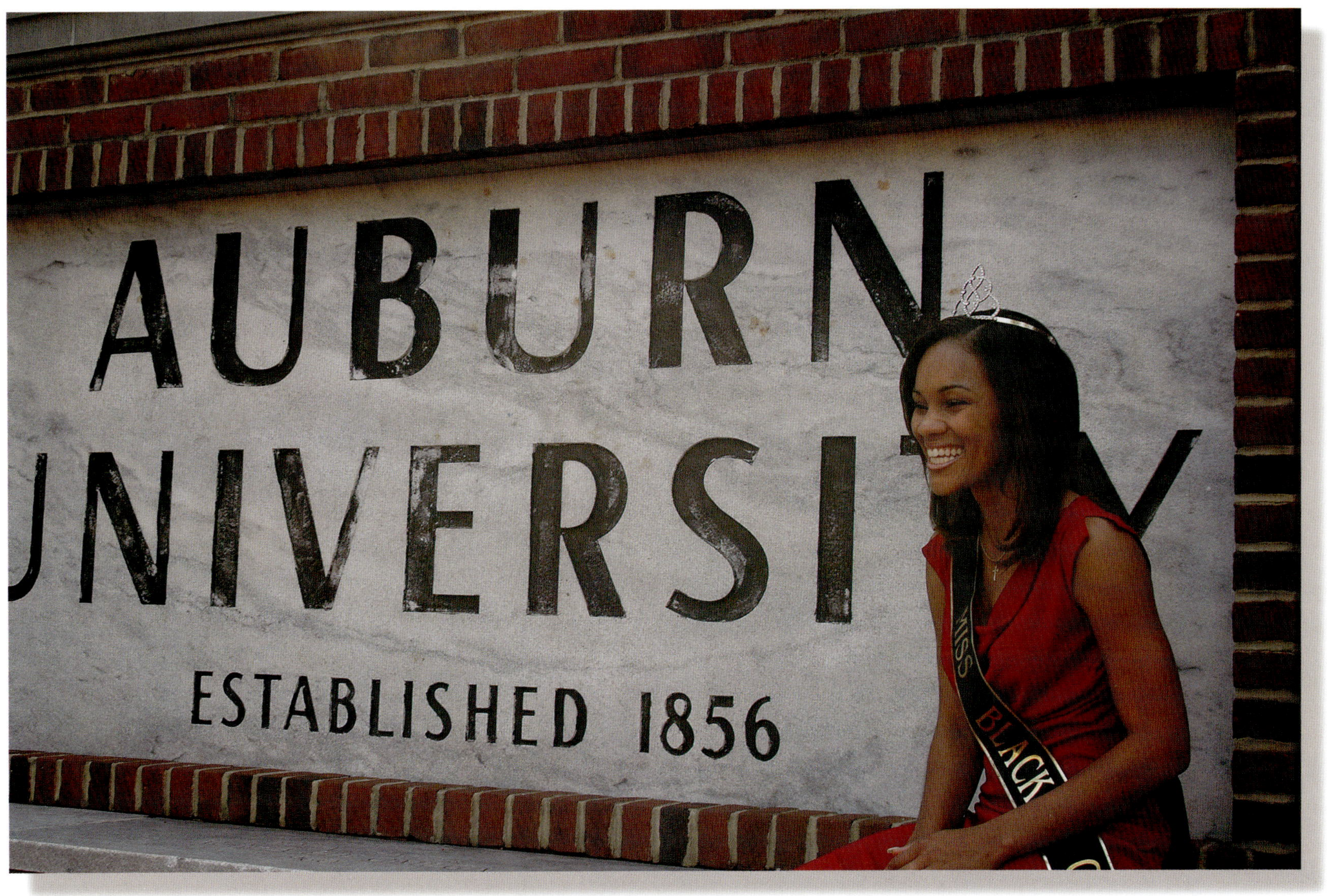

Since I was born in the city and lived there for the first seven years of my life, moving to Alabama was a dramatic change, yet one for the better. I've grown up in Alabama practically all my life now and this is what I call home. To be an Alabamian means being part of a country-enriched family, and there is no place like my Home Sweet Home, Alabama!

Rebecca Ferguson
[STUDENT, AUBURN UNIVERSITY]

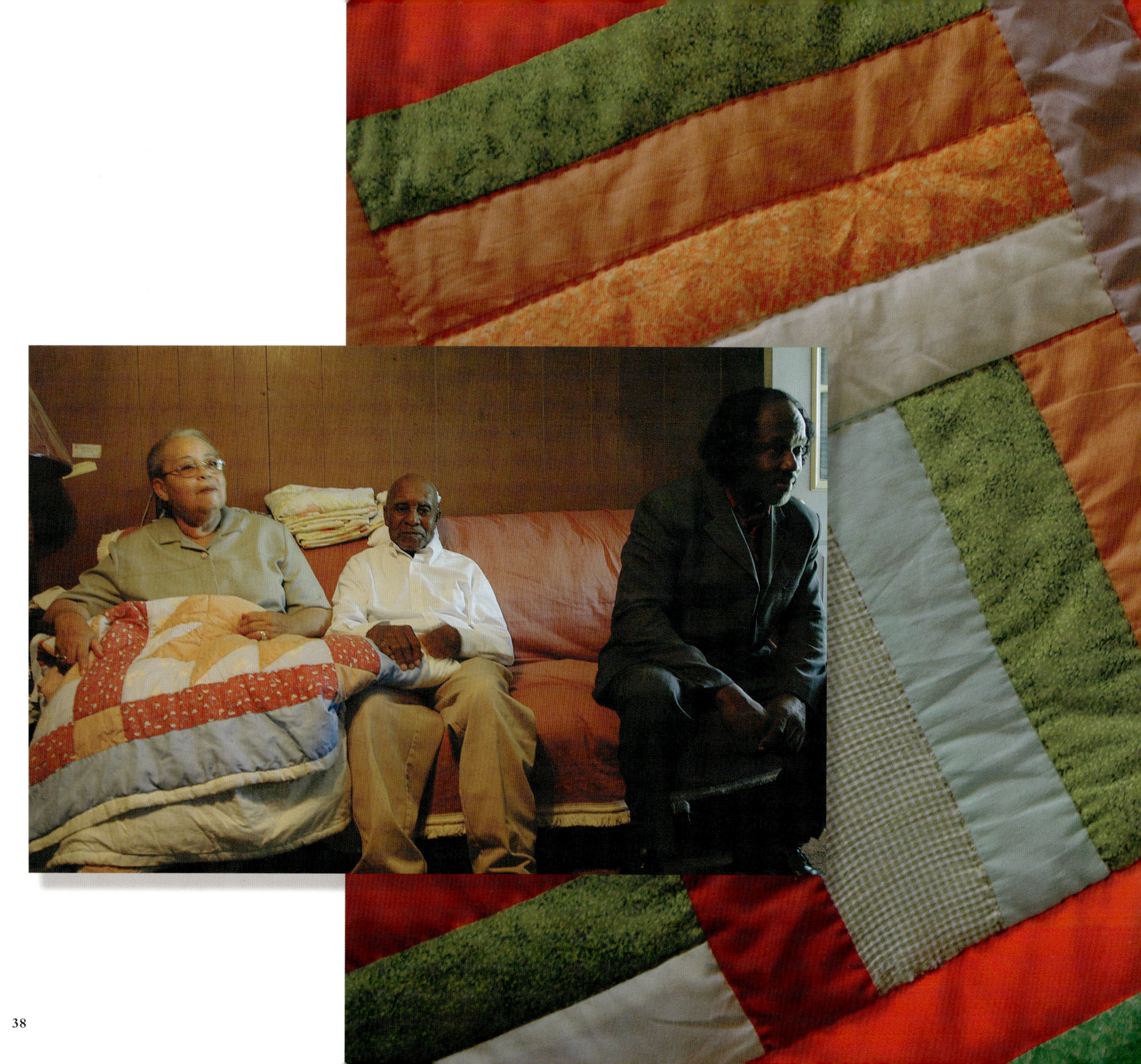

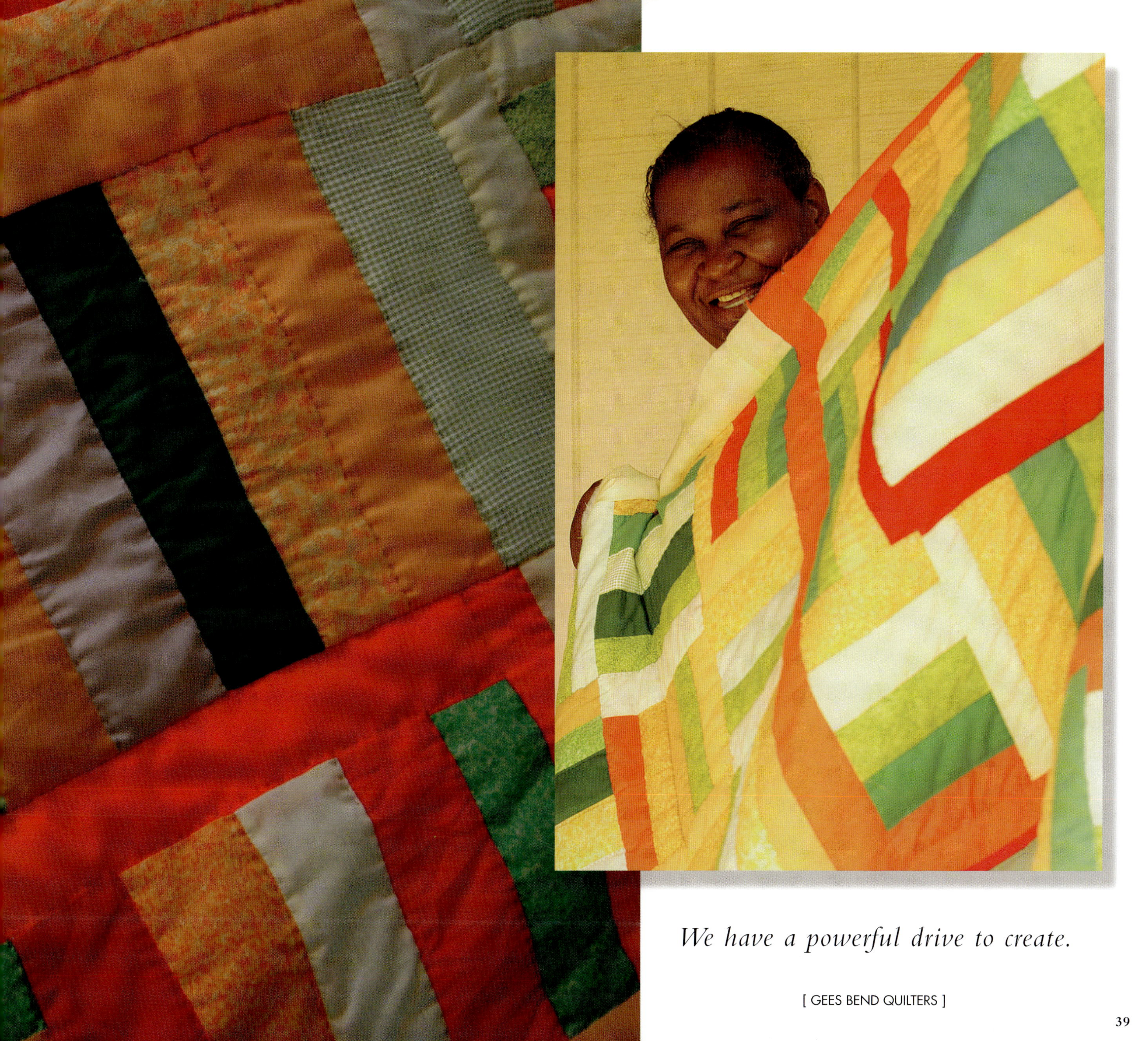

We have a powerful drive to create.

[GEES BEND QUILTERS]

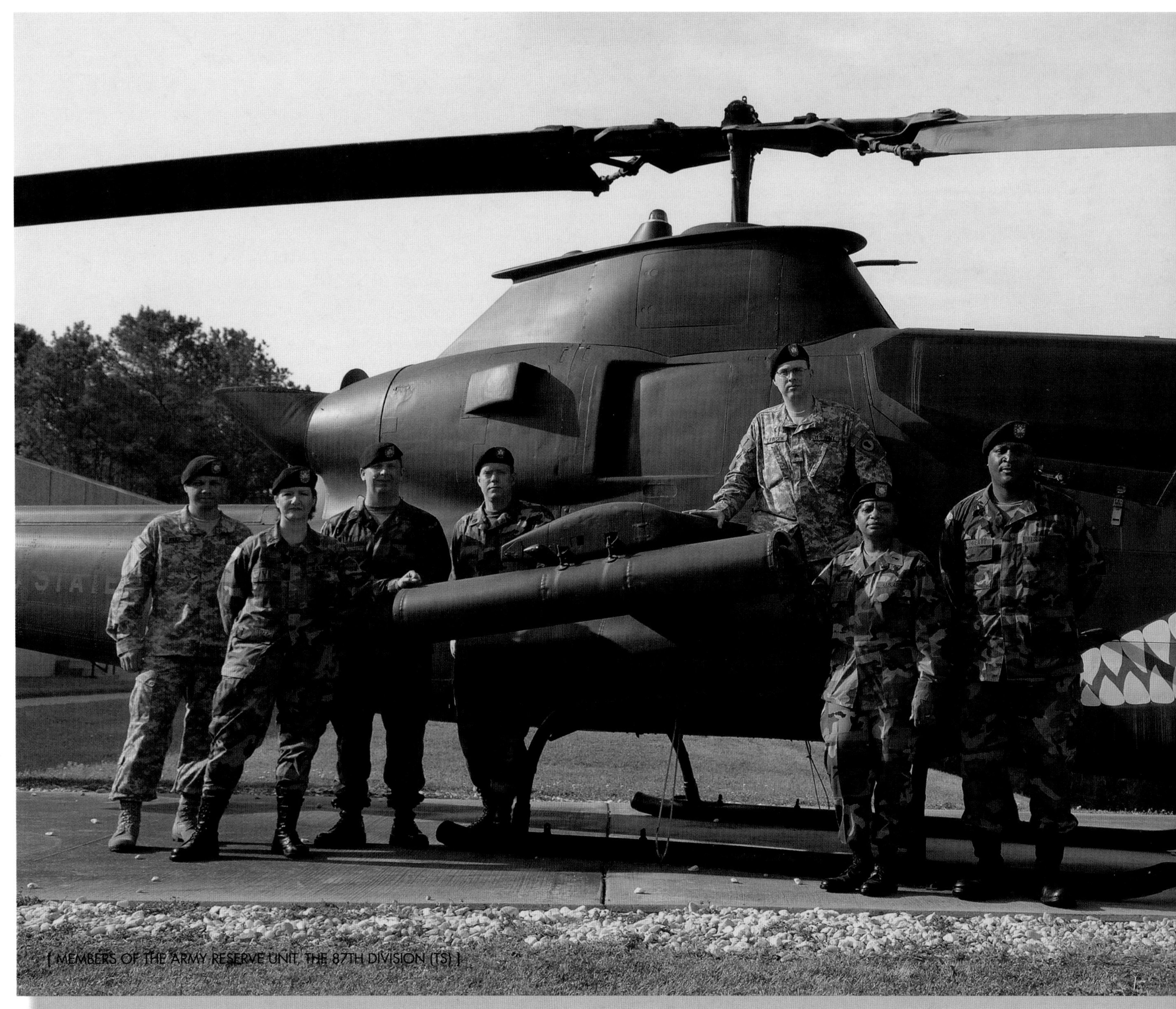

[MEMBERS OF THE ARMY RESERVE UNIT, THE 87TH DIVISION (TS)]

I've lived all over the Southeastern states and nothing comes close to Alabama. It's the only place I would want to raise my daughter.

MEGAN PAIGE LEE ELLARD
[E4/CADET 1343RD CHEMICAL COMPANY]

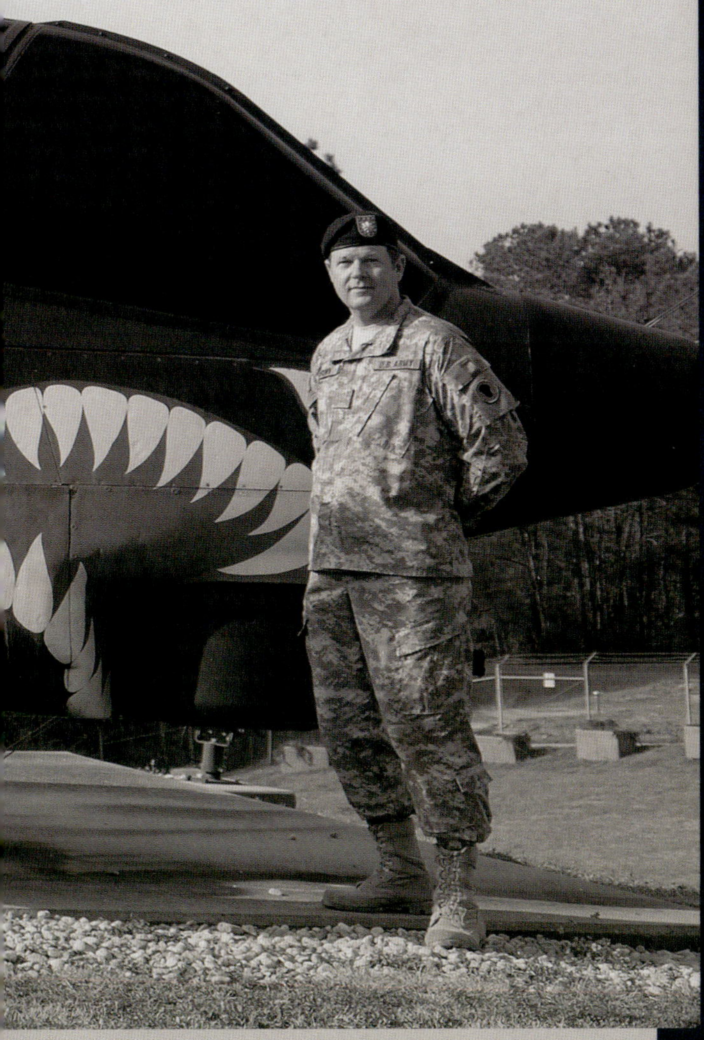

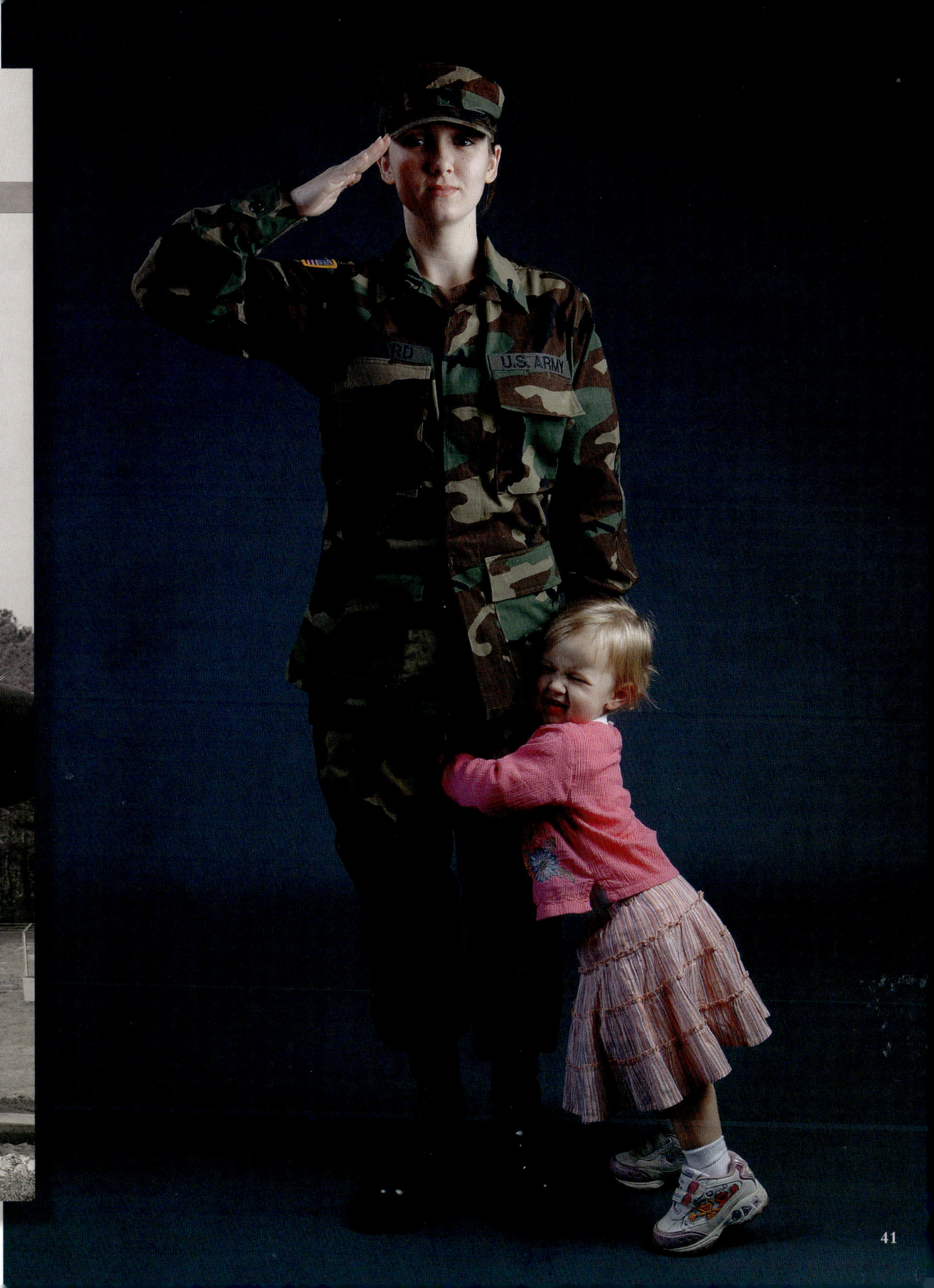

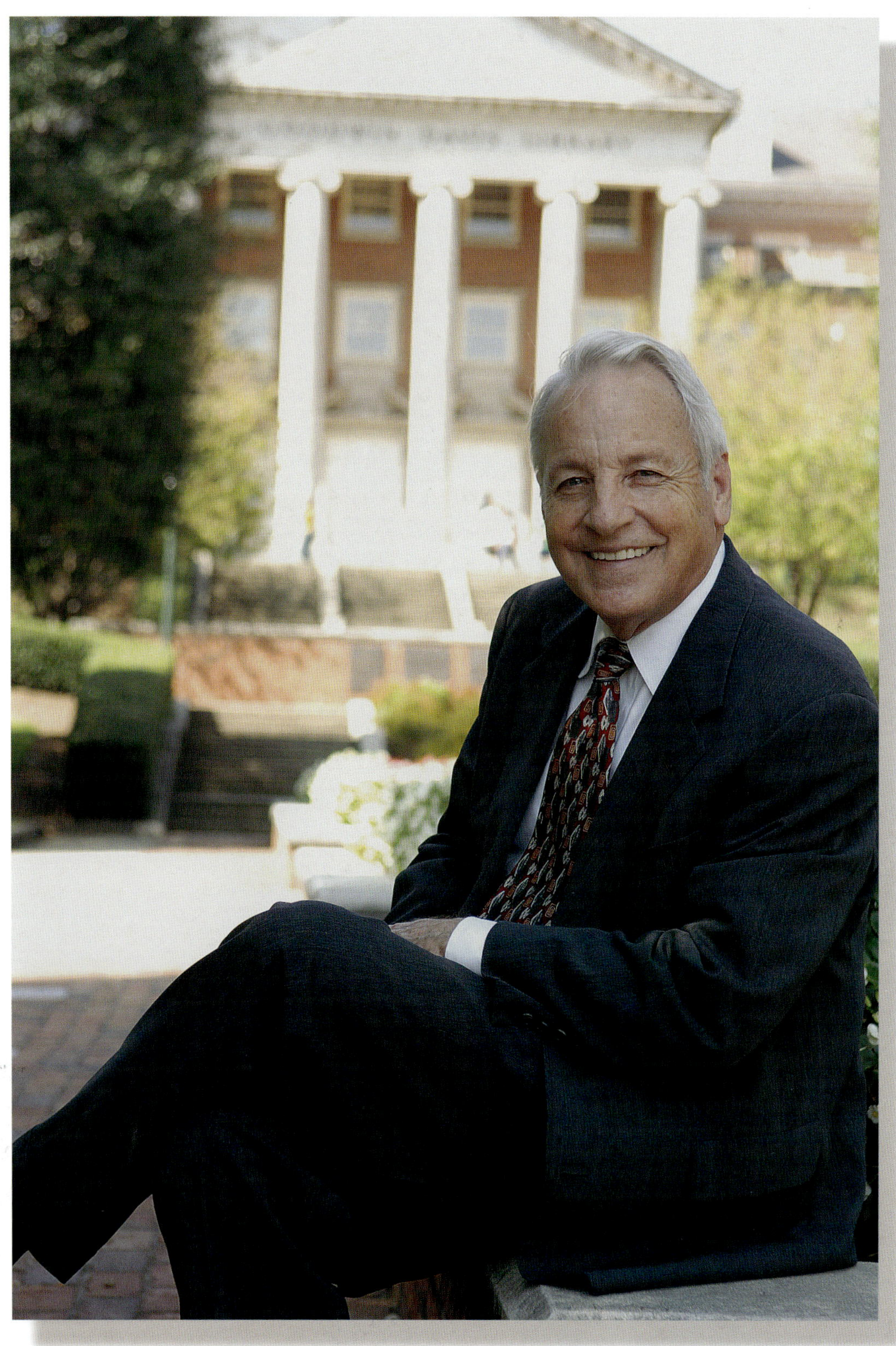

Alabama is known for its abundant natural resources, its mountains and beaches, its rivers and streams, and its natural beauty, but Alabama's real strength lies in its people. Strong in virtues and values, loyal and patriotic, and genuinely caring and compassionate, the people of Alabama have made my career in law, politics, and teaching rewarding and satisfying. Truly, Alabama is a great place in which to live and work.

Albert Brewer
[FORMER GOVERNOR; DISTINGUISHED PROFESSOR OF LAW & GOVERNMENT, SAMFORD UNIVERSITY]

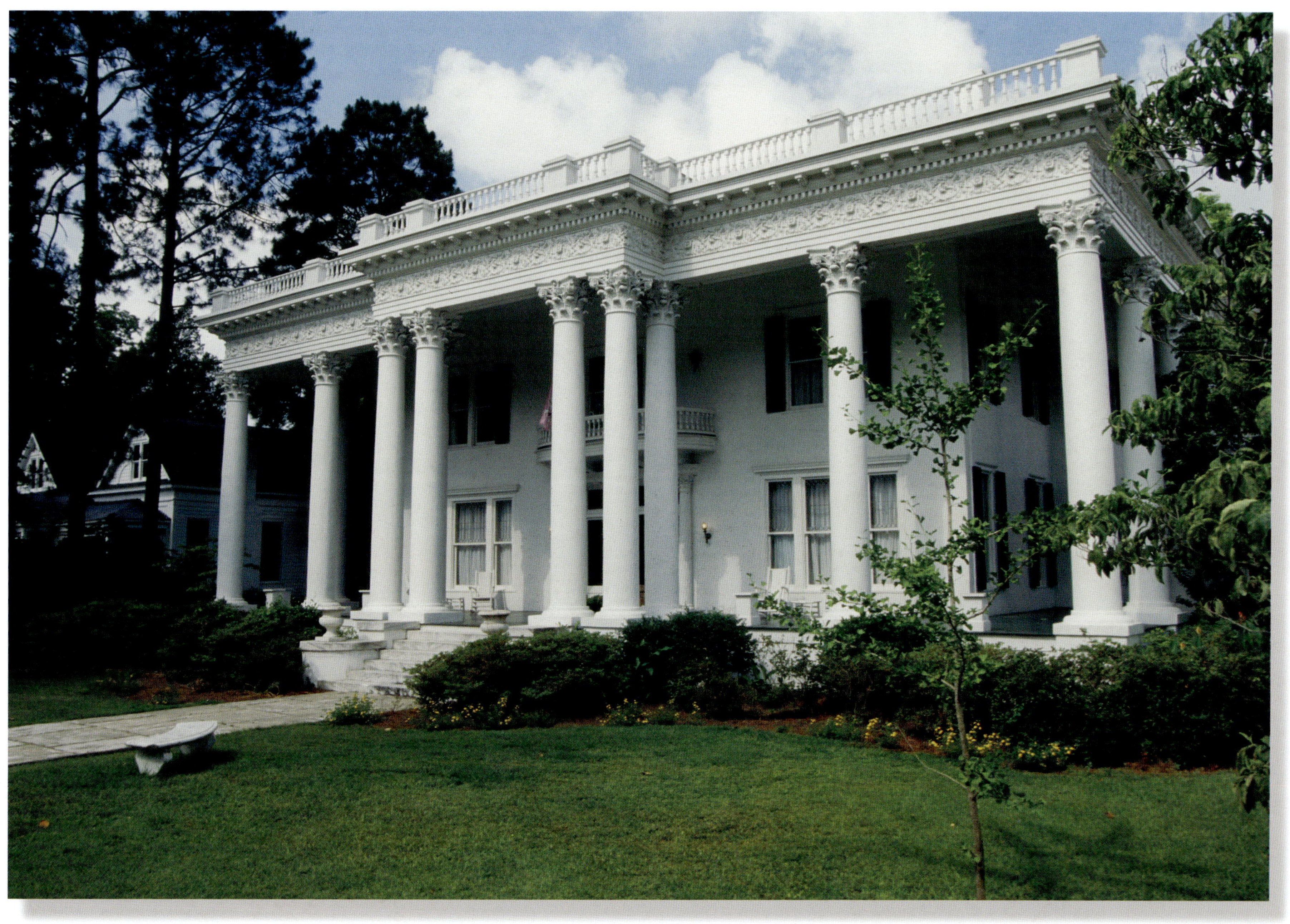

[EUFAULA]

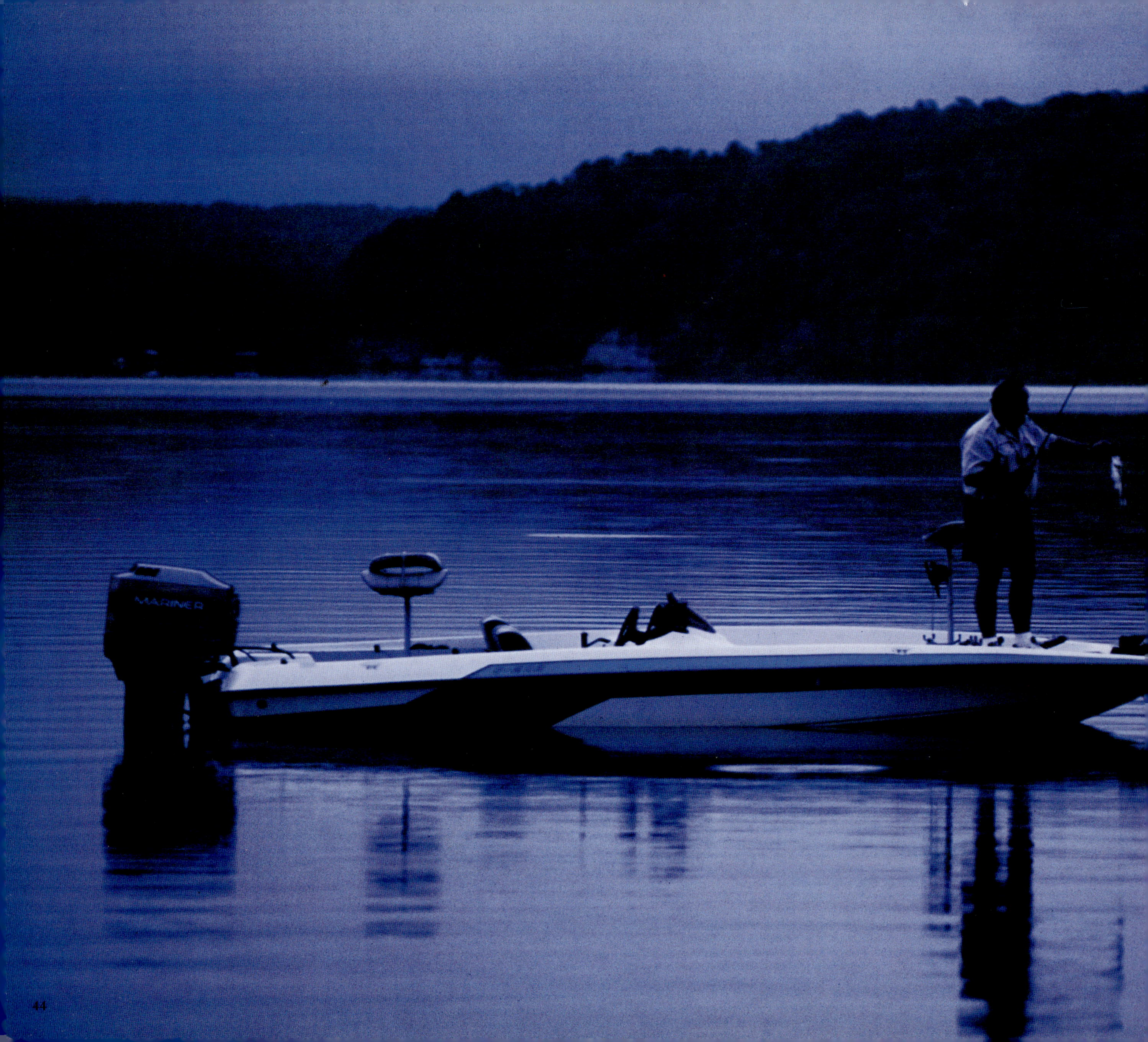
MARINER

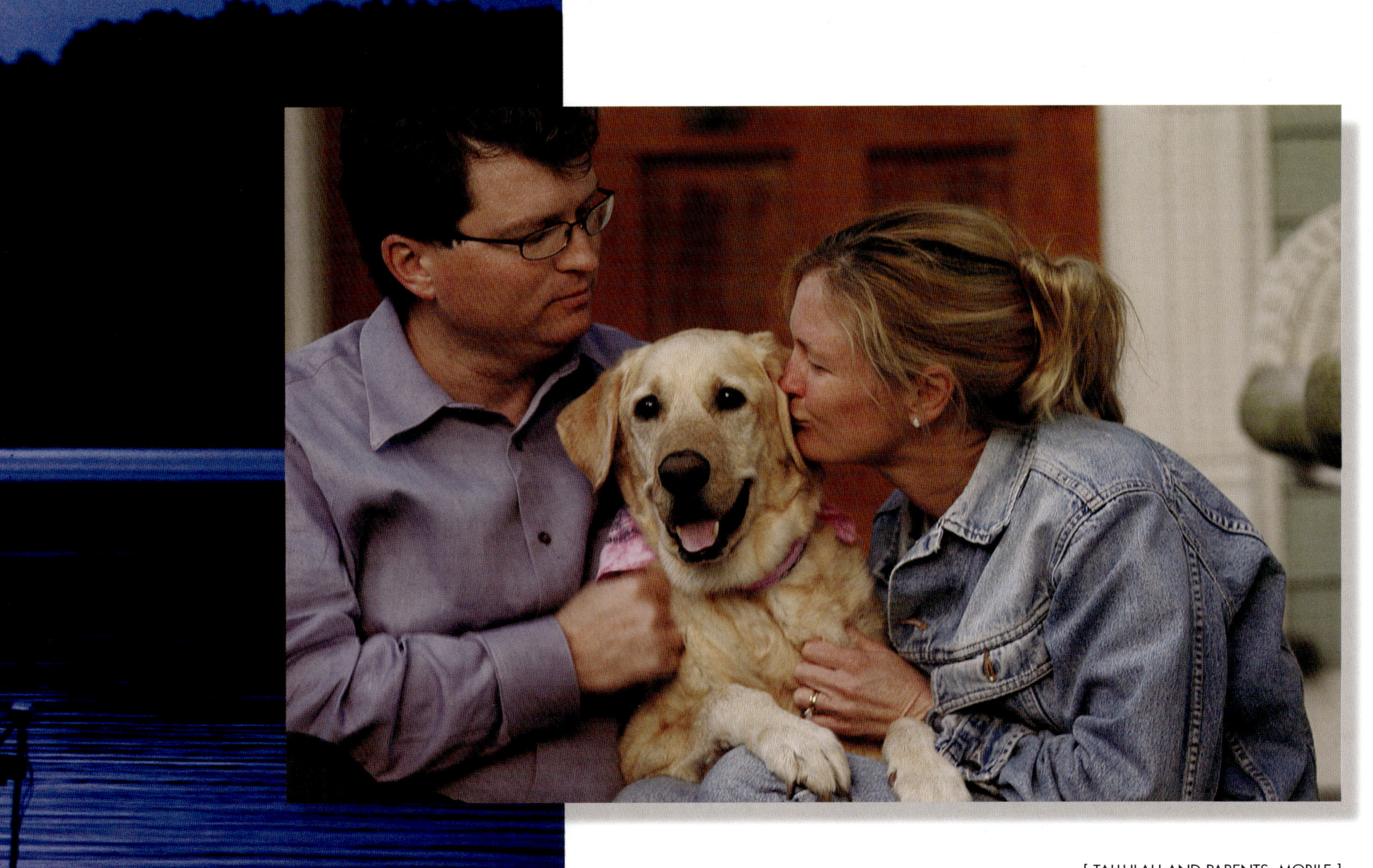

[LAKE EUFAULA]

[TALLULAH AND PARENTS, MOBILE]

There is a deep place
in the soul of Alabama.

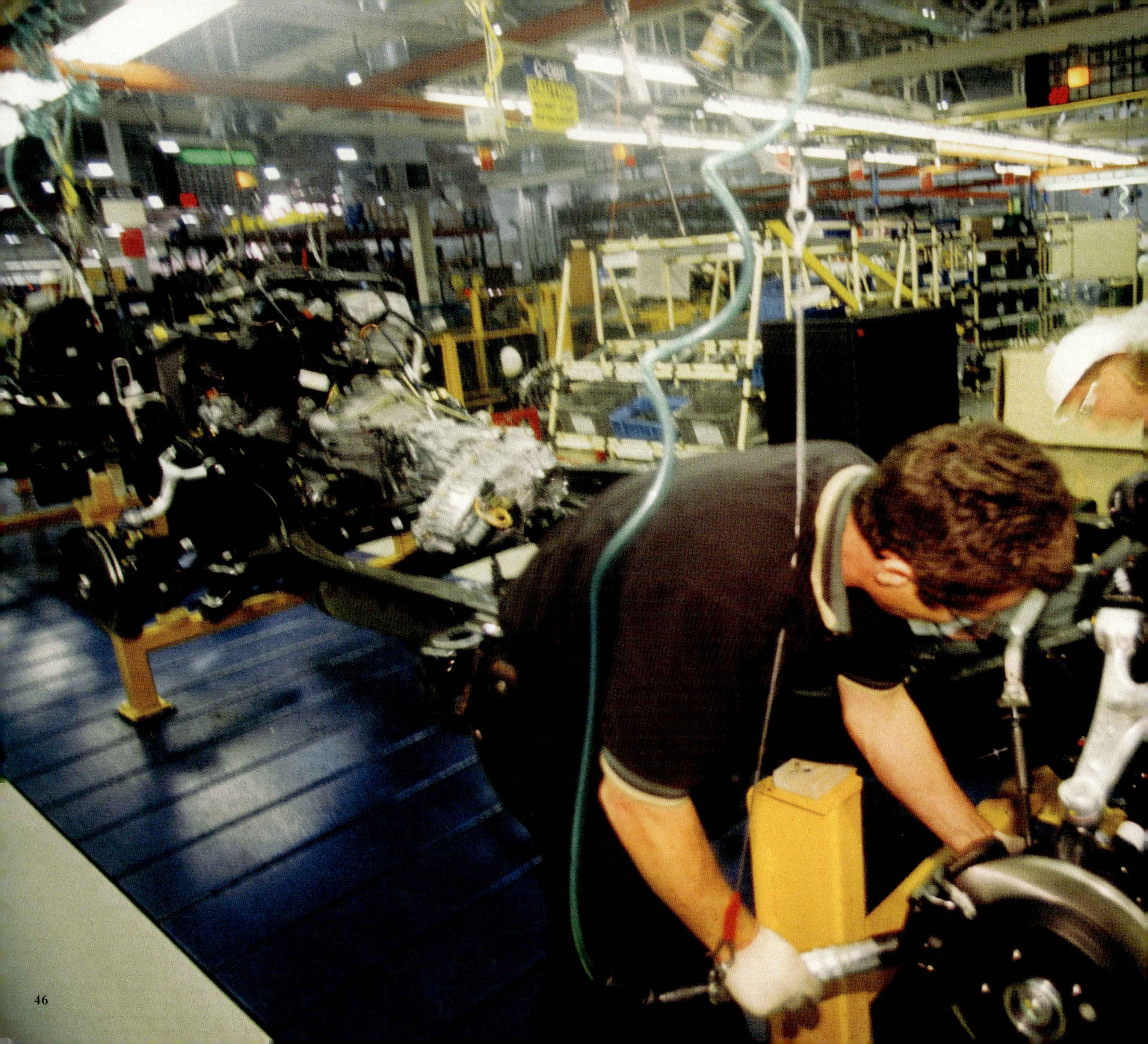

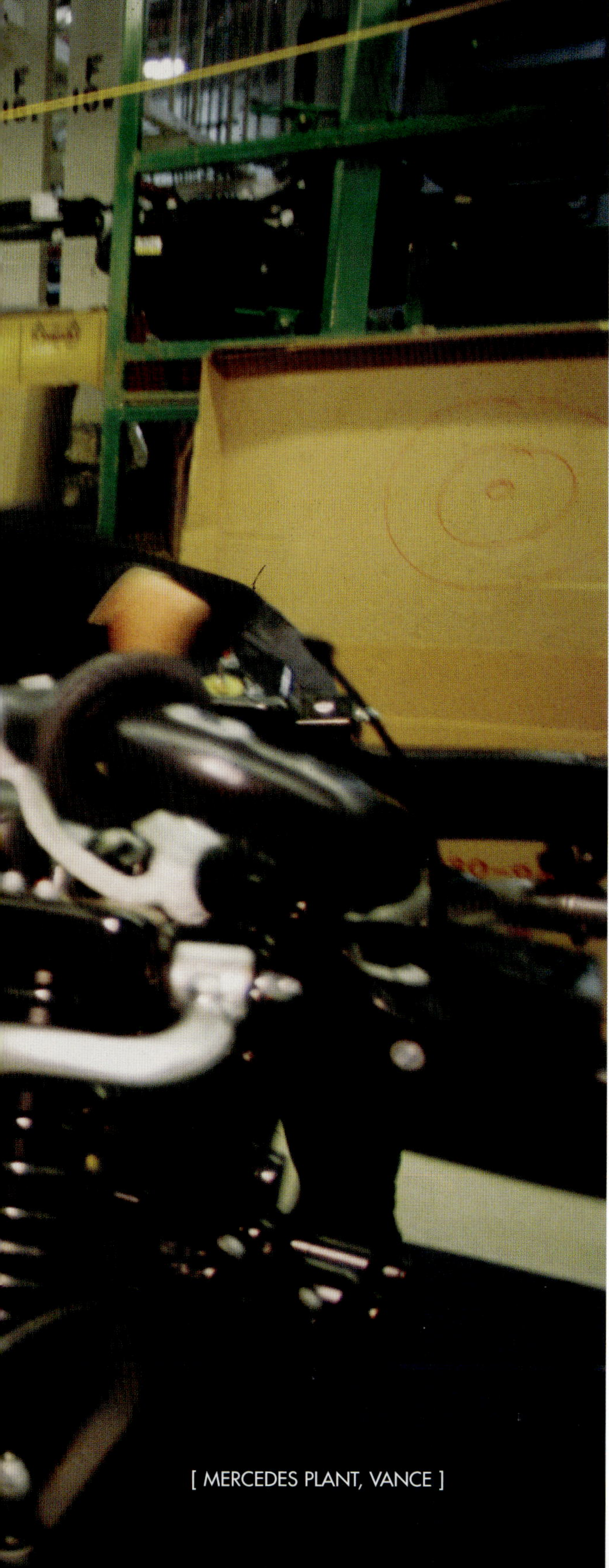

[MERCEDES PLANT, VANCE]

The Way We Work

Working hard is a large part of what defines us. We don't do anything half way. We take pride in everything we do. We are always finding new ways to push ourselves ahead, and to excel. We can do anything.

Steel and iron still burn in our veins.

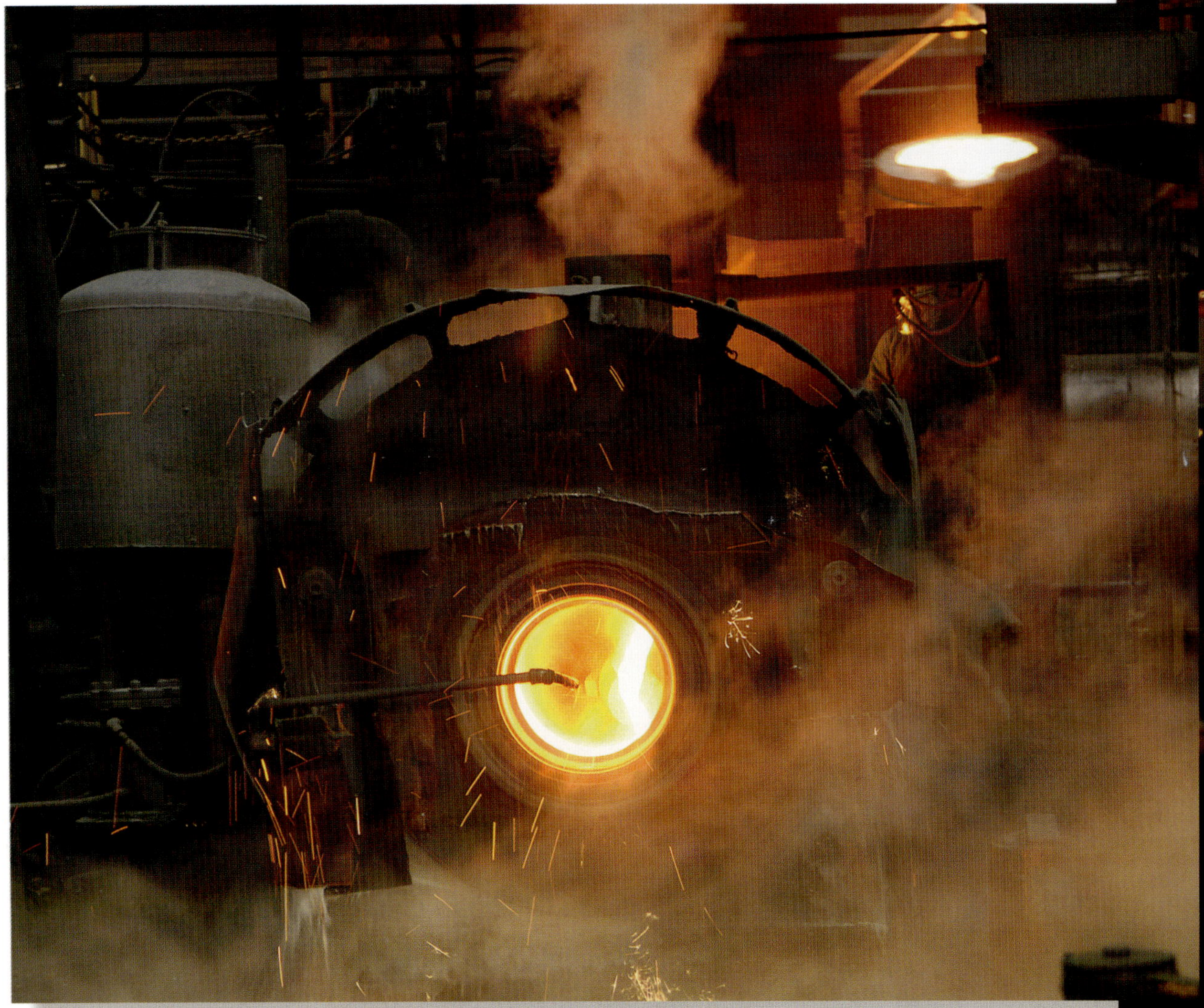

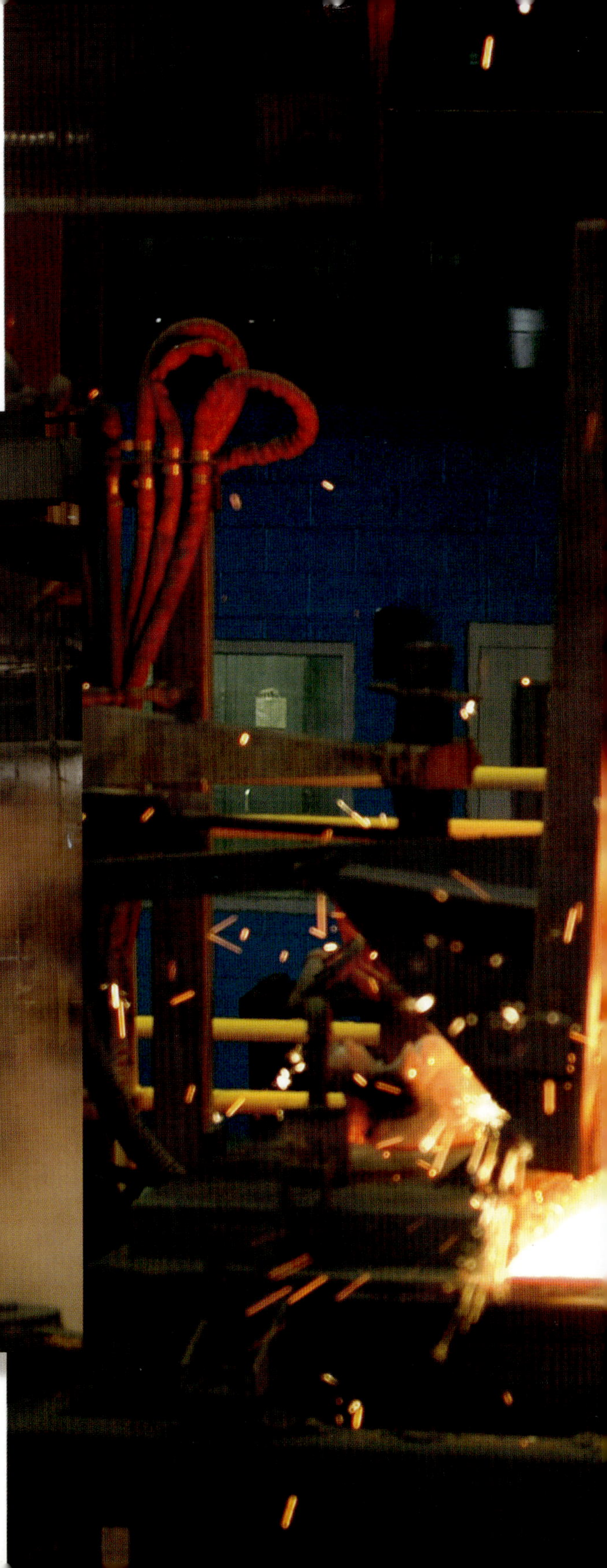

[McWANE CAST IRON PIPE, BIRMINGHAM / ANNISTON]

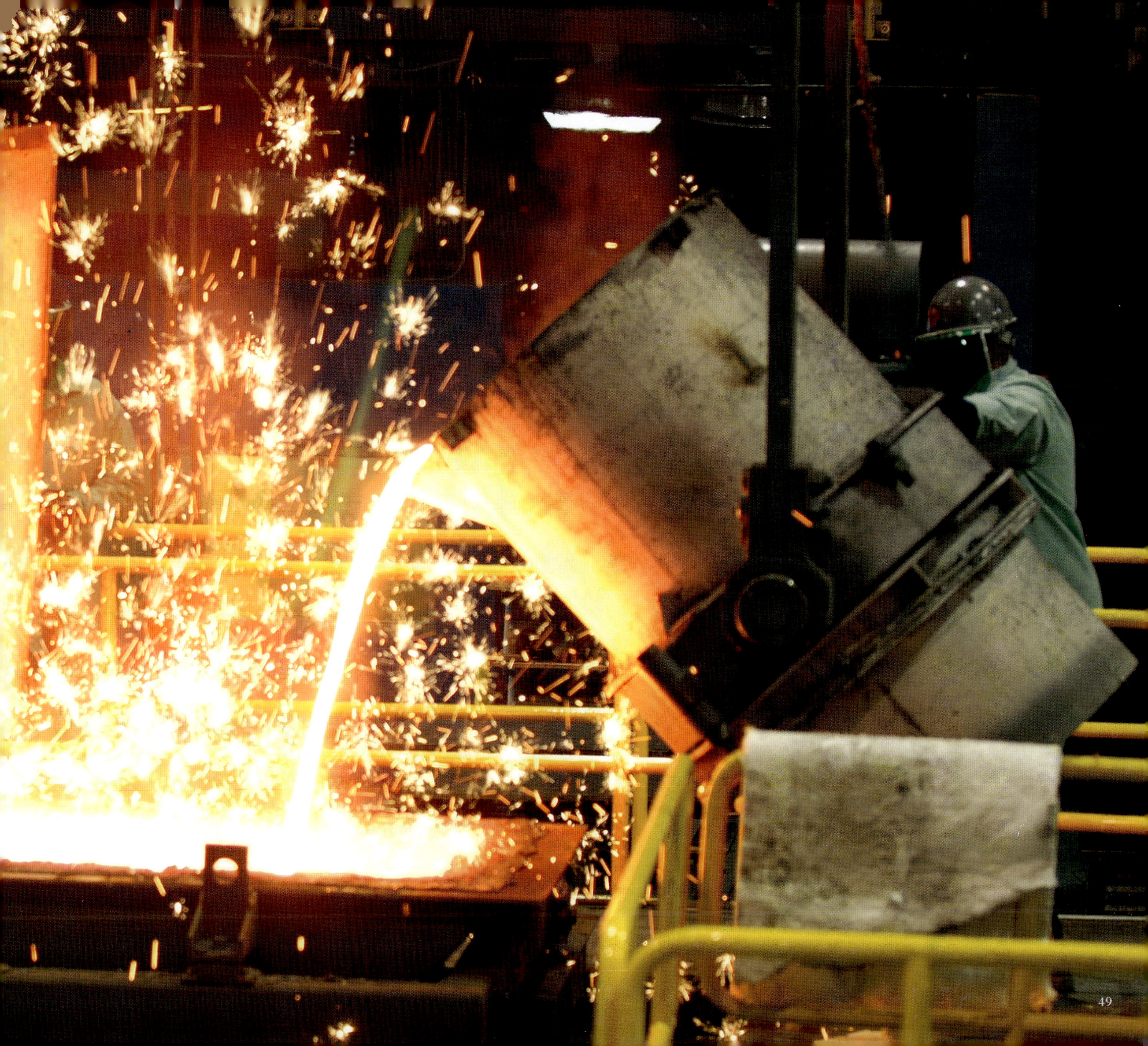

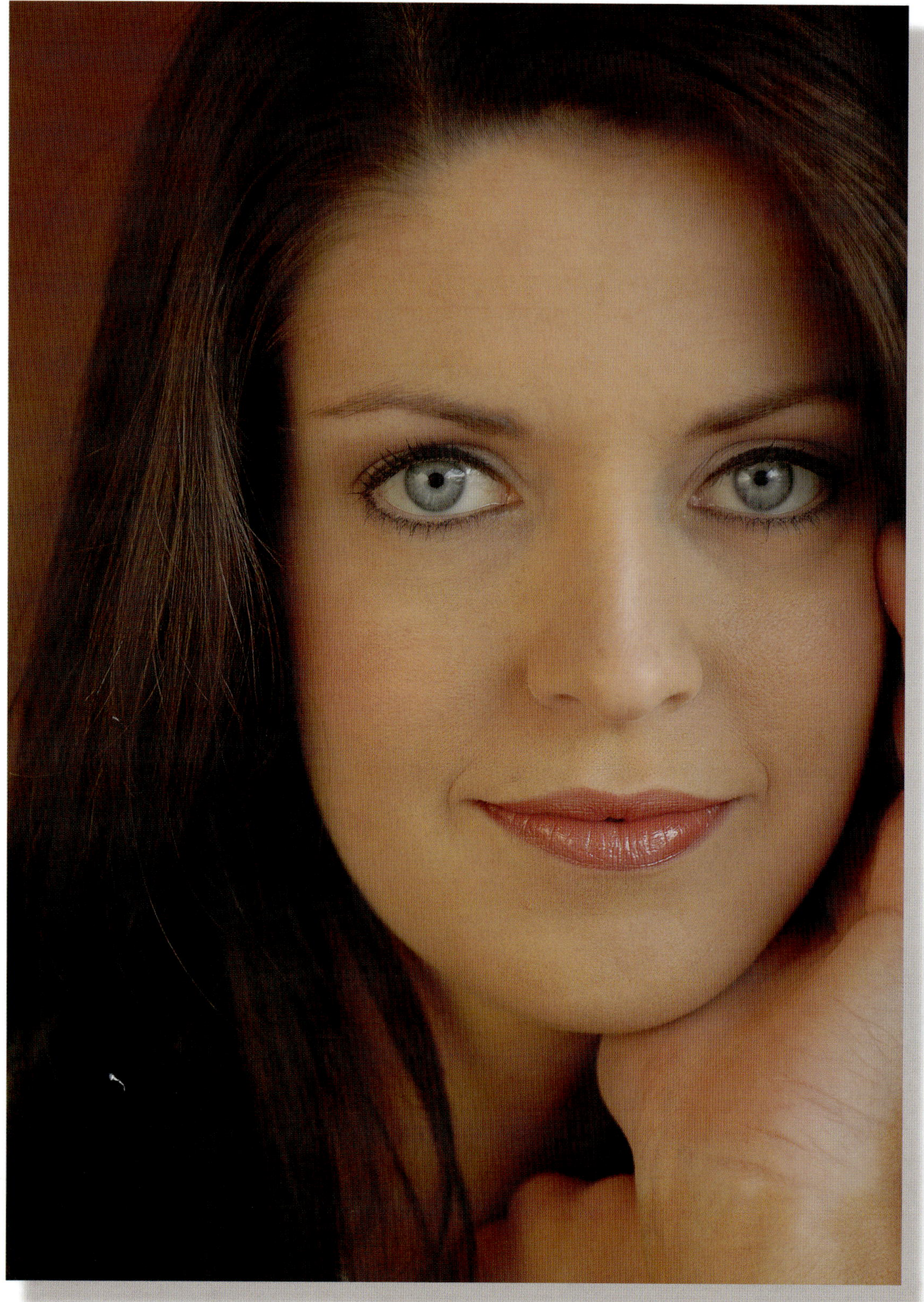

Alabama has been my home since childhood. It is a beautiful state with so much to offer, so many hidden treasures – but one of the things I love best is the people. As Miss America, I spent sixteen months traveling around the country, and every time I returned to Alabama, I received such a warm welcome. No matter where I was in Alabama, simply being here gave me an indescribably comforting sense of security, of belonging, and of being in the place I'm meant to be.

I chose to stay in Alabama to attend medical school at UAB, and I hope to pursue a career here as a pediatrician. It was an honor to represent the state of Alabama as Miss America 2005, and my hope is that in the future, I can give back to the people of this state – by continuing to promote pediatric cancer research through the *Curing Childhood Cancer* license plate, and by using my career as a physician to improve children's healthcare in Alabama.

DEIDRE DOWNS
[MISS AMERICA 2005]

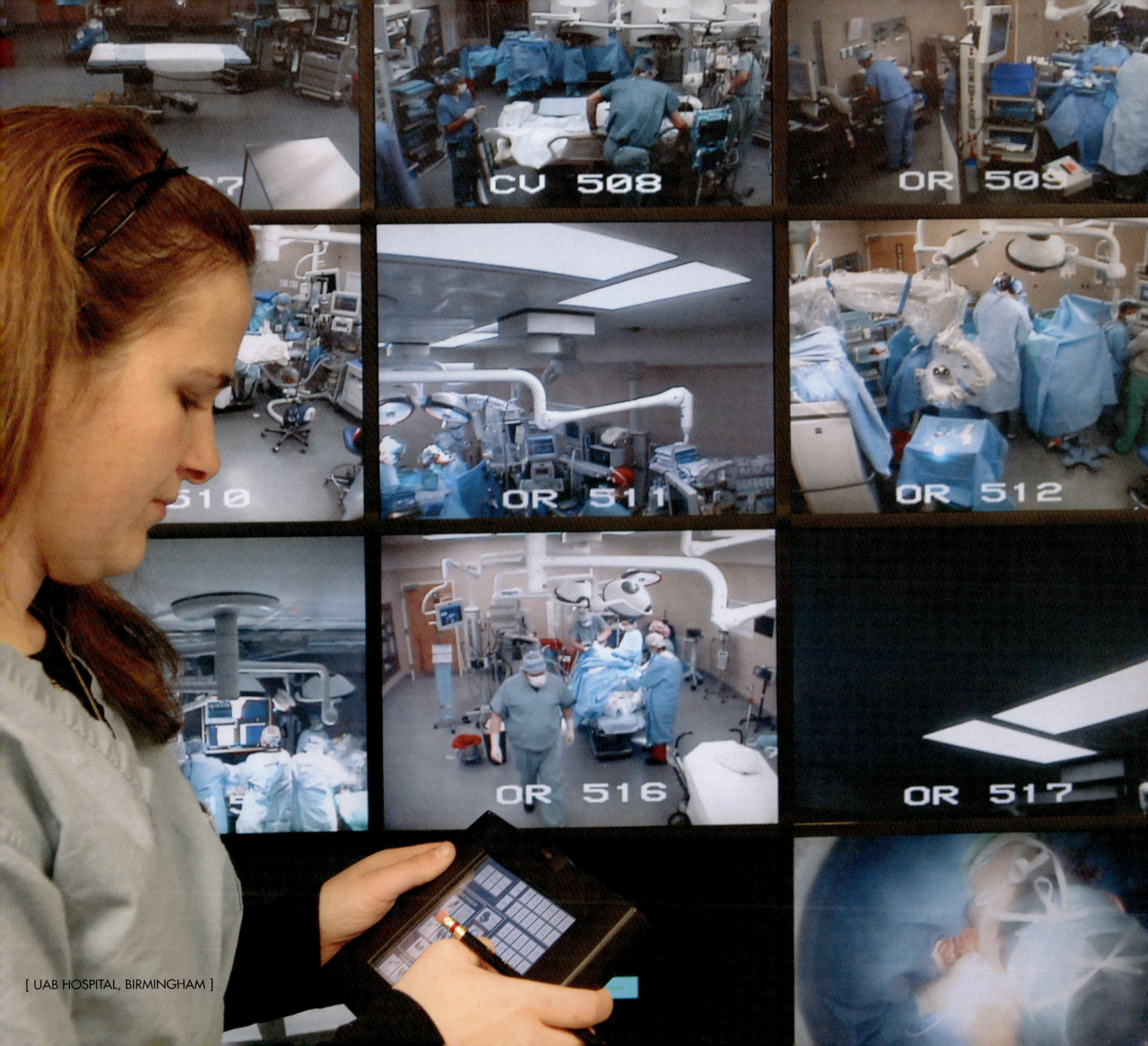

[UAB HOSPITAL, BIRMINGHAM]

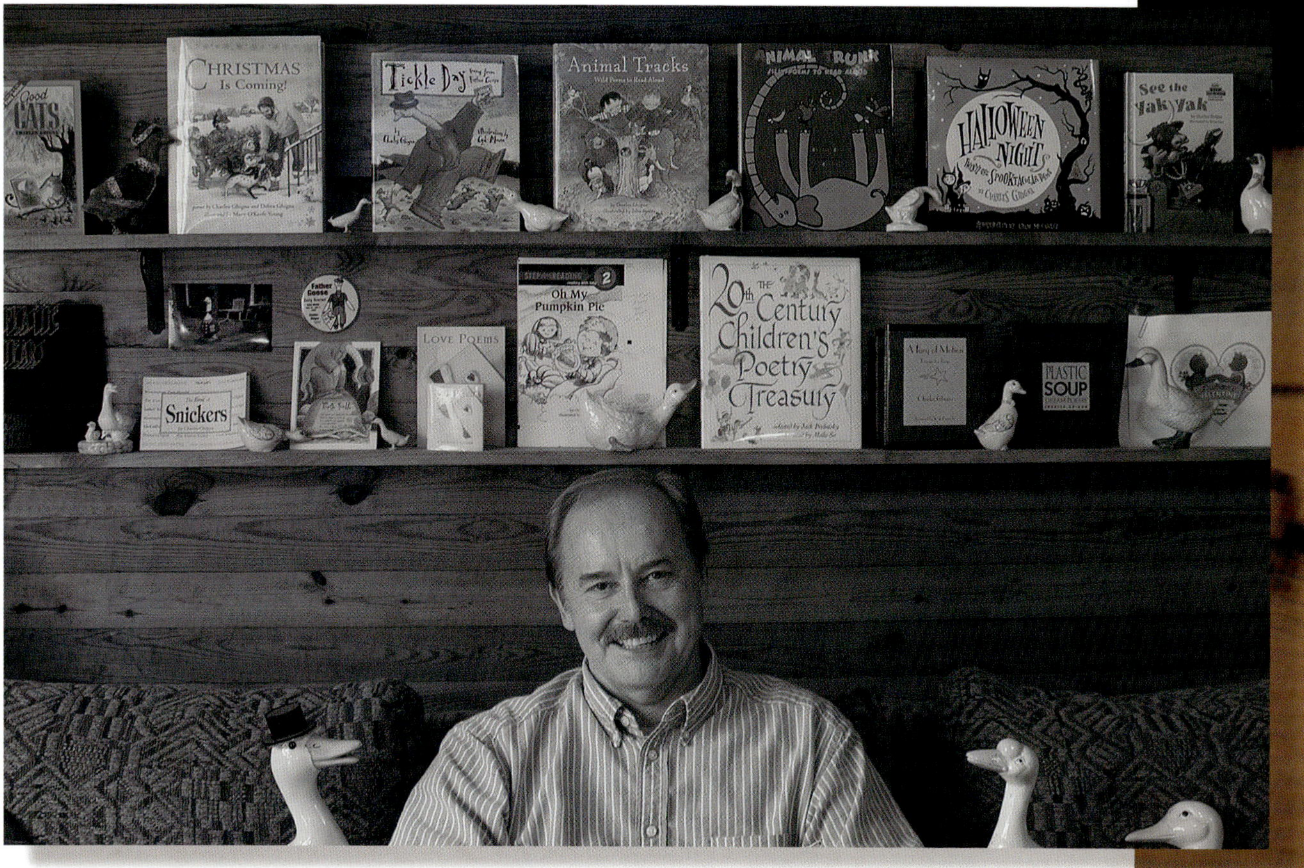

Alabama's a great place to raise a family. It's friendly, safe, and inspiring. It has a rich history of heartaches and heroes, as well as a vast cross section of hardworking people from all cultures and backgrounds, from rocket scientists and brain surgeons, to peanut farmers and poets. And if you love football, there is no better place on earth than Alabama.

Alabama's also a nature lover's paradise. We have some of the prettiest mountains, beaches, lakes, forests, rivers, caves, and canyons to be found anywhere in the South – and beyond.

For my family and me, living in Alabama is like living in a storybook world. It's down-home comfortable and just the right size. As Goldilocks said when she stumbled into the Three Bears' house and found the bed of her choice, "It's not too big. It's not too small. It's just right." Right on, Alabama. Write on!

CHARLES GHINGA (FATHER GOOSE)
[AUTHOR]

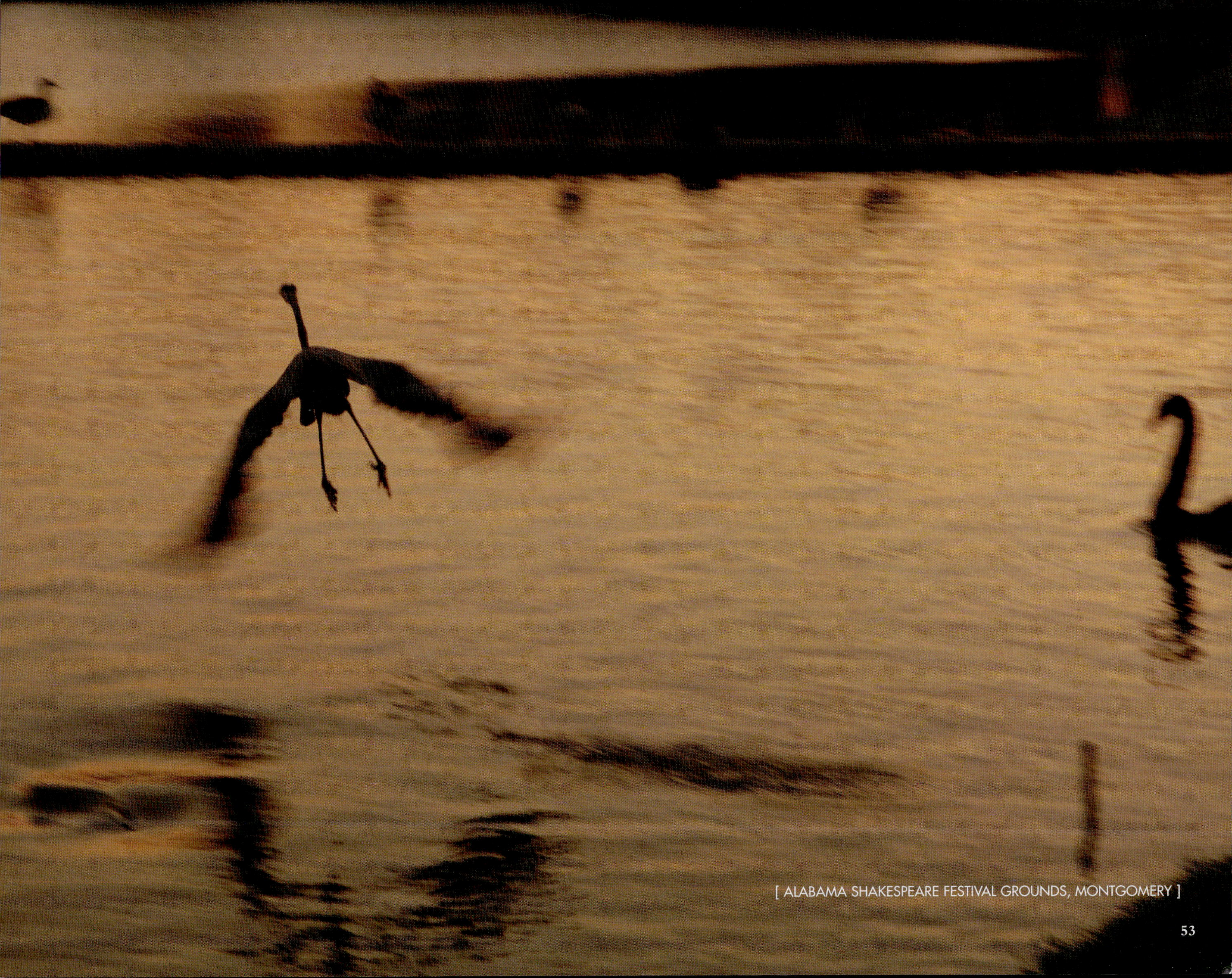

[ALABAMA SHAKESPEARE FESTIVAL GROUNDS, MONTGOMERY]

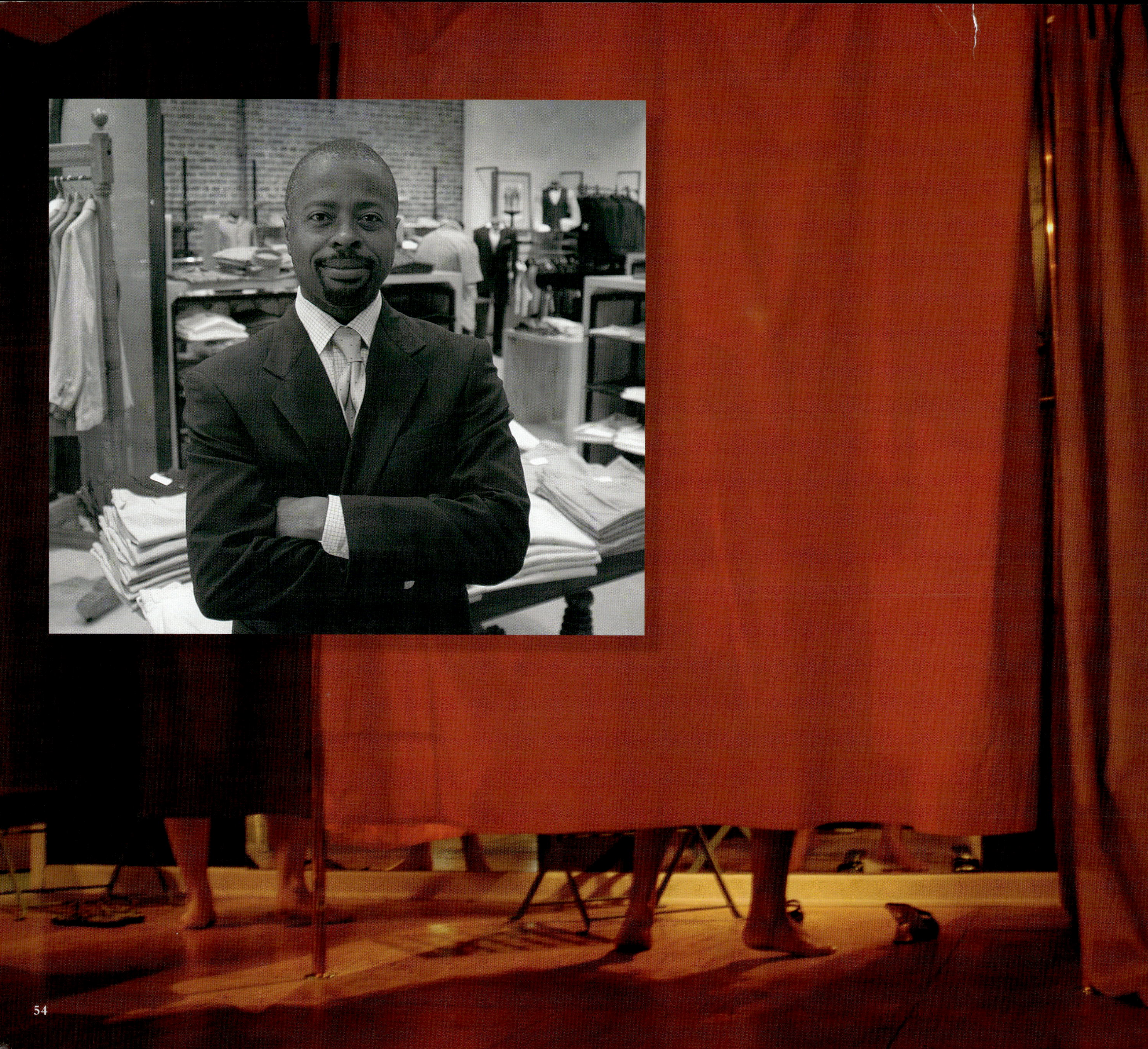

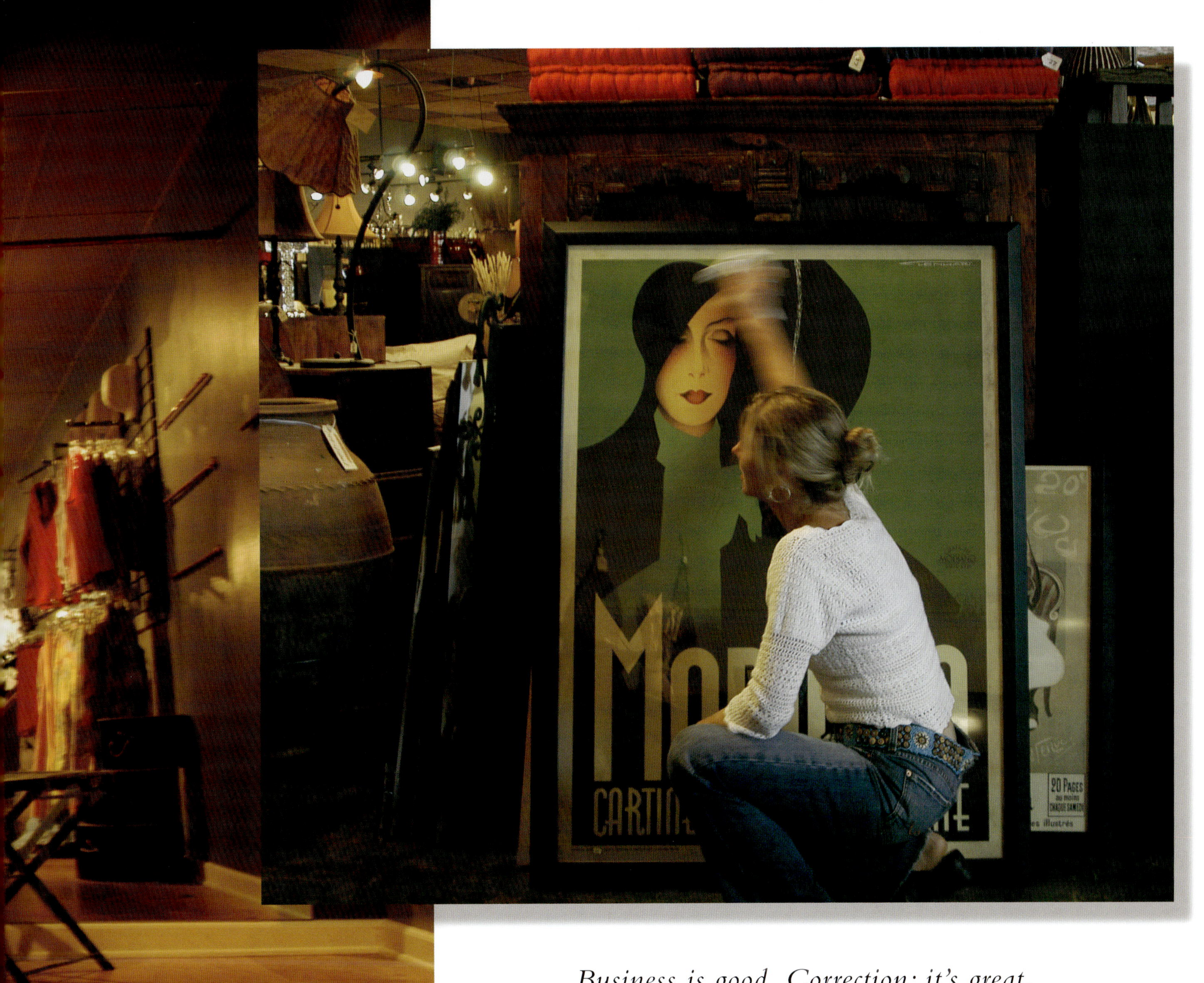

Business is good. Correction: it's great.

[SHAIA'S, *LEFT;* A.K.A. GIRL STUFF, *CENTER;* AT HOME FURNISHINGS, *RIGHT*]

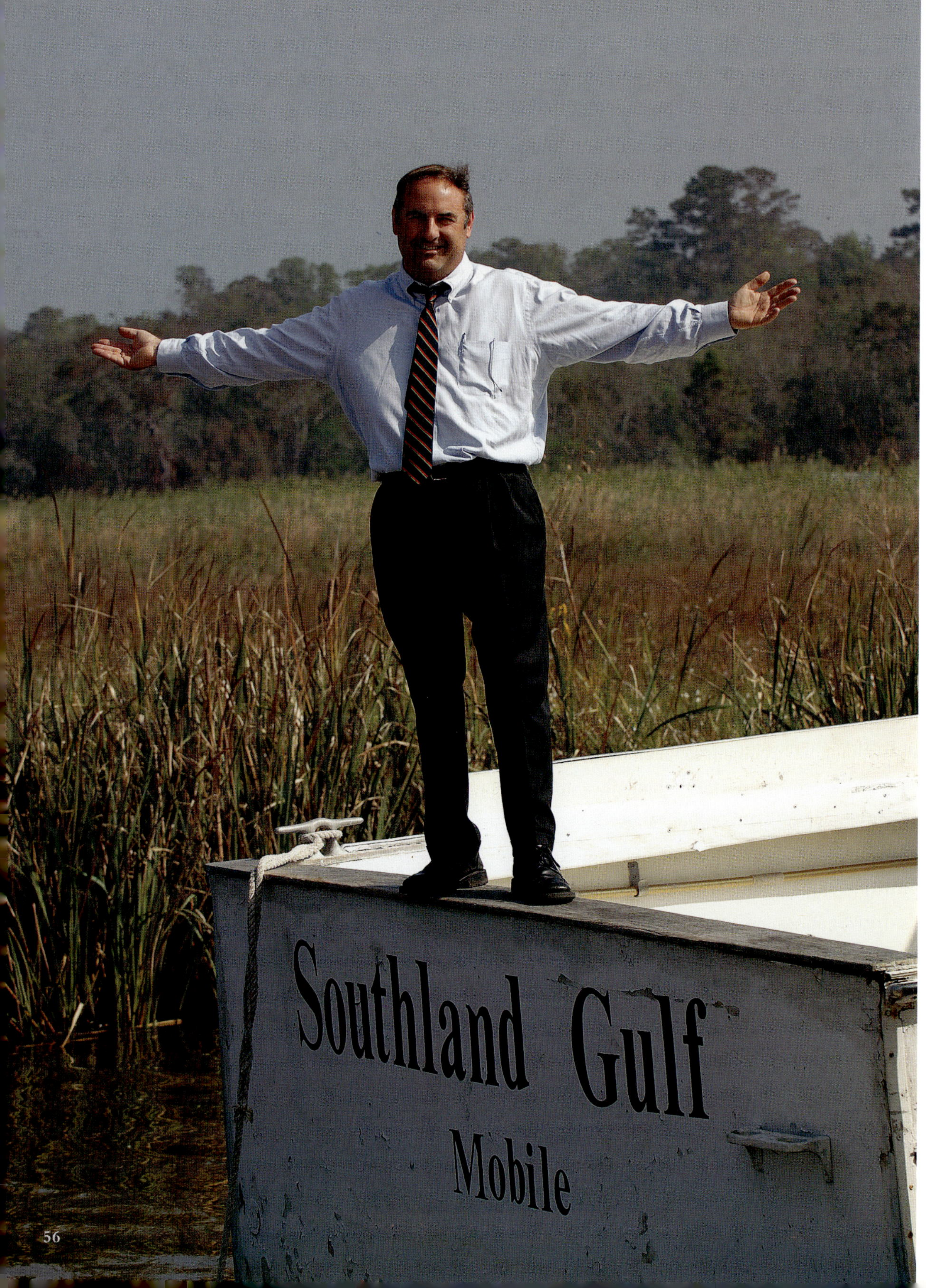

The south Alabama I know is unknown to others ... it is a secret delta swamp on the Gulf of Mexico where alligators and blue marlin and bald eagles live ... where rich and poor and black and white share lives simply ... people are friendly, and the smart ones move slowly. Mobile is the home of Hank Aaron and Forrest Gump. We are the home of a place only now discovered by tourists, developers, snowbirds, and migrants. And for those of us from here, that's a reason to string barbed wire and say, "thanks, but no thanks, we're full."

Robin Delaney
[CREATIVE DIRECTOR, WKRG NEWS 5, MOBILE]

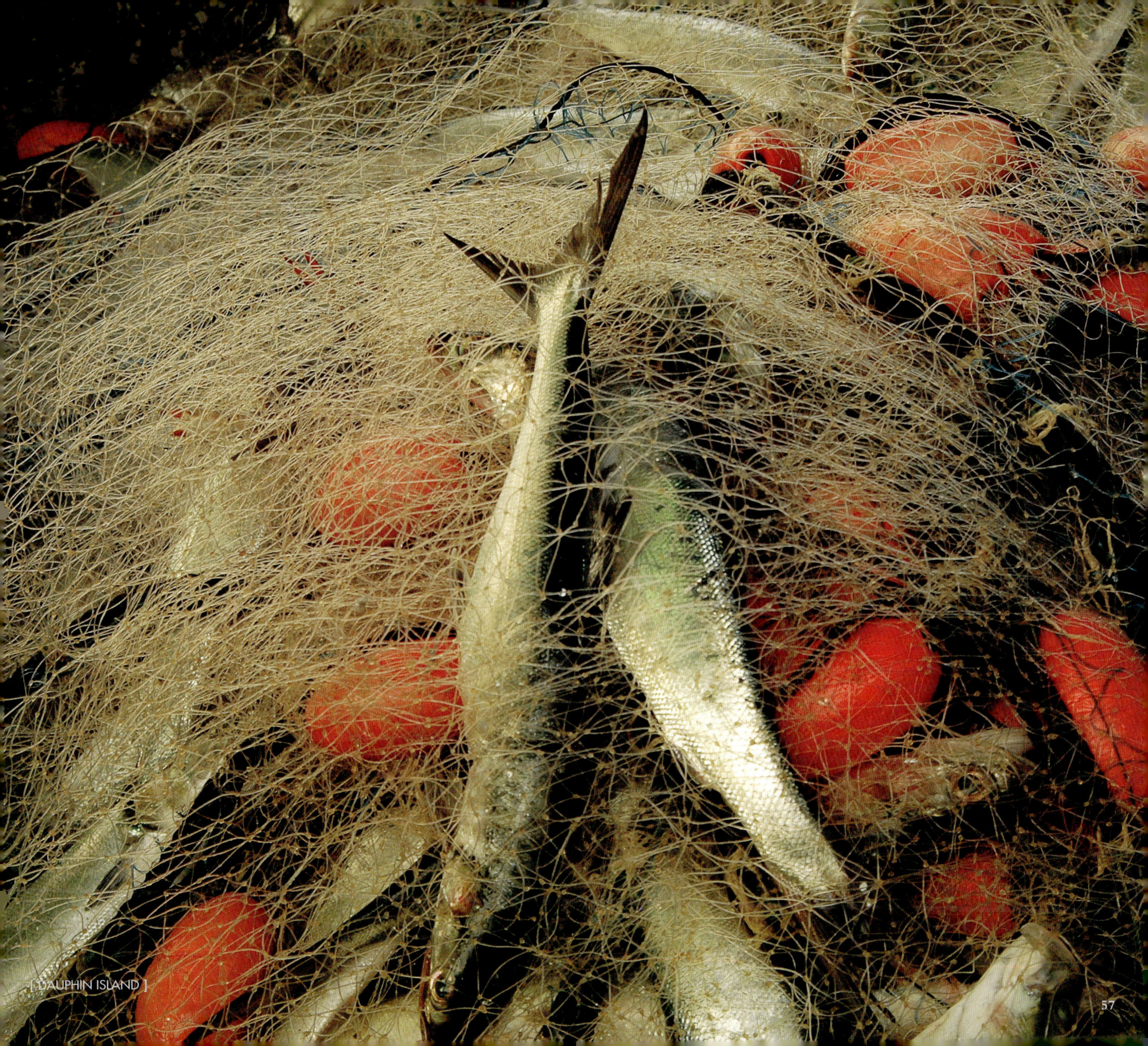

[DAUPHIN ISLAND]

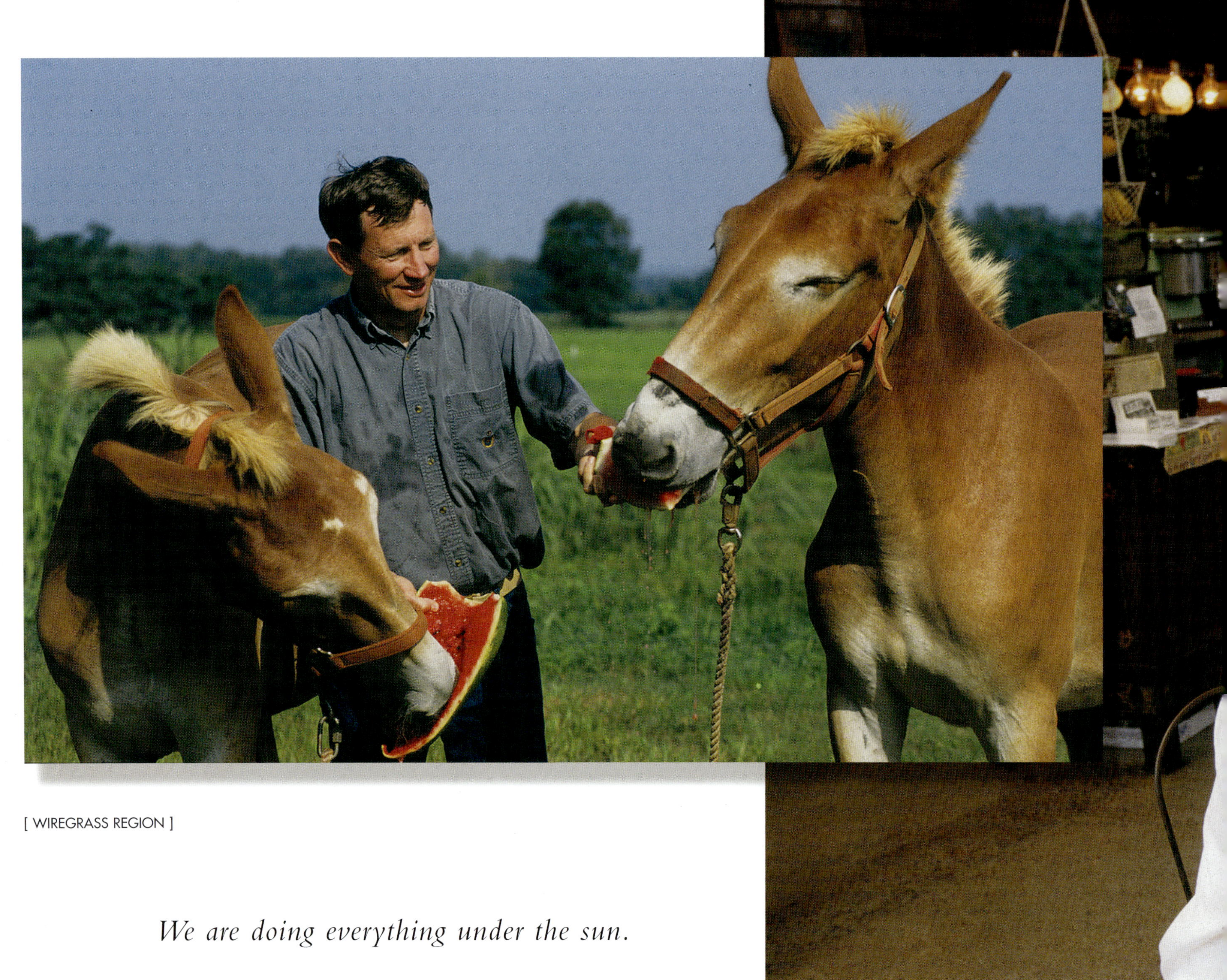

[WIREGRASS REGION]

We are doing everything under the sun.

[FOLEY SODA FOUNTAIN]

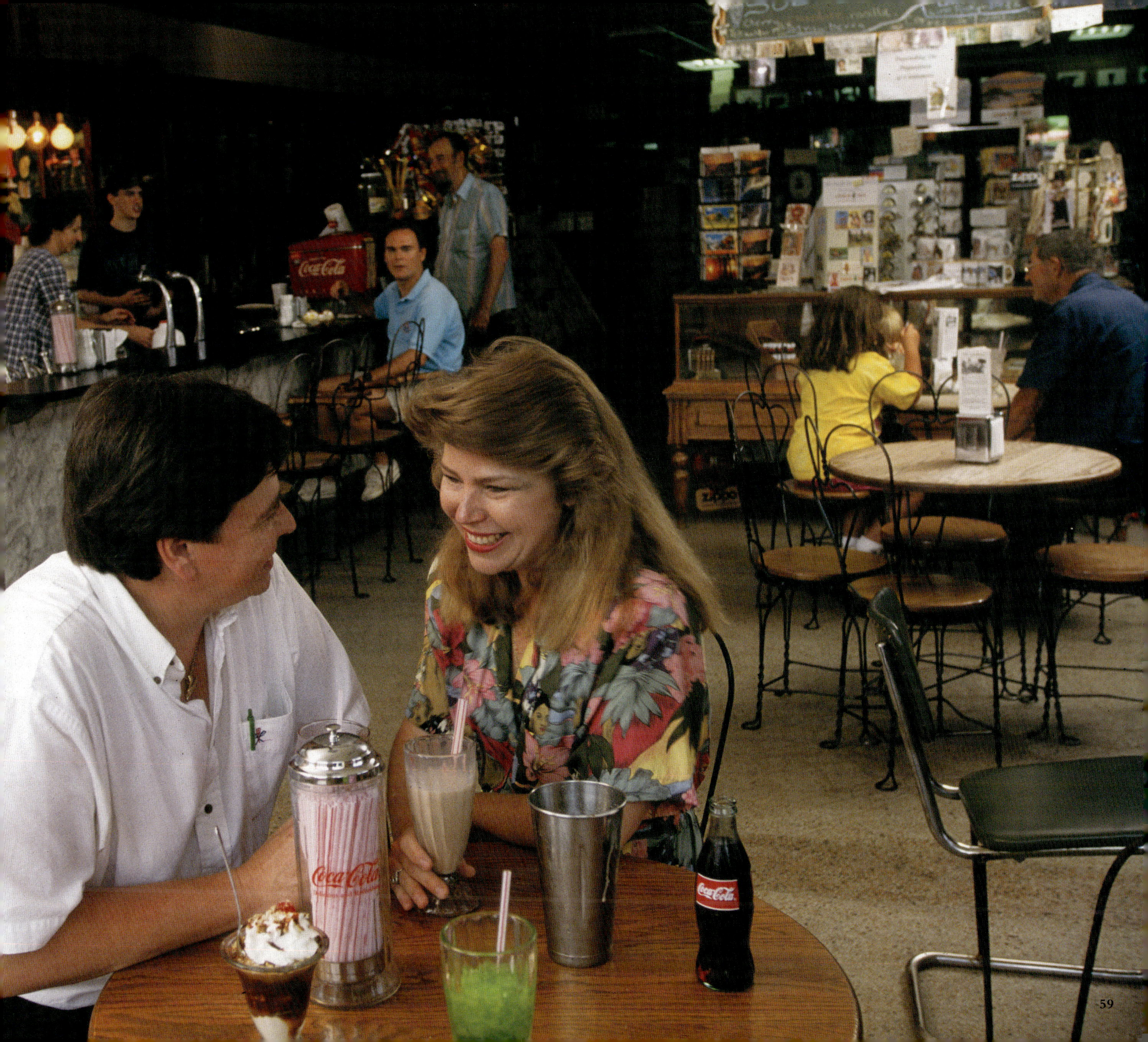
Coca-Cola
Coca-Cola
Coca-Cola

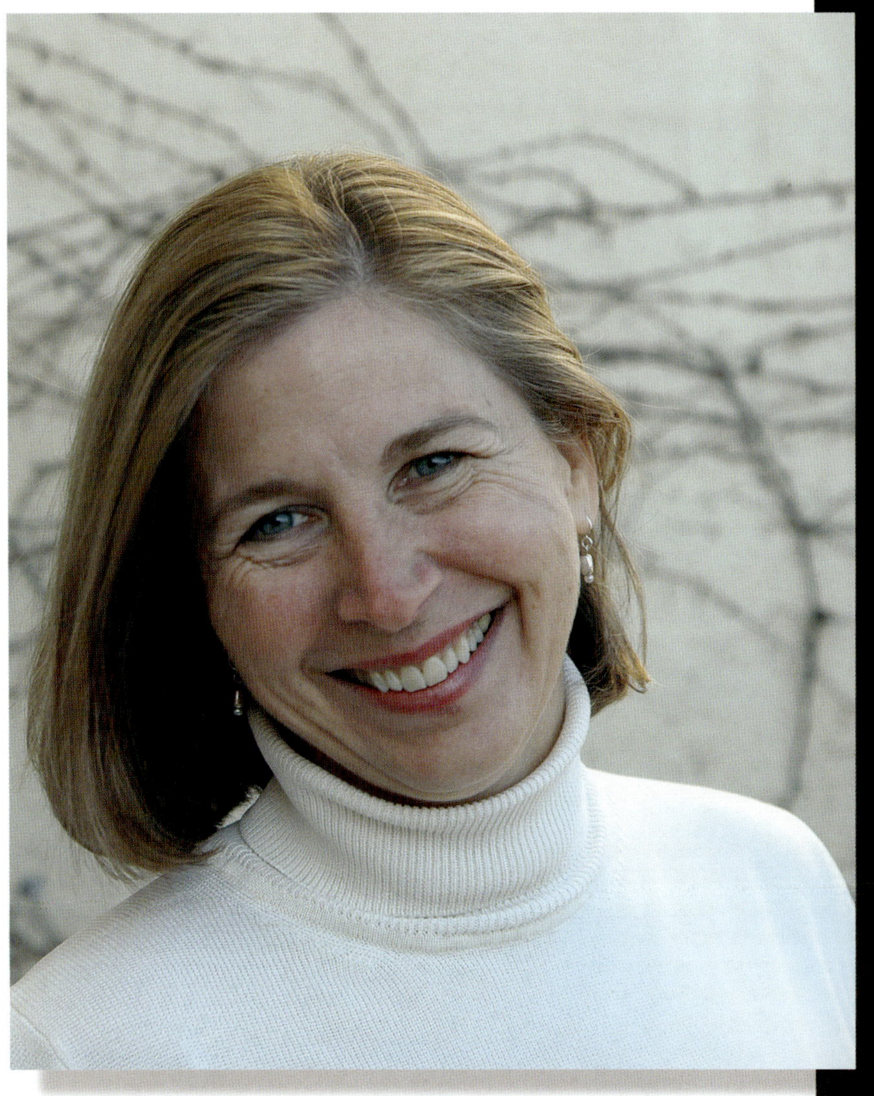

One thing I love about living in Alabama is the surprise people experience when they come here to visit. They don't expect mountains, or the incredible loveliness of the land, or the genuine warmth of the people, or how far we have come with race relations. They love our food, our art, and our authentic city. Seeing Alabama through their eyes reminds me again and again of the wonder and beauty of this place.

Cathy Crenshaw
[REAL ESTATE DEVELOPER]

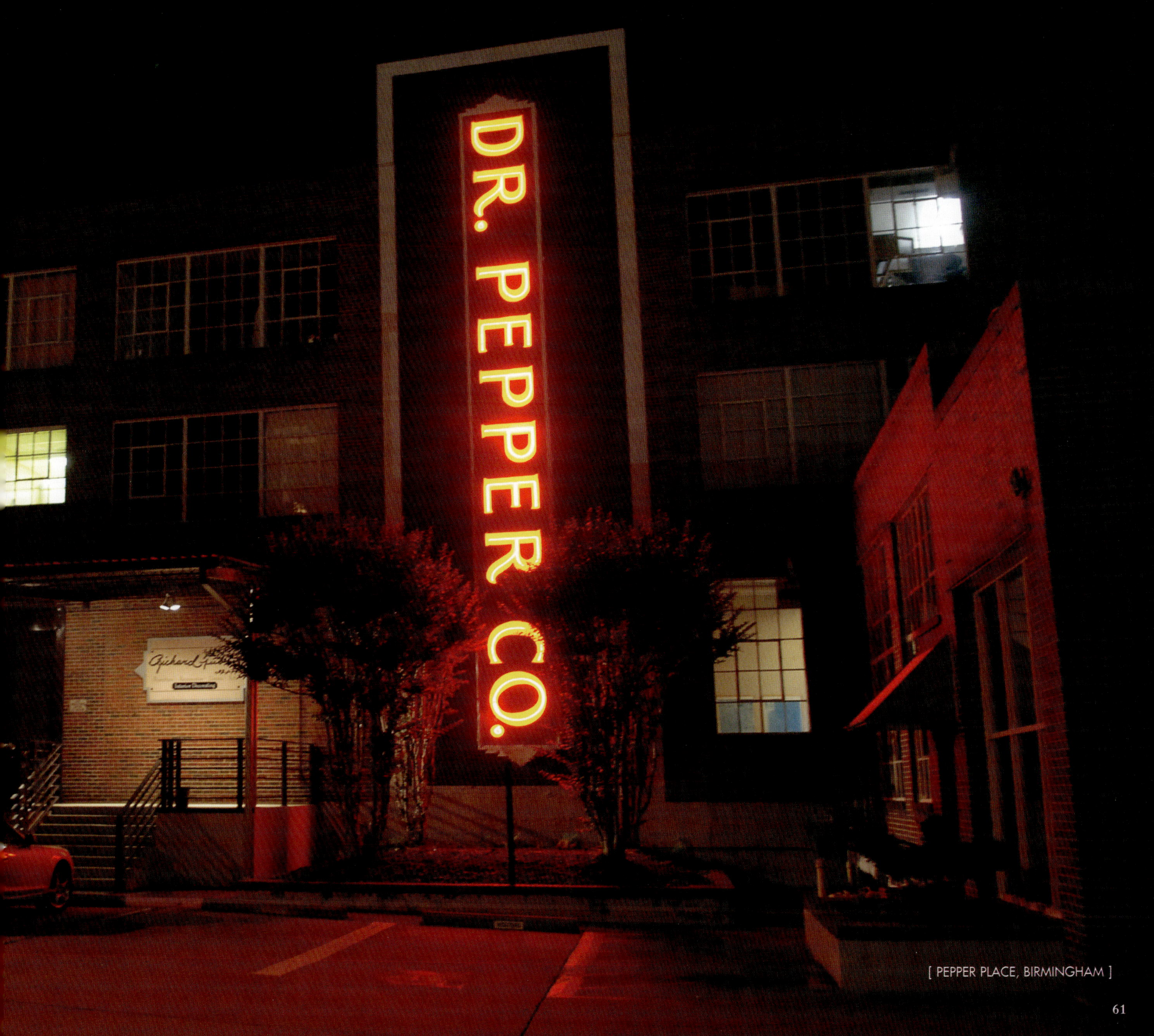

[PEPPER PLACE, BIRMINGHAM]

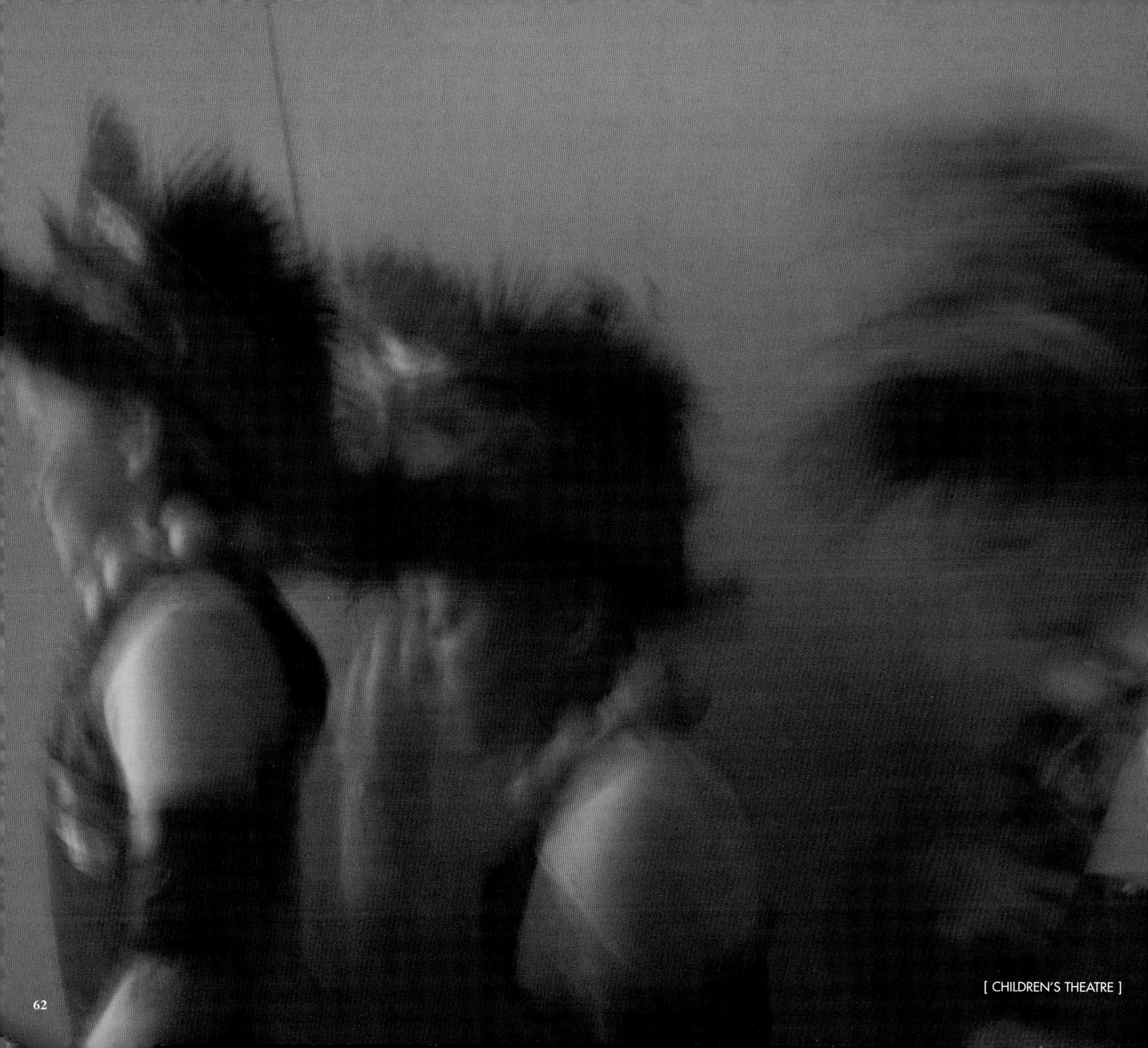

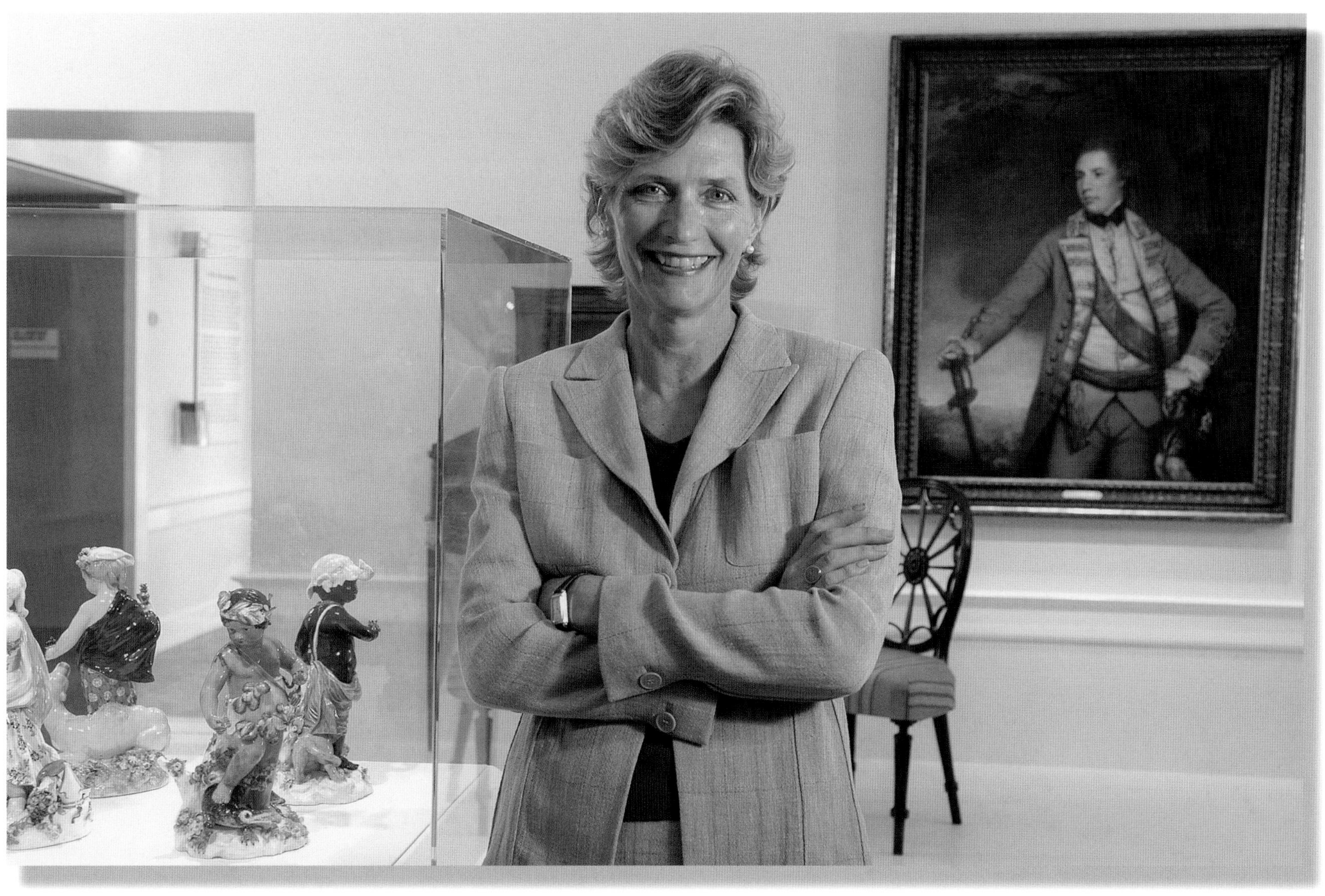

I love the strong sense of narrative that lies at the heart of Alabama. There is always a story, a history, to amplify daily events, the people we meet, the places we live. Whether fact or fiction, this tradition enlightens, but it also builds and deepens community and creates bonds with newcomers. Great storytellers come from Alabama and their gifts have shaped this place. We need these stories; they connect us to each other in a unique and powerful way, grounding us as we try to understand the past and negotiate the future.

Gail Trechsel
[DIRECTOR, BIRMINGHAM MUSEUM OF ART]

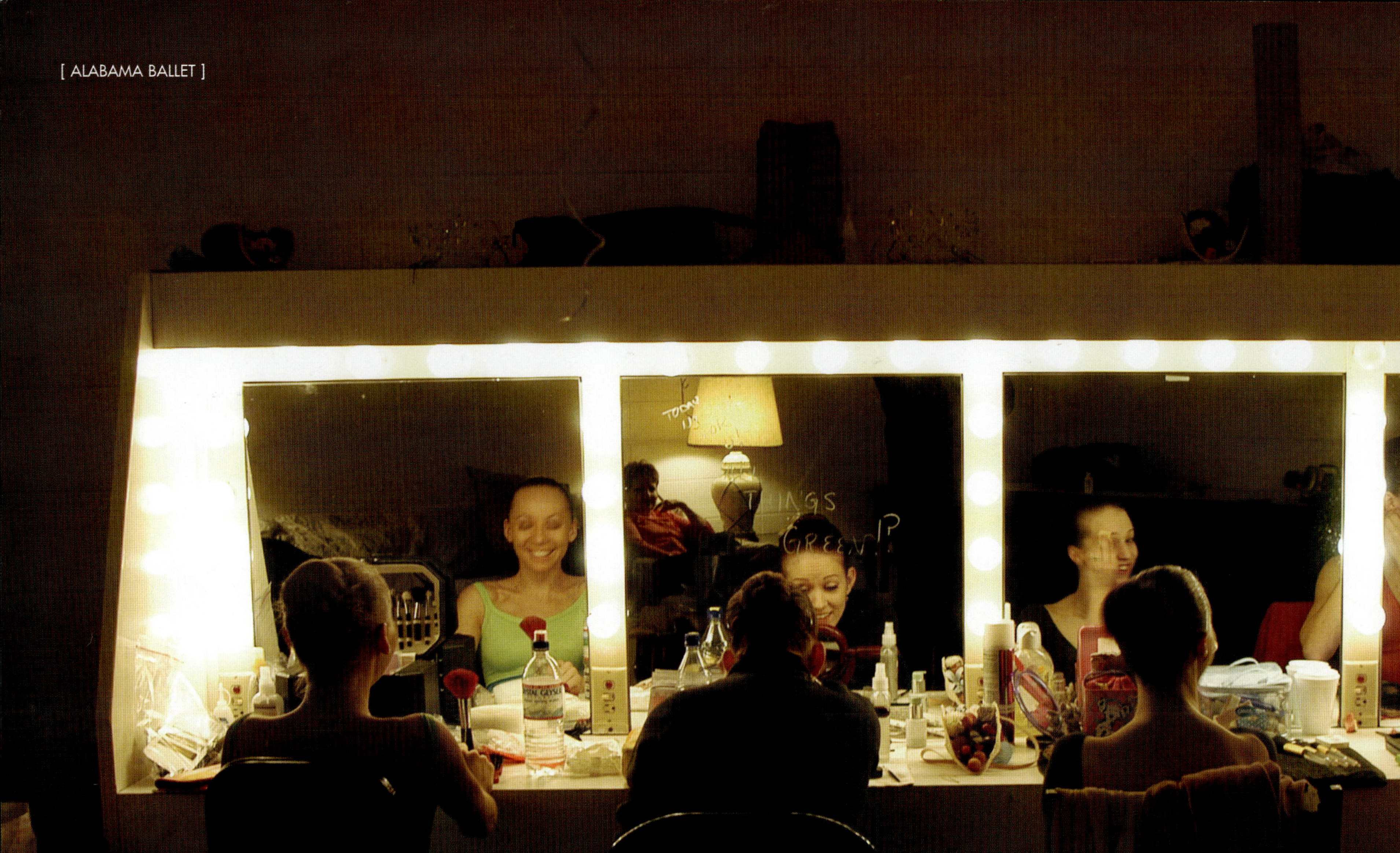

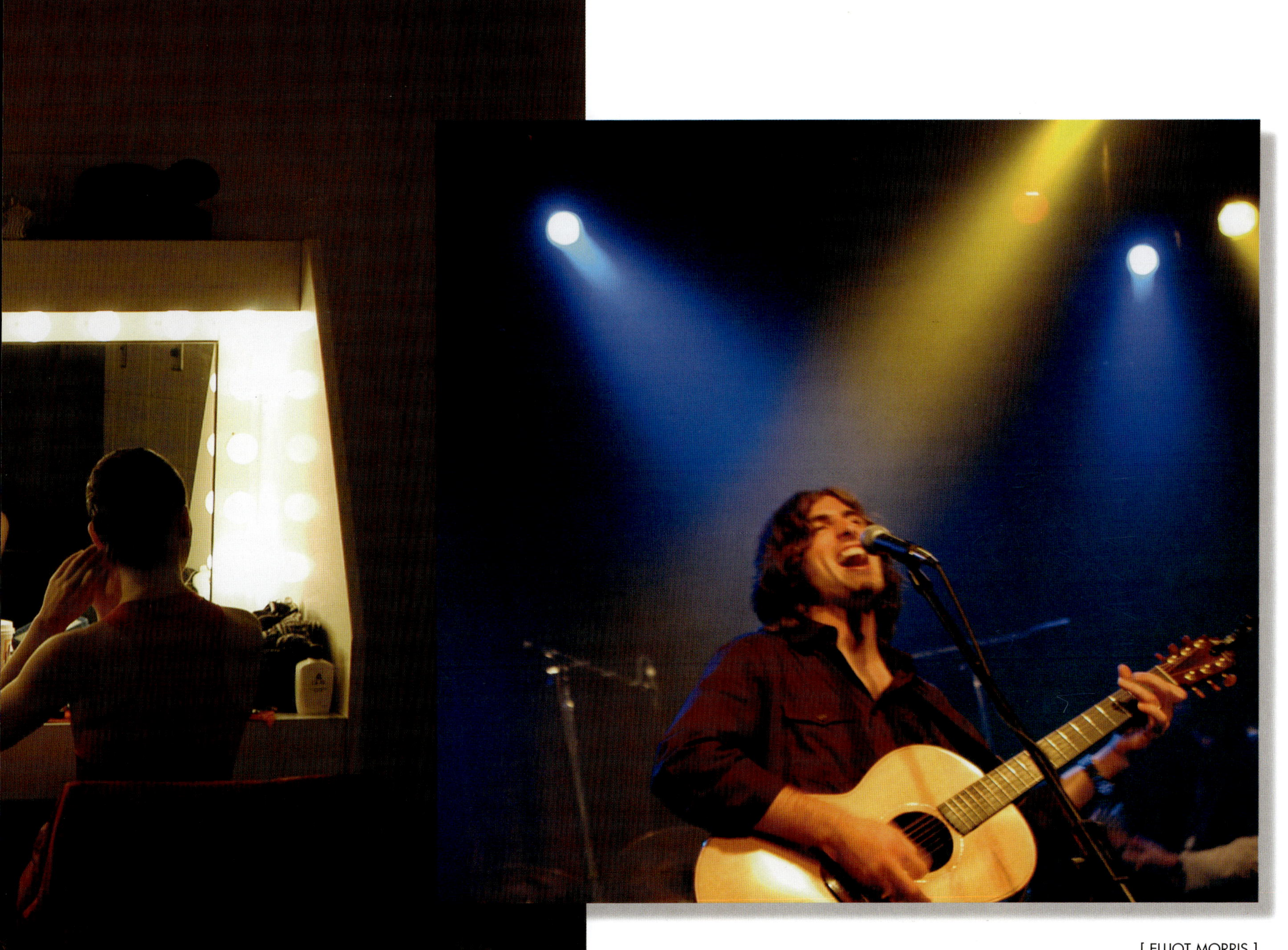

[ELLIOT MORRIS]

The arts are part of our way of work – and life.

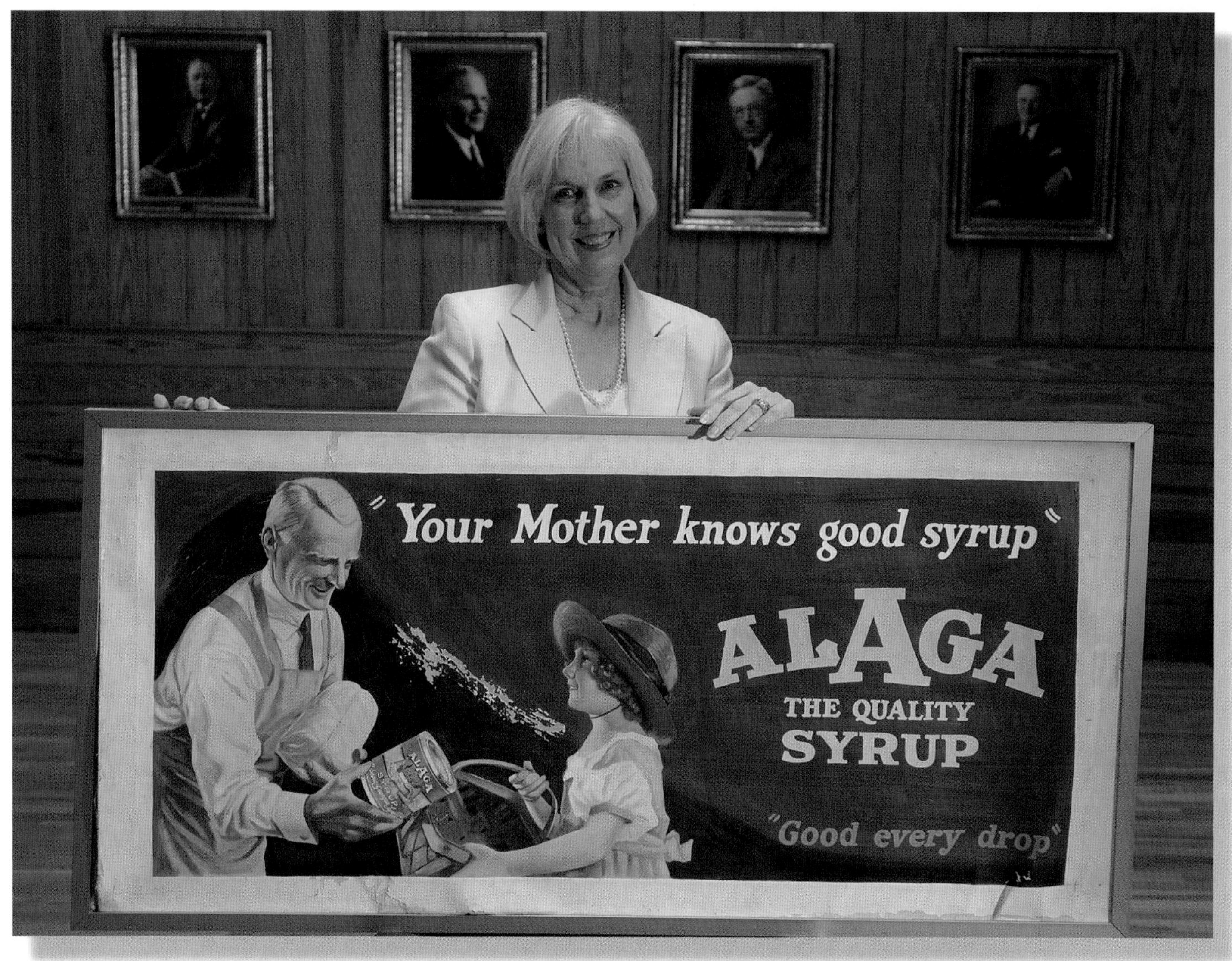

My memories of love began here with my mother, father, and sister, and continued to create the most beautiful hues among the colors of my life. There is always the memory of a first love, the love of your life, the unconditional love a mother feels for a child, the love of family, friends, and now, love of grandchildren, and the peace from a loving God.

Even Alaga (Alabama-Georgia Syrup Company) was born out of the love of a woman from Alabama and a man from Georgia. The love which started Alaga syrup has flowed through four generations of the Whitfield family into the kitchens of Alabamians for one hundred years.

Virginia Whitfield
[DIRECTOR OF PUBLIC RELATIONS, WHITFIELD FOODS (100 YEAR-OLD FAMILY BUSINESS)]

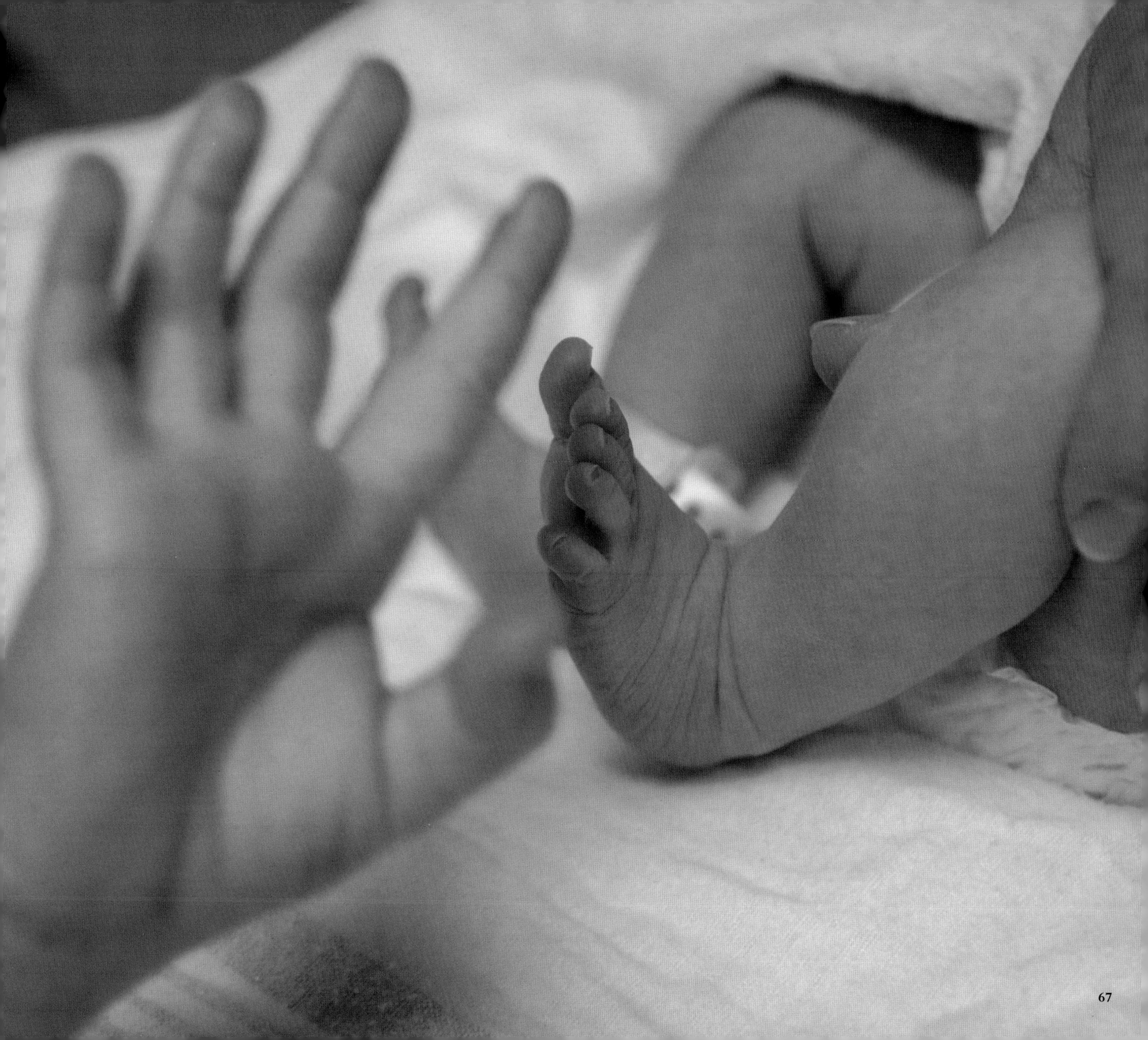

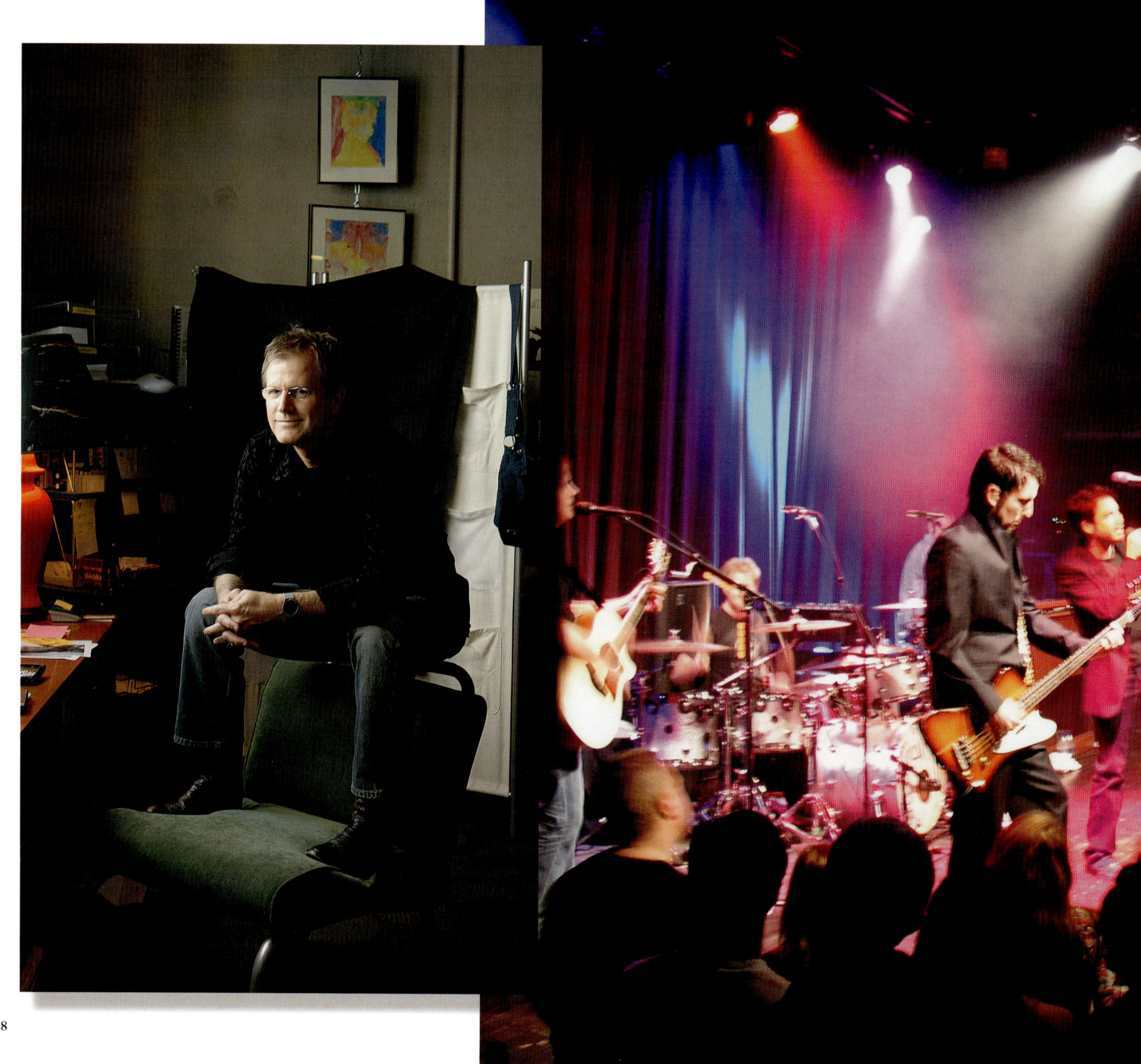

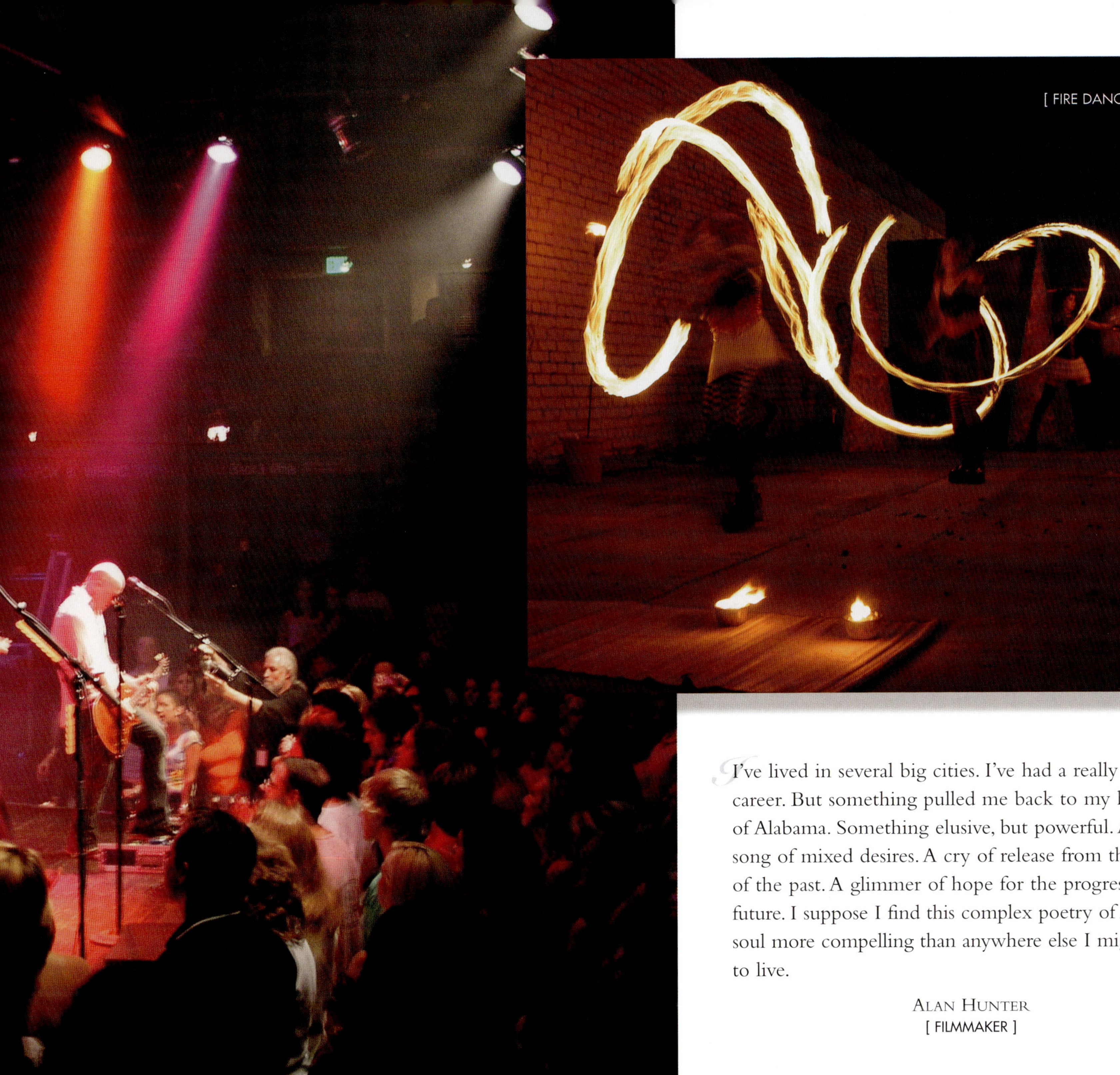

[TRAIN PERFORMING AT WORKPLAY, BIRMINGHAM]

[FIRE DANCERS]

I've lived in several big cities. I've had a really exciting career. But something pulled me back to my home state of Alabama. Something elusive, but powerful. A siren's song of mixed desires. A cry of release from the pain of the past. A glimmer of hope for the progress of the future. I suppose I find this complex poetry of Alabama's soul more compelling than anywhere else I might choose to live.

Alan Hunter
[FILMMAKER]

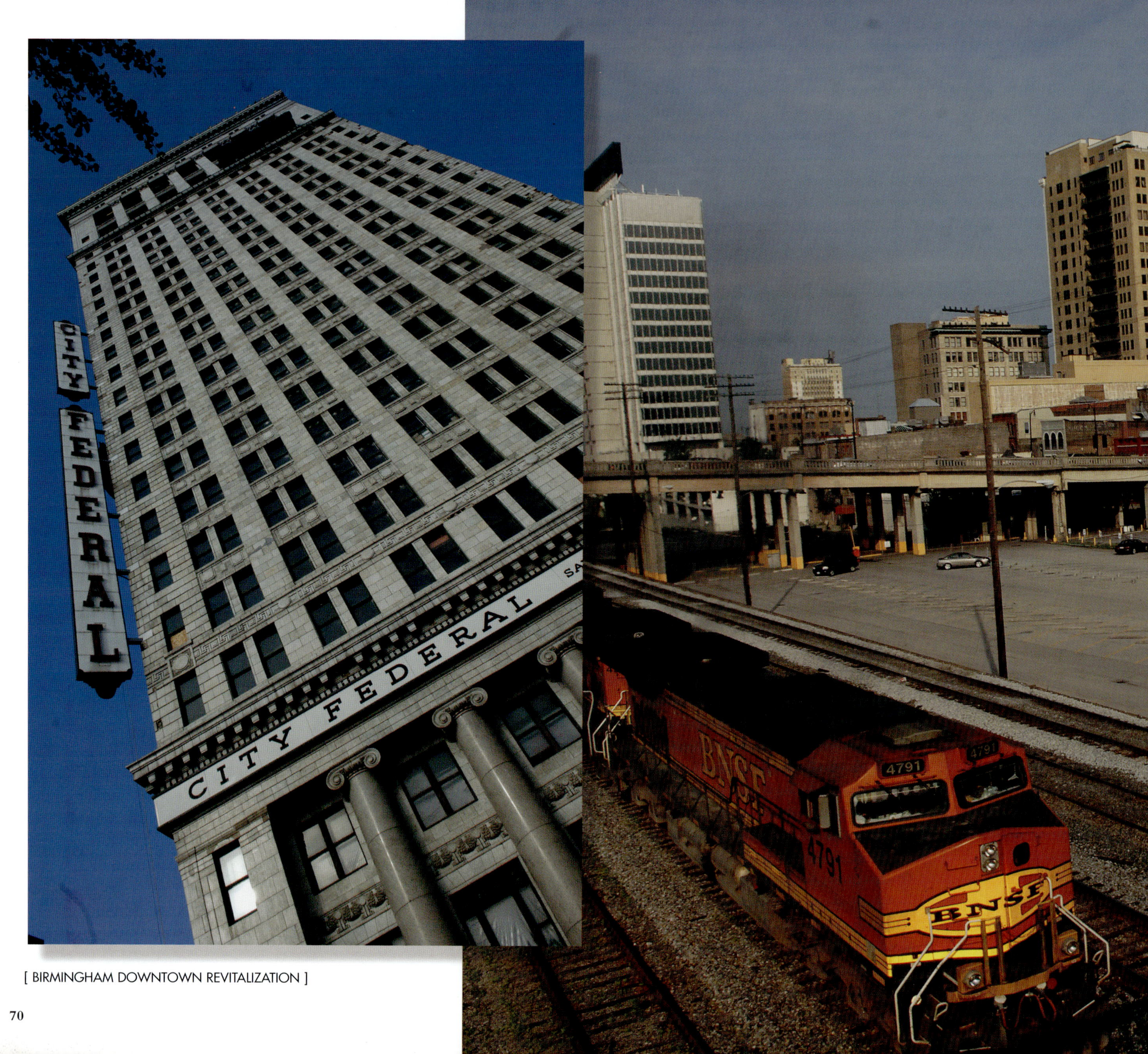
CITY FEDERAL
CITY FEDERAL
BNSF
4791
BNSF

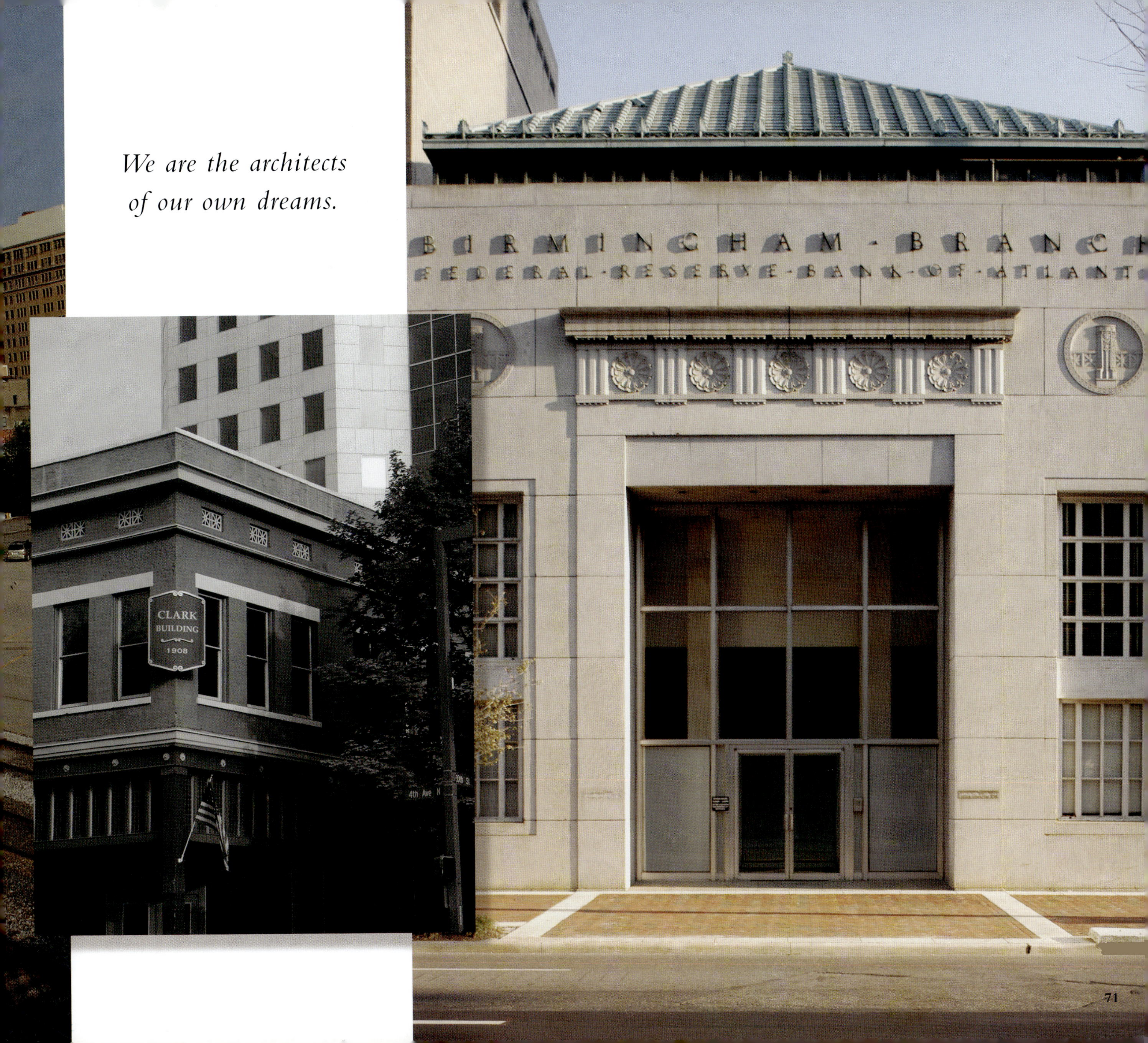

We are the architects
of our own dreams.

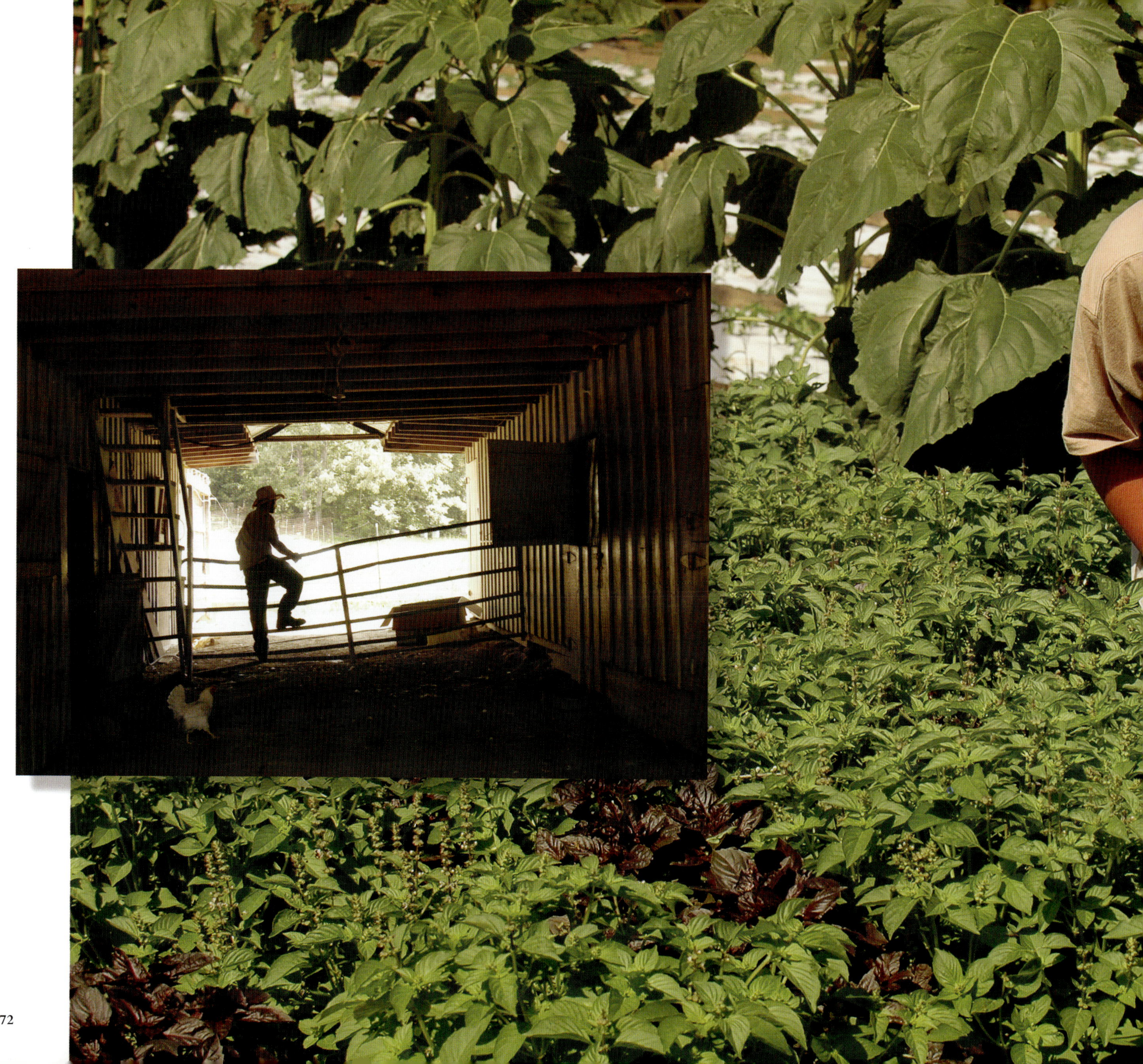

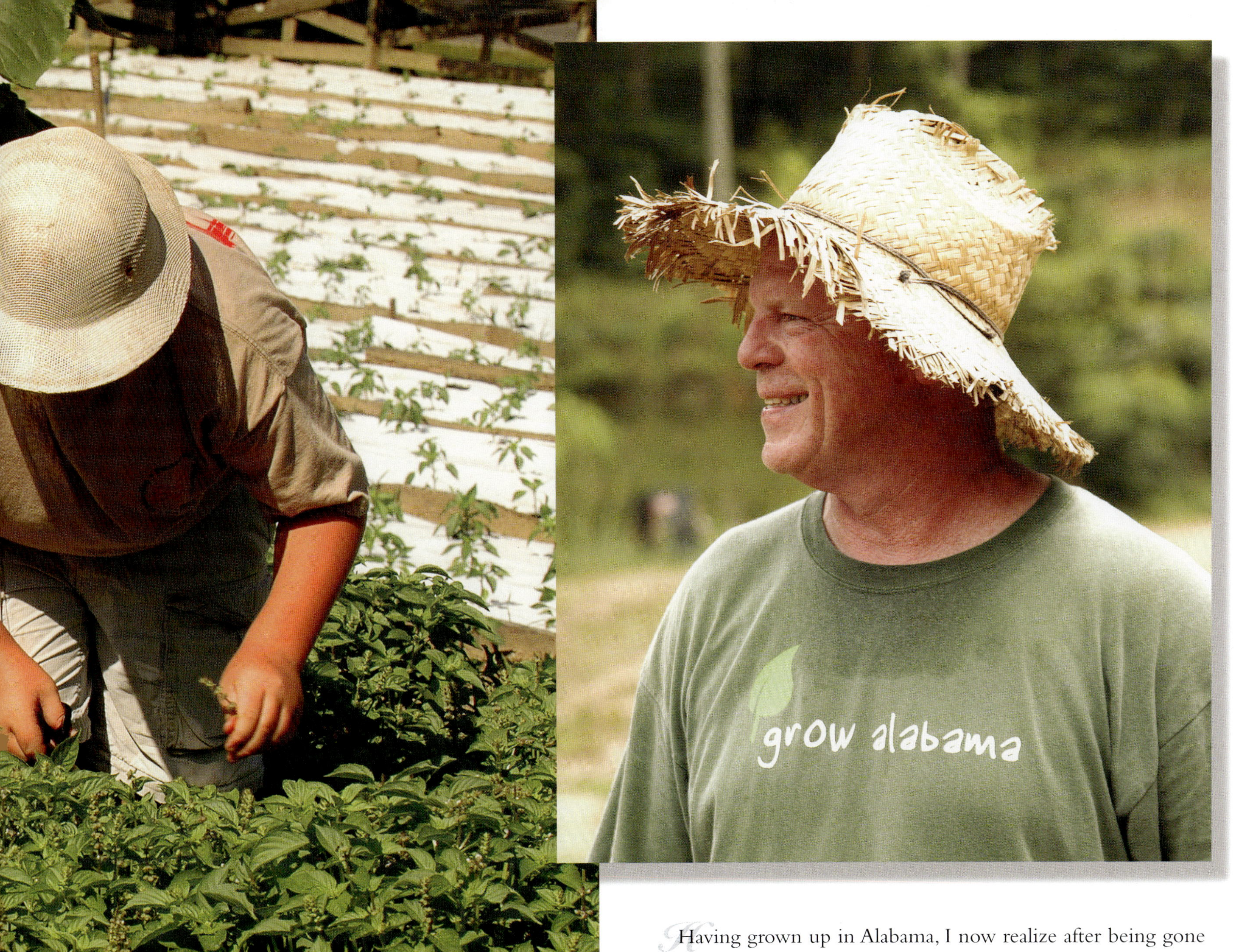

[GROW ALABAMA ORGANIC FARMS]

Having grown up in Alabama, I now realize after being gone for over twenty years, that one of the great things about Alabama is being able to have Alabama Grown foods. Most people don't realize that Alabama Grown is not readily available in the stores.

JERRY SPENCER
[FARMER]

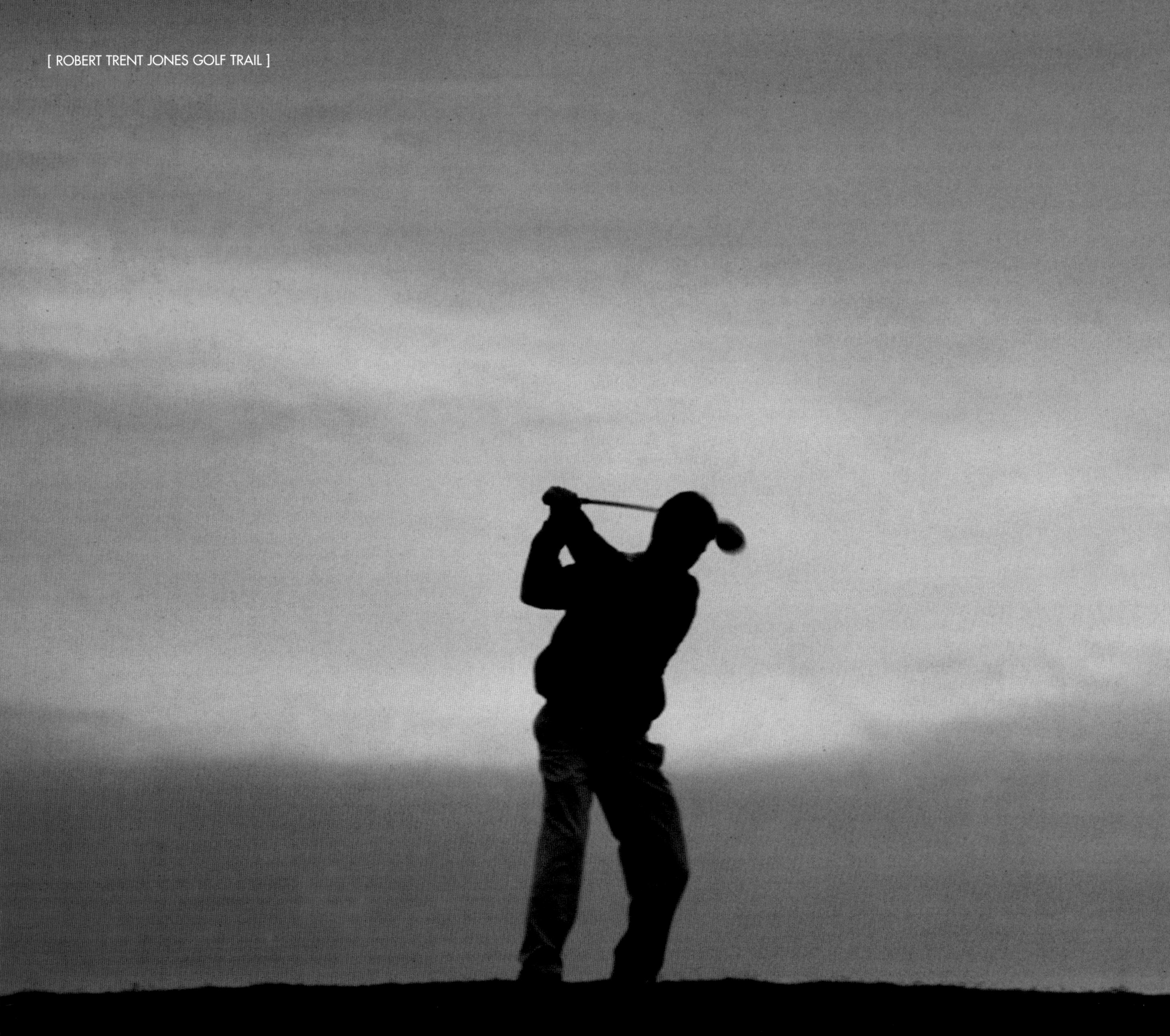

The Way We Play

We definitely wrote the book on this one. We play as hard as we work. We play ball. We hunt. We drive fast cars. We climb mountains. We raft rivers. We hike trails. We dance. We laugh. We know how to stop and smell the roses. And they smell so good.

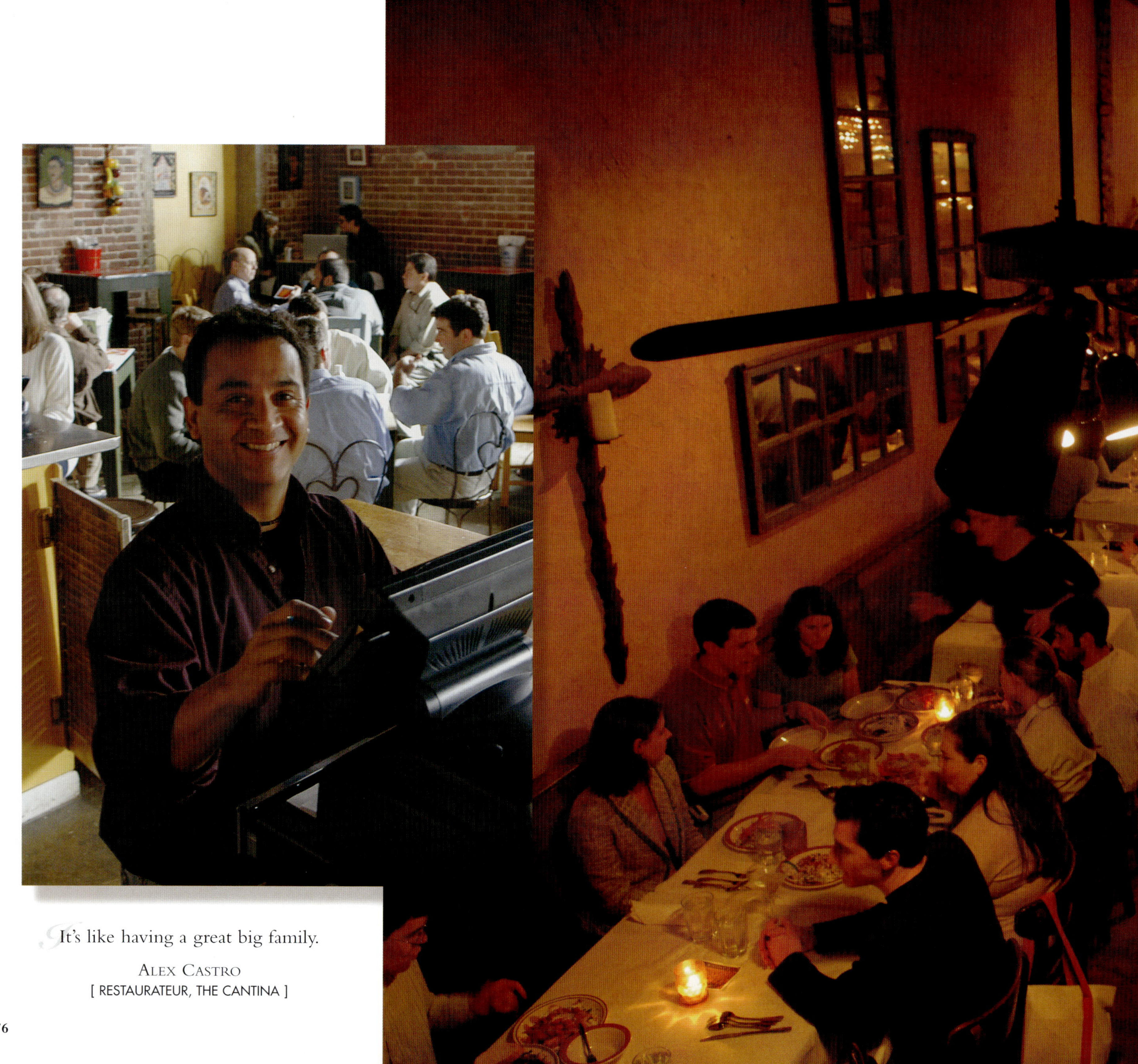

It's like having a great big family.

Alex Castro
[RESTAURATEUR, THE CANTINA]

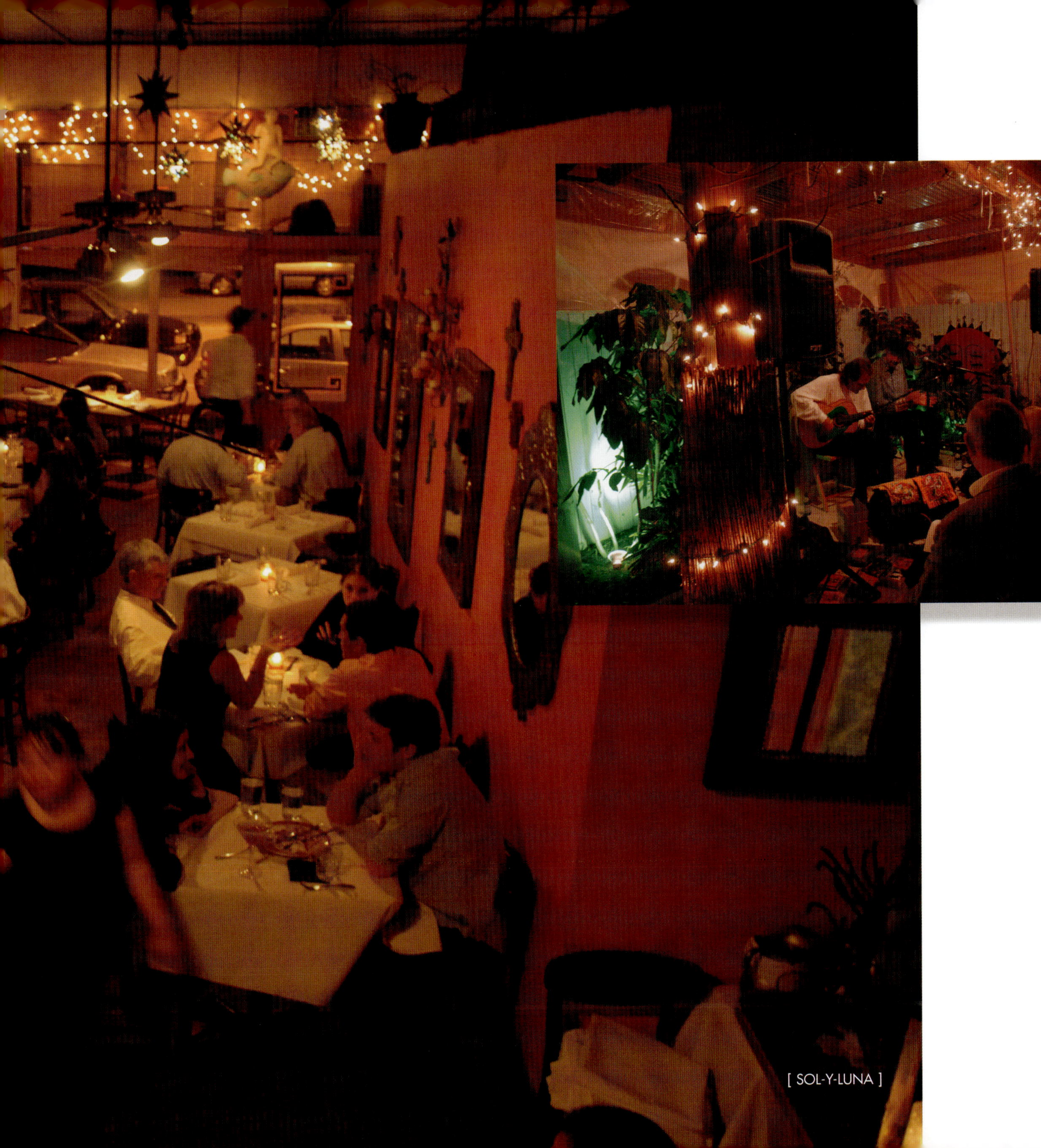

[SOL-Y-LUNA]

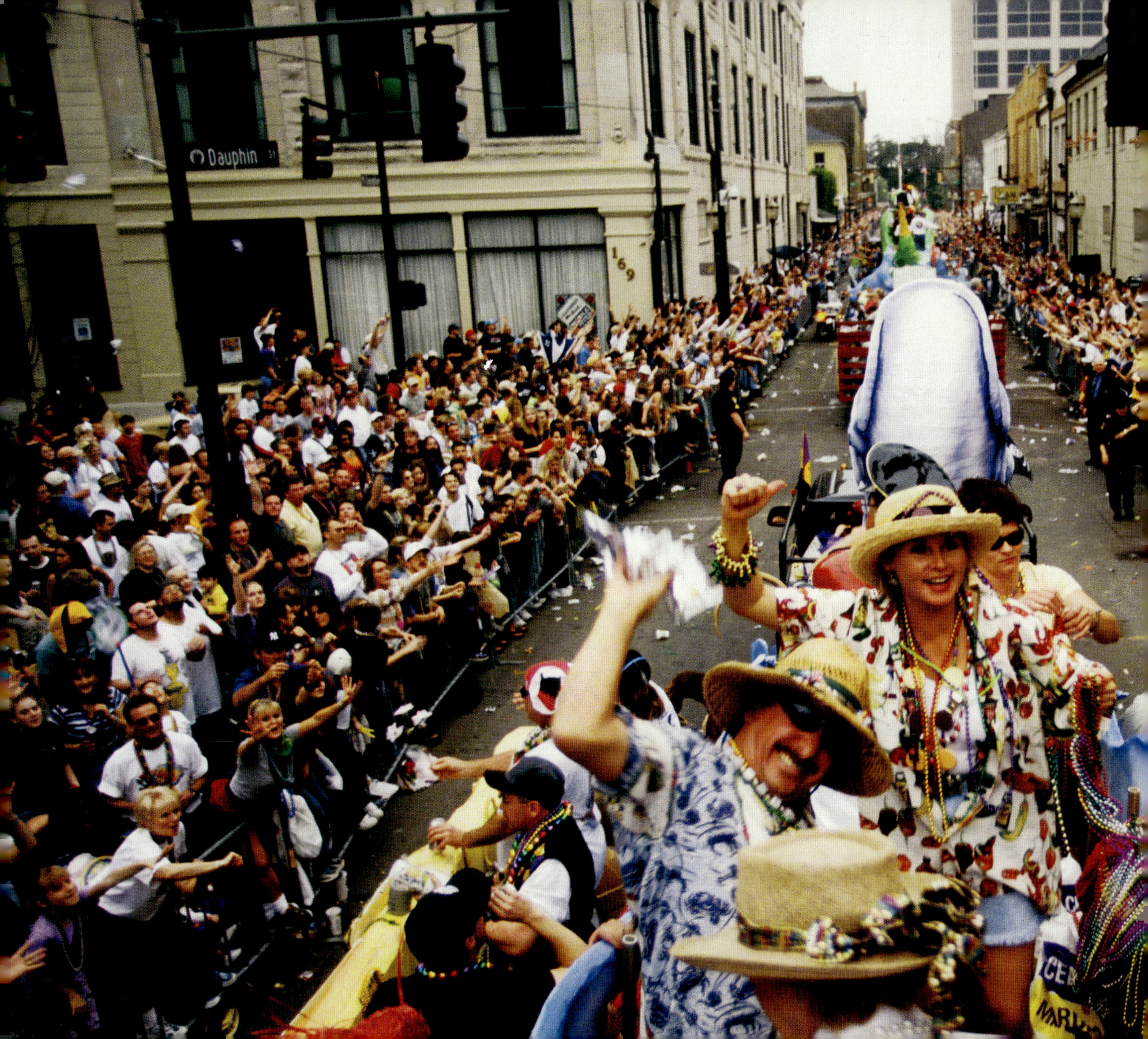
Dauphin
169

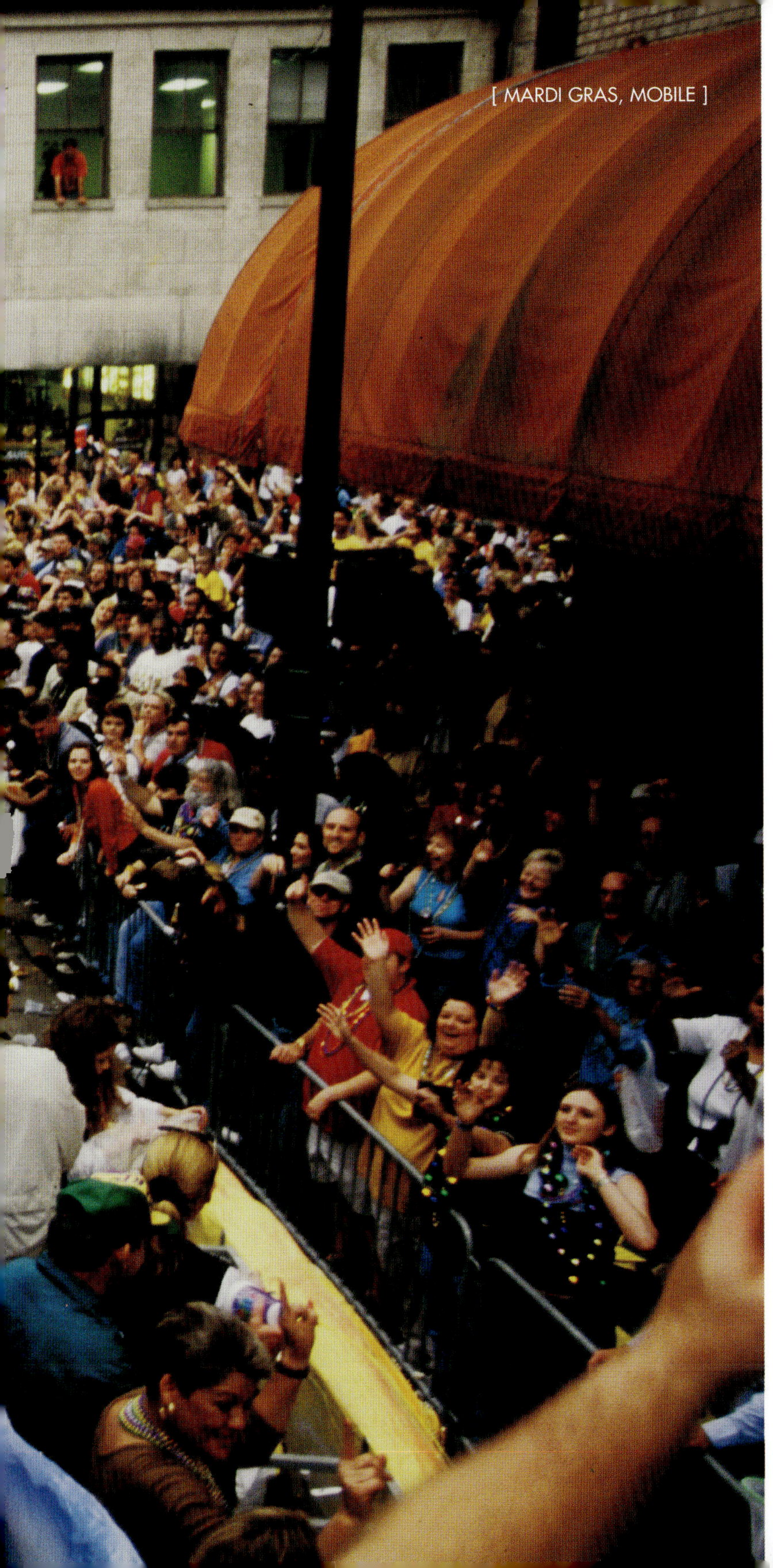

[MARDI GRAS, MOBILE]

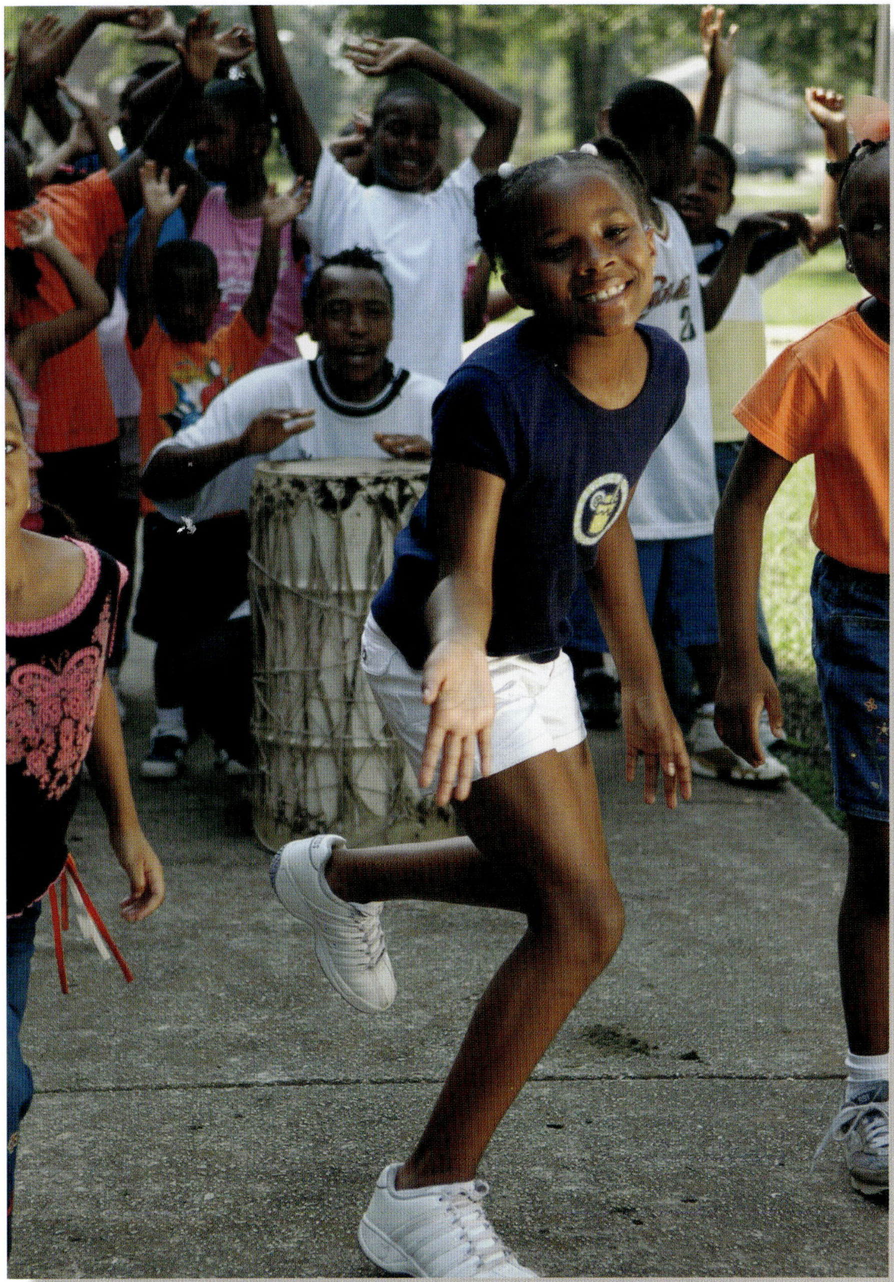

[NORTH BIRMINGHAM COMMUNITY CENTER]

There's pretty much something to have a party about all the time.

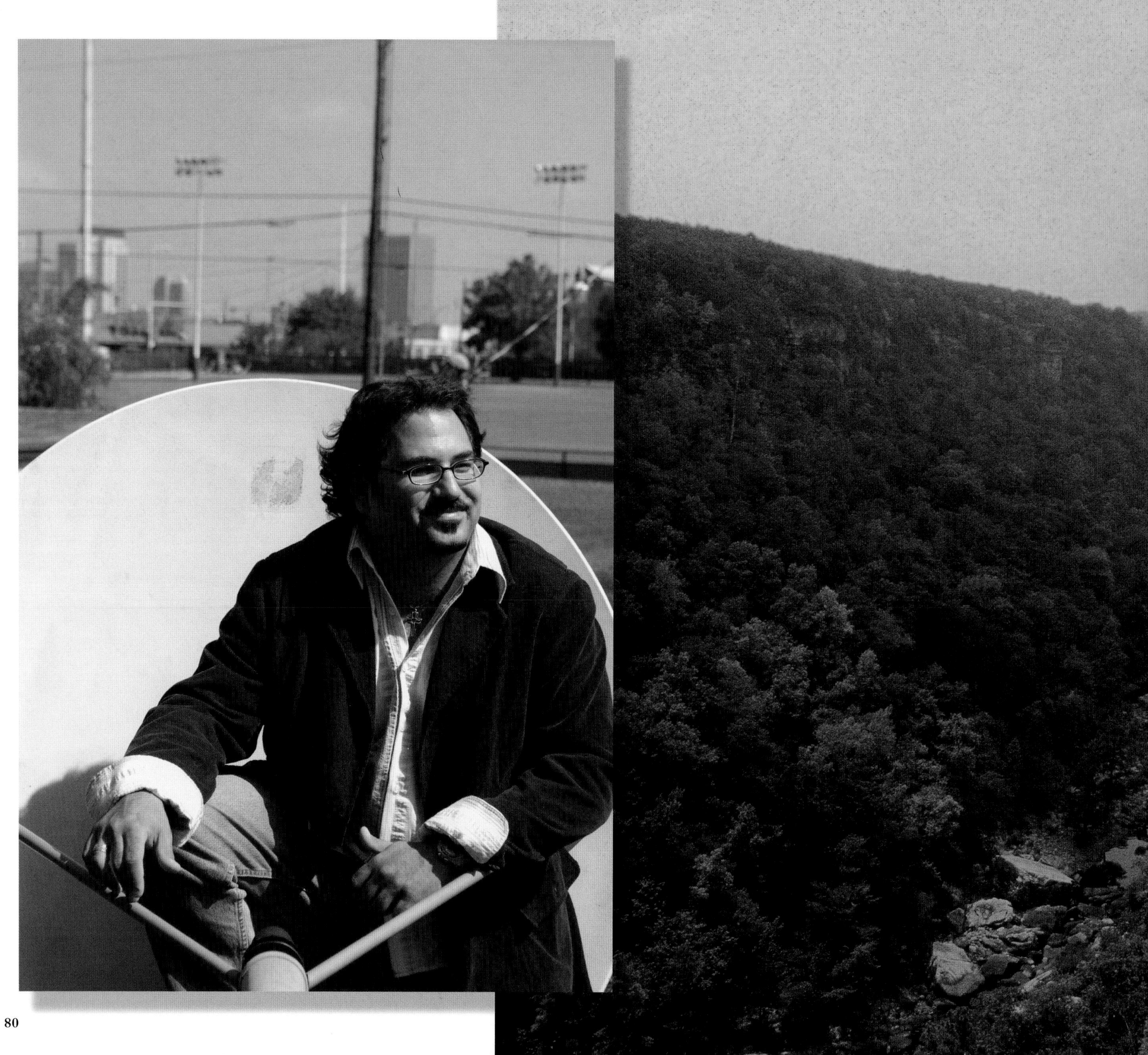

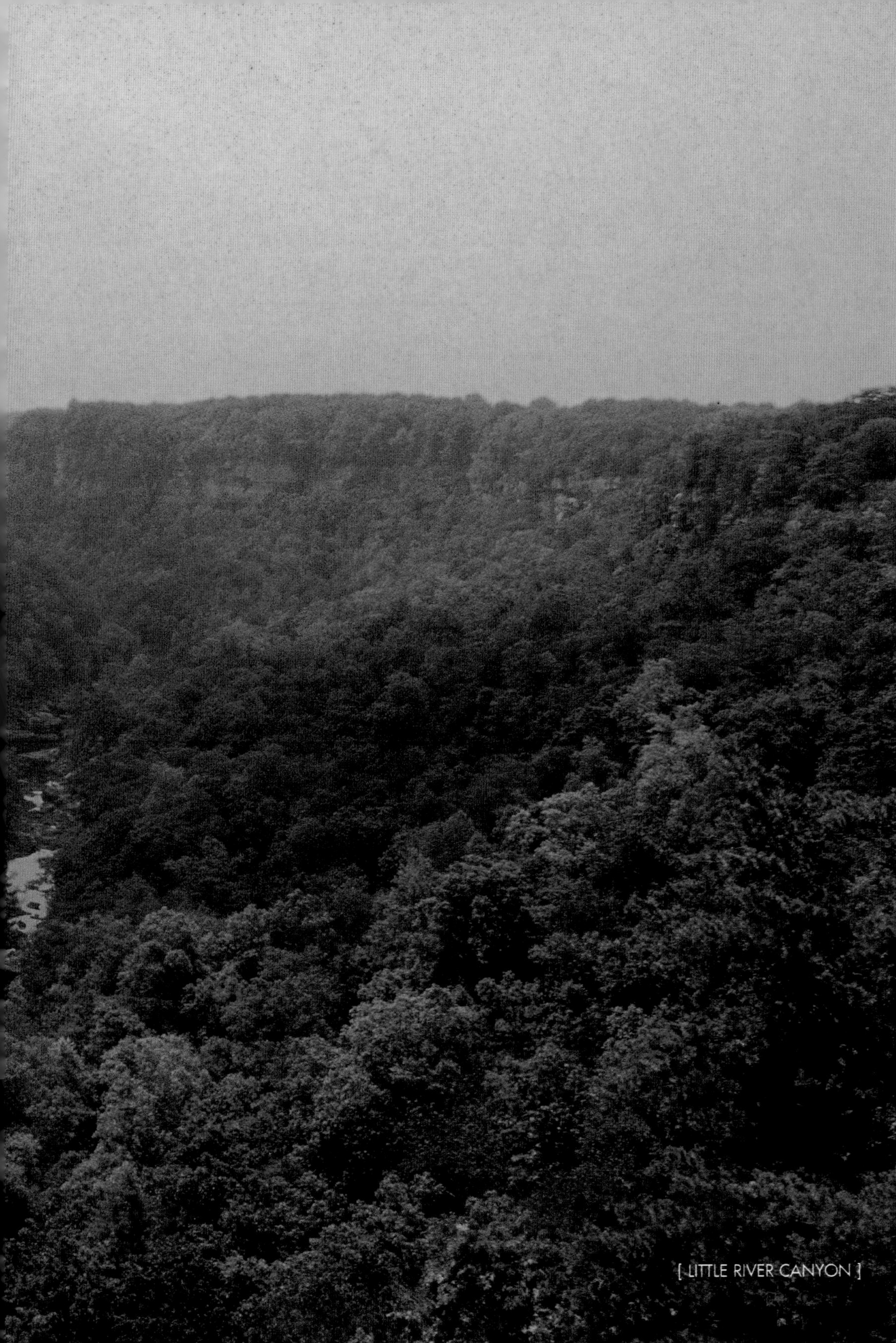
[LITTLE RIVER CANYON]

Away from the city, from the bustle and buildings, from the satellites, transmitters and microphones, I see serenity.

Alabama is a place of unlimited natural beauty. I've been to what seems like every square inch of this place, and am no longer surprised by what's around the bend or over the crest. I live for Little River Canyon — a special place for me to unwind and meander. I cherish my time at Cheaha, hop to the beach, ascend the mighty Monte Sano, cross the cool and cavernous Natural Bridge, and am in awe of the awesome Tennessee of the Shoals. I can't get enough of it.

There may be some who belittle this place, but they don't know it and certainly don't see it and feel it like I do. For most of my life, I've been a witness to its beauty – natural and otherwise. And no matter where my path leads, Alabama will always be beautiful and will always be home.

Steve Chiotakis
[HOST / PRODUCER, 90.3 WBHM]

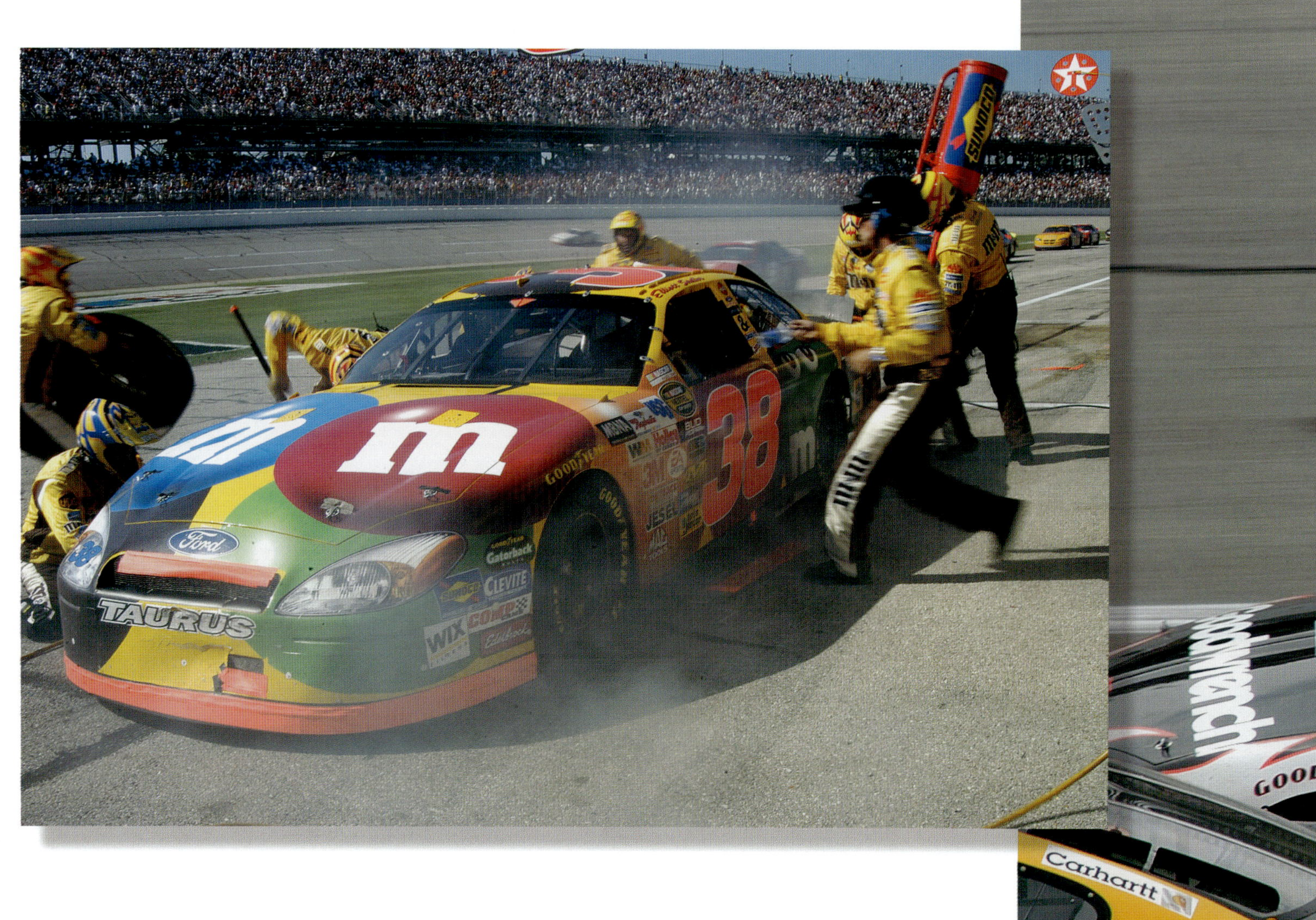

We still have a Southern drawl
at 200 miles per hour.

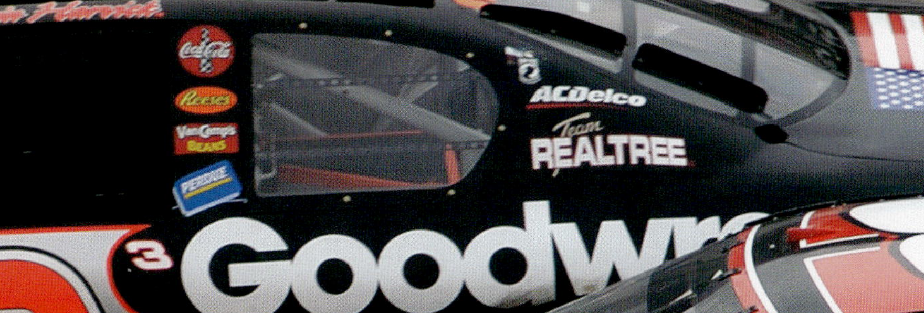
ACDelco
Team
REALTREE

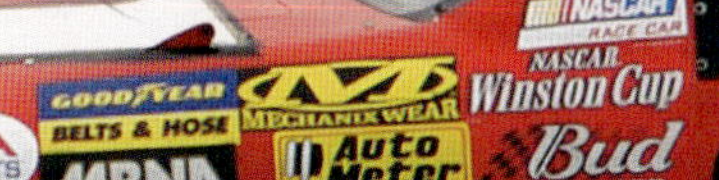
NASCAR
Winston Cup
Bud

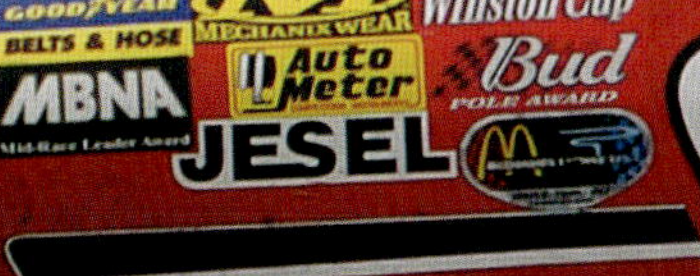
MBNA
Auto Meter
JESEL

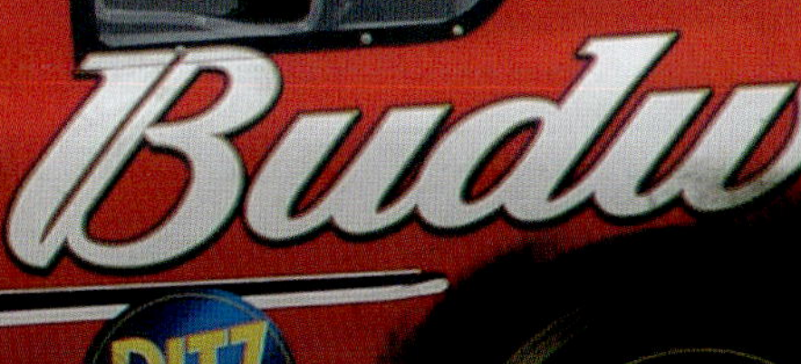
DaleEarnhardtInc.com

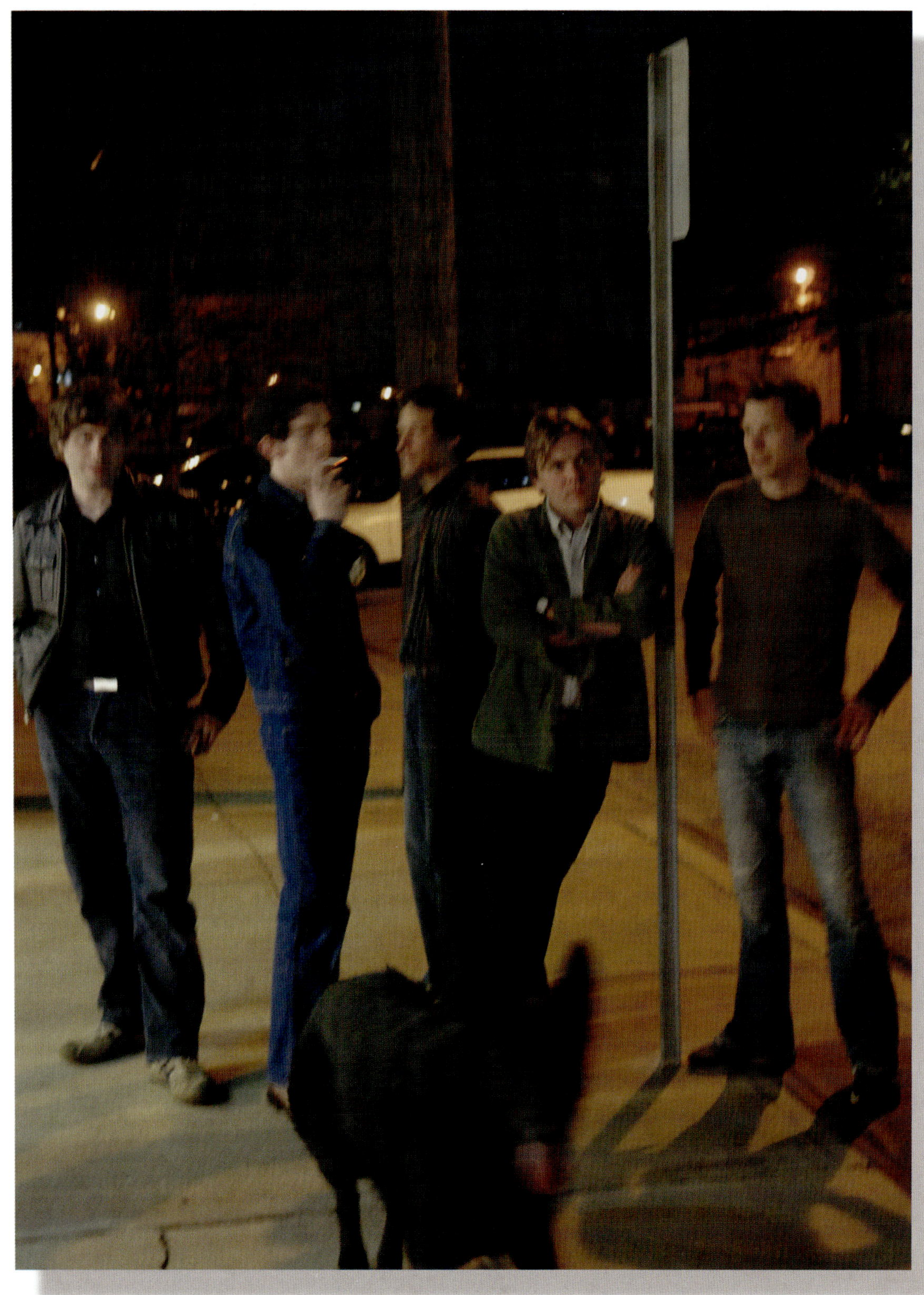

We always know when we've come home. There's something here that nobody else has.

THROUGH THE SPARKS
[PROGRESSIVE/PSYCHEDELIC ROCK & ROLL BAND]

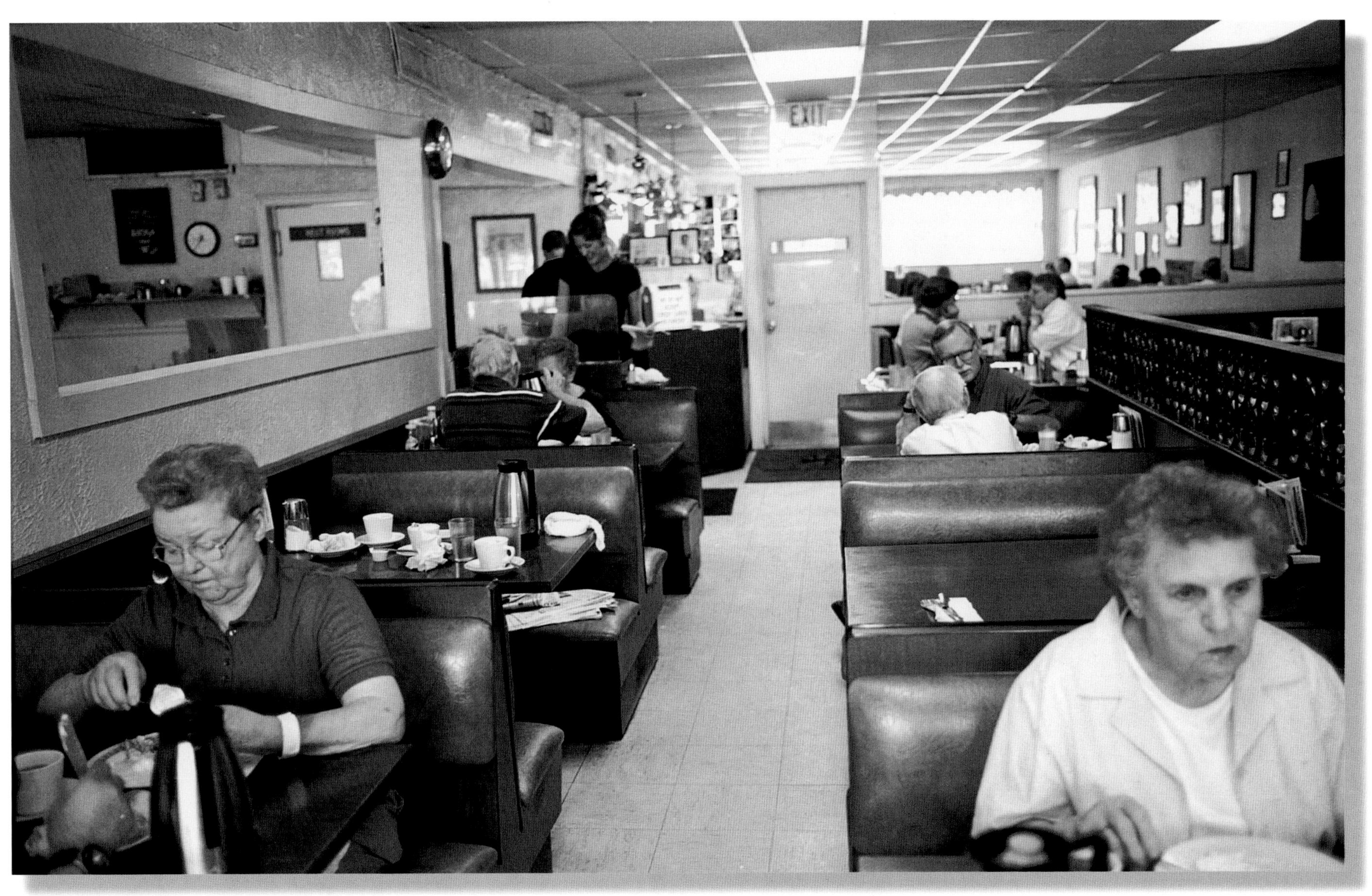

[BOGUE'S RESTAURANT]

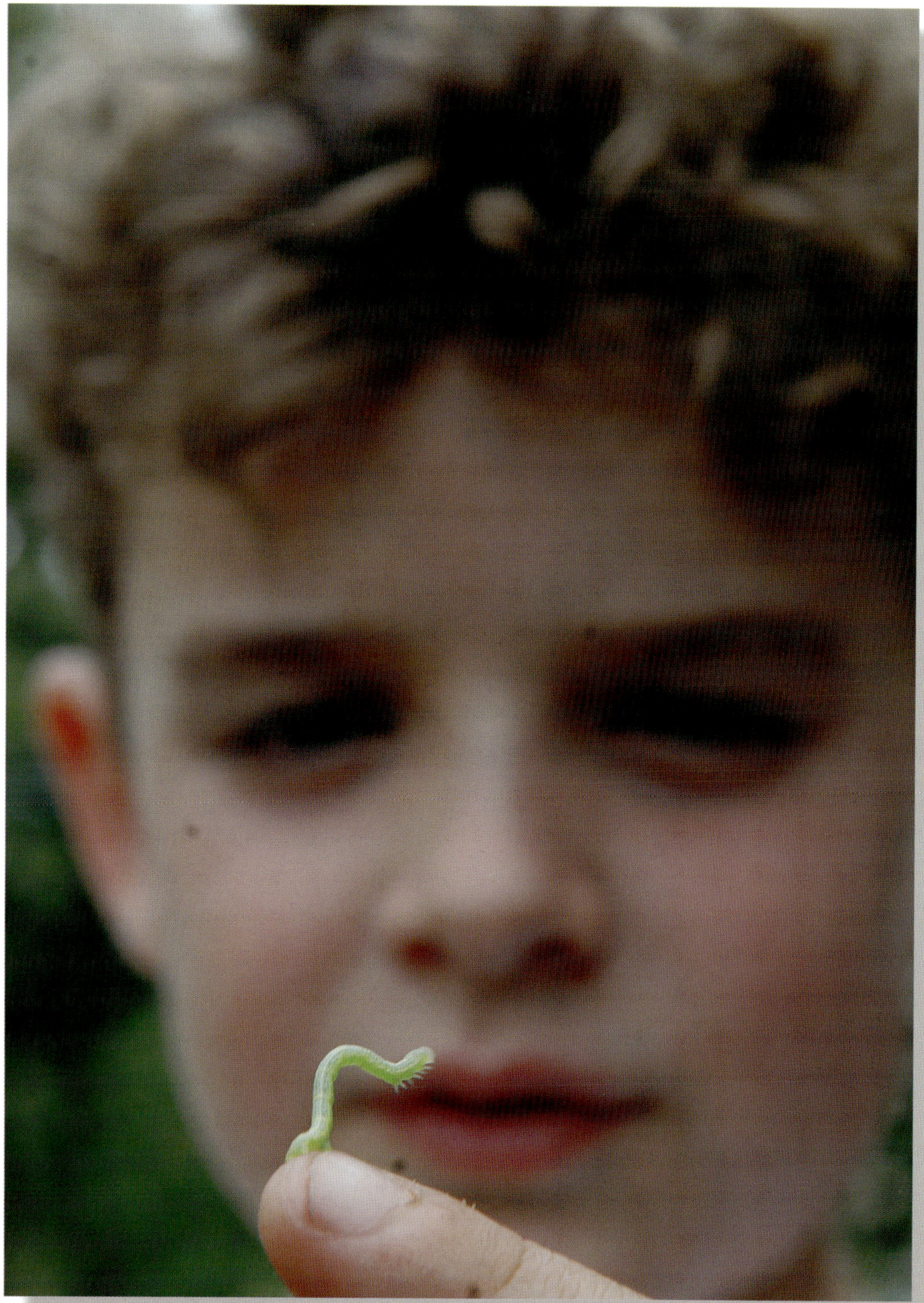

[DURY, AGE 8, WITH INCHWORM]

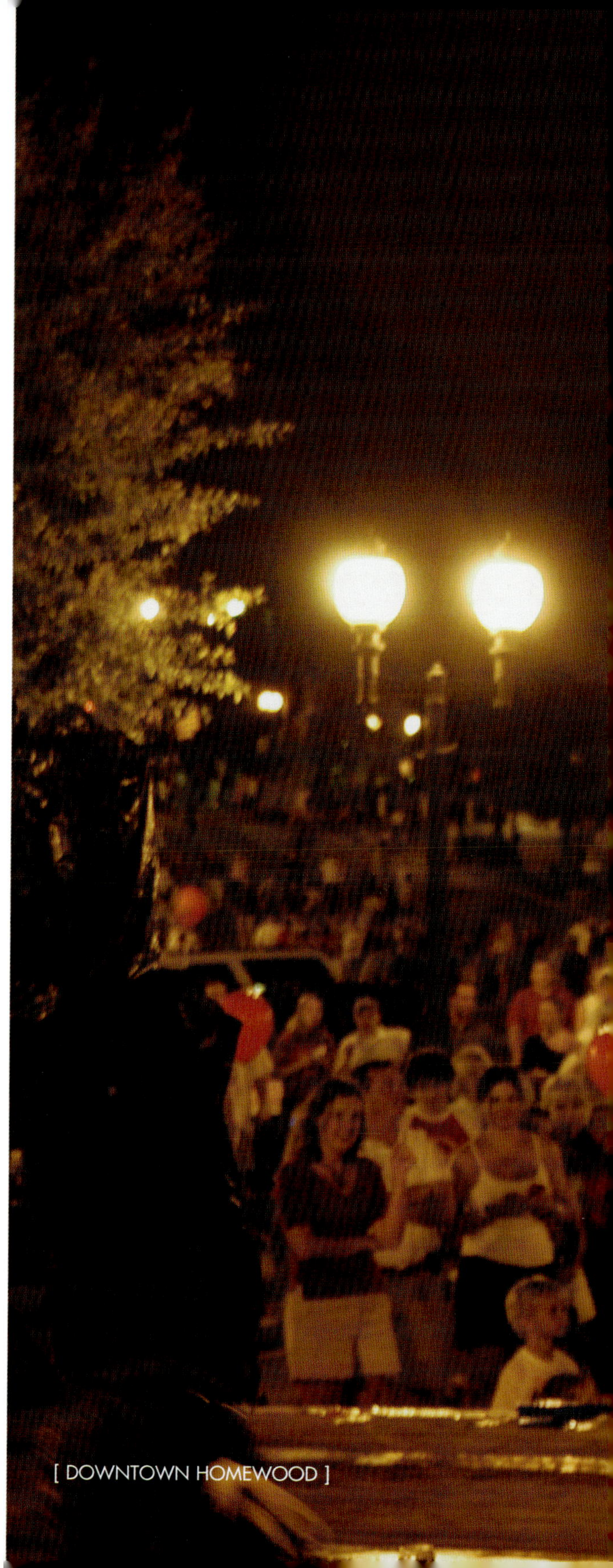

[DOWNTOWN HOMEWOOD]

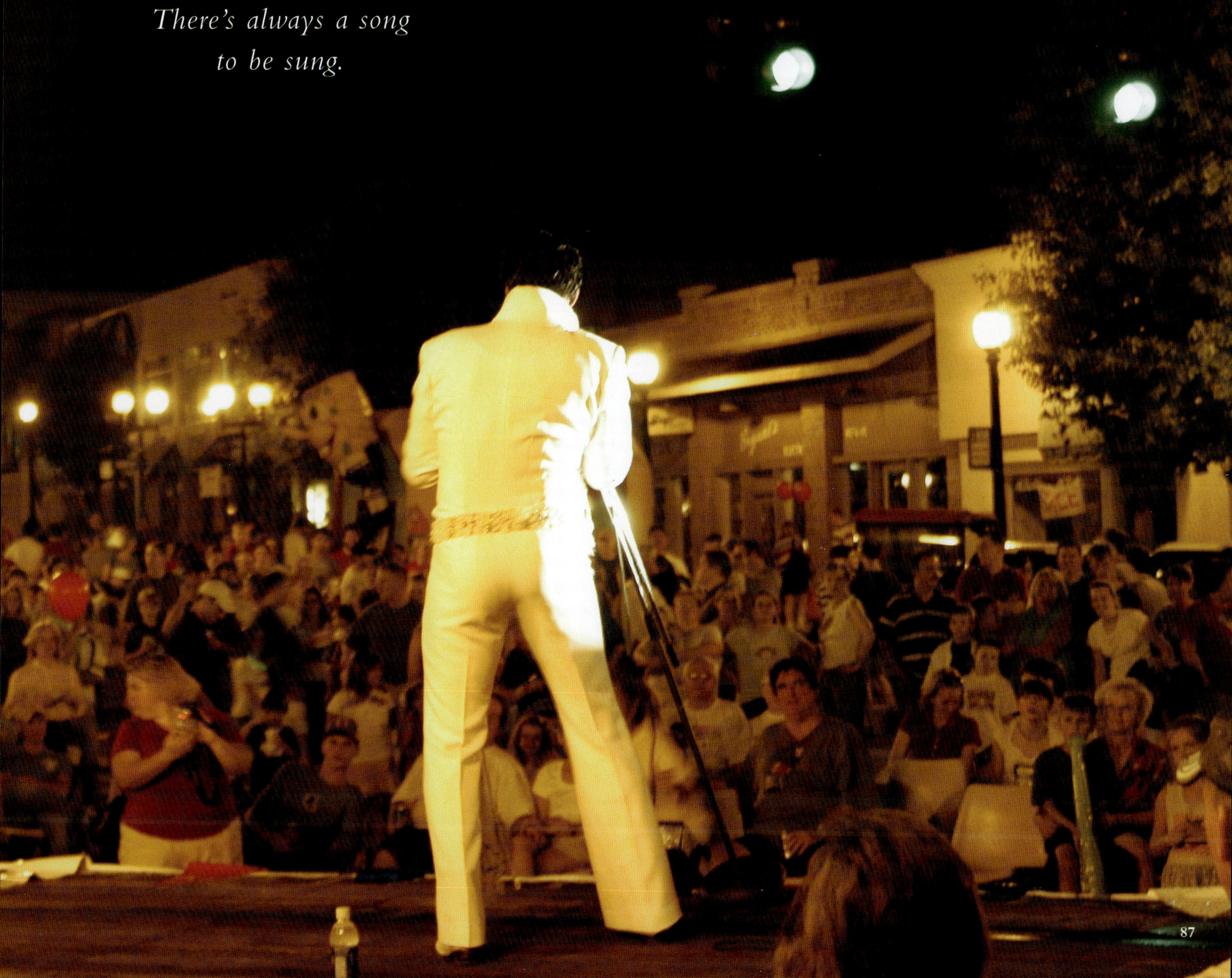

There's always a song
to be sung.

"Alabama the beautiful!" This quote says it all: we love Alabama. We were born in Birmingham, and remain here with our family, no matter where our travels have taken us. There is nothing like this state—the beautiful rolling mountains, the lakes, the seasons, and, of course, the people. Alabamians make this state more beautiful than just its natural appearance. The people here with their southern ways and hospitality make it home for us. The smell of sweet wisteria vines and the beautiful tulips, irises, and azaleas bring out happiness for the spring. The summer nights will take your breath away with the sounds of the evening and warm air. Next, the changing of the leaves in the fall brings out the football fans and tailgating parties. Finally, a crisp winter to enjoy our family times and holidays as we grow into a new year. If you haven't been to Alabama, don't miss this awesome state. ... stop in for a while and maybe picnic or go for a hike at one our state parks like Oak Mountain, Mount Cheaha, Desota Caverns, Wind Creek, and many more. This is a great place to check out ... we love to fish, hike, camp, play softball, and listen to some country music. Alabama is beautiful x 2!

NATALIE CARROL & ADRIA KLEIN
[OWNERS, "THE FITNESS TWINS"]

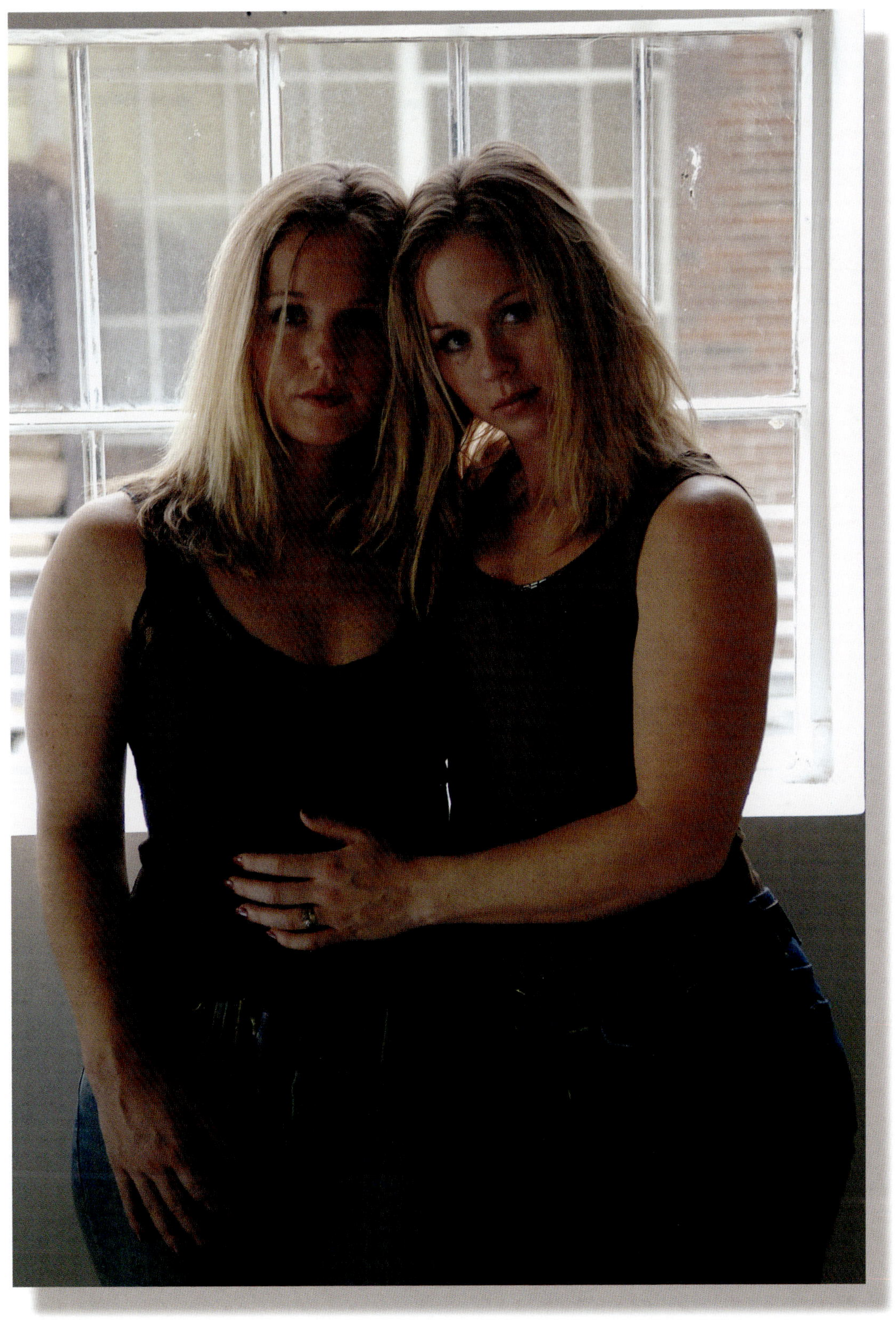

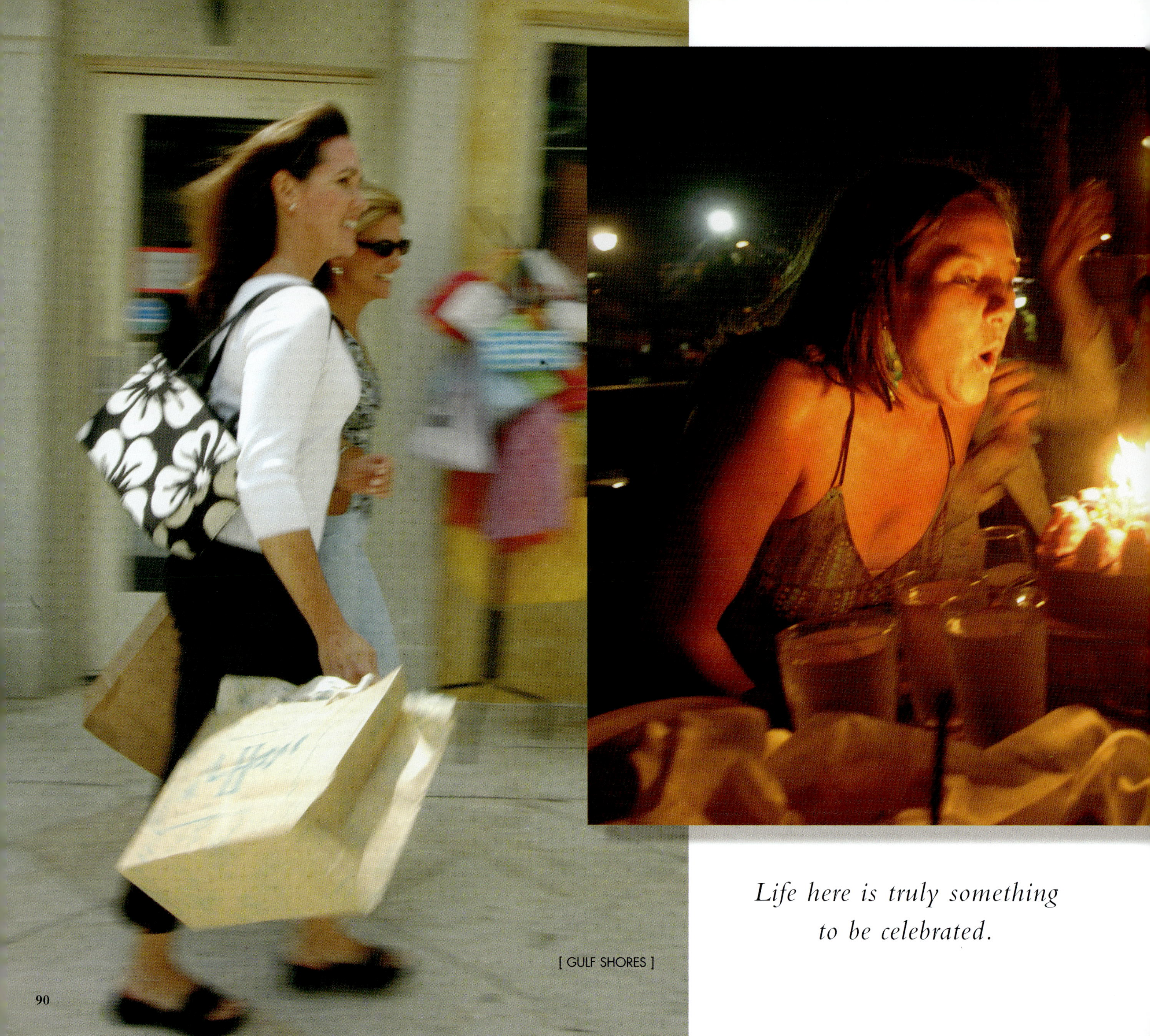

[GULF SHORES]

Life here is truly something to be celebrated.

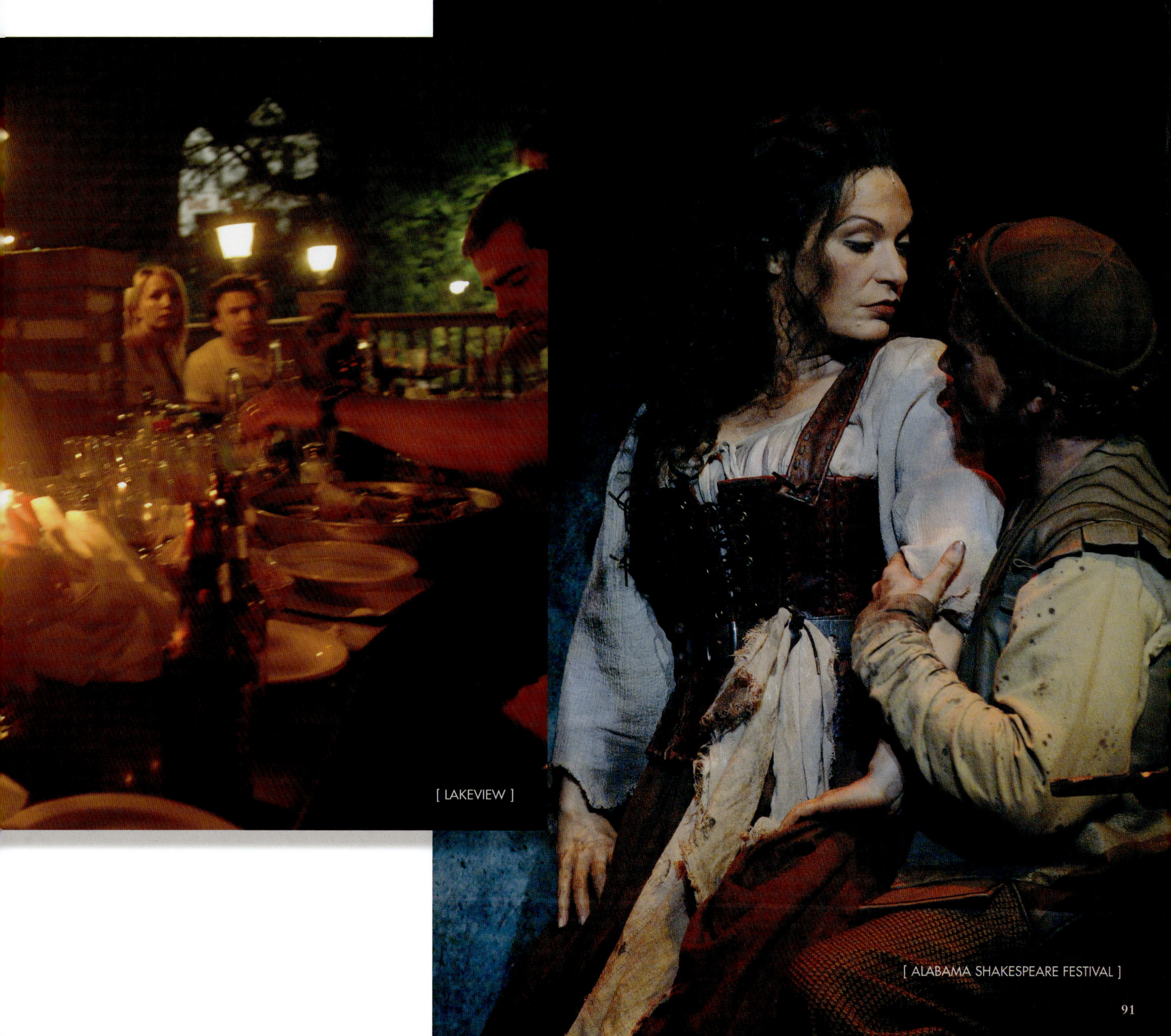

[LAKEVIEW]

[ALABAMA SHAKESPEARE FESTIVAL]

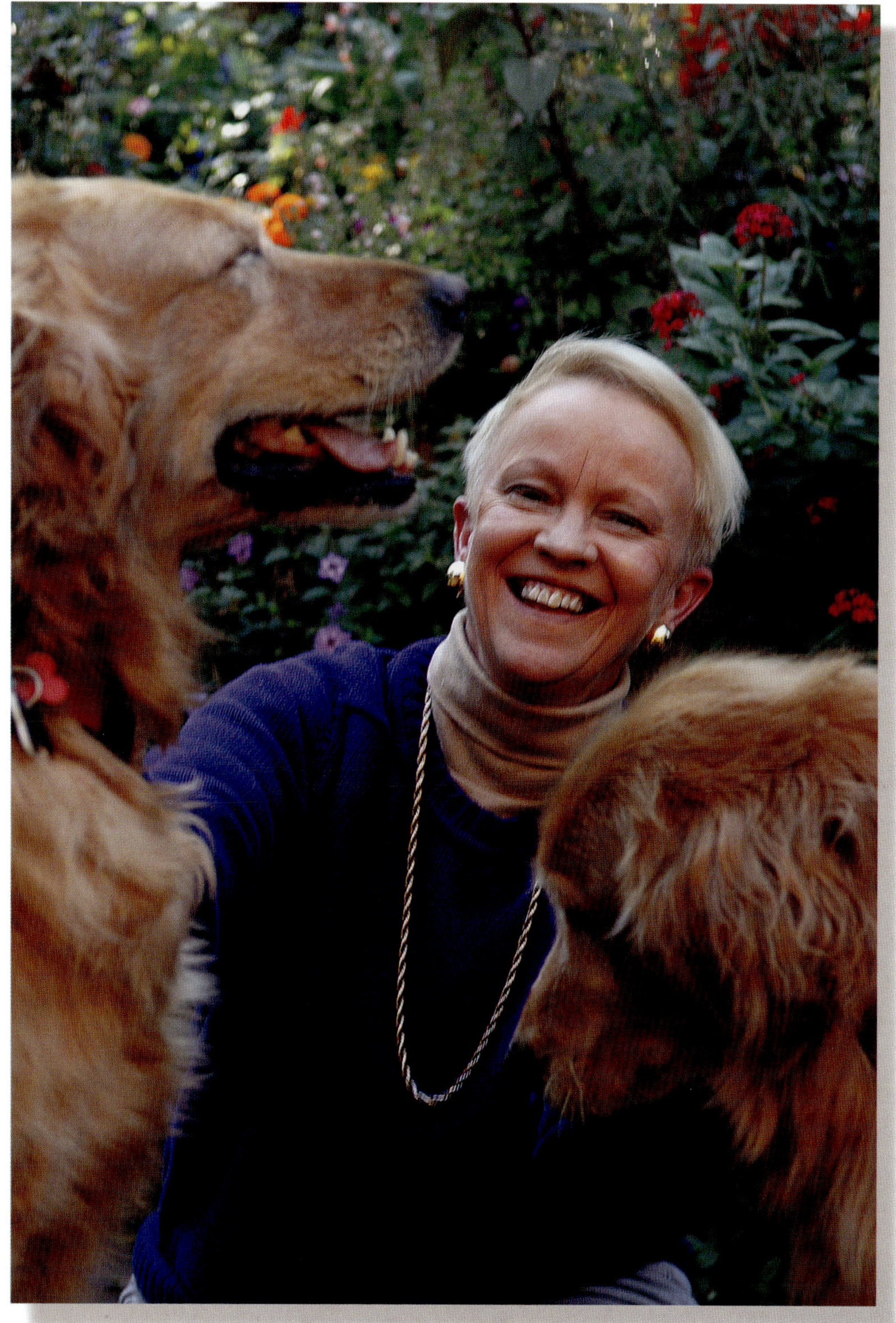

I appreciate living in a place in which nature changes through four distinct seasons, each enjoying its own merits. There is nothing softer than the air in Alabama April, when the azaleas and cherry trees are blooming, or sweeter smelling than a June morning just after the grass has been cut. The fall is at the same time outrageous and poignant, with foliage colors competing like flamboyant lawyers arguing their final statements. For those of us who garden compulsively, winter provides an interlude; bare branches dripping with red berries, or, even better, dappled with a few snowflakes, provide small miracles in a brown landscape.

Alabama's Mother Nature, like any remarkable woman, has that one small character flaw. Alabama is infamous for having a hellishly humid fifth season called August, best visited through long distance telephone calls back home placed from cooler vantage points of mountains or ocean. But even in August, almost always in August, we are treated to one or two days of a cold front stirring the air around, teasing us with promise, and reminding us that while Mama Nature's not perfect, she's still at heart our favorite good old girl.

Cathy Adams
[WRITER, GARDENER]

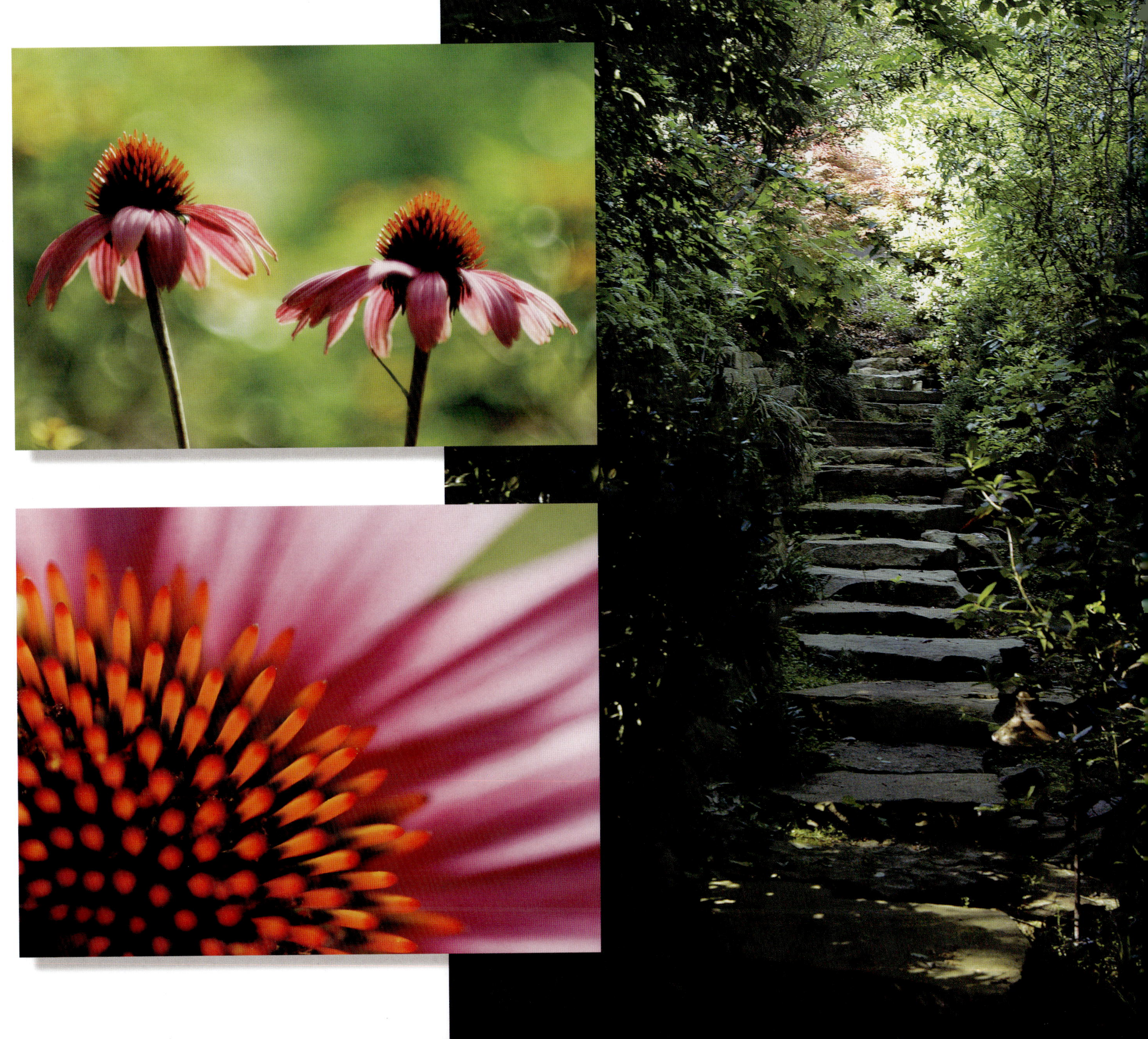

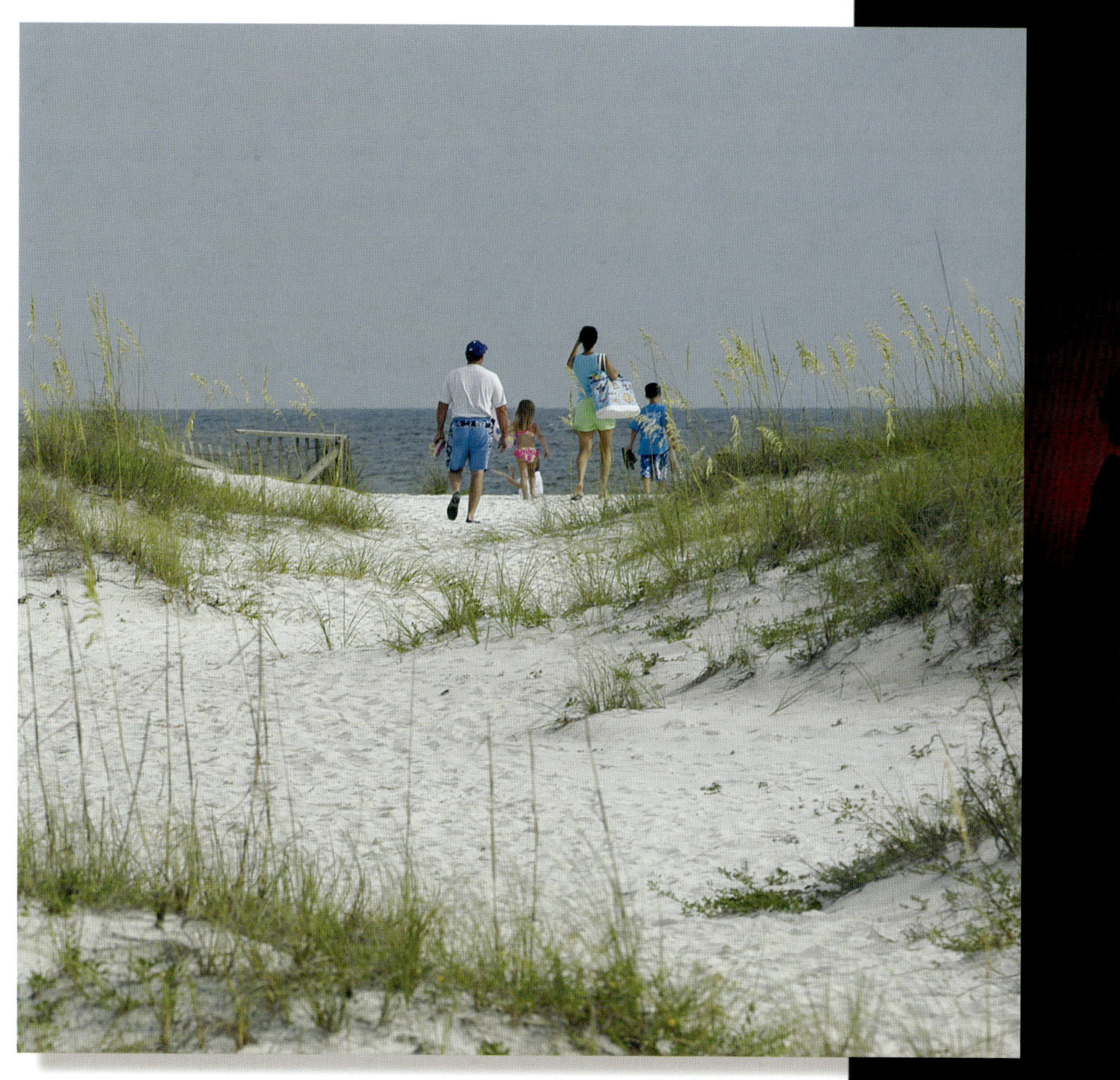

We play in the most beautiful places in the world.

[GULF SHORES]

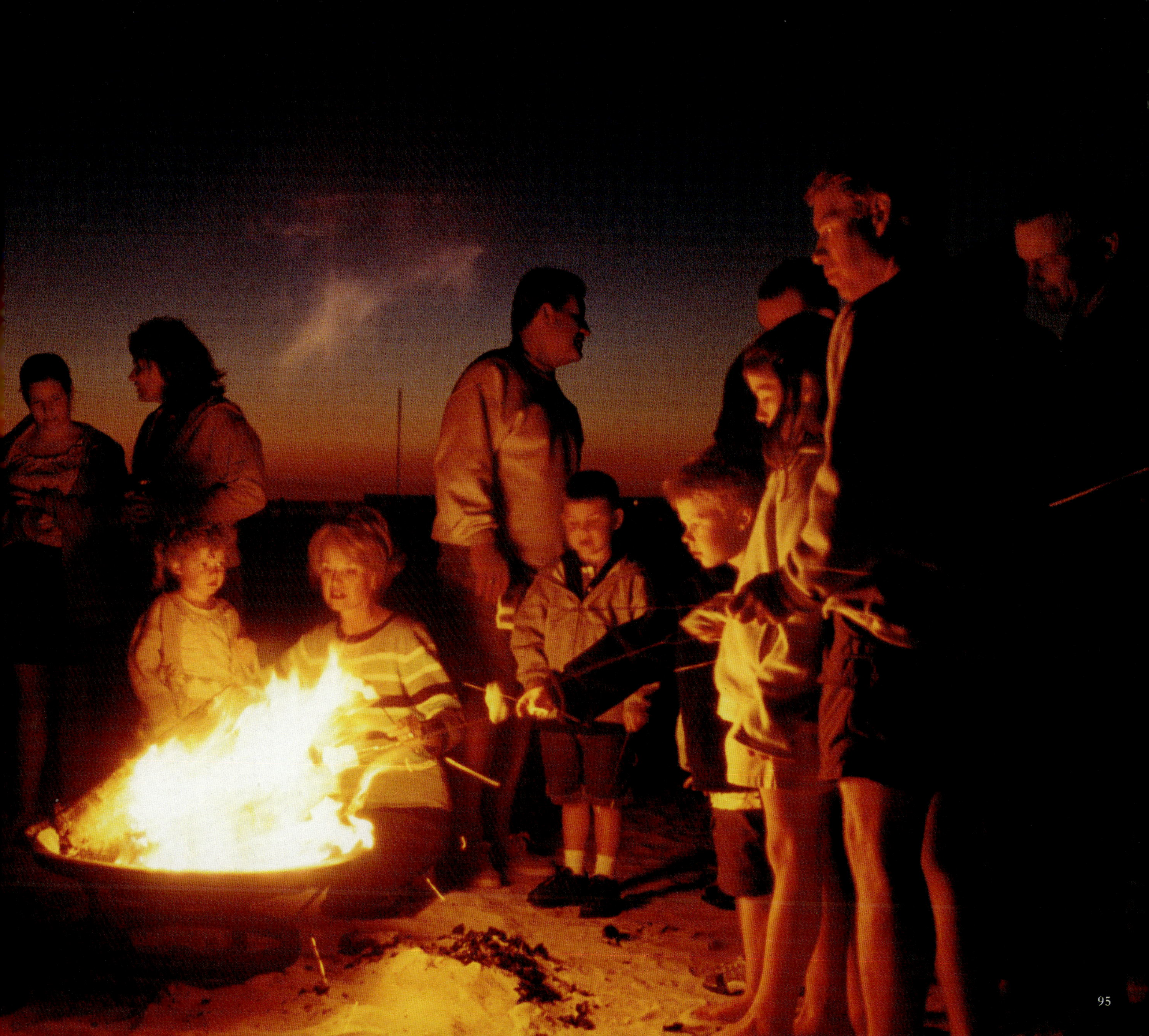

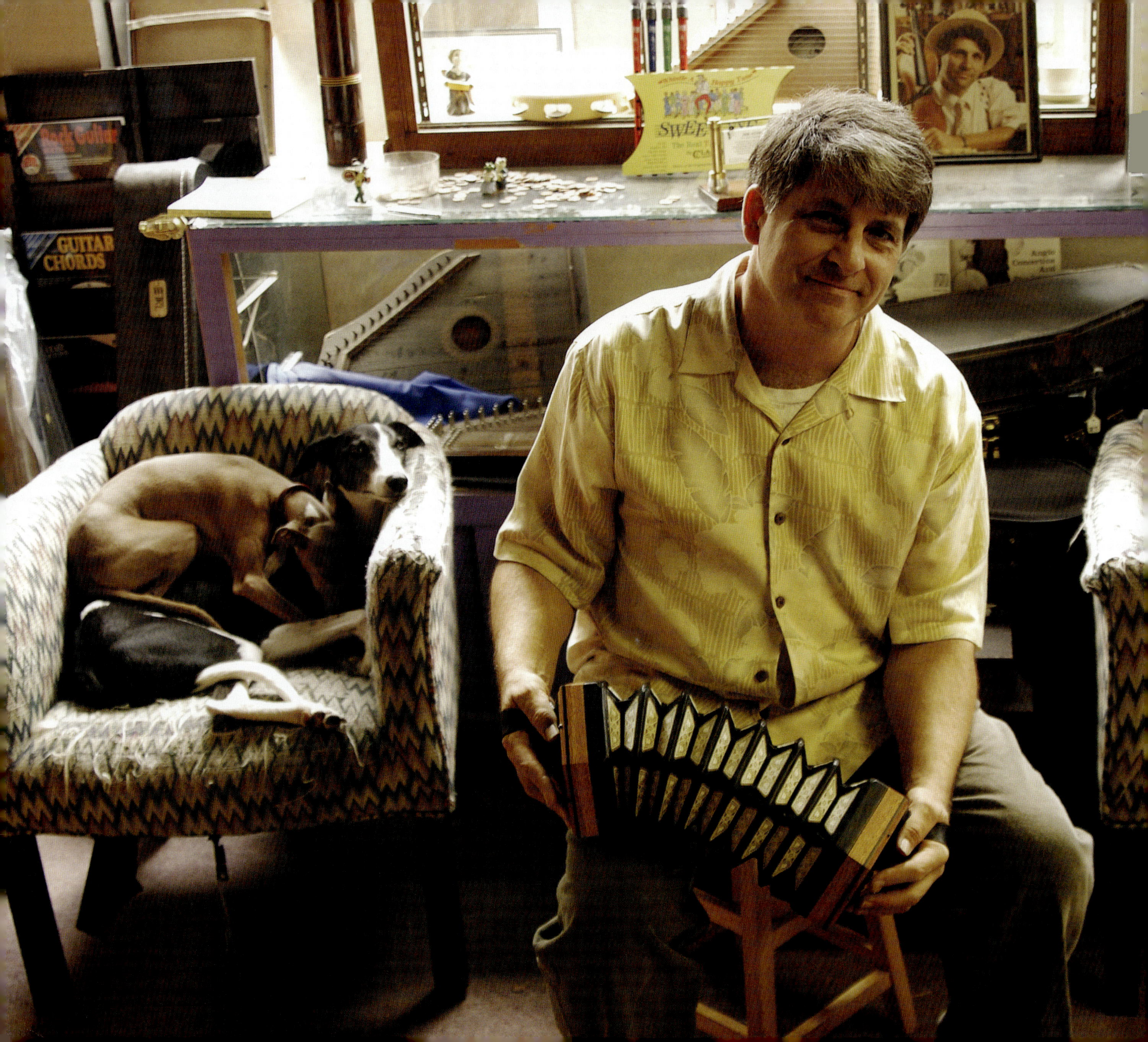
Rock Guitar
GUITAR CHORDS

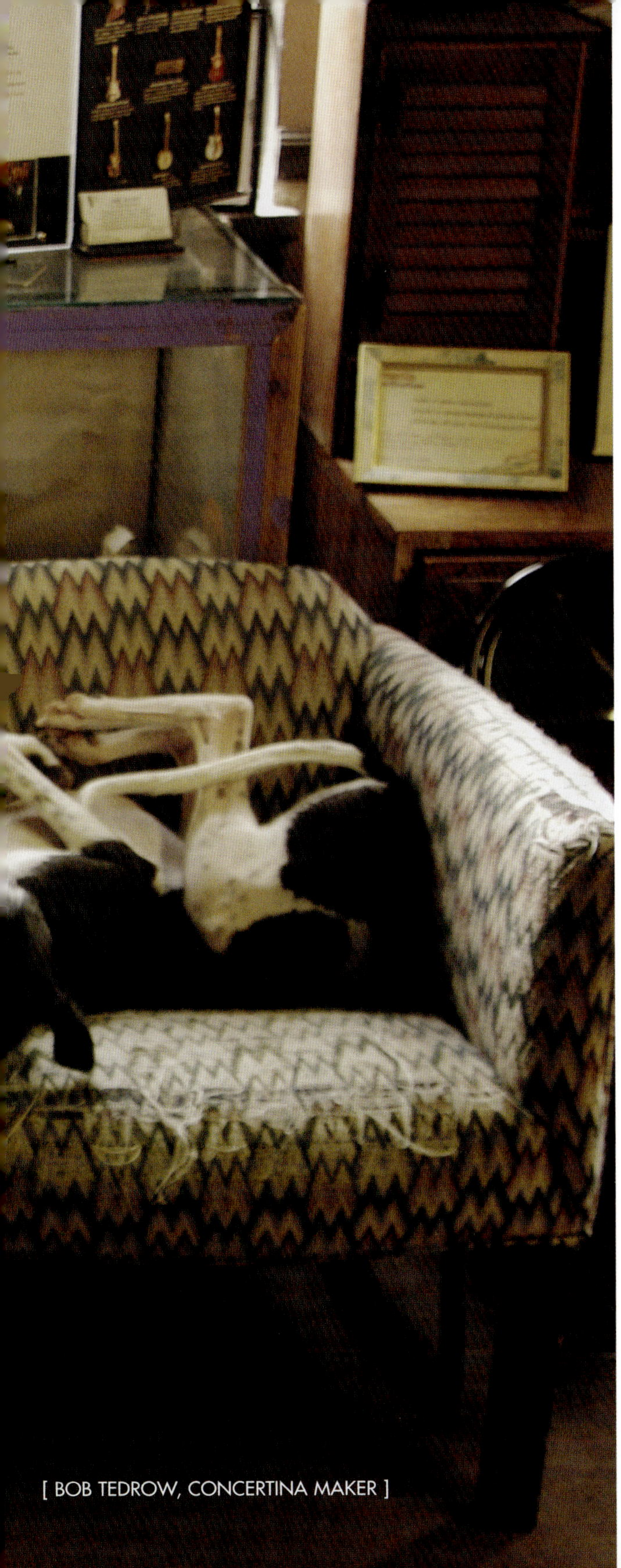
[BOB TEDROW, CONCERTINA MAKER]

The Way We Live

We have our own style. It flourishes freely, growing like a flowering tree with many blooms, varied as the rainbow ... and as unified. We live a tapestry that is true to who we are, down to the depths of our sweet Alabama souls.

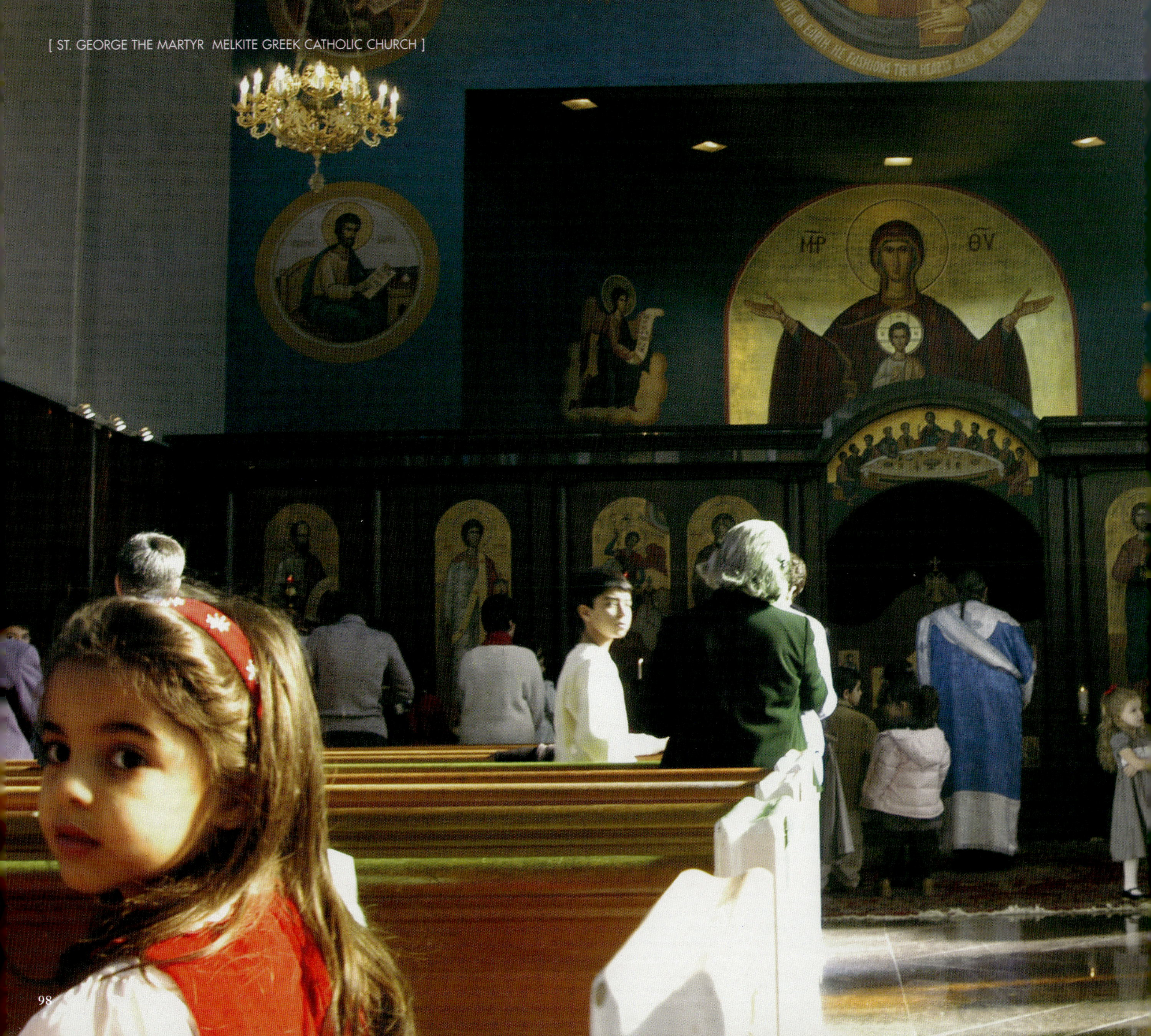

[ST. GEORGE THE MARTYR MELKITE GREEK CATHOLIC CHURCH]

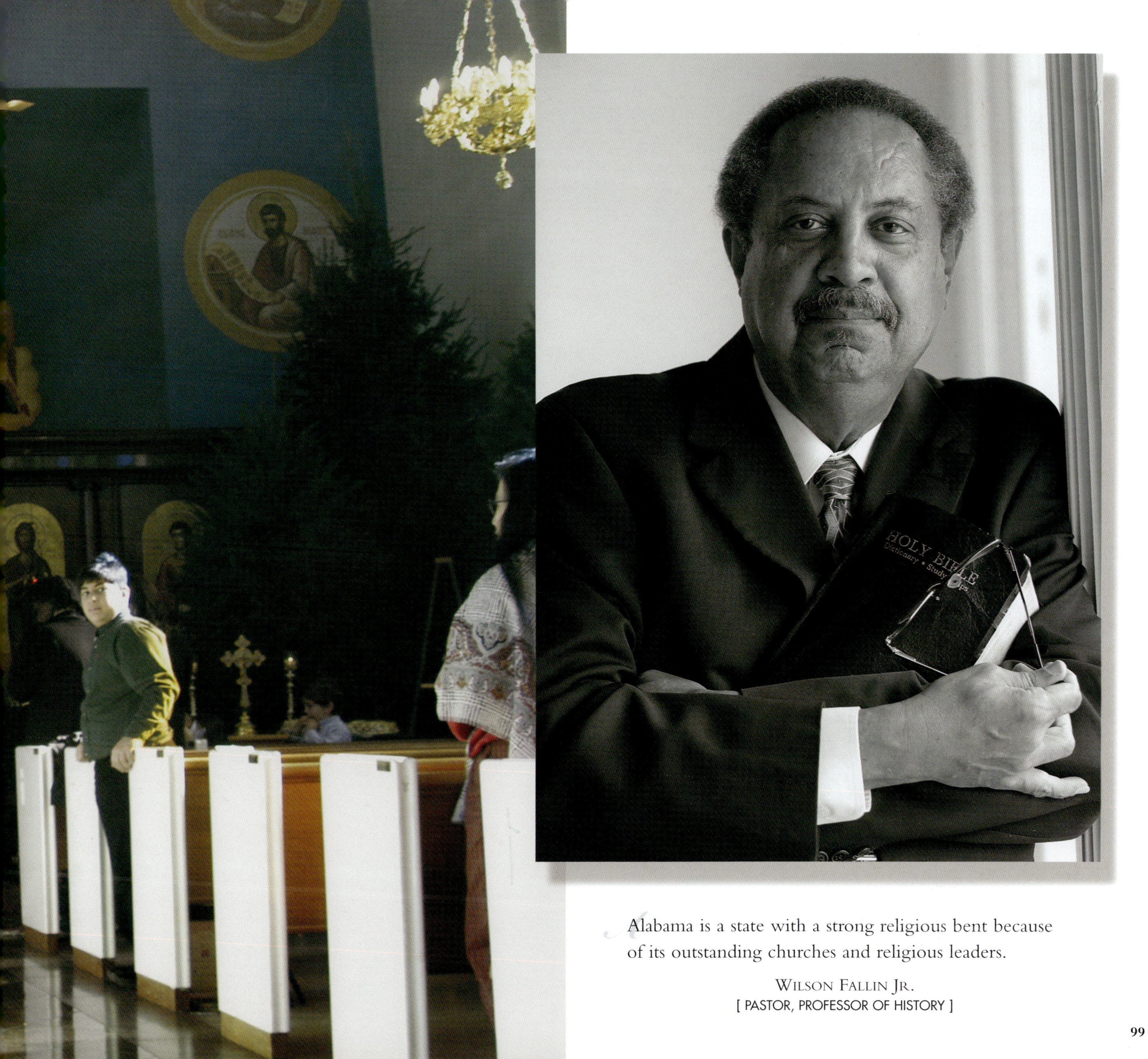

Alabama is a state with a strong religious bent because of its outstanding churches and religious leaders.

WILSON FALLIN JR.
[PASTOR, PROFESSOR OF HISTORY]

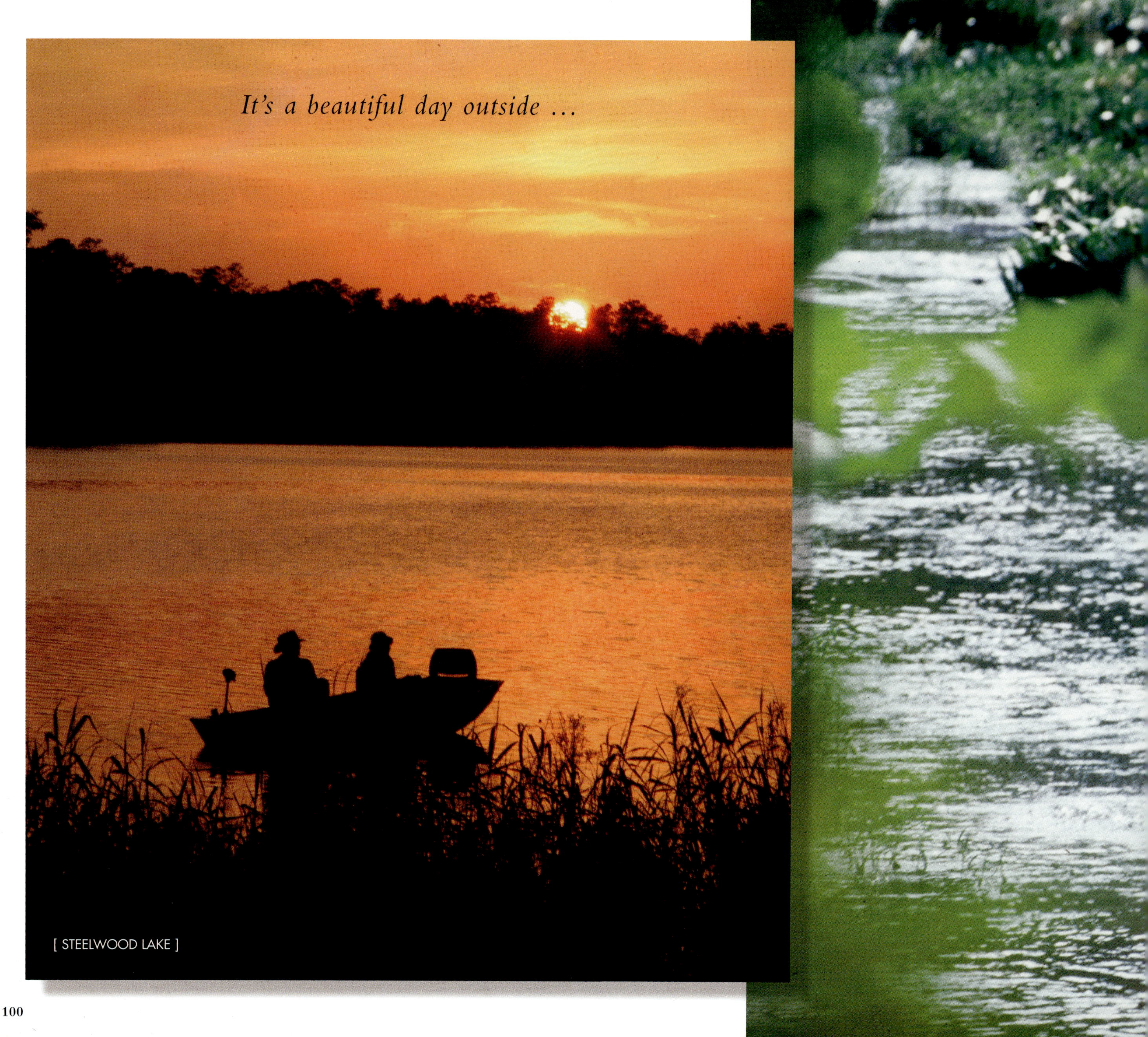

[STEELWOOD LAKE]

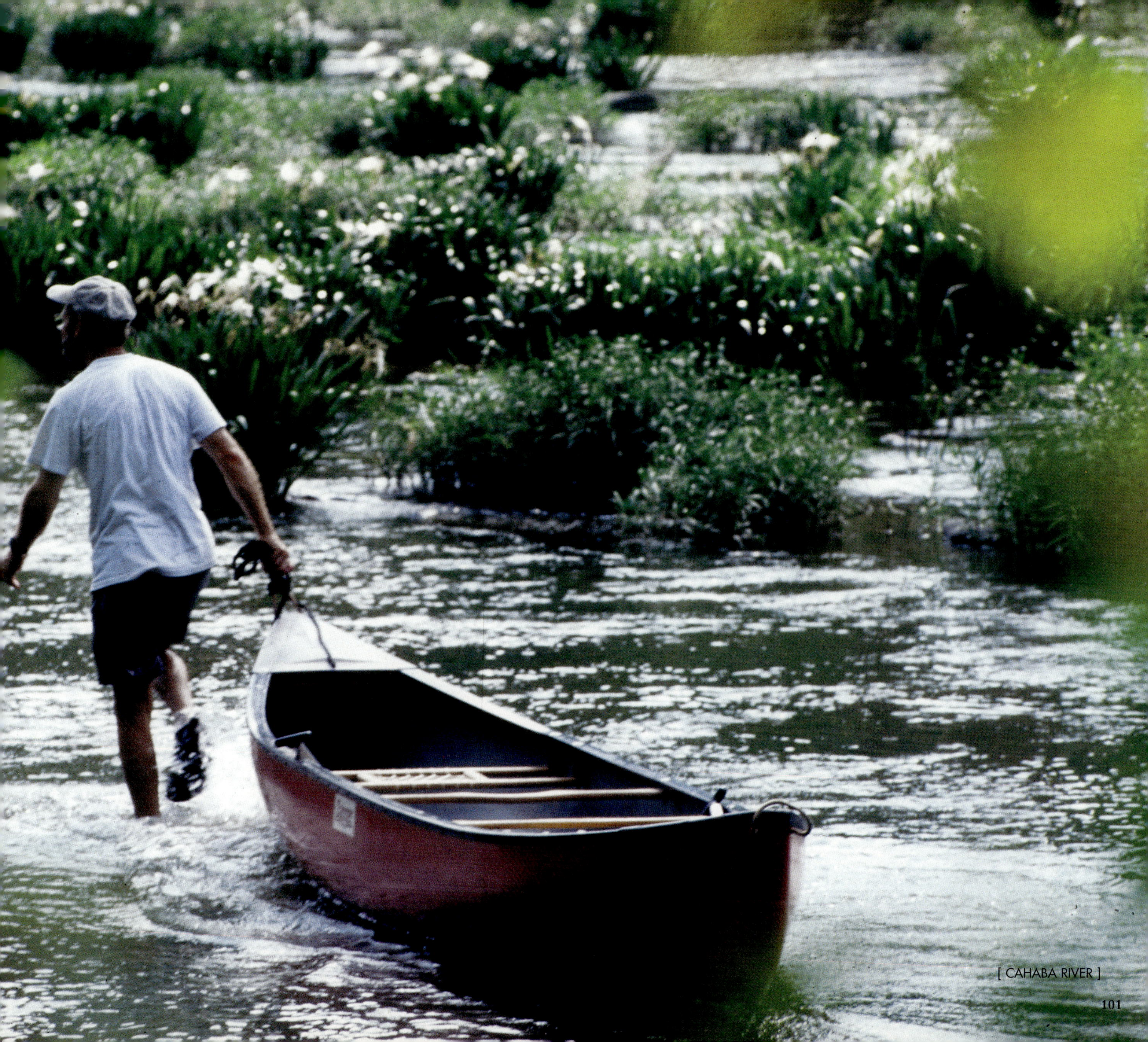

[CAHABA RIVER]

And it's beautiful inside, too.

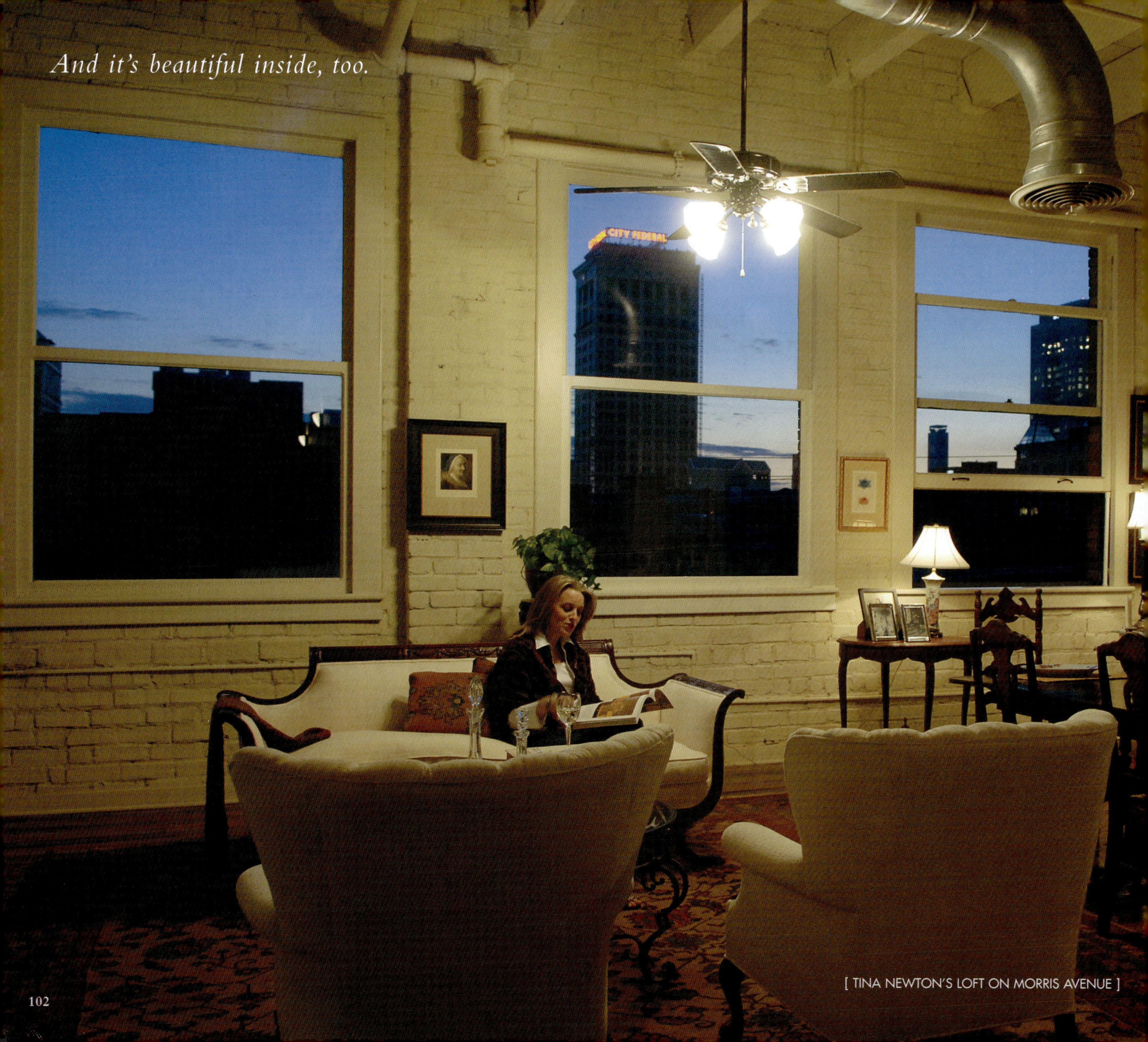

[TINA NEWTON'S LOFT ON MORRIS AVENUE]

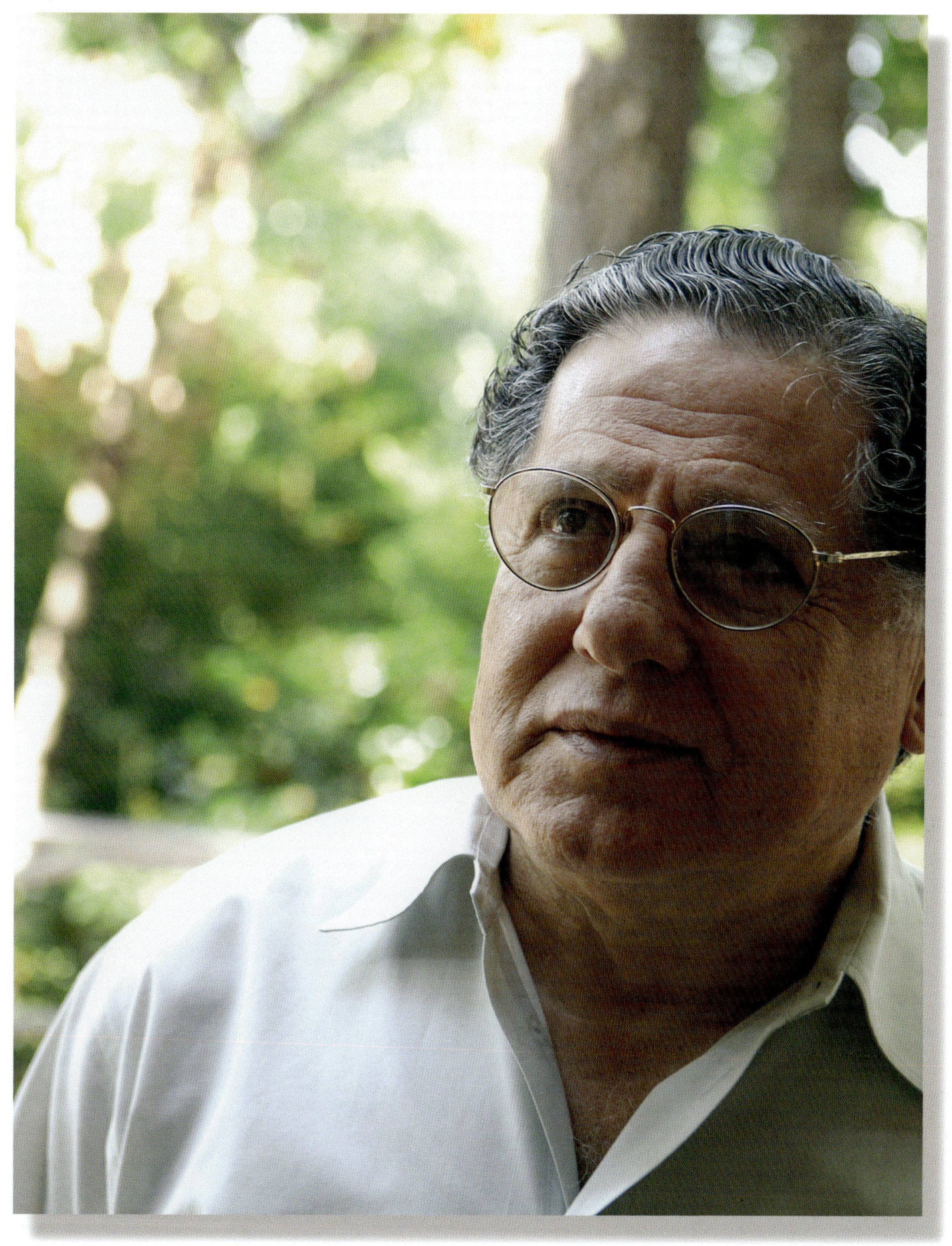

Alabama is home away from home.

IBRAHIM "ABE" FAWAL
[FILMMAKER, AUTHOR]

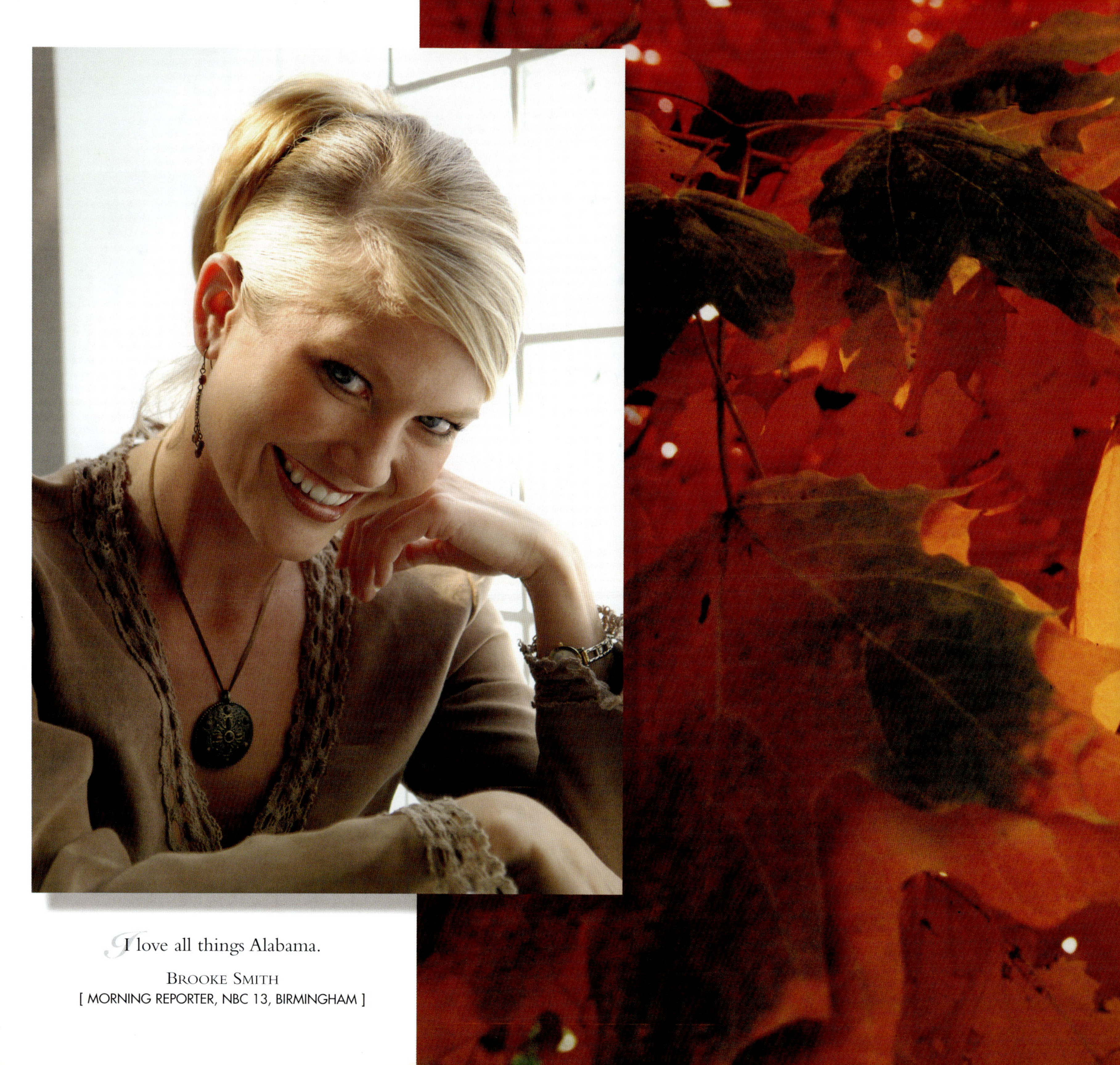

I love all things Alabama.

BROOKE SMITH
[MORNING REPORTER, NBC 13, BIRMINGHAM]

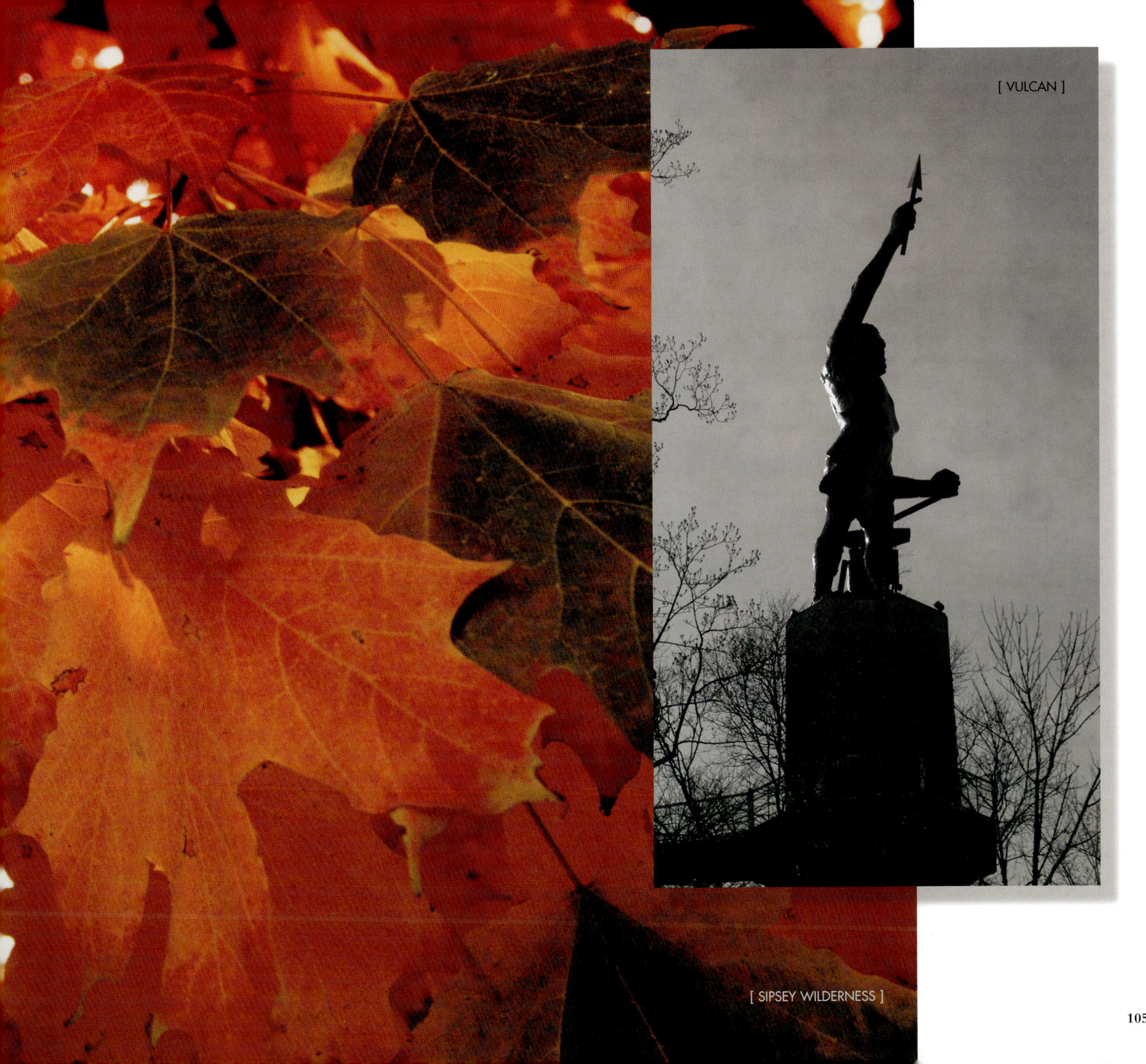

[VULCAN]

[SIPSEY WILDERNESS]

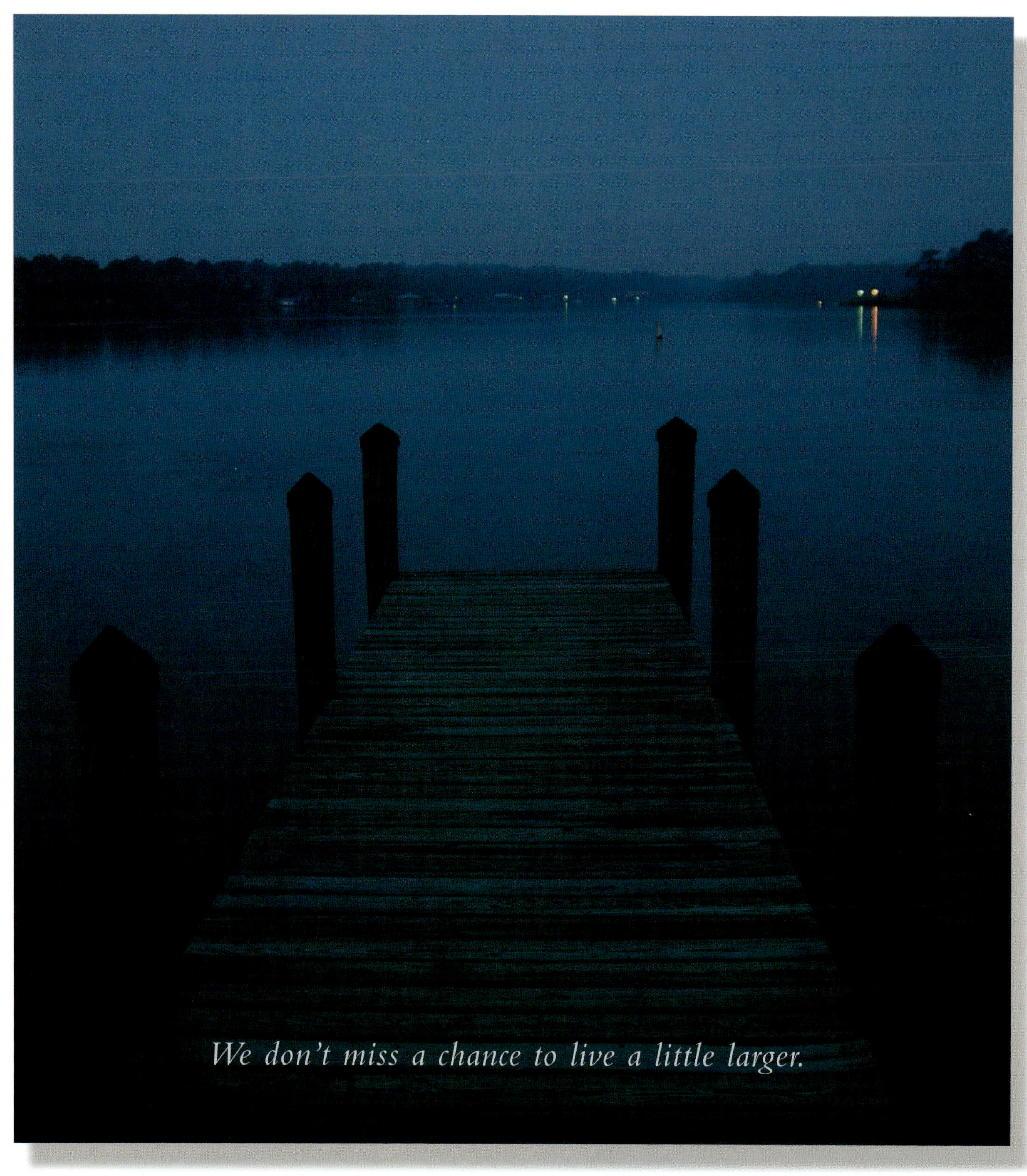
We don't miss a chance to live a little larger.

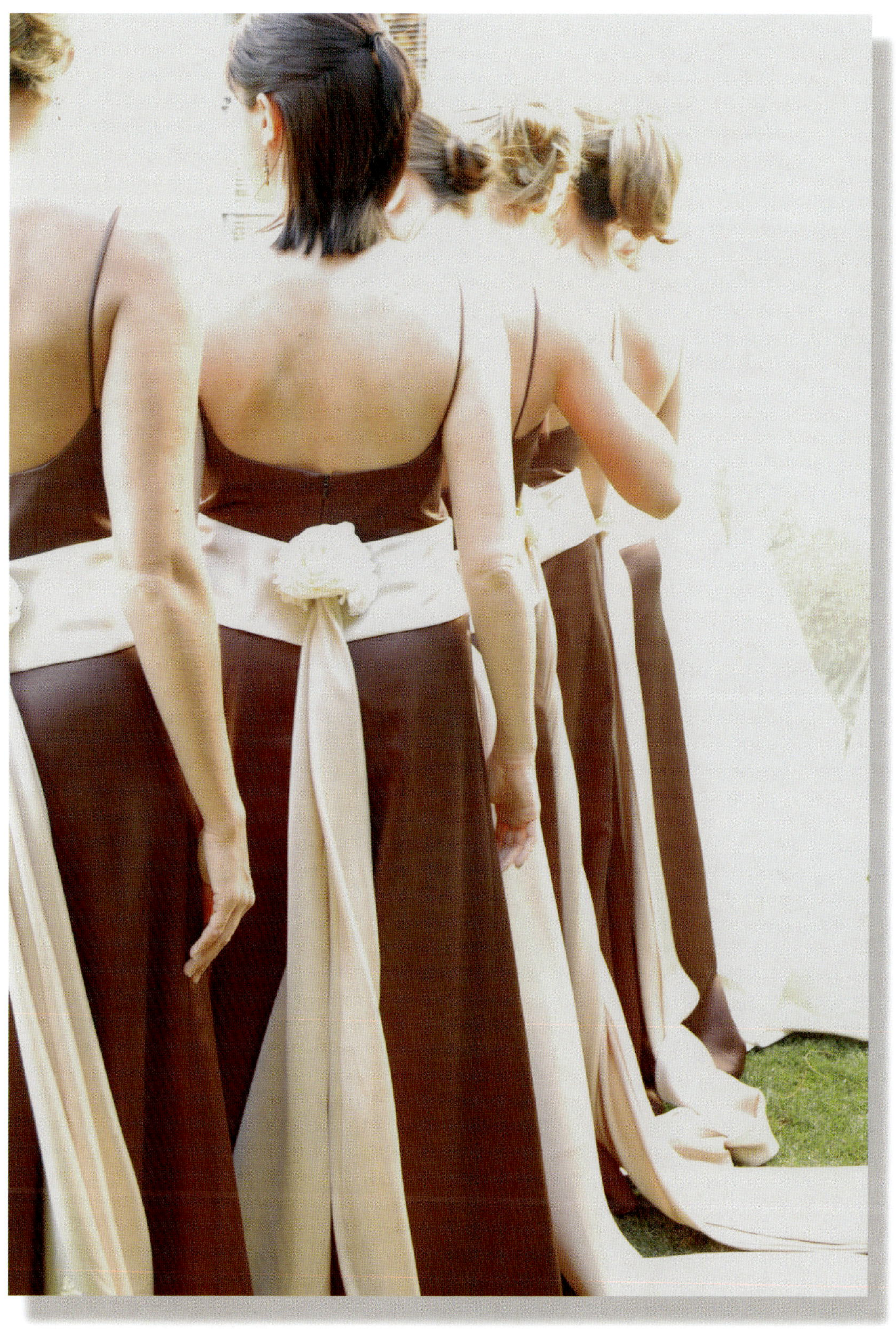

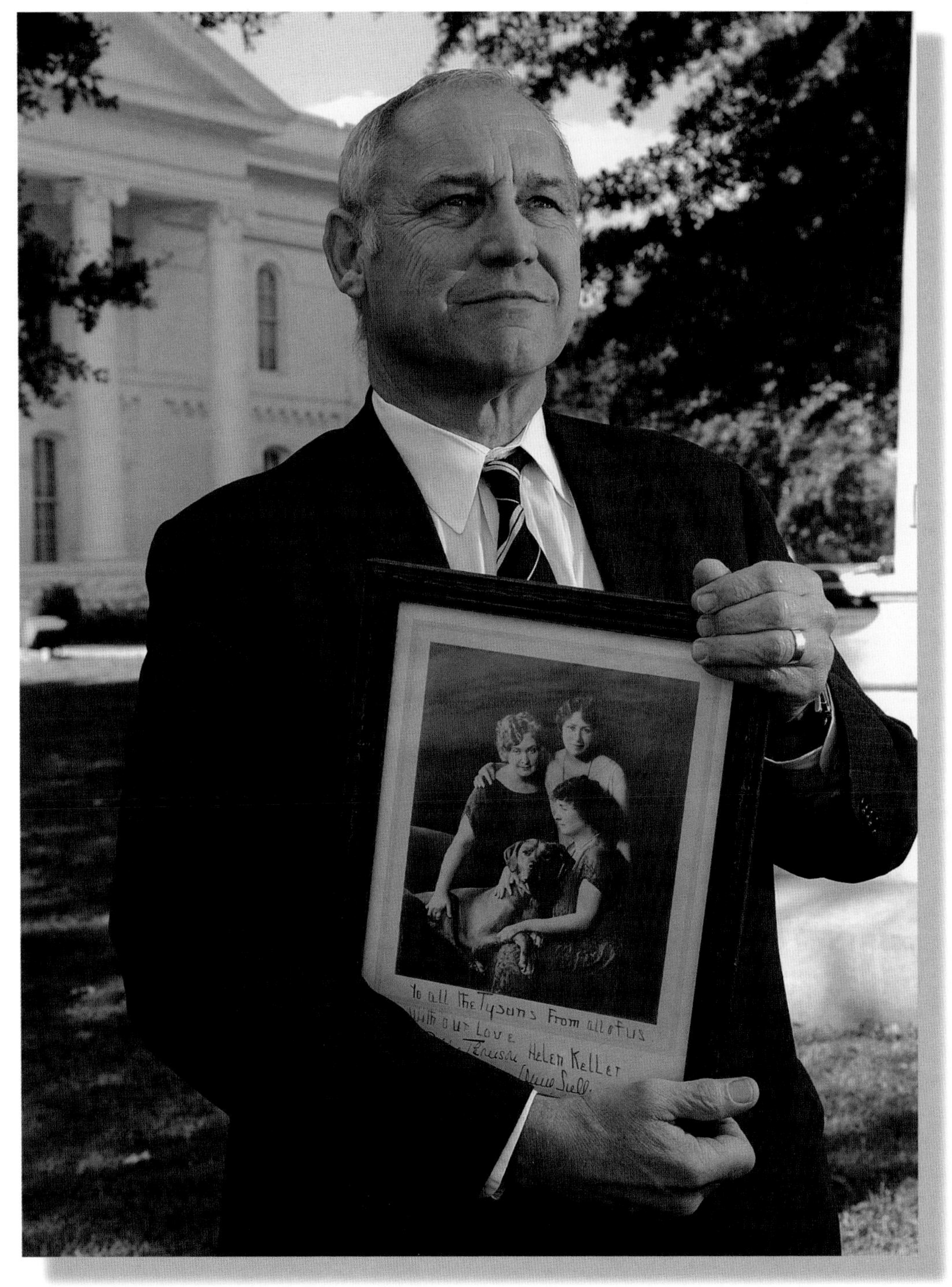

Alabama is the center of my universe.

William Johnson
[ATTORNEY, GREAT NEPHEW OF HELEN KELLER]

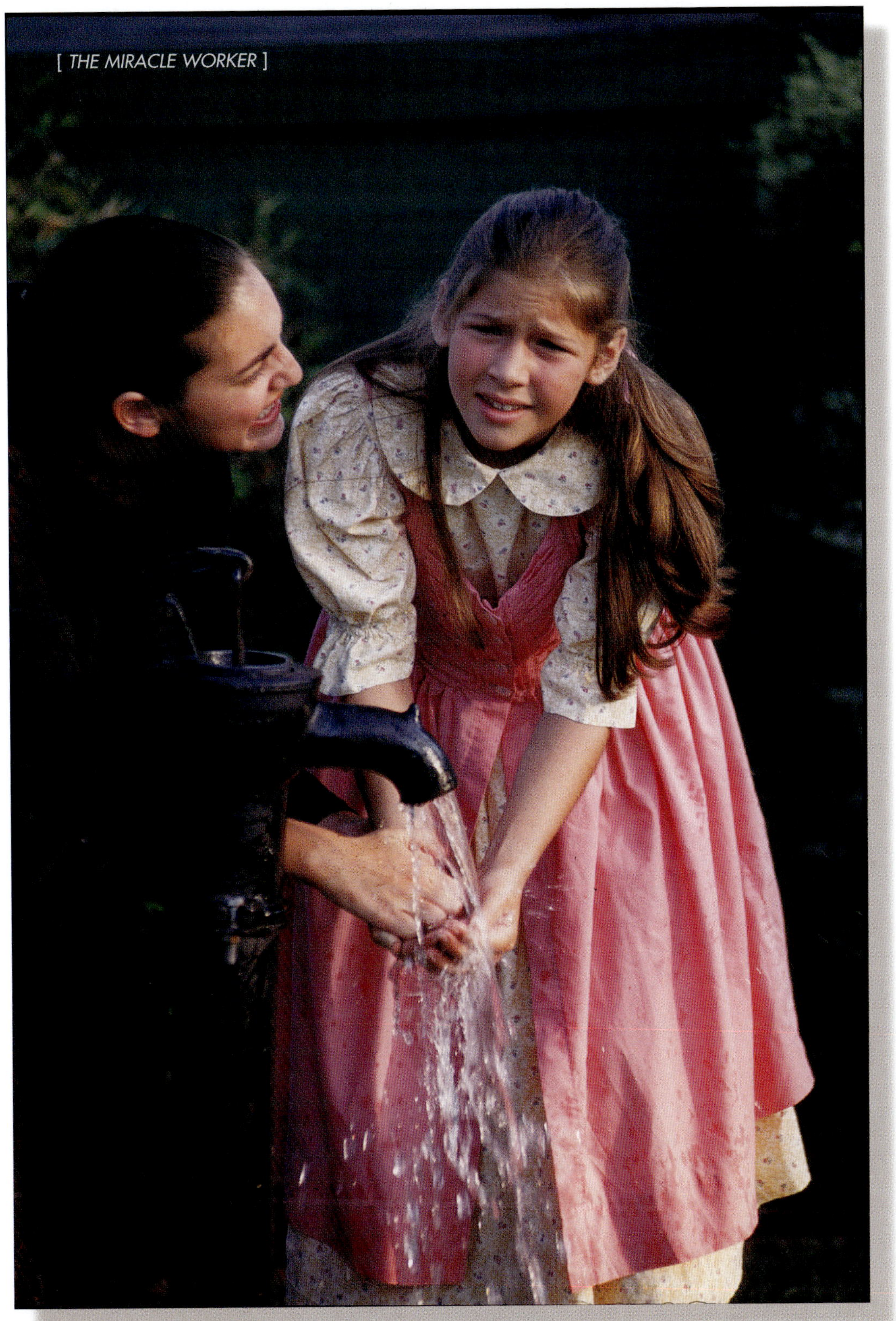
[THE MIRACLE WORKER]

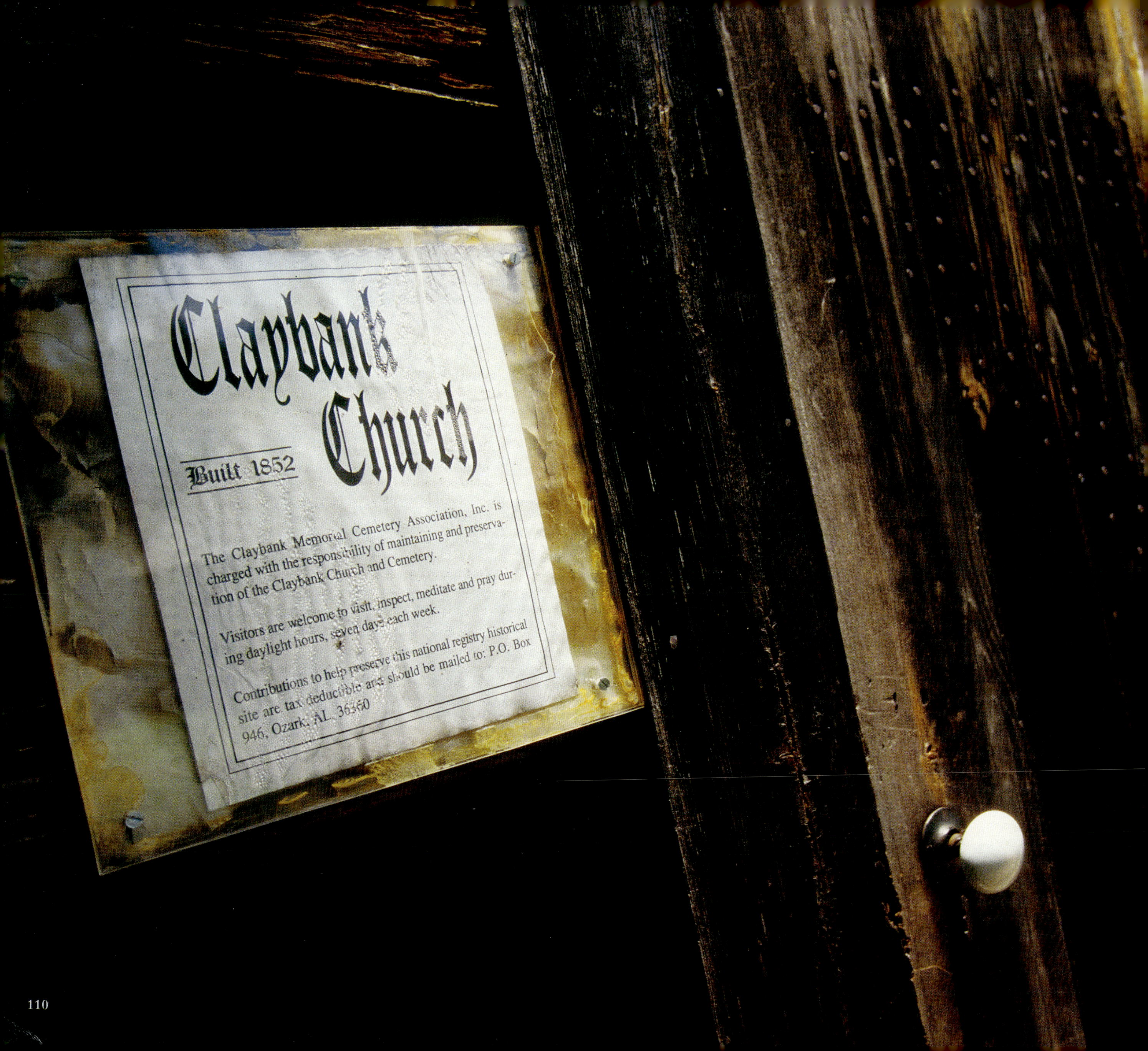
Claybank Church
Built 1852
The Claybank Memorial Cemetery Association, Inc. is charged with the responsibility of maintaining and preservation of the Claybank Church and Cemetery.
Visitors are welcome to visit, inspect, meditate and pray during daylight hours, seven days each week.
Contributions to help preserve this national registry historical site are tax deductible and should be mailed to: P.O. Box 946, Ozark, AL 36360

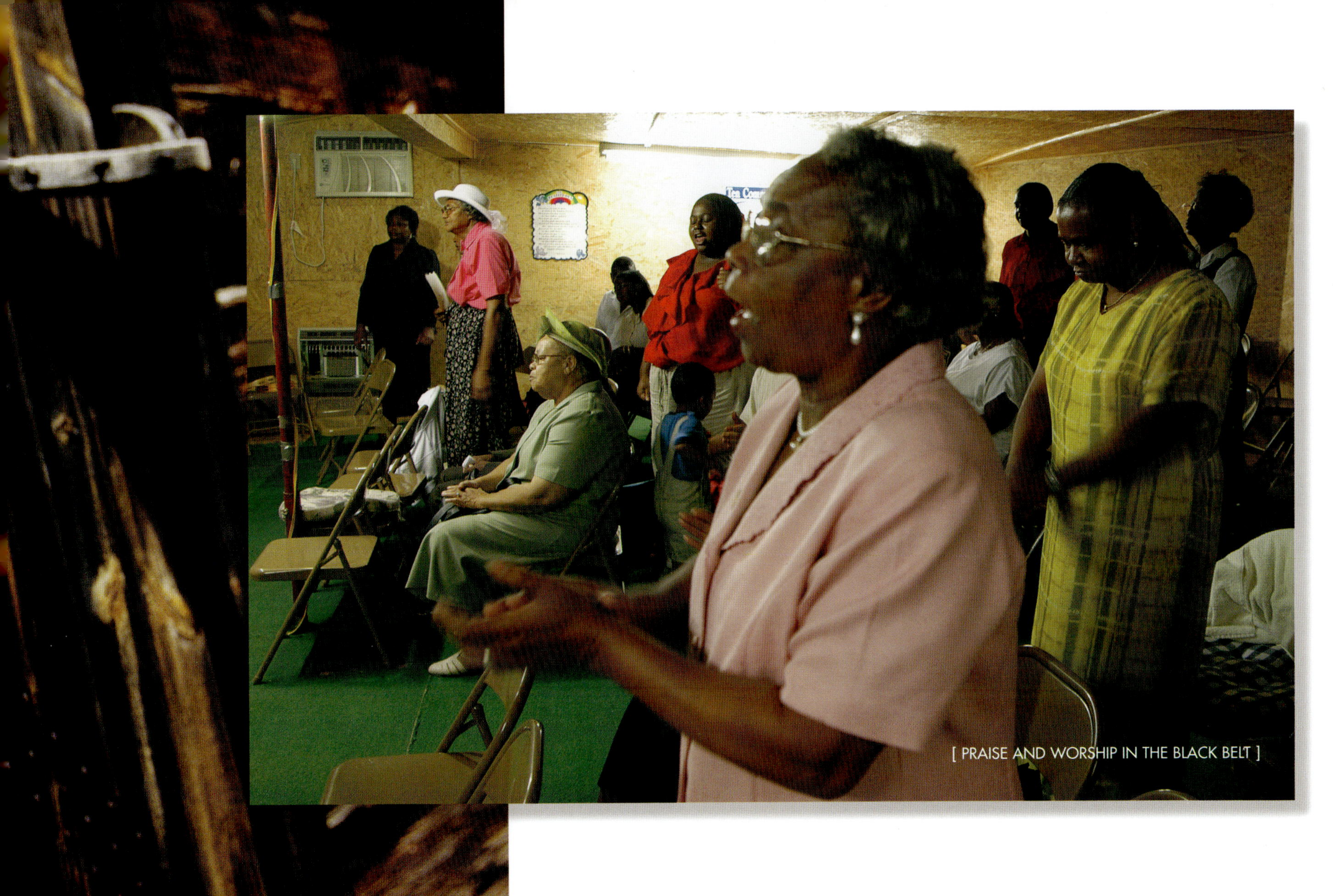

[PRAISE AND WORSHIP IN THE BLACK BELT]

And we sing every Sunday.

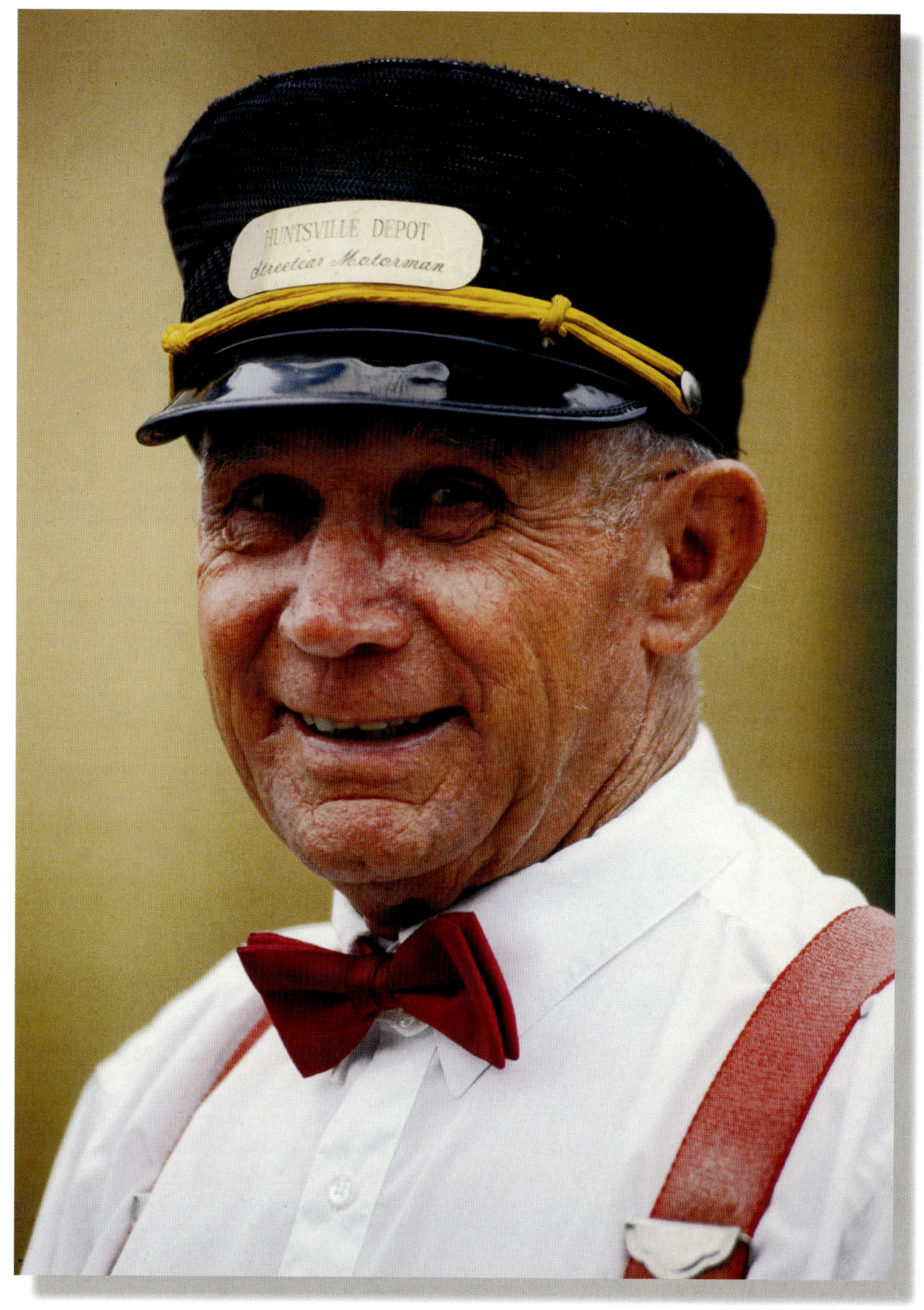
HUNTSVILLE DEPOT
Streetcar Motorman

"Alabama has been good to me."

Jimmy Carter
[SINGER, THE BLIND BOYS OF ALABAMA]

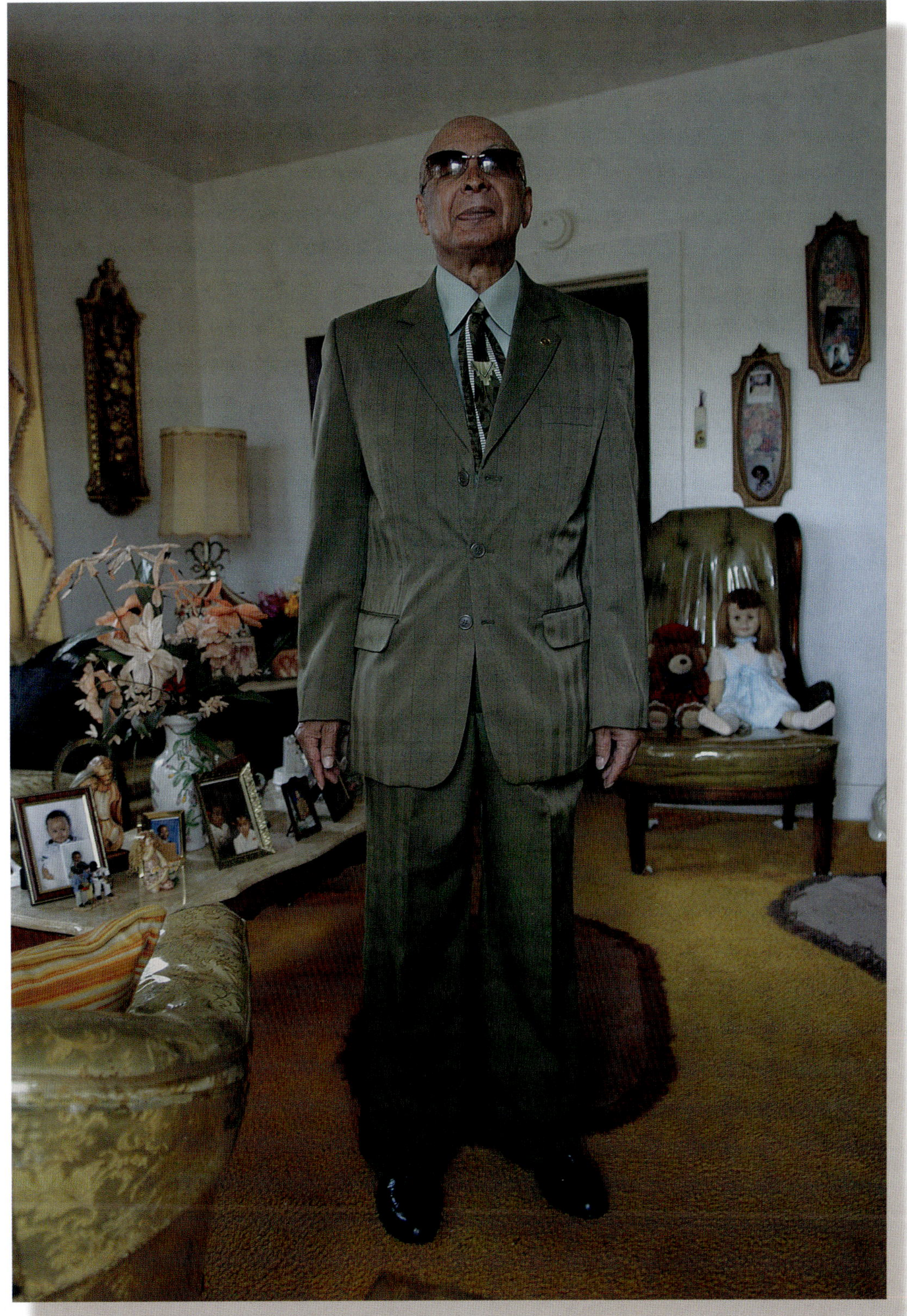

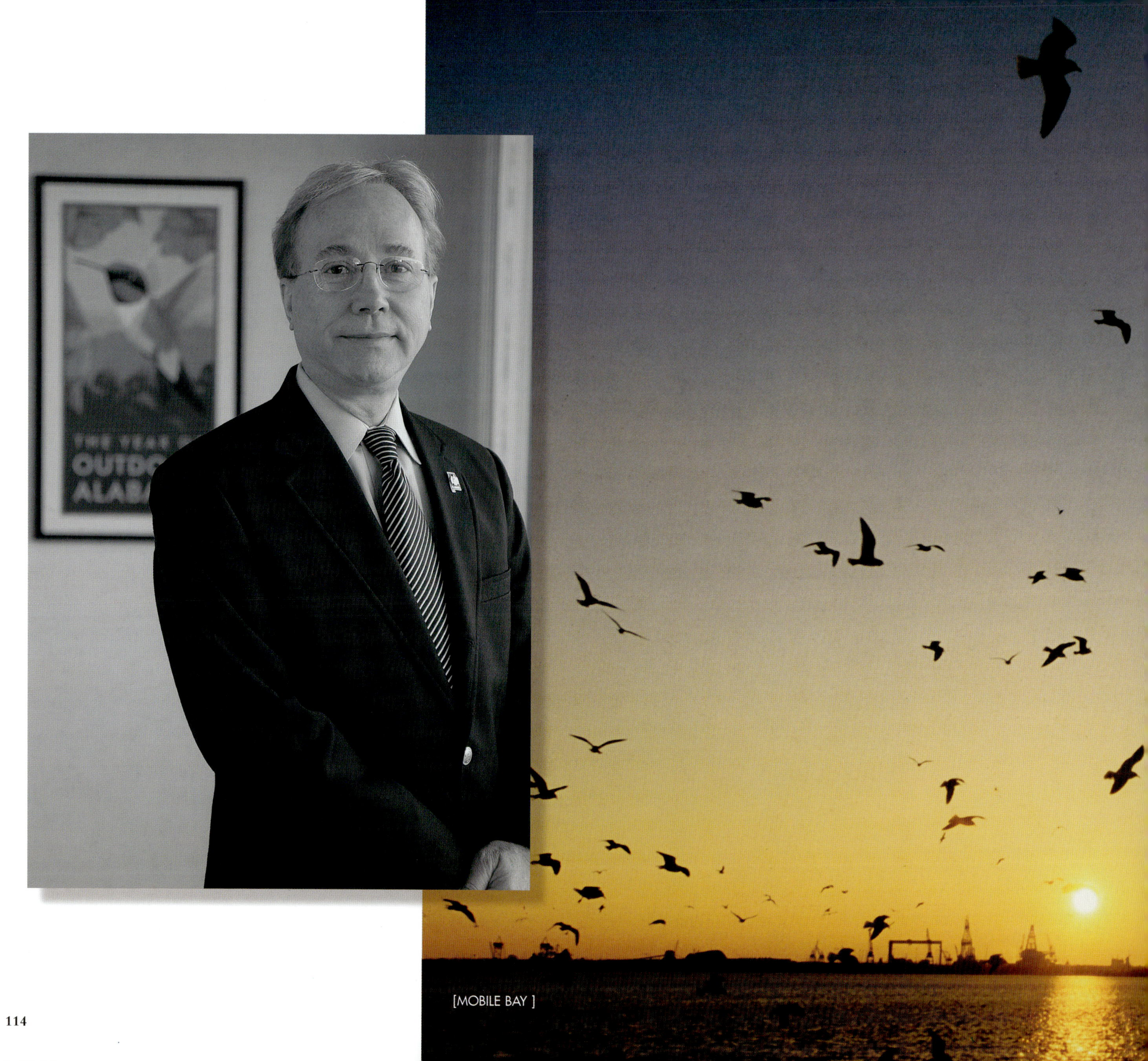

[MOBILE BAY]

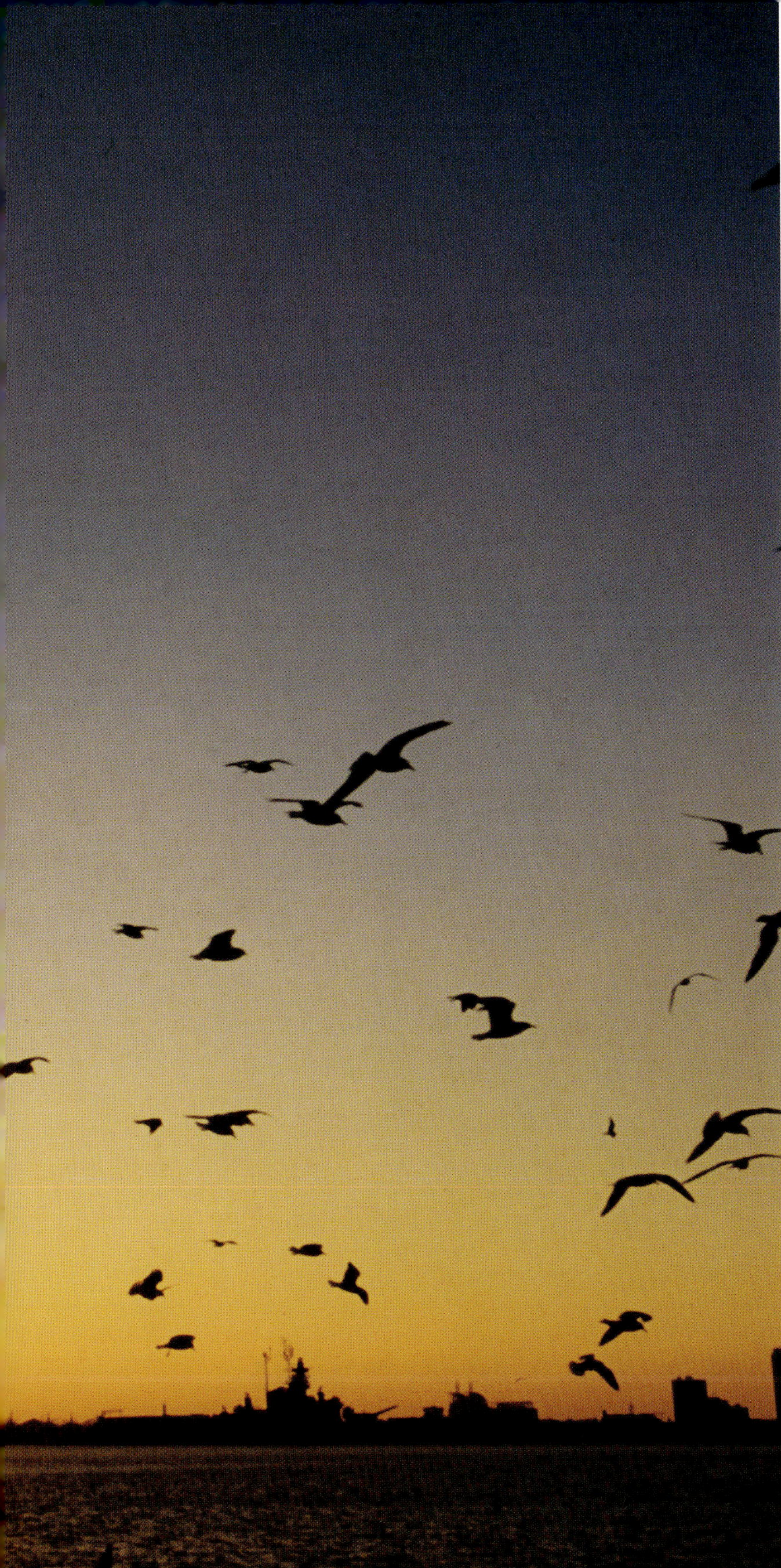

The title of the song "Sweet Home Alabama" was a popular phrase in the mid 1970s and surged back into favor a few years ago, thanks to Reese Witherspoon's romantic comedy of the same name. Bo Bice made the song his personal anthem on *American Idol.*

It's become our unofficial state catch phrase, and it's more popular than ever. Why? I think it's because we're more confident as Alabamians. We've got a governor we're proud of. We've given ourselves permission to love our state and acknowledge it out loud. We like celebrating with our own soundtrack.

Our unique history defines the South as a complicated region apart, to be studied, albeit frequently misunderstood. Alabama isn't only the birthplace of the Confederacy, but also of the civil-rights movement.

The first comment from tourists is usually, "Alabama is such a beautiful state." And we are a friendly people. Northerners phone just to hear our "ac-cents."

Our topography ranges from Mount Cheaha and Lookout Mountain to the rolling pastureland around Montgomery, down to the silent rivers that mingle above Mobile. We've got the most beautiful beaches in America and the freshest shrimp.

Our juicy tomatoes, sweet potatoes, cornbread, and okra are to die for. Birmingham's top chefs have even transformed grits into haute cuisine.

Many of our older towns are arranged around a stoic courthouse square. Even in cities, sidewalks, shade trees, and churches bring us together.

We work hard, love football and our neighbors, and practice the Golden Rule. We are sweet. This is home. We are Alabama.

LEE SENTELL
[DIRECTOR, ALABAMA BUREAU OF TOURISM & TRAVEL]

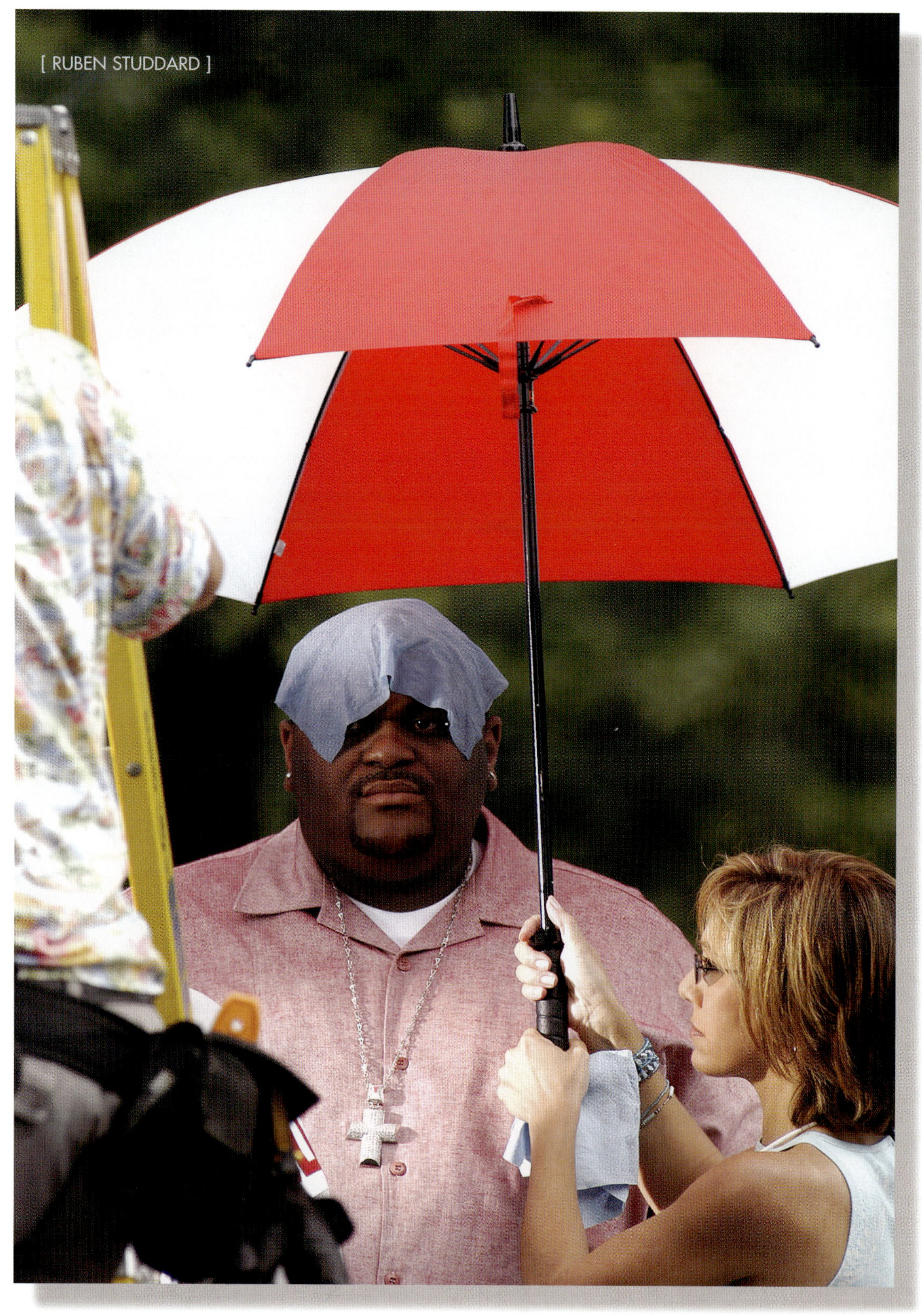
[RUBEN STUDDARD]

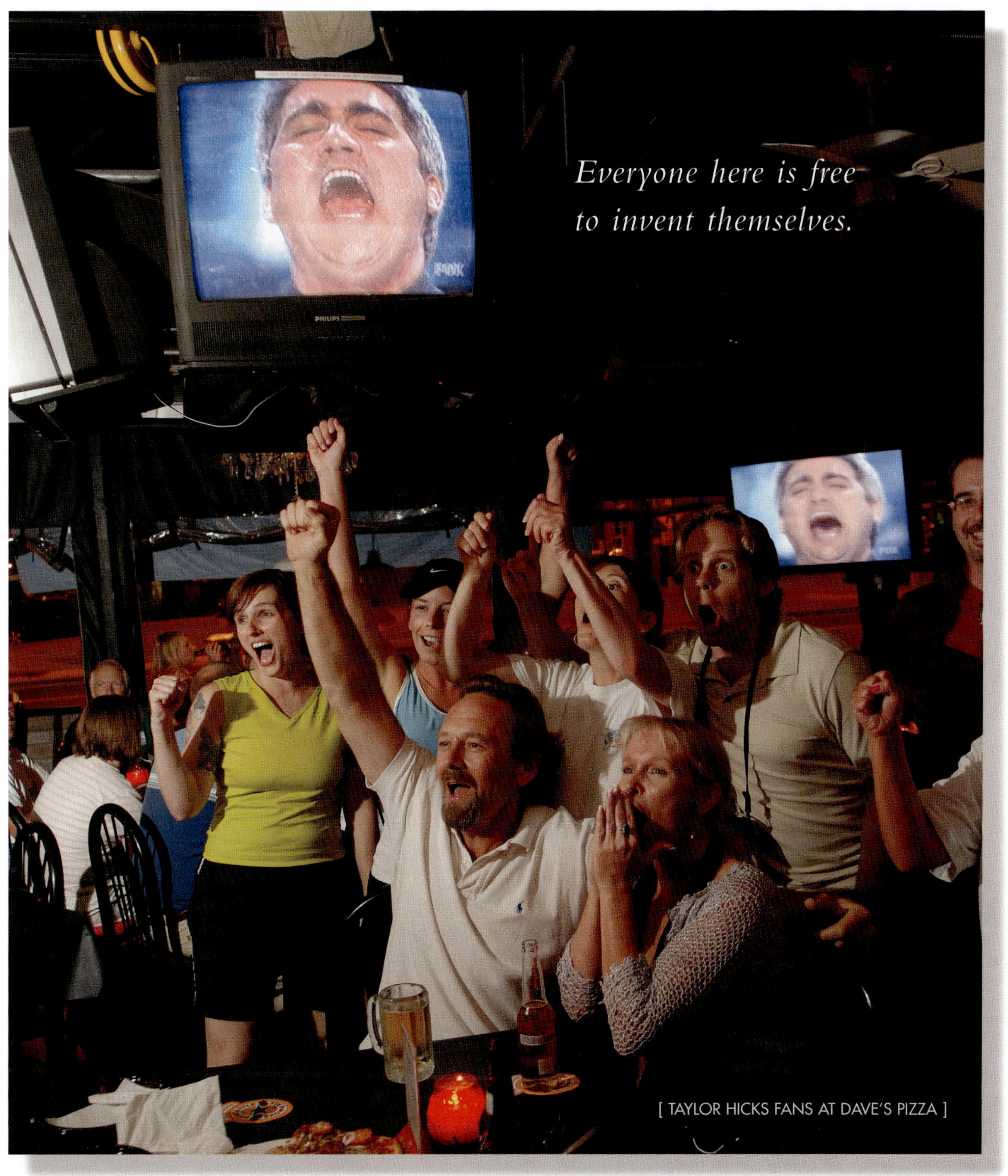

Everyone here is free to invent themselves.

[TAYLOR HICKS FANS AT DAVE'S PIZZA]

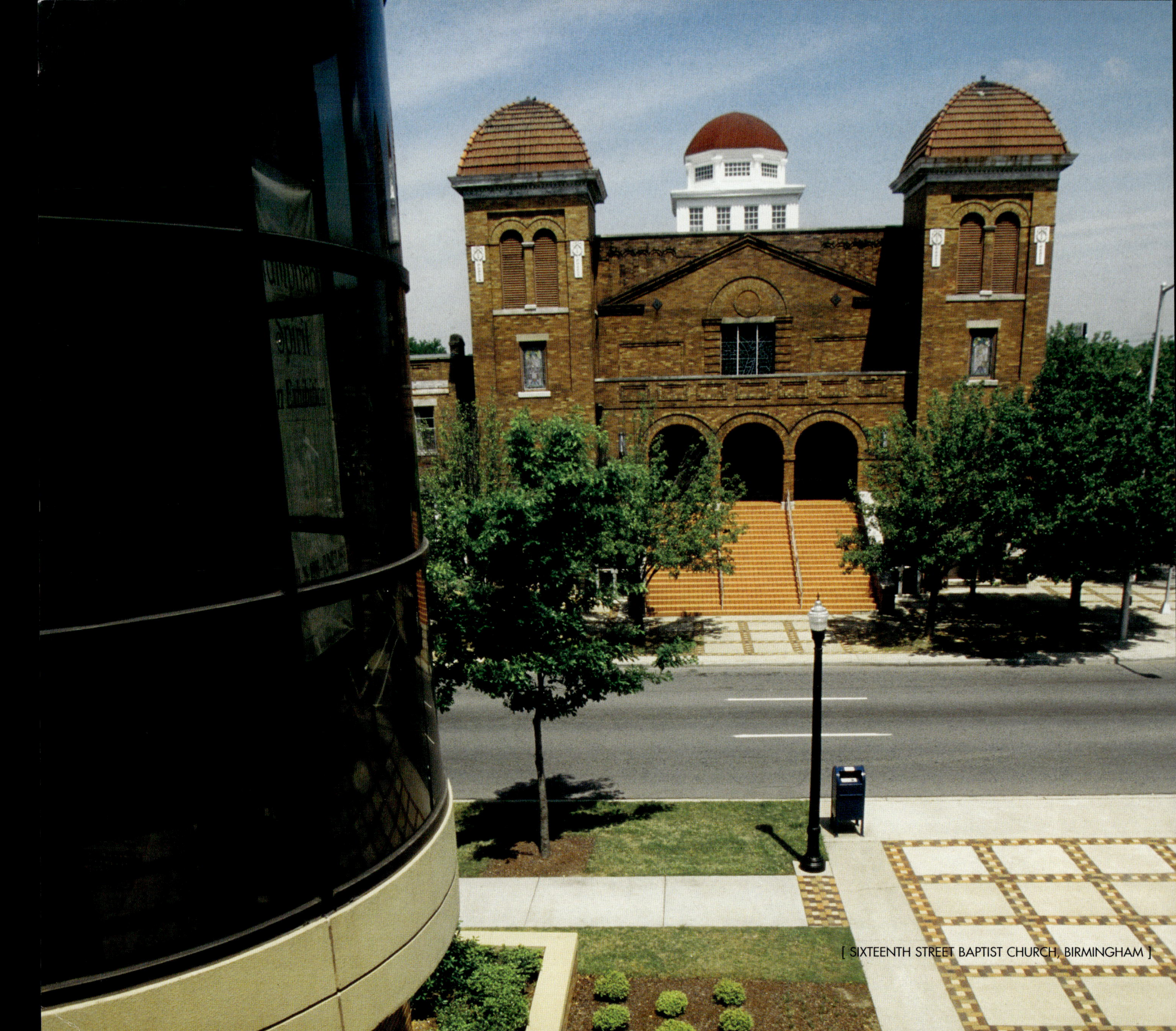

[SIXTEENTH STREET BAPTIST CHURCH, BIRMINGHAM]

I am an Alabama native proud of my deep roots in this state. Born in the Auburn University infirmary, I grew up in Fort Payne, and have many fond memories of our farm there and of my grandfather's farm in Clarke County. Along the way, I developed a deep and abiding love of the land that we call Alabama, and of its people.

Over the years, I have watched our state, and particularly my now hometown of Birmingham, progress from the early days of the civil rights movement to become a world leader in efforts to eliminate racism and other forms of injustice wherever they exist. In the process, I found myself inspired to offer a public affirmation addressing the racial issues that have divided us over the years. In 1997, I wrote what came to be known as the Birmingham Pledge as my individual commitment to honor and respect the worth and dignity of all people, hoping to inspire others to make a similar commitment and a positive difference, one person at a time. Since that time, people from all over the globe and from all walks of life have made that commitment. The process continues.

James E. Rotch
[ATTORNEY]

THE BIRMINGHAM PLEDGE

I believe that every person has worth as an individual.

I believe that every person is entitled to dignity and respect, regardless of race or color.

I believe that every thought and every act of racial prejudice is harmful; if it is my thought or act, then it is harmful to me as well as to others.

Therefore, from this day forward I will strive daily to eliminate racial prejudice from my thoughts and actions.

I will discourage racial prejudice by others at every opportunity.

I will treat all people with dignity and respect; and I will strive daily to honor this pledge, knowing that the world will be a better place because of my effort.

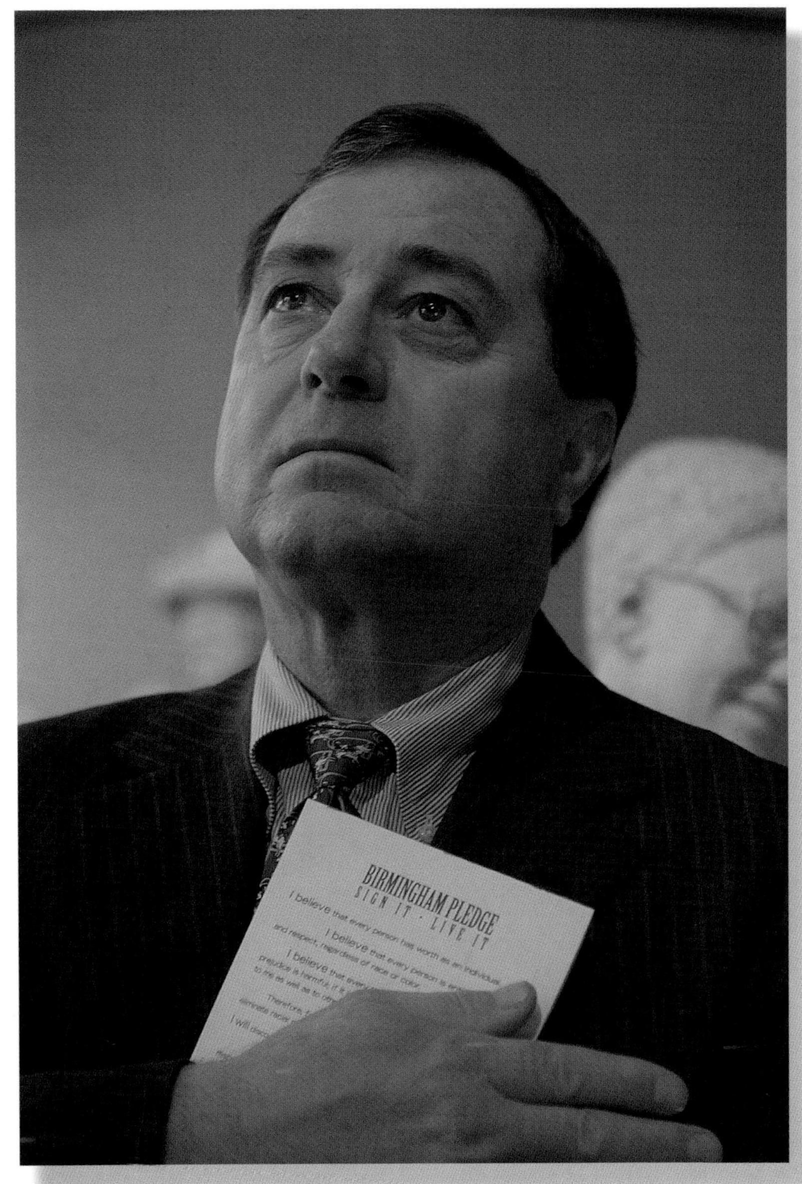

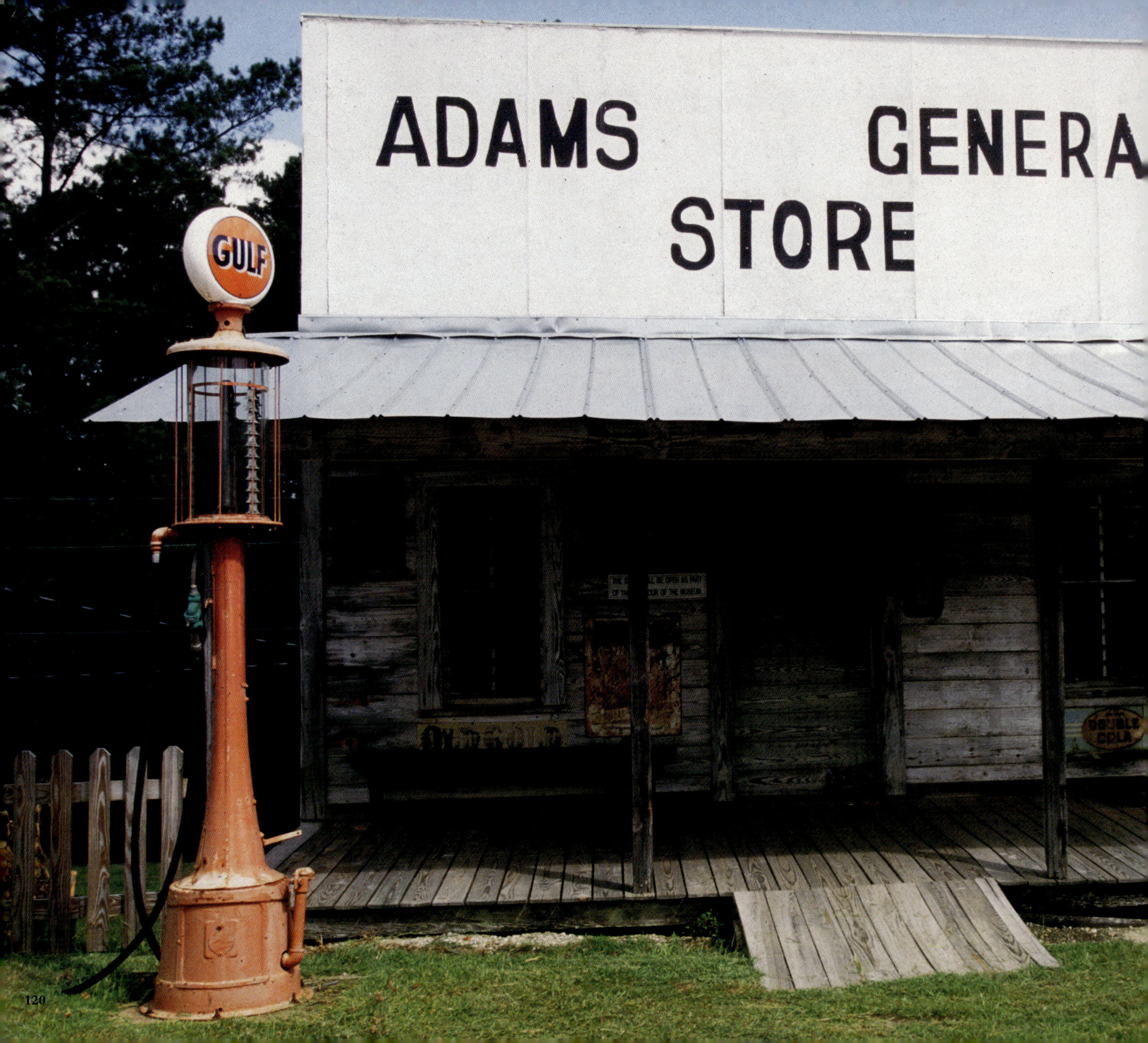
ADAMS GENERA
STORE
GULF
DOUBLE COLA

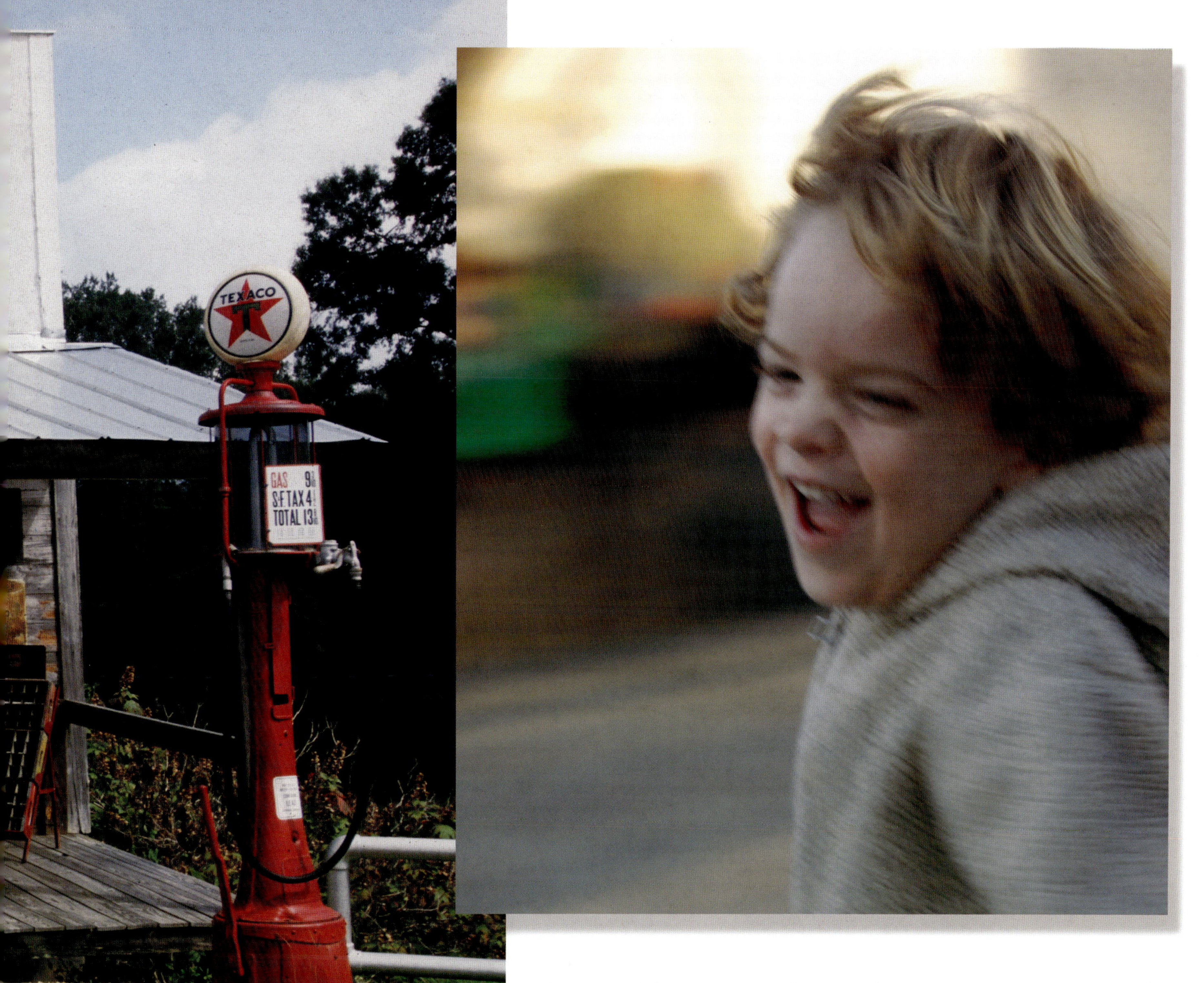

[PIONEER MUSEUM, TROY]

When we need something, we just run down to the corner.

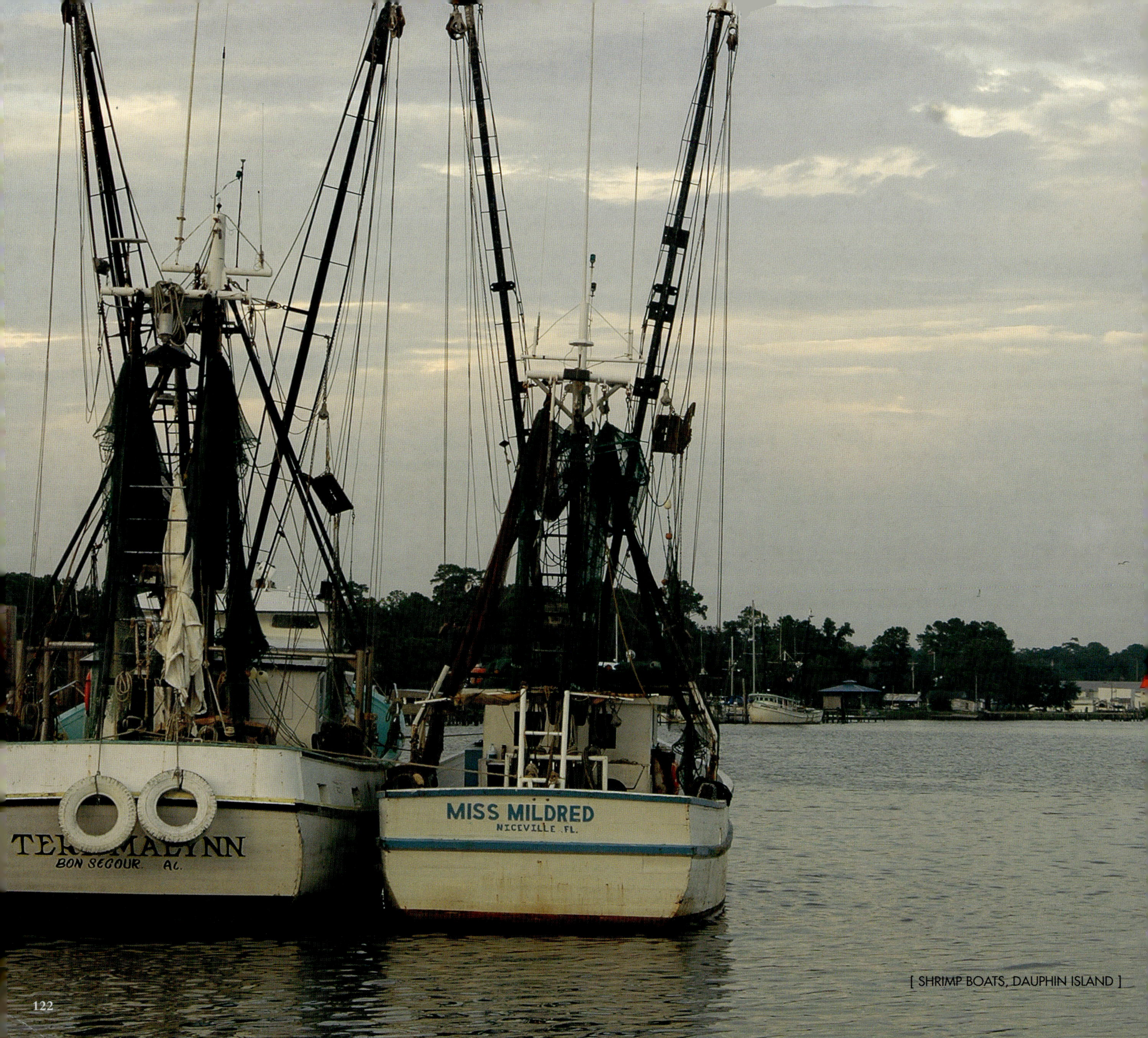

[SHRIMP BOATS, DAUPHIN ISLAND]

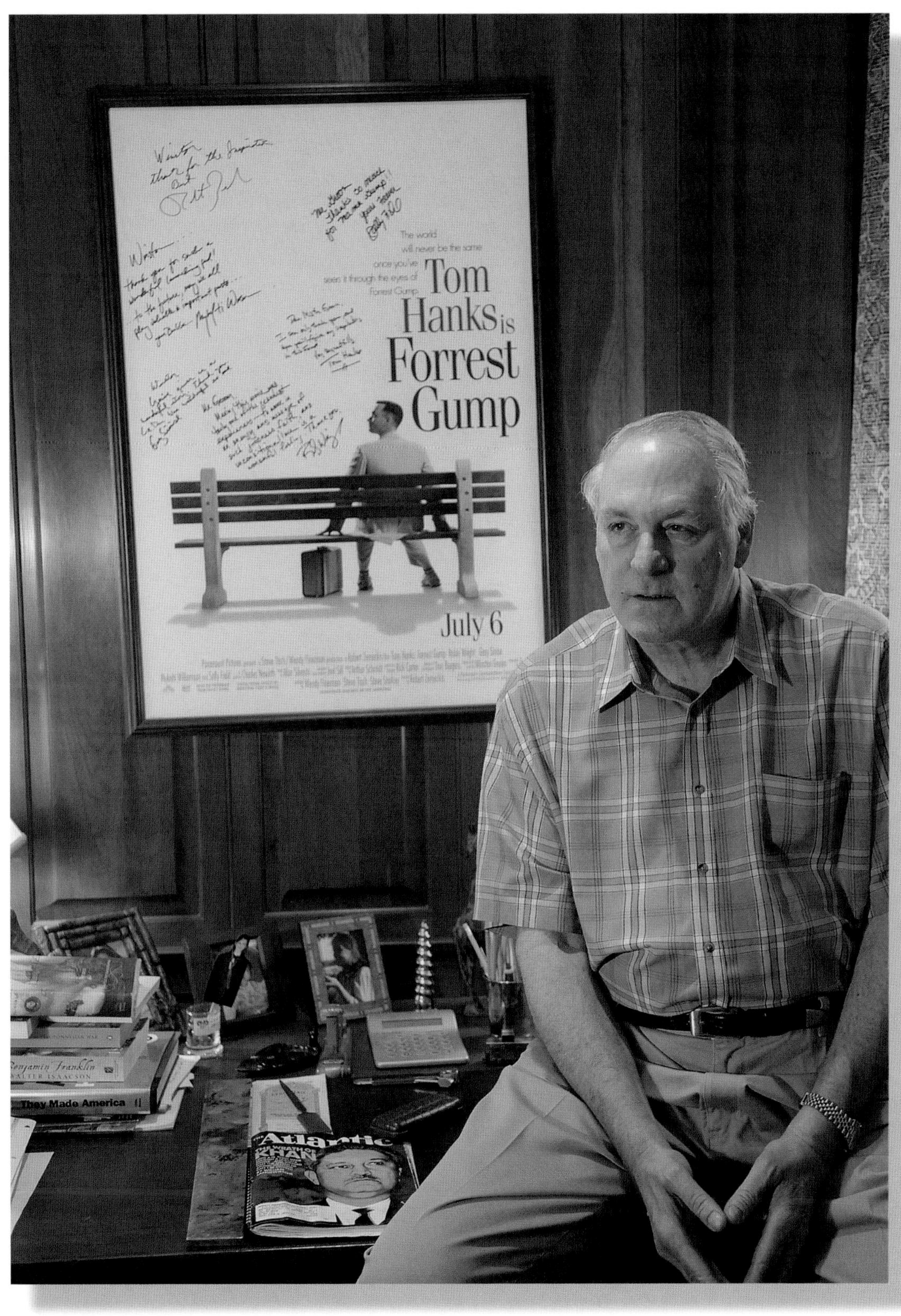

I love Alabama because it's my home. I was in Washington, D.C. and New York for nearly two decades, and while those places have their particular charm, Alabama is where I want to be. My old, dear friends are here, and it's a great place to raise children. My daughter, Carolina Montgomery Groom, age 7, loves it here, and here I am.

WINSTON GROOM
[AUTHOR]

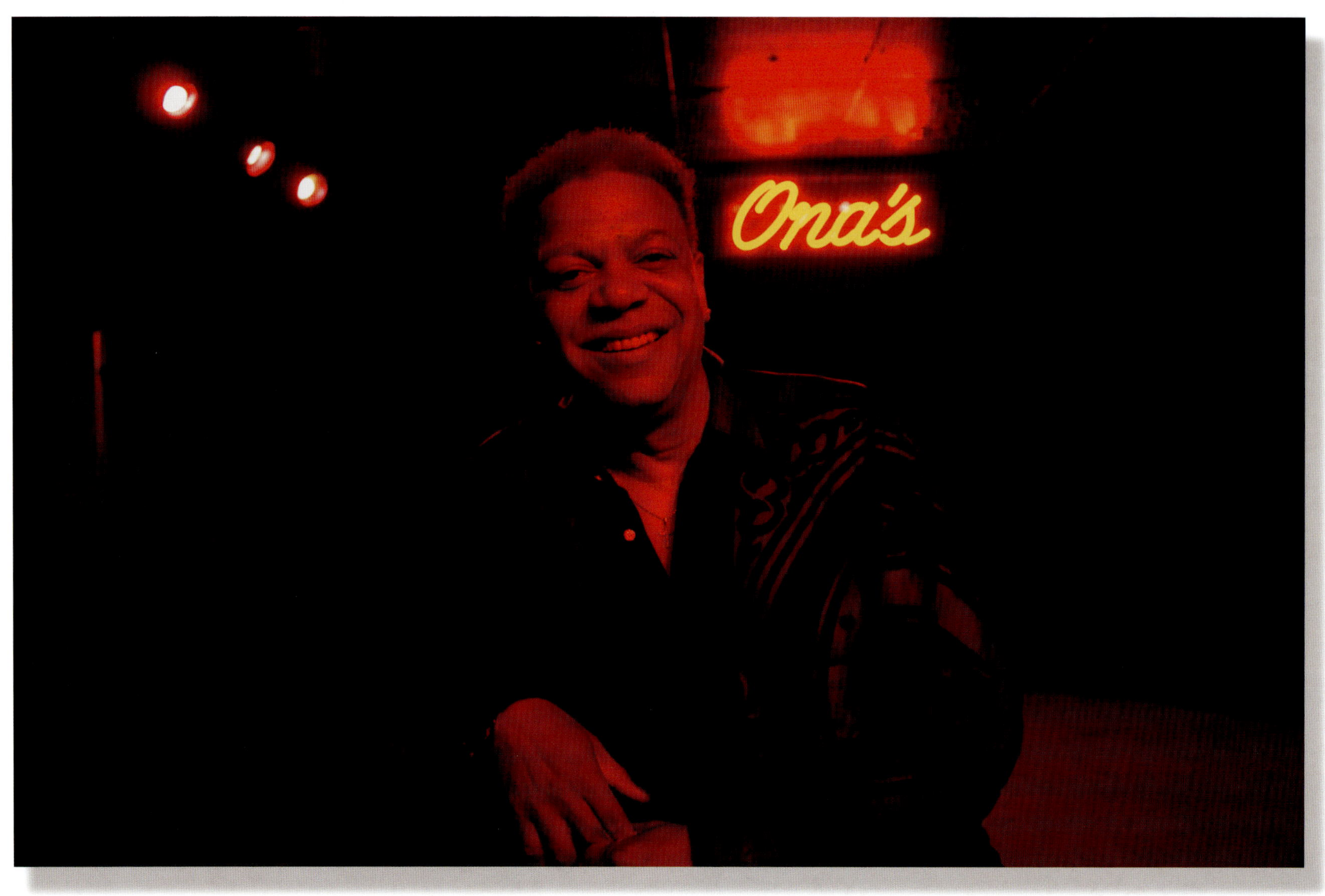

I love Alabama because it's my home. I've seen it embrace so many wonderful, positive things that allow all people here to fulfill their dreams.

ONA WATSON
[SINGER, CLUB OWNER]

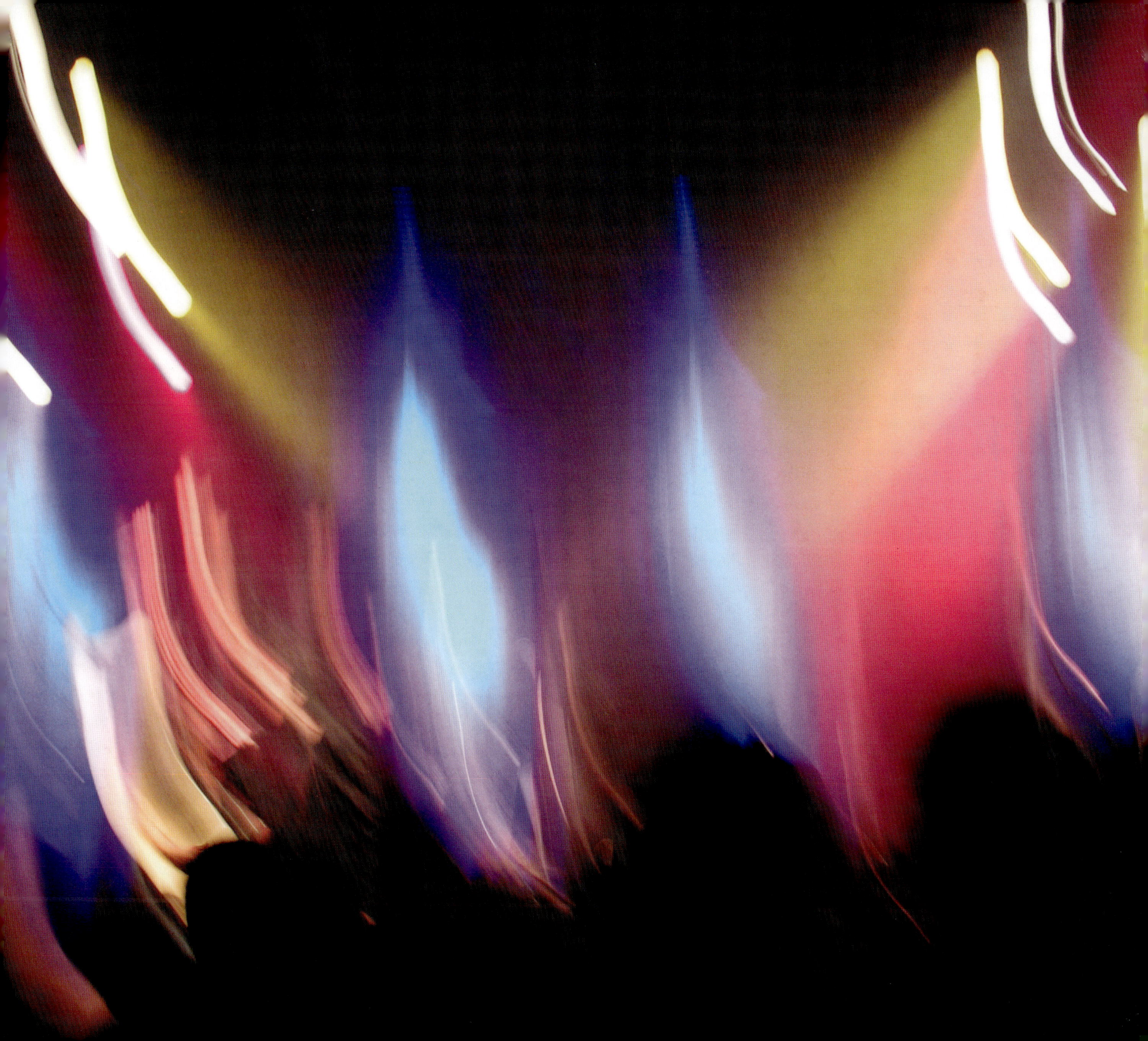

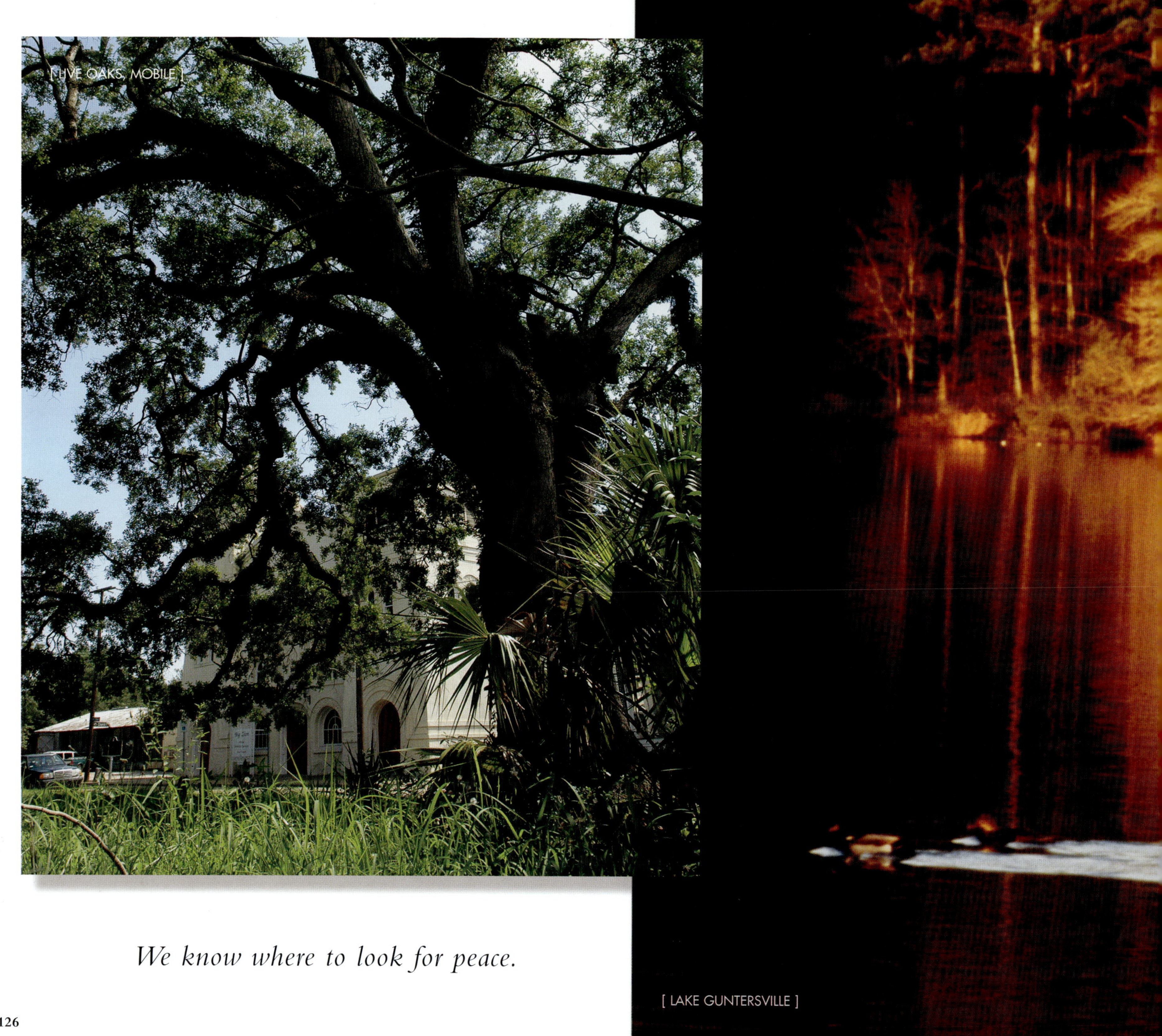

We know where to look for peace.

[LAKE GUNTERSVILLE]

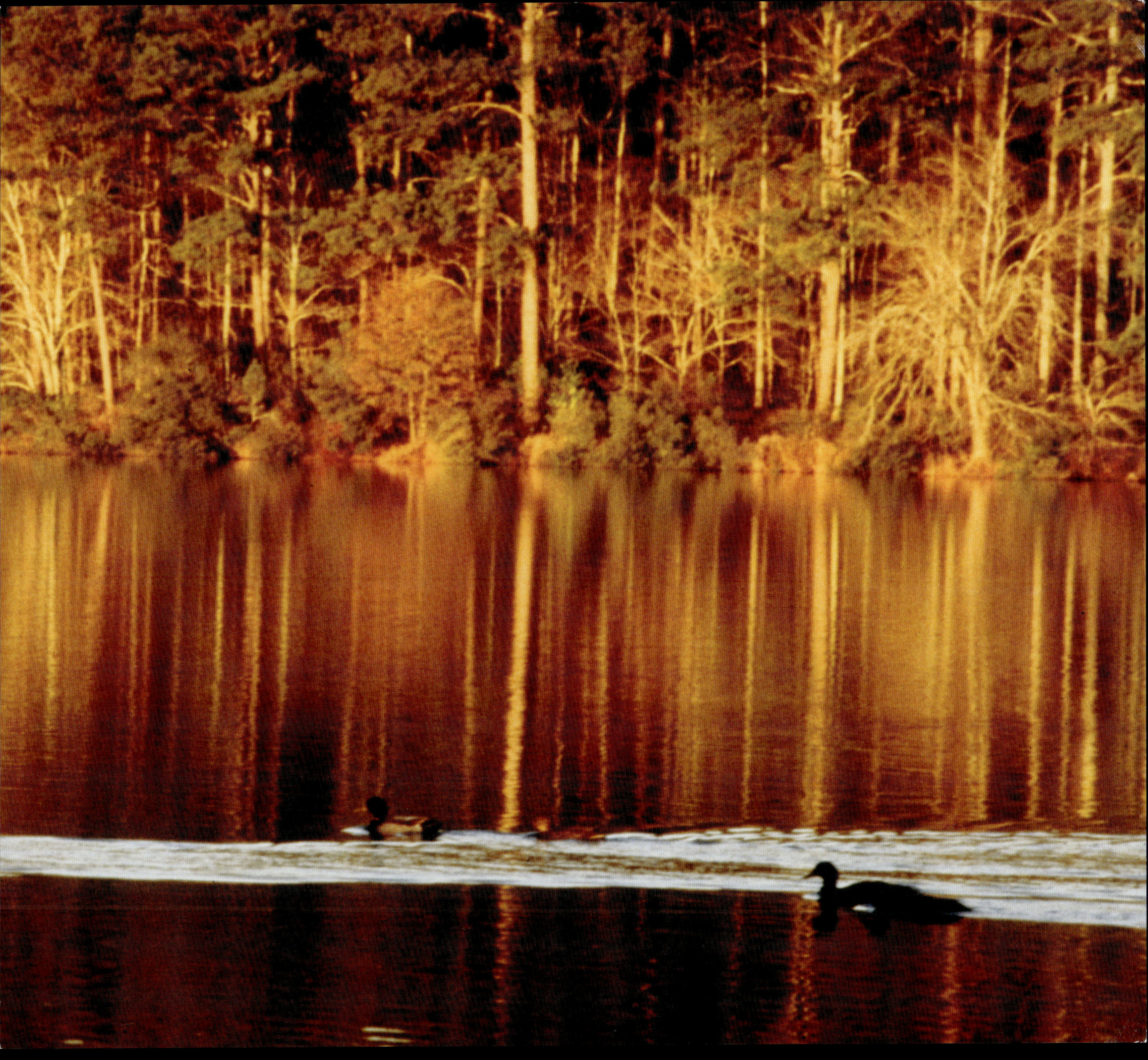

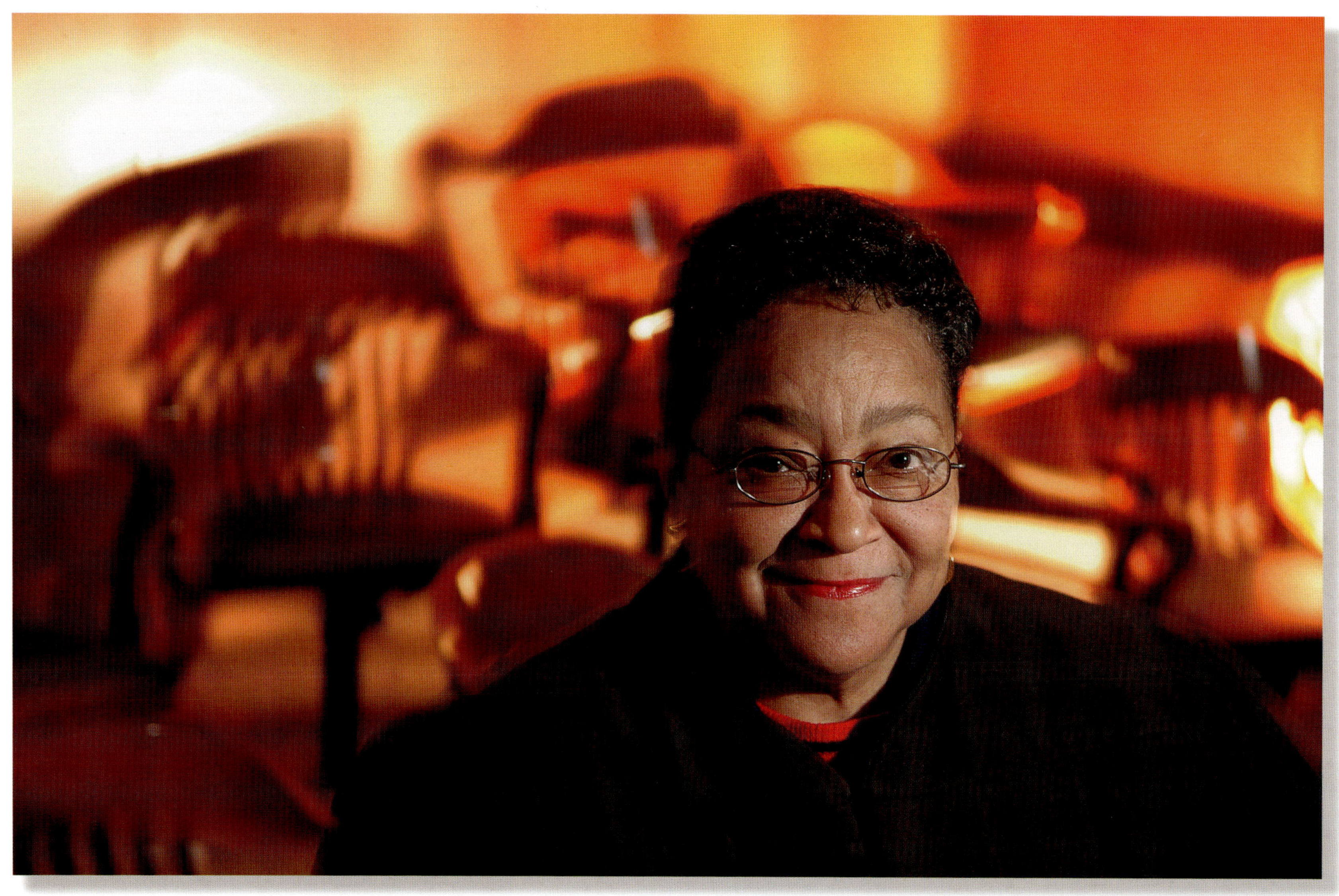

The best decision I ever made was to move back to Alabama where my children could grow up around their grandparents and learn their history and heritage. I am proud to be part of the change that is taking place here in Alabama – a change that is directed at full integration, full participation in government, equal justice in the courts, and complete and unconditional recognition of African-Americans for their worth.

Helen Shores Lee
[CIRCUIT JUDGE]

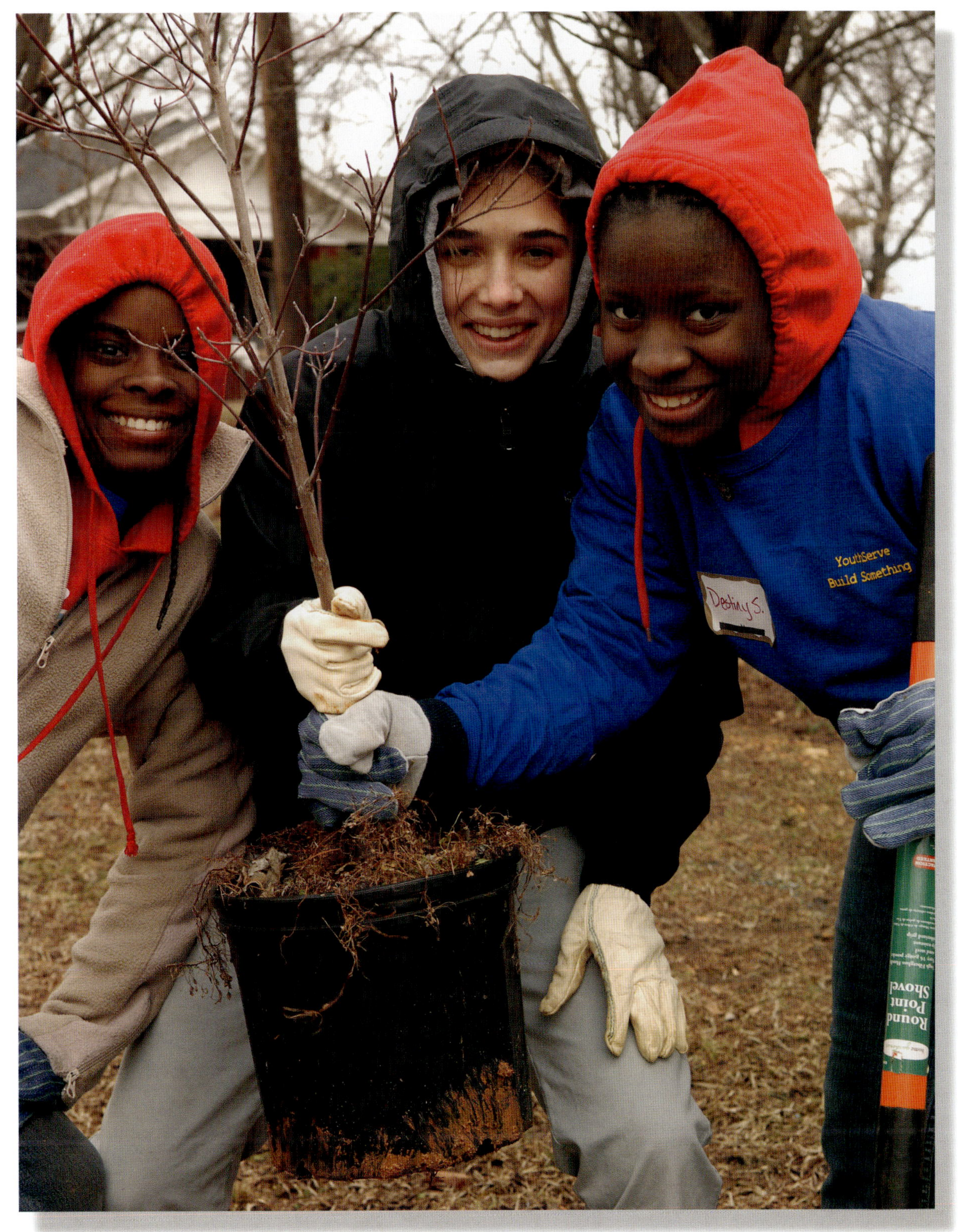

[NORWOOD BOULEVARD TREE PLANTING - COMMUNITY VOLUNTEERS]

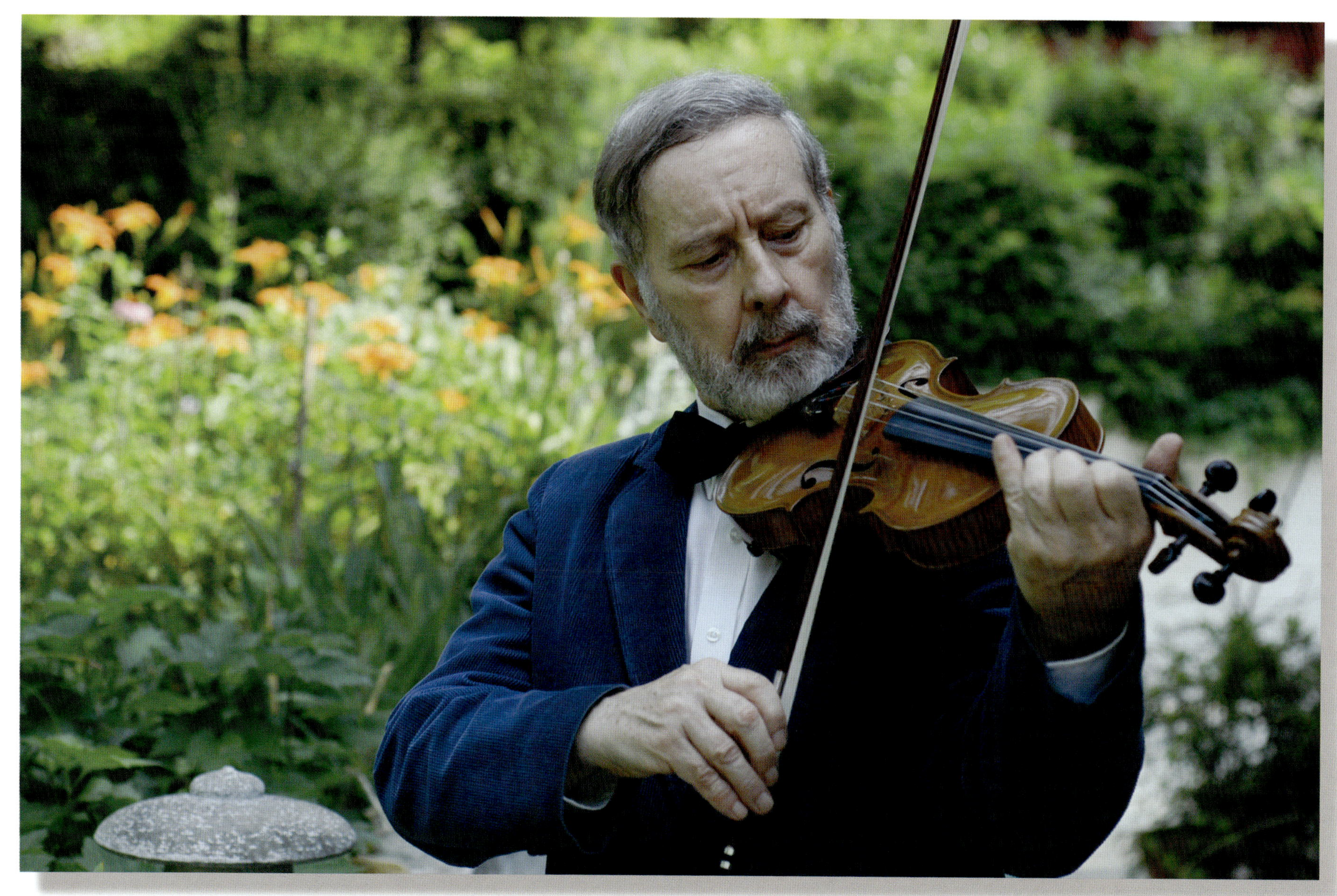

[THEODORE HADDIN IN HIS GARDEN]

We live our priorities.

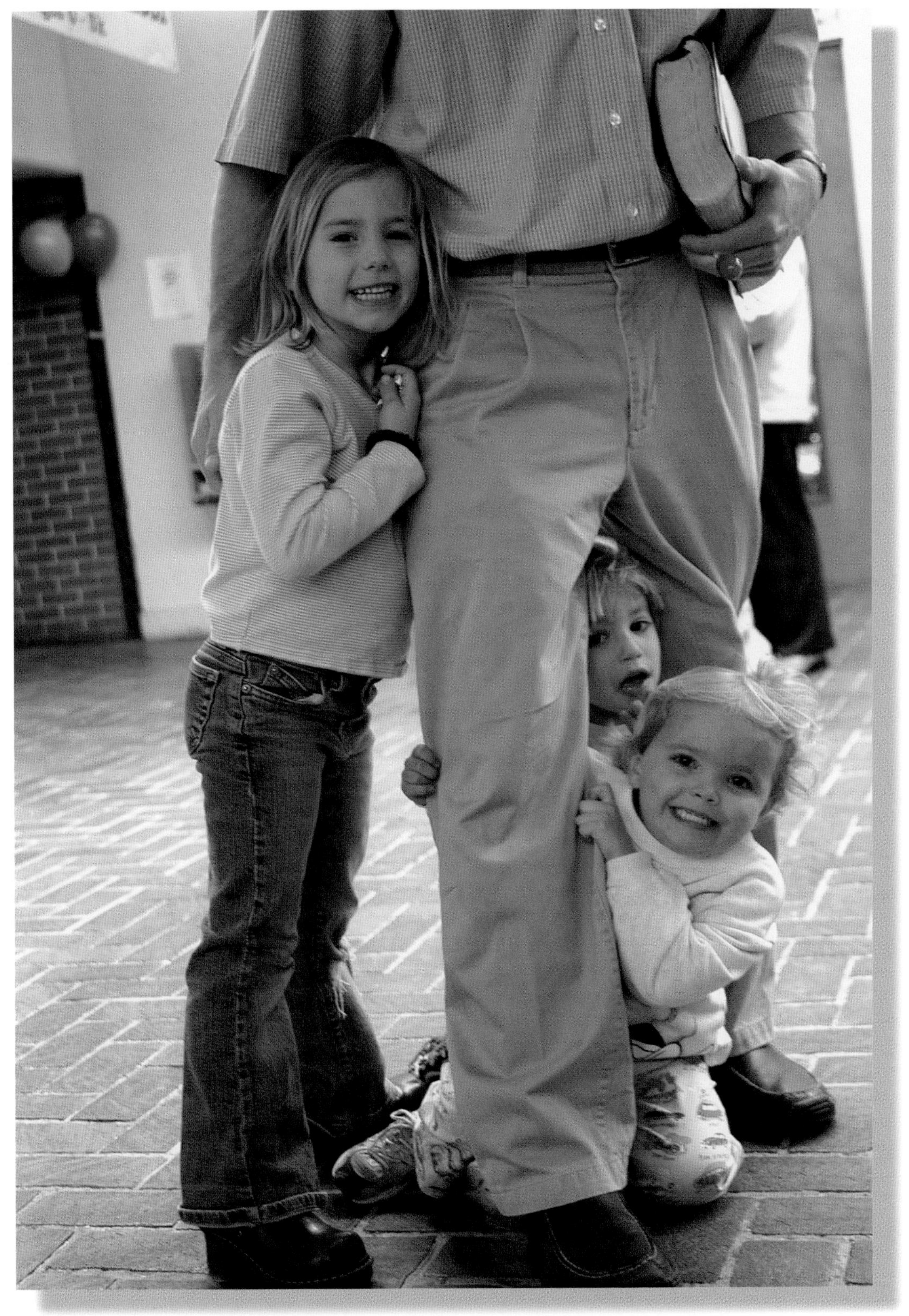

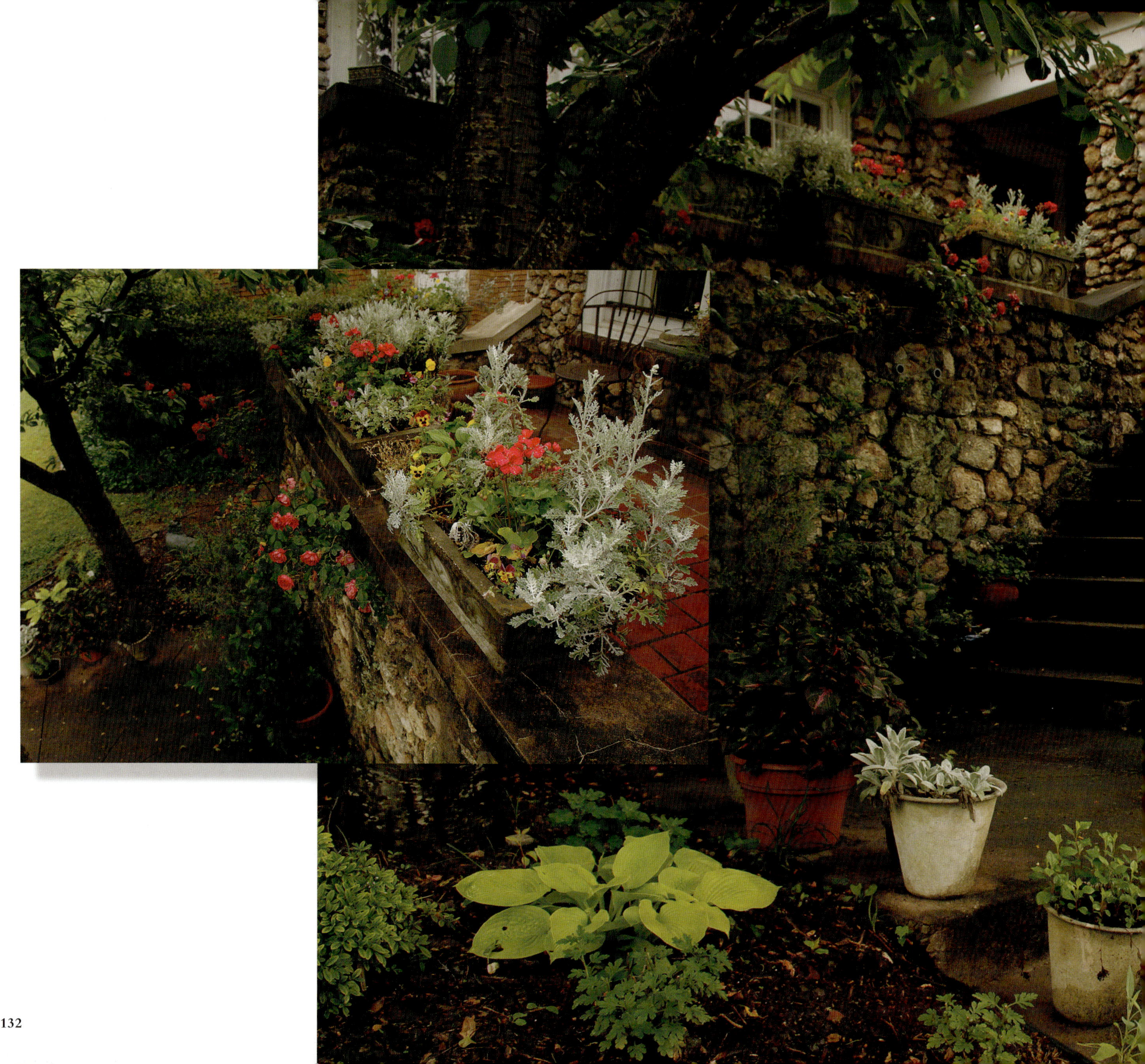

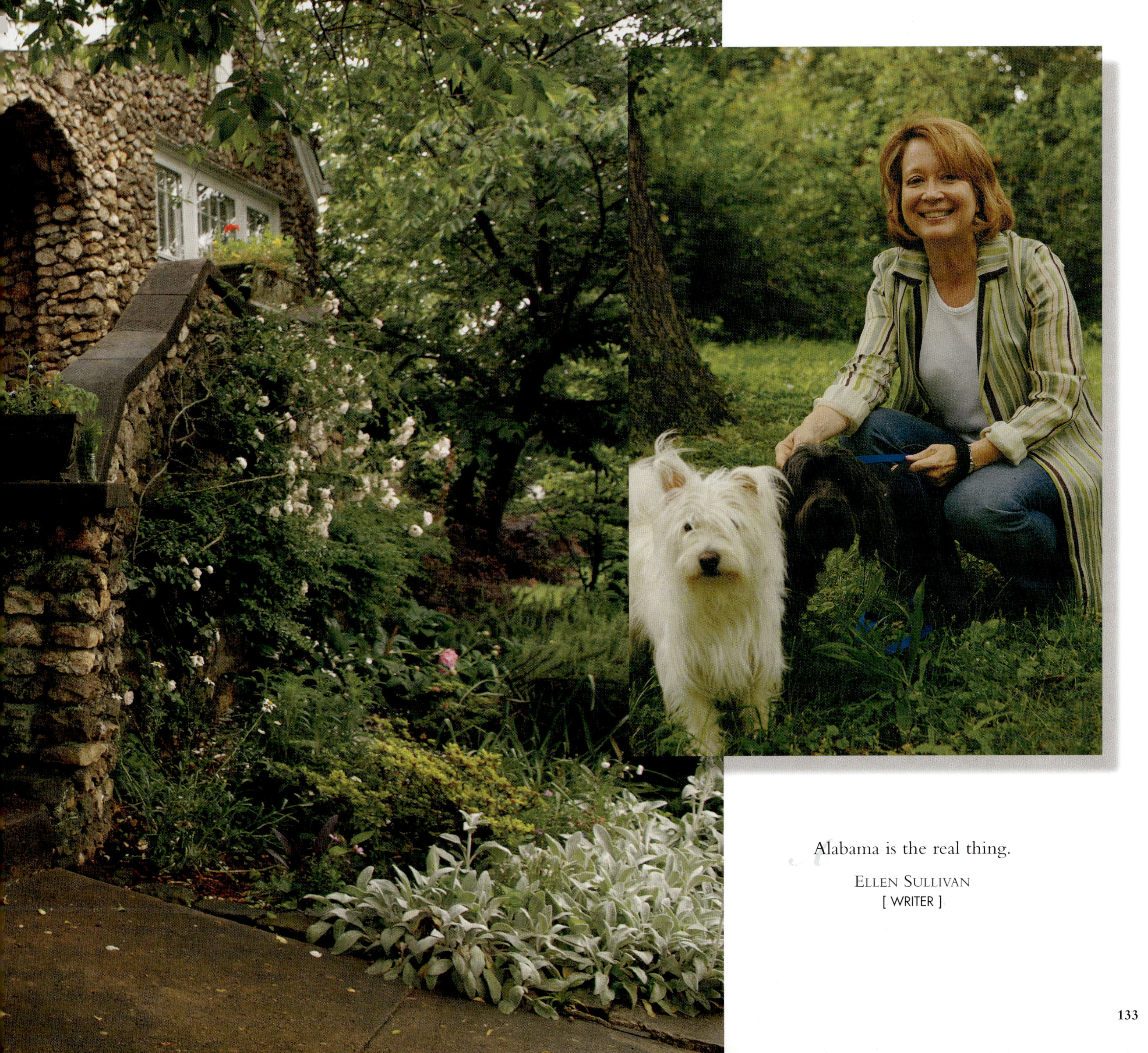

Alabama is the real thing.

ELLEN SULLIVAN
[WRITER]

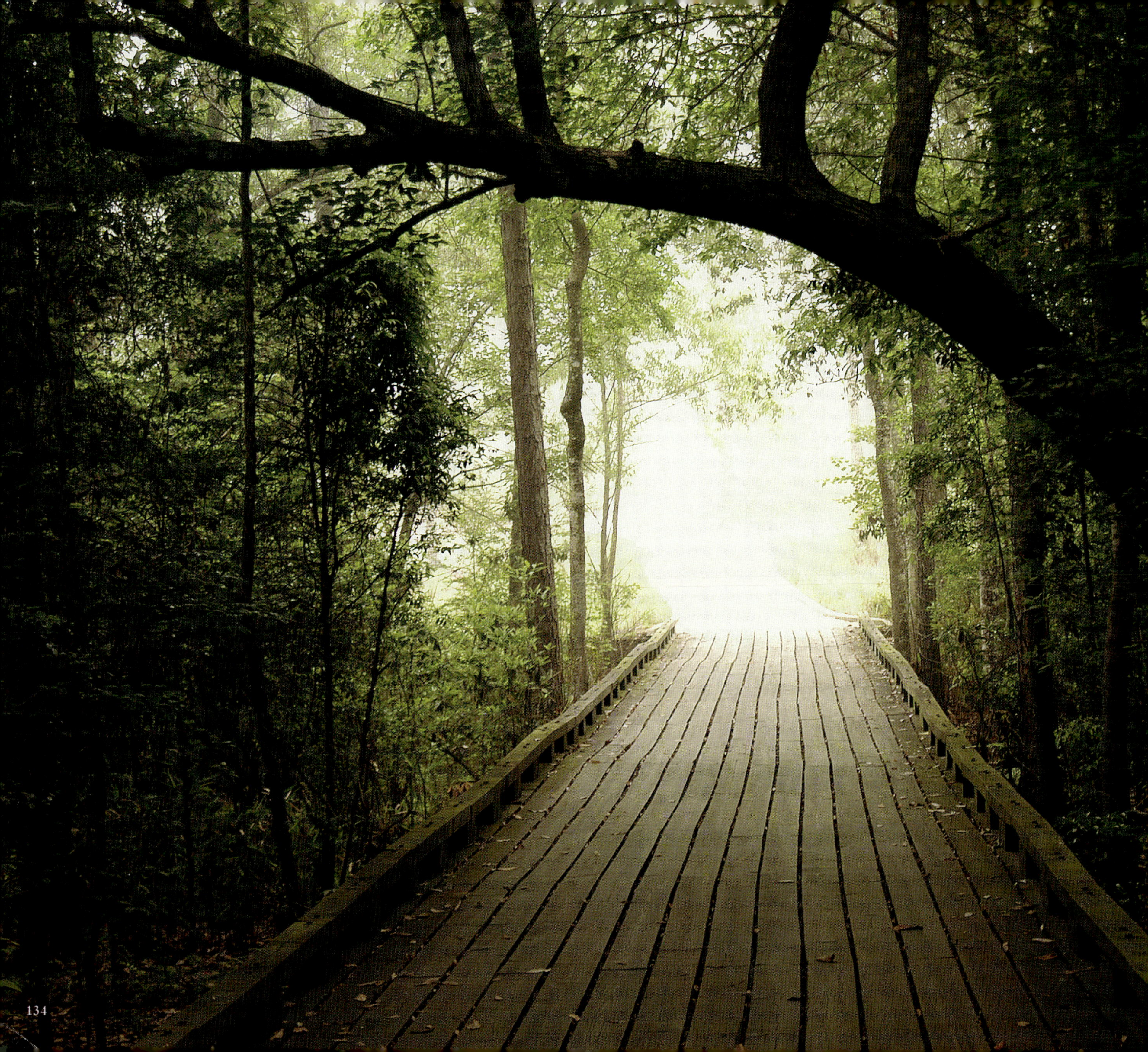

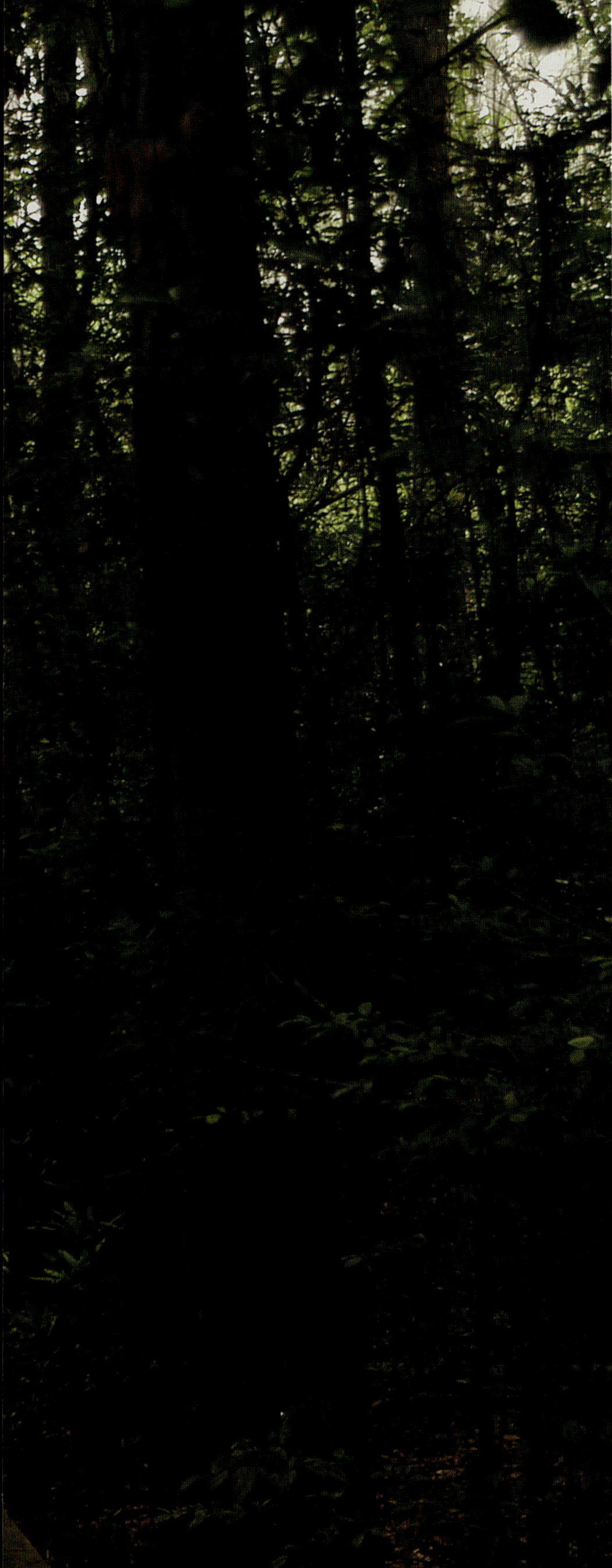

Where We're Going

There's a place inside we're always aiming for. It's filled with light, and dappled shade. It's very new and very old. A place where our families can grow, we can be safe and happy, and love one another. We find here in Alabama that the journey to that place is what life is all about.

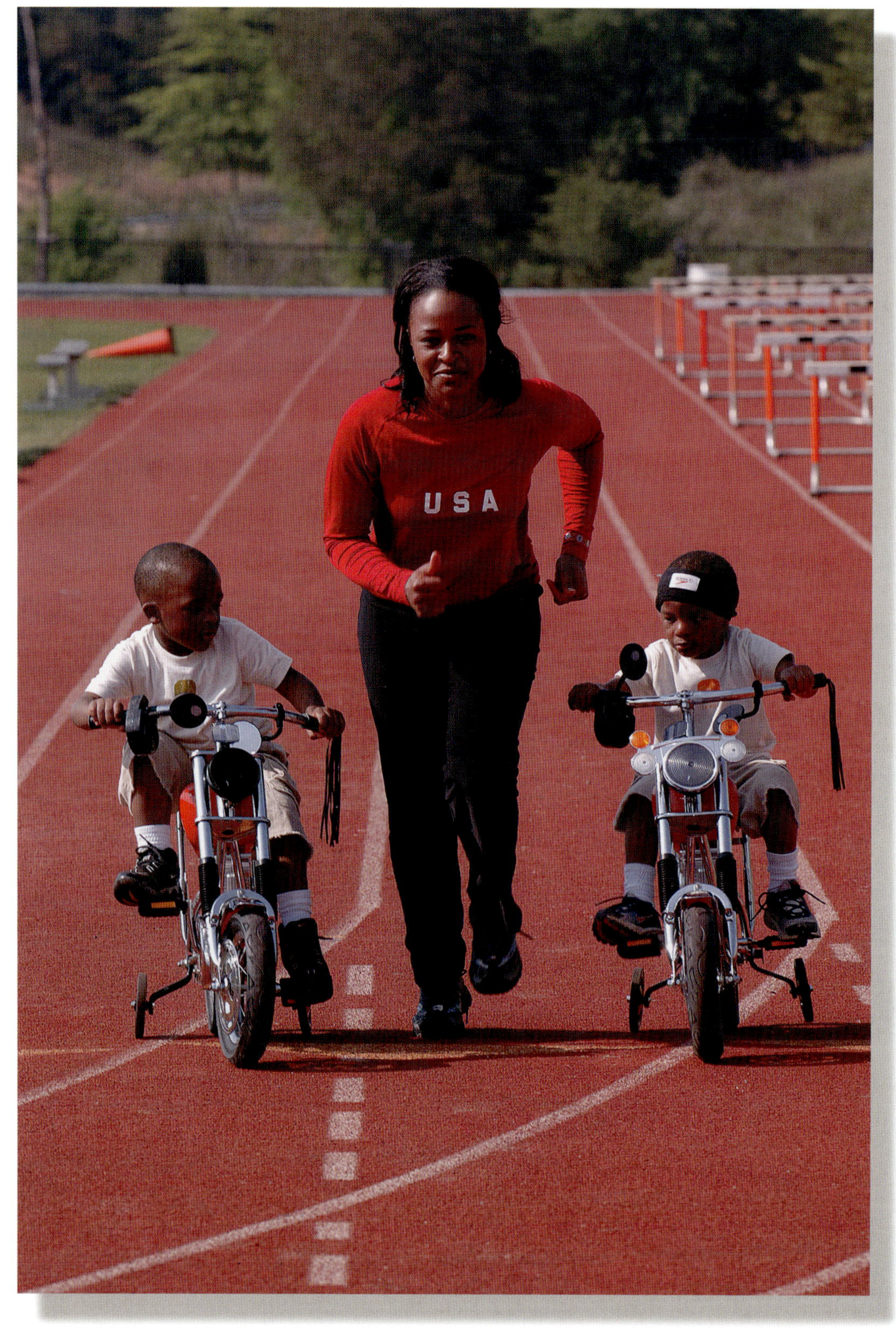
USA

Traveling around the world, I always compare the different cultures, the food, the cities, and the people to my life in Birmingham. There are times when the scenery and the events are so beautiful that I often say…"I could live here." But then I think about my childhood days and what has brought me to this point in my life. I think about my humble beginnings and how I started my career on a very small asphalt track in Bessemer, Alabama.

I think about how I stood in 100 degree heat, on the corners at busy intersections, to help support my track team (The Birmingham Striders). I think about all of the stories that I will one day share from my childhood, and how we survived living in the projects and getting by on what we had. I think about all of the good times that I've shared with many of my friends and about my decision to attend college at UAB. The reason is simple. My family lives in Birmingham. Wherever I go, I am always thinking of the people in Alabama with whom I've spent countless hours laughing, playing, eating, praying, and worrying, and I wish that they could share in my experiences. This is who I am. I LOVE Birmingham and if you have family here, you probably do too!

Vonetta Flowers
[OLYMPIC GOLD MEDALIST]

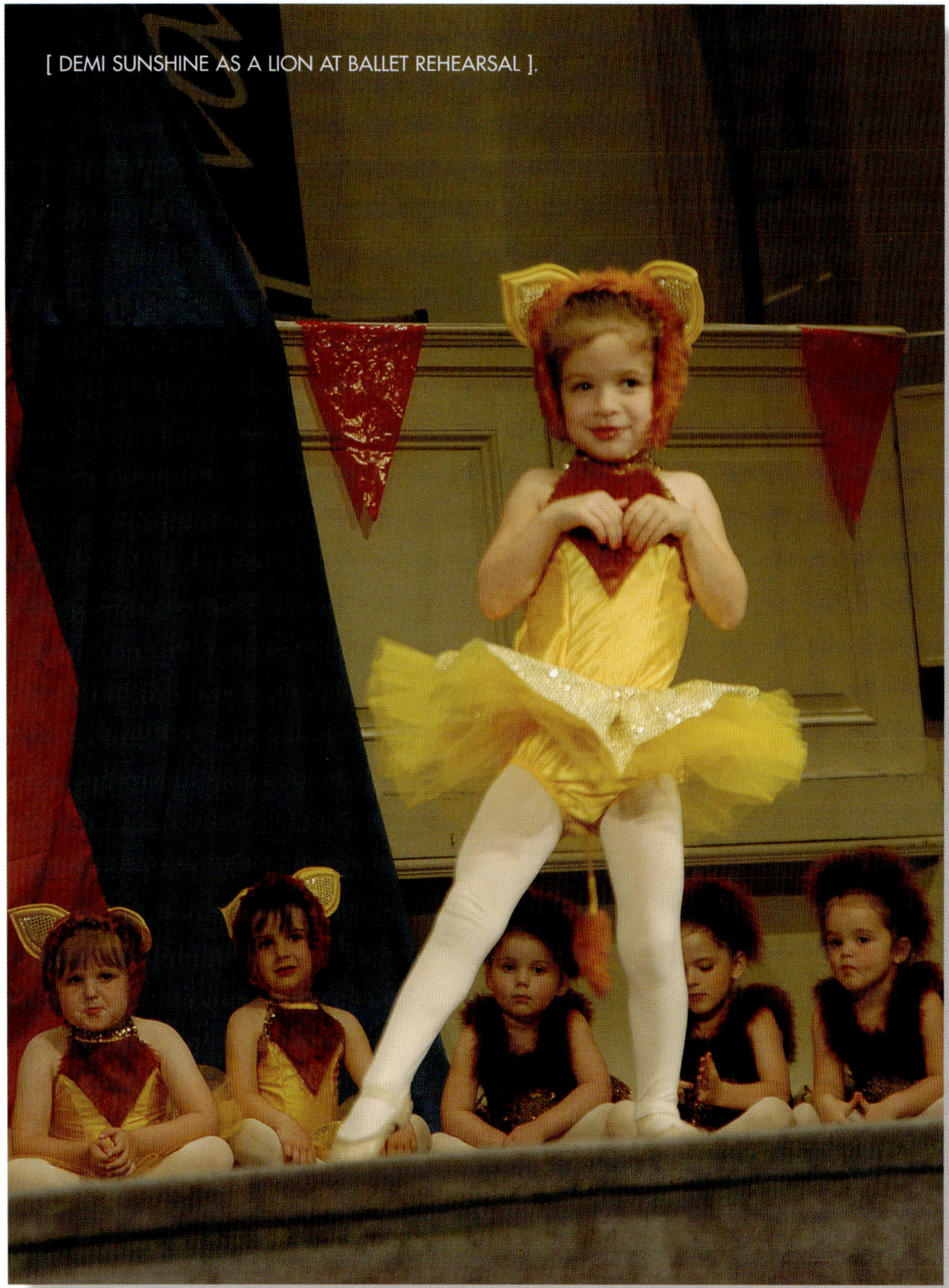

[DEMI SUNSHINE AS A LION AT BALLET REHEARSAL].

The creative force is alive within us.

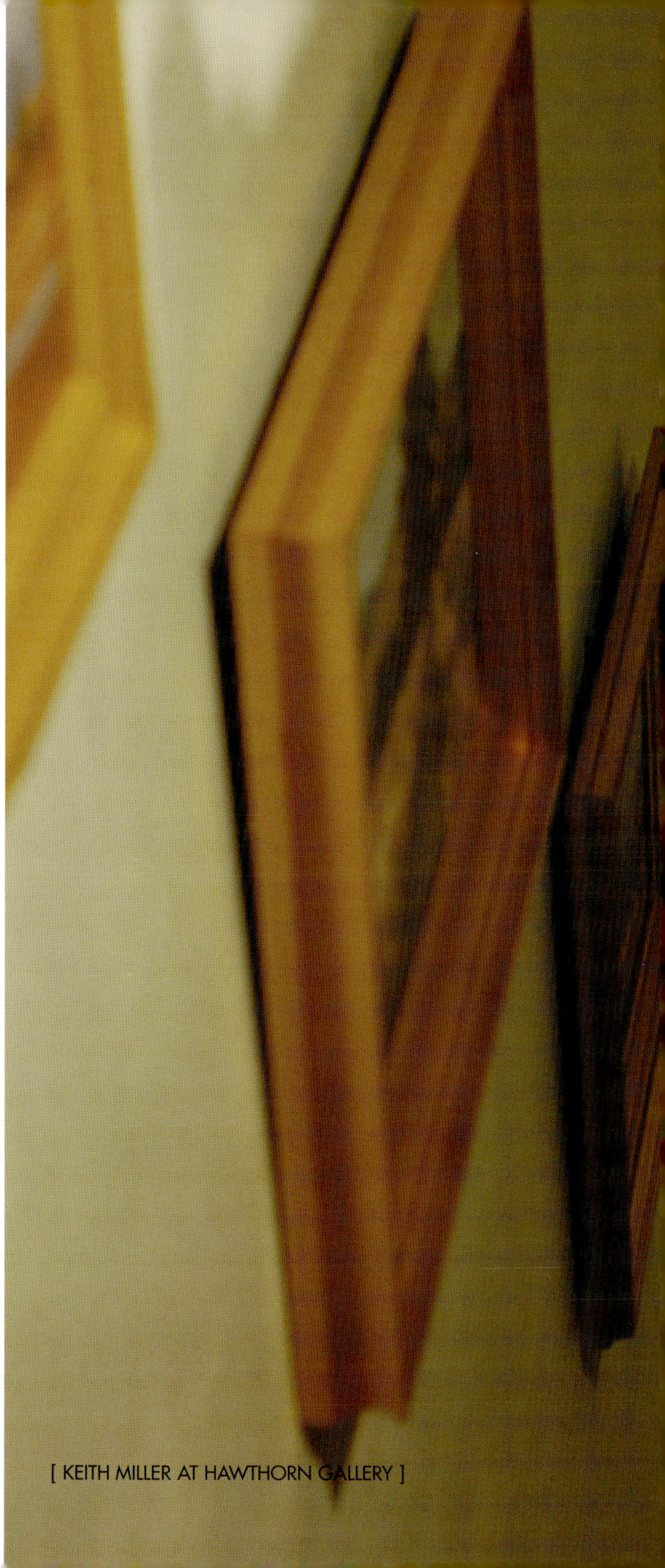

[KEITH MILLER AT HAWTHORN GALLERY]

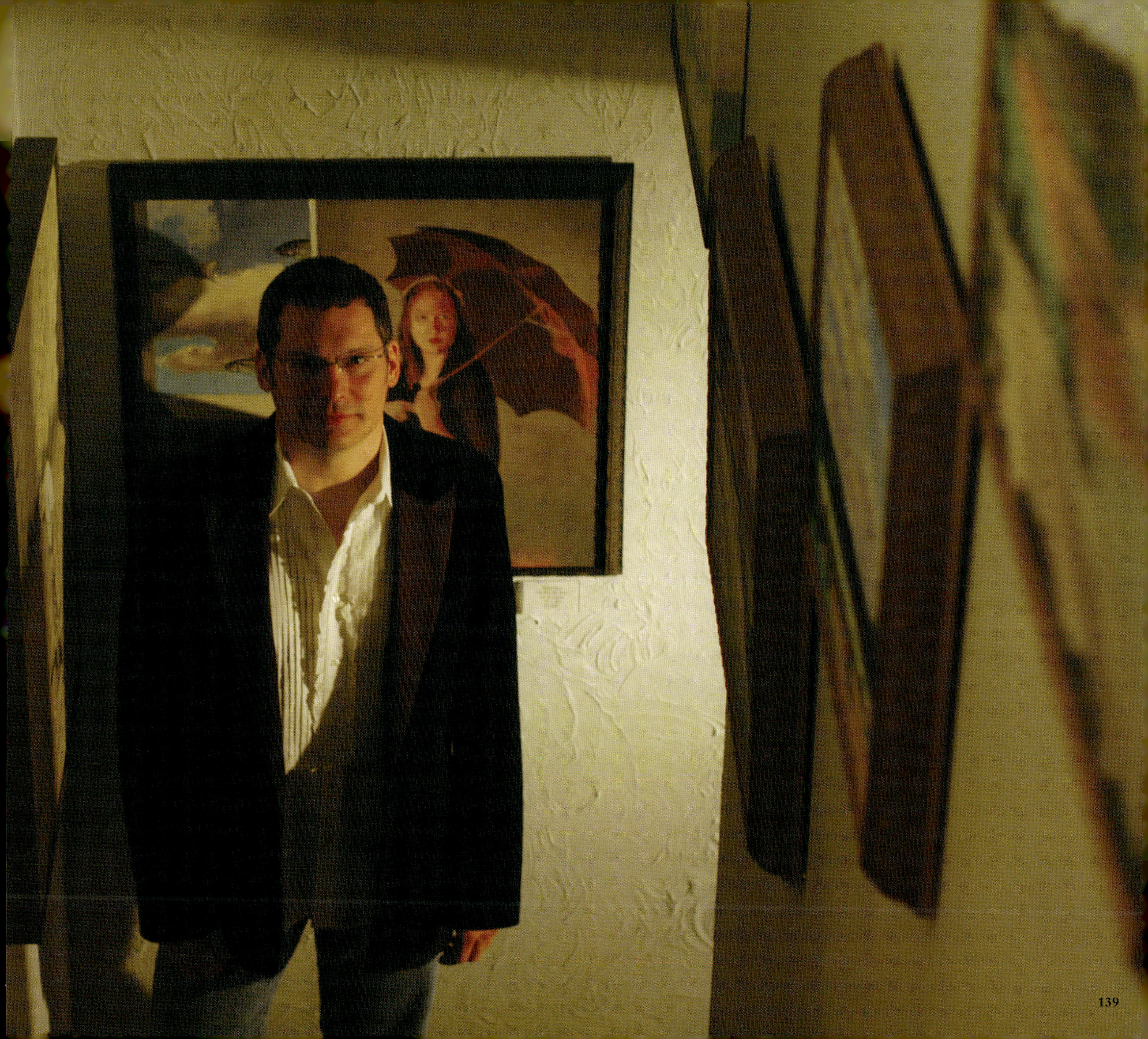

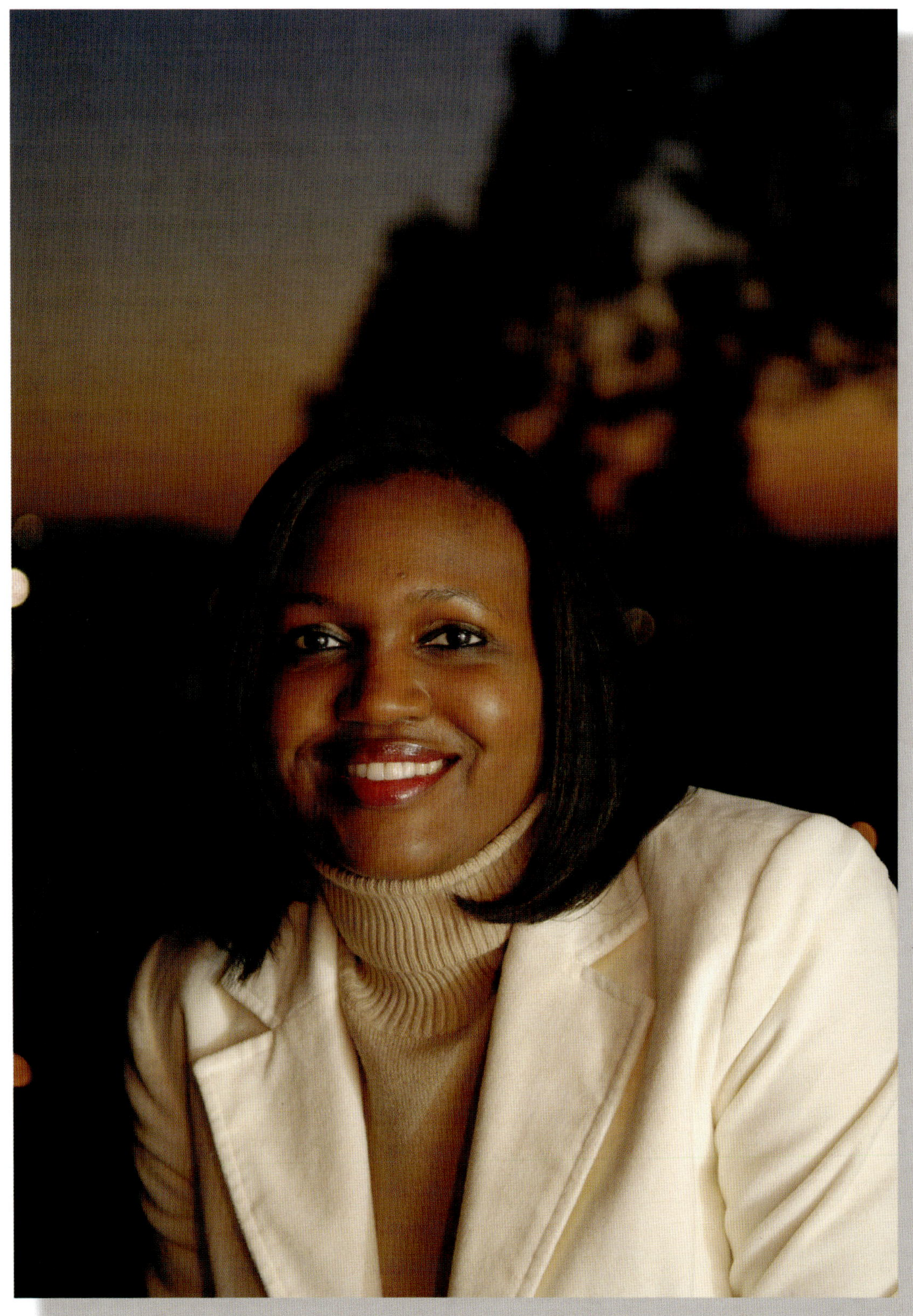

I love Alabama because of its rich history. Like my dad, I am fascinated by history and majored in it in college. In fact, I did my senior paper on *Women in the Civil Rights Movement.* It was a labor of love because one of the subjects that I interviewed was Addine Drew, my godmother. "Deenie," as she was affectionately called, was a den mother of the movement in Birmingham and integrated several public faculties, including the Birmingham Public Library. Deenie was originally from Philadelphia and moved to Alabama in the 1940s to work for Red Cross. Twenty years later, she found herself participating in and contributing to America's most significant sociopolitical movement of the twentieth century. That's why I love Alabama. This is a place in which some of the most unlikely people make a difference.

MICHELLE CLEMON
[VICE-PRESIDENT, HUMAN RESOURCES & PUBLIC AFFAIRS, MCWANE, INC.]

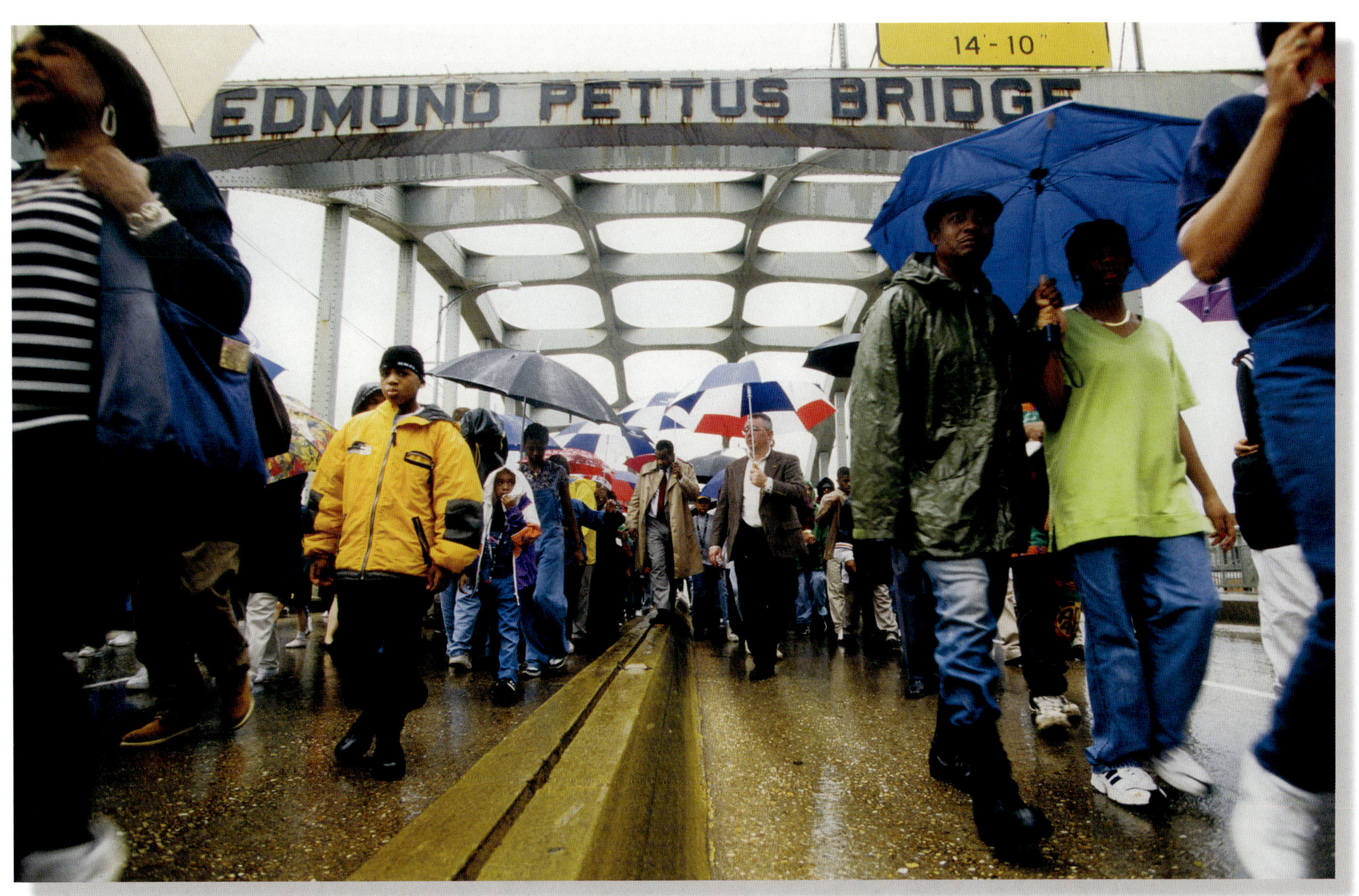

[SELMA MARCH COMMEMORATION]

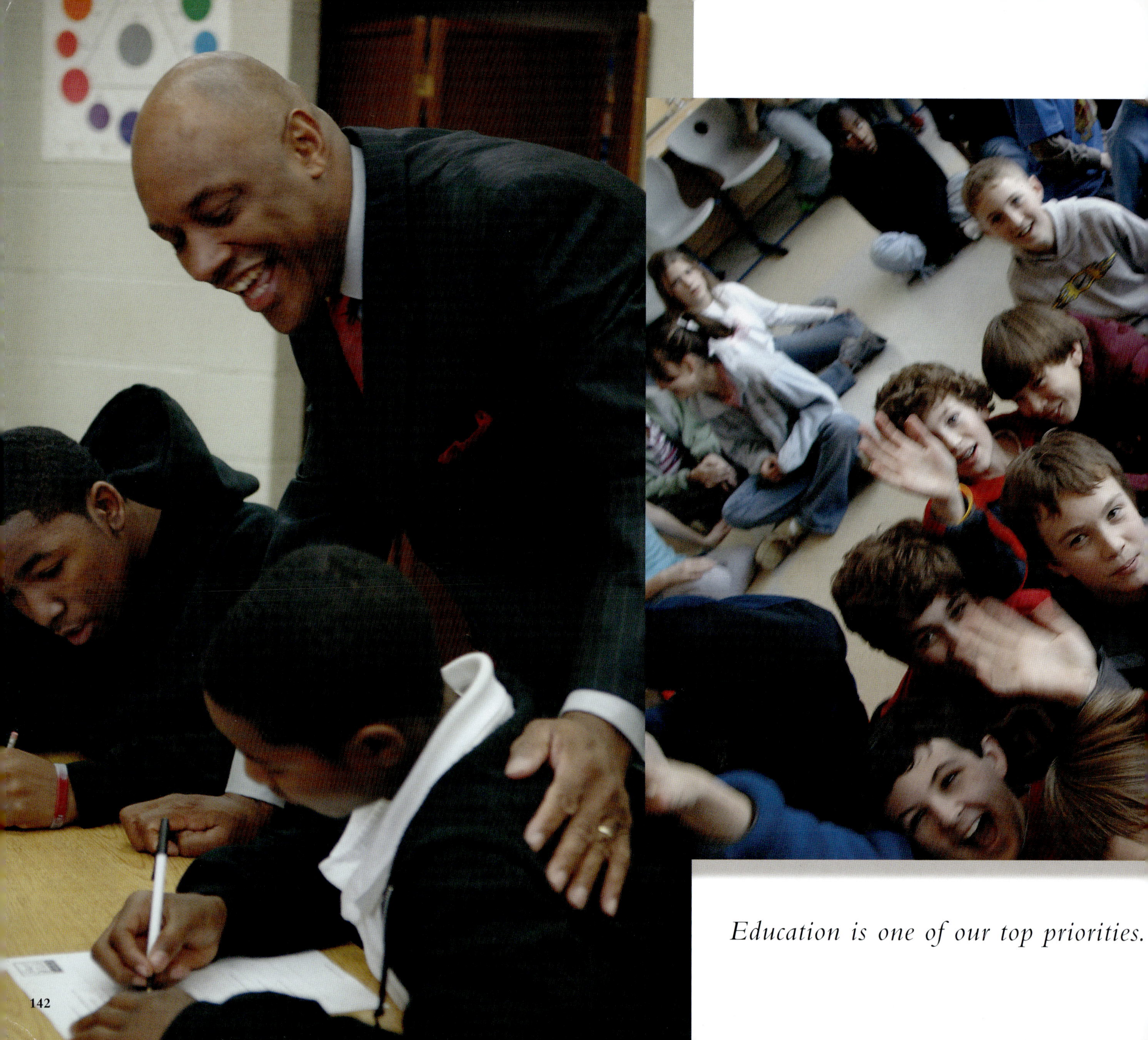

Education is one of our top priorities.

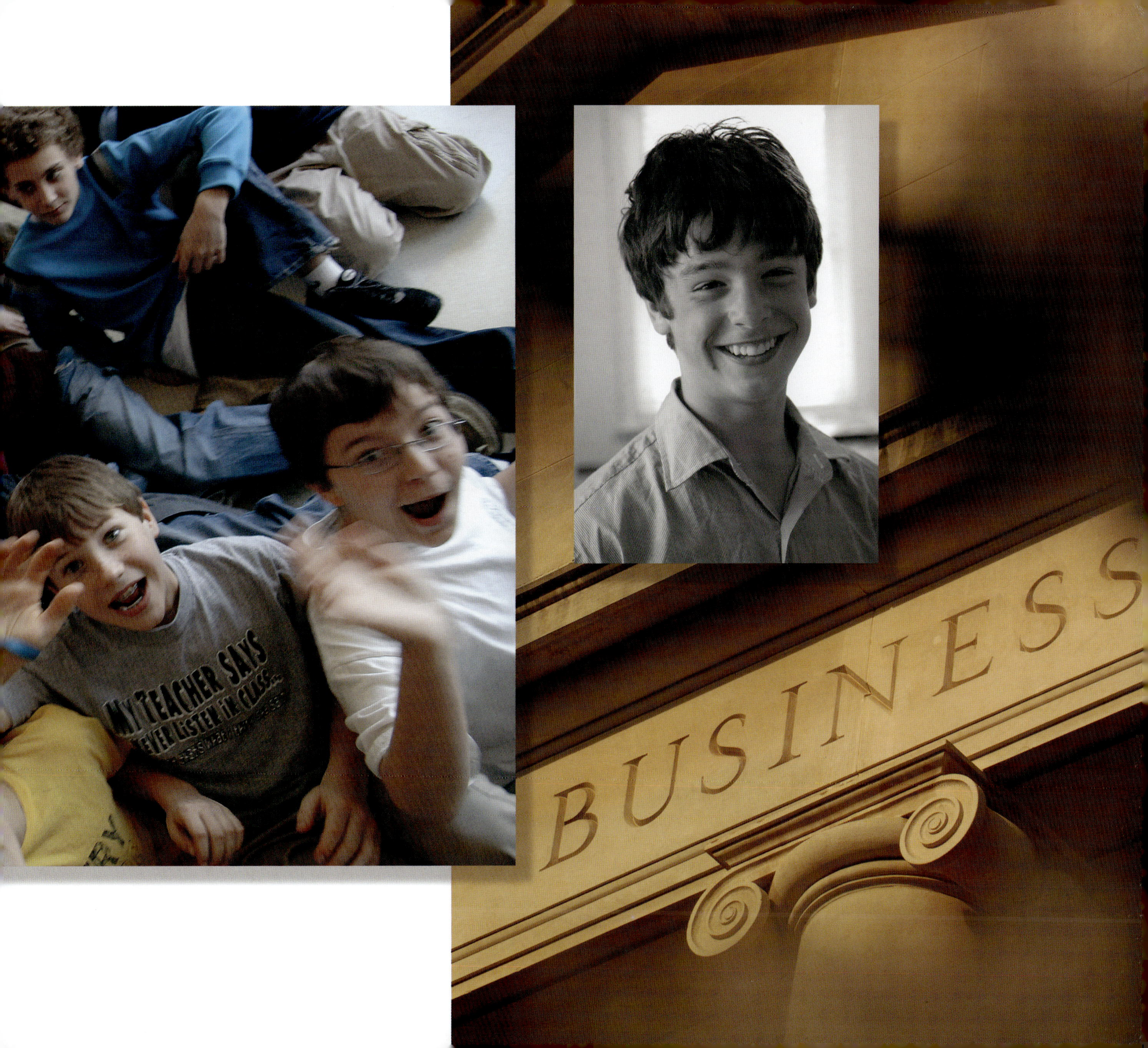
MY TEACHER SAYS
NEVER LISTEN IN CLASS...
BUSINESS

I was born and grew up in the state of Alabama. While attending school in other parts of the country, both north and south, I really began to appreciate home and found myself longing to come back here to stay. That is exactly what I did in 1993 when I graduated from Berklee College Of Music after spending a few years in Boston.

I suspect that because of my involvement in the music industry, I am frequently asked the question, "Why haven't you settled in Los Angeles, New York, or perhaps Atlanta or Nashville?" The answer is simple: I love Alabama. This is where I am from. I know a lot of people that spend a good portion of their lives trying to escape where they came from and who they are. I am not one of those folks. I have a lot to be proud of and much to embrace as an Alabamian. We are strong people. We have endured much. Nothing bows our heads or weakens our resolve. Those things that are not beautiful about our state, we are committed to change; those things that are beautiful, we try our best to preserve. I am inspired by those qualities. It is the kind of person I want to be ... a true Alabamian.

ERIC ESSIX
[JAZZ MUSICIAN]

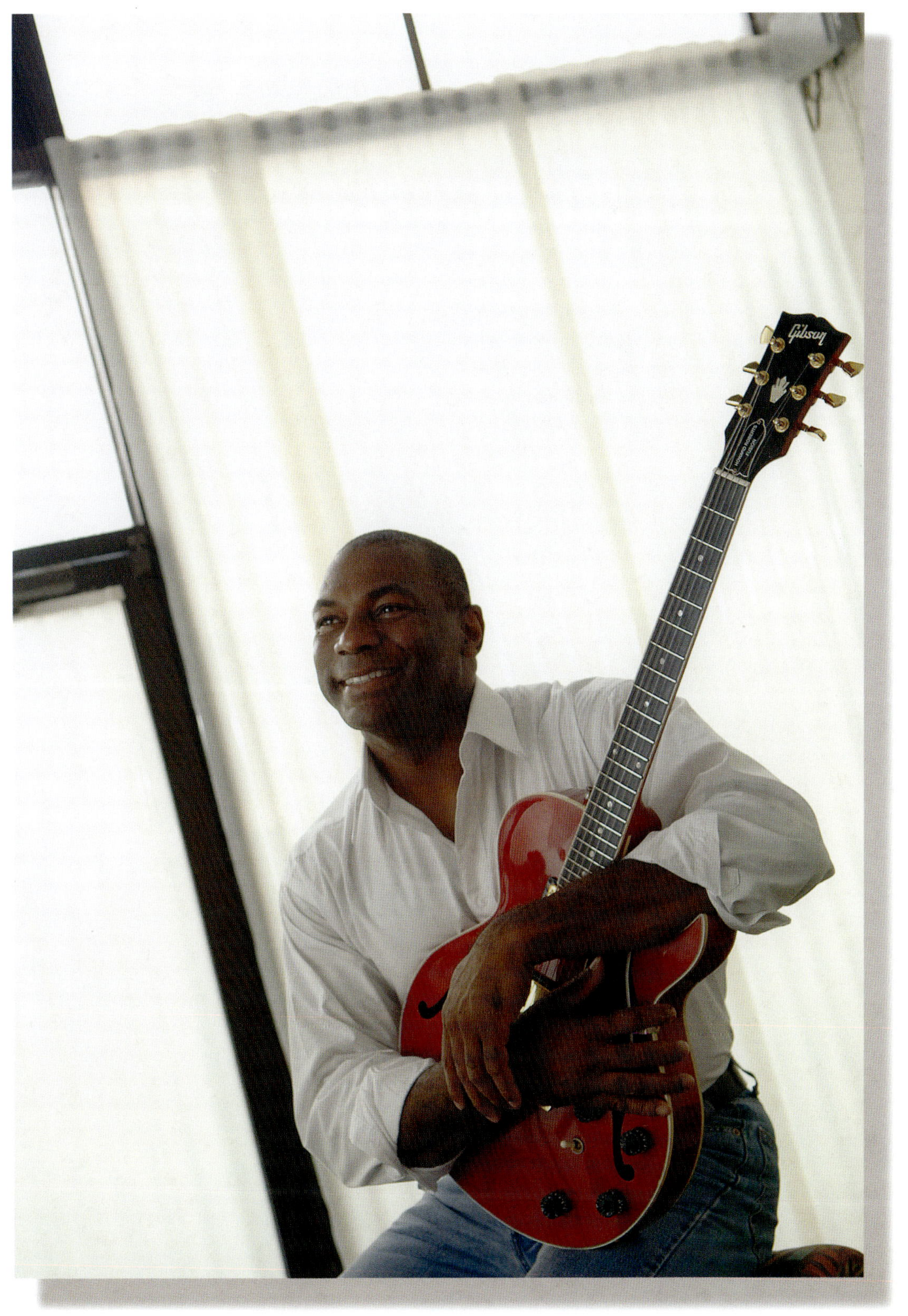
Gibson

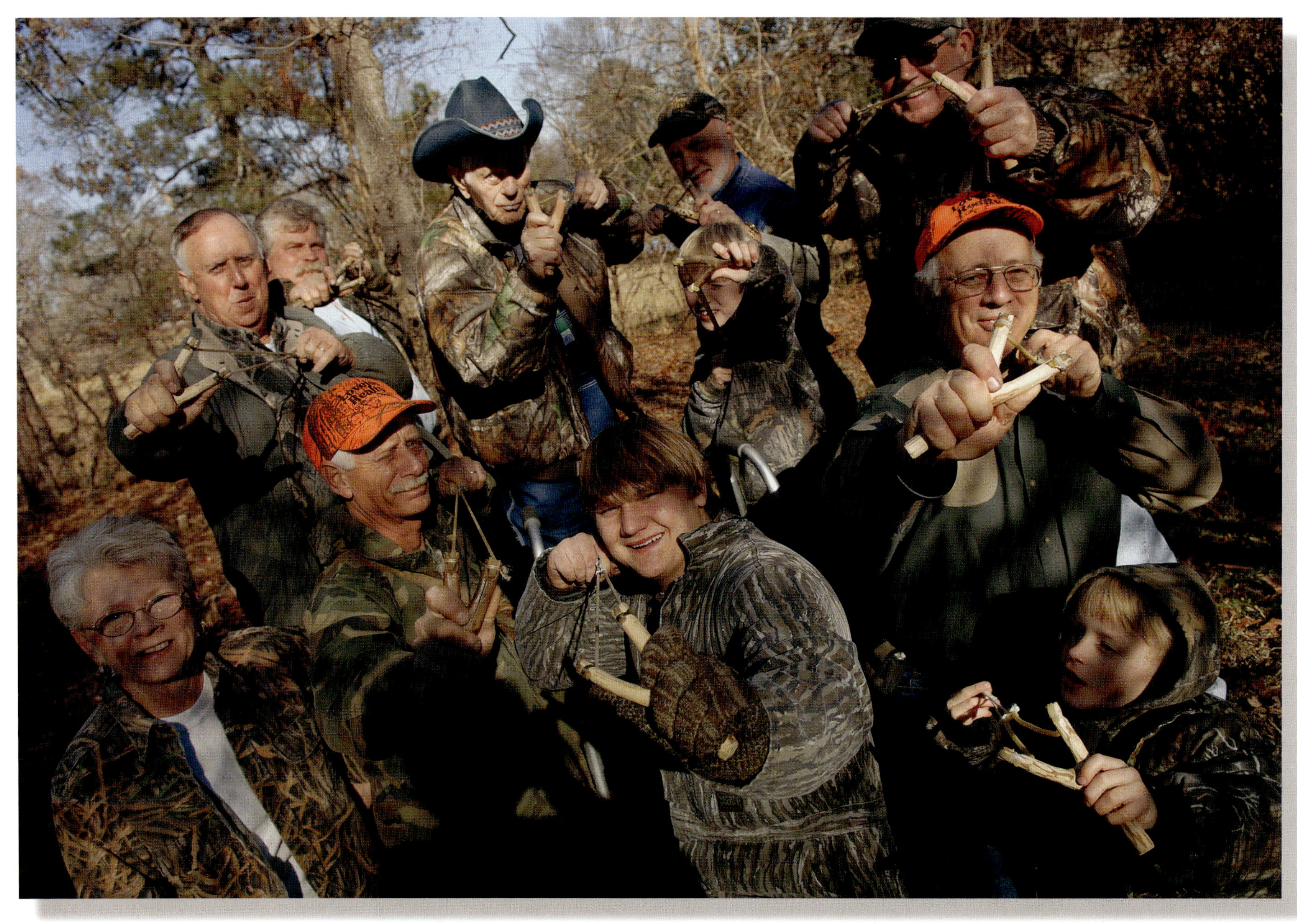

[ST. CLAIR COUNTY]

We're ready for anything.

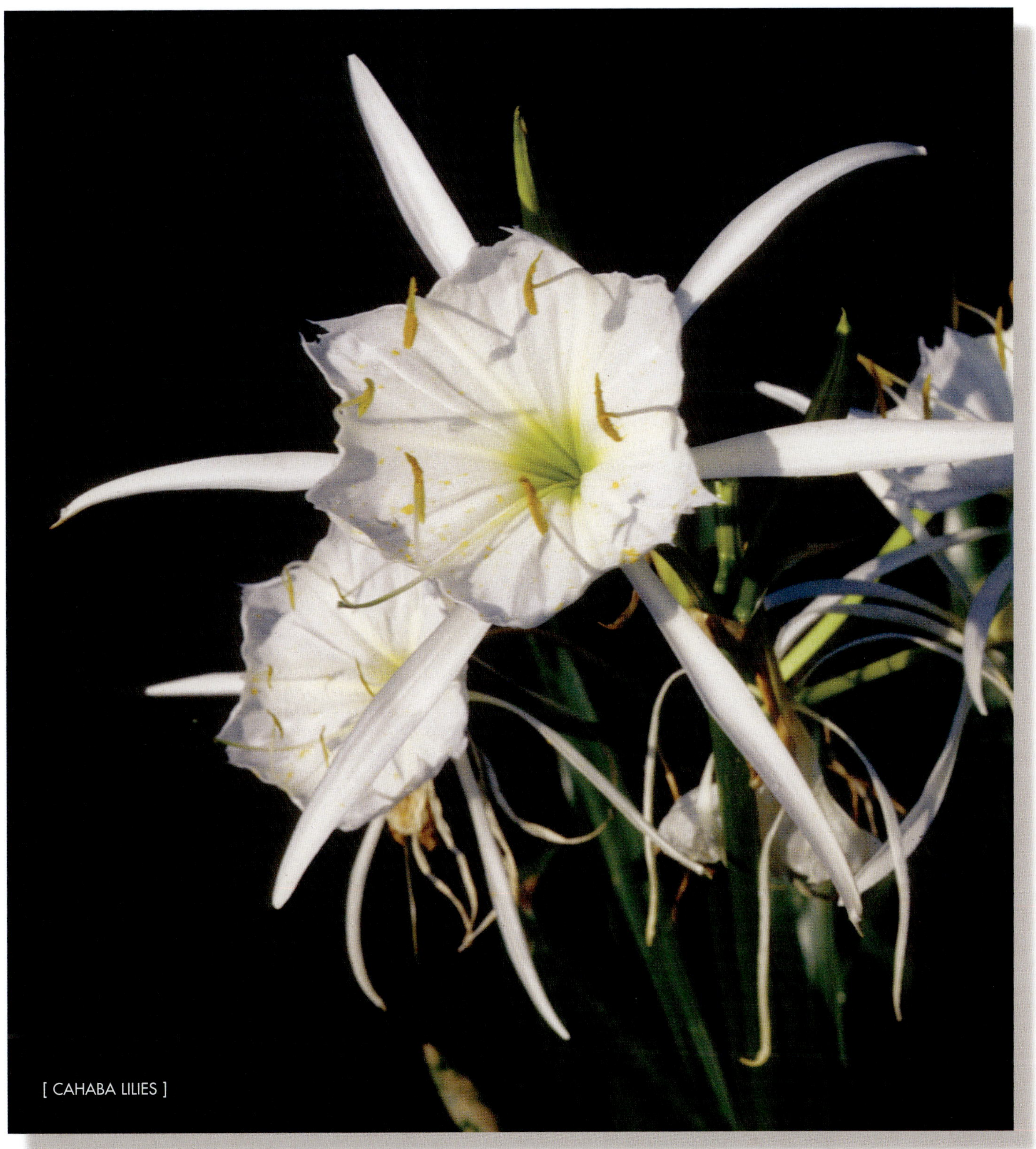

[CAHABA LILIES]

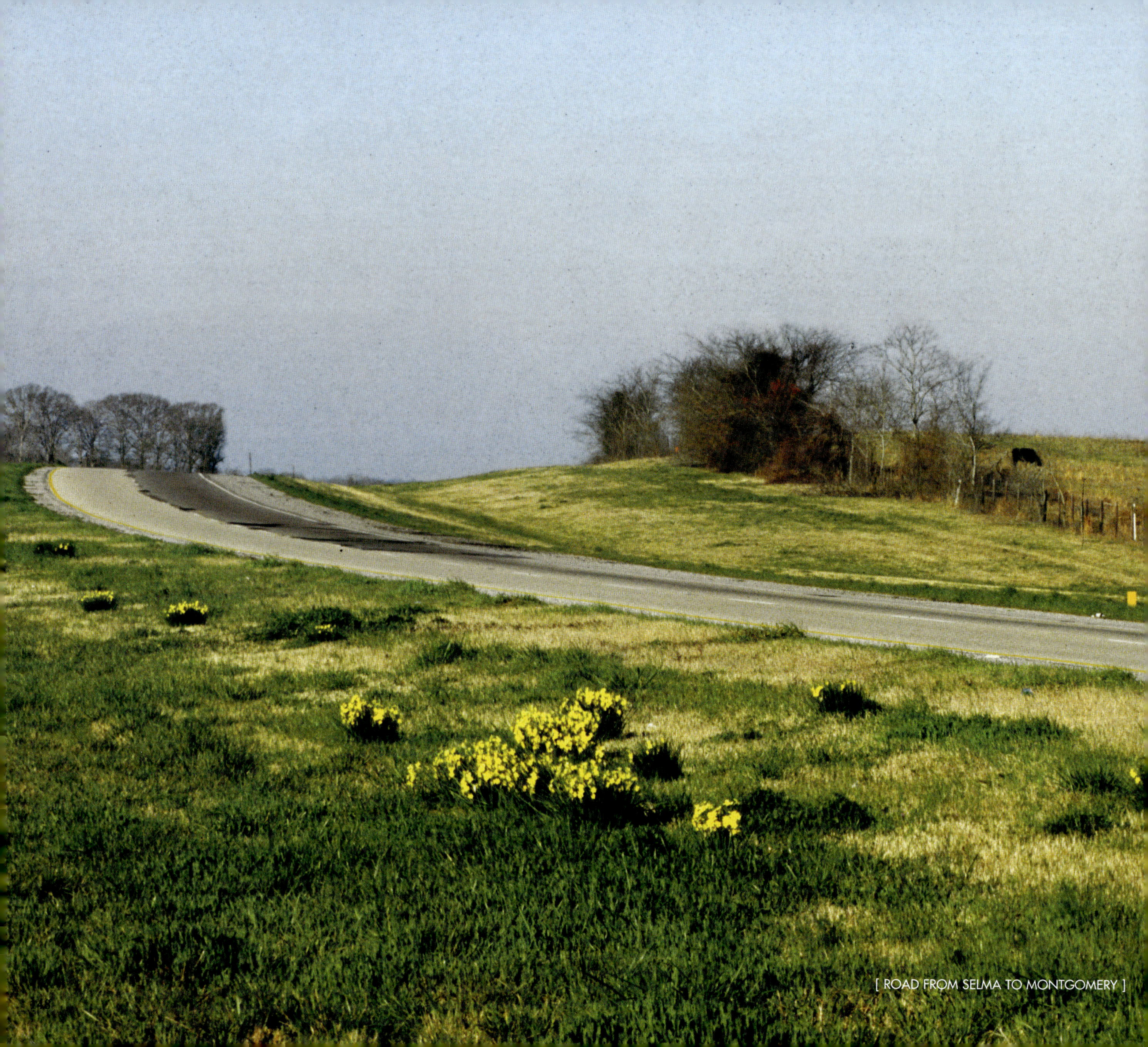

[ROAD FROM SELMA TO MONTGOMERY]

"Alabama ... unforgettable to me because I can stand on the rim of Little River Canyon and watch the sunrise while day-dreaming about the beaches of Gulf Shores, and before sunset, I can be there. This is my Alabama: a Civil War survivor and a Civil Rights champion. This is civilization!

AUBREY MILLER
[PRESIDENT, BAPTIST HEALTH FOUNDATION]

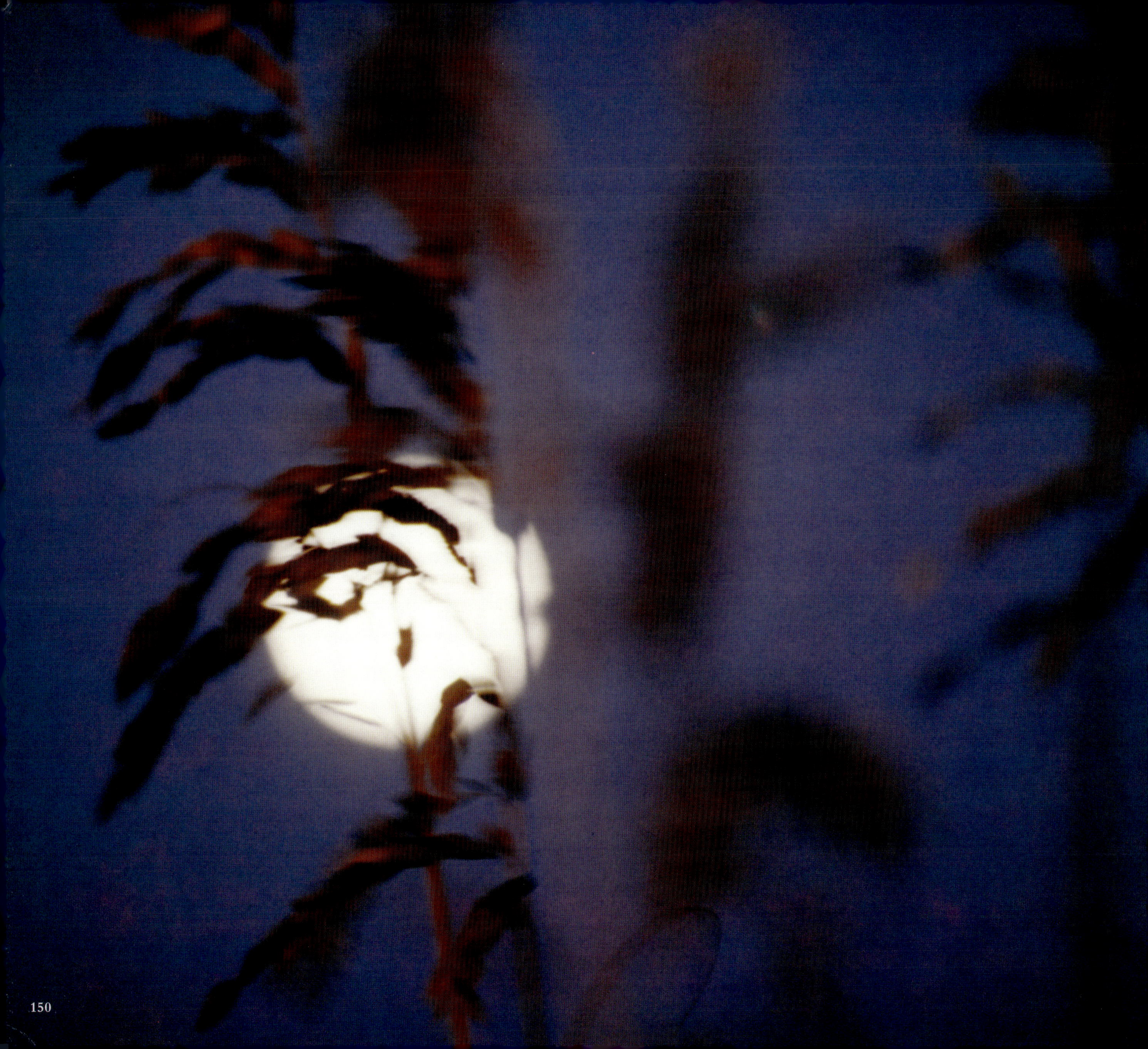

The soul of an explorer lives in us all. America's astronauts rode the Saturn V rocket to the moon. They stood on the shoulders of the men and women of Alabama who developed the rocket and made sure their part worked. That's the legacy we leave to the explorers of today and tomorrow—make sure your part works.

Ed Buckbee
[FOUNDER OF SPACE CAMP
AUTHOR, *THE REAL SPACE COWBOYS*]

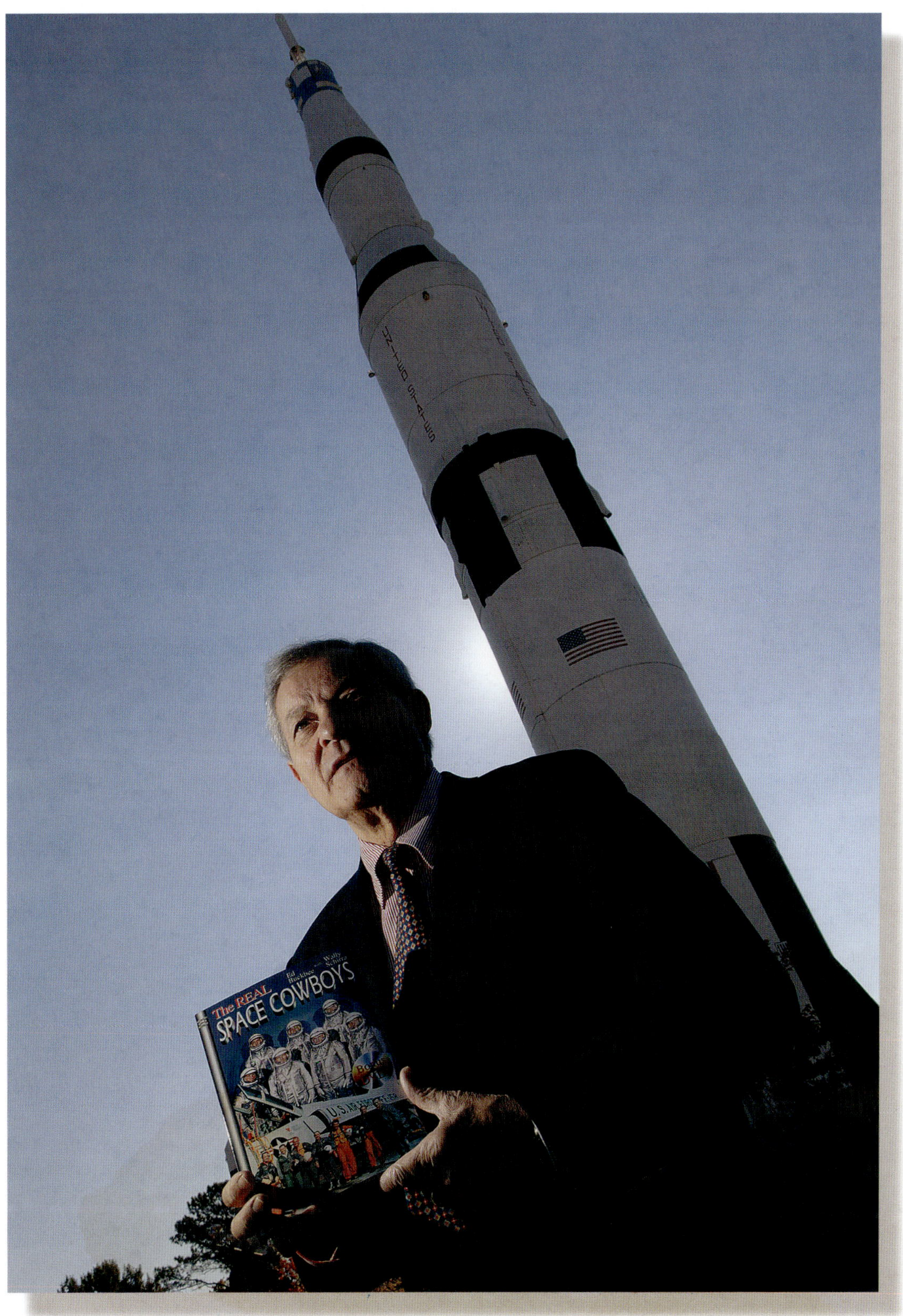

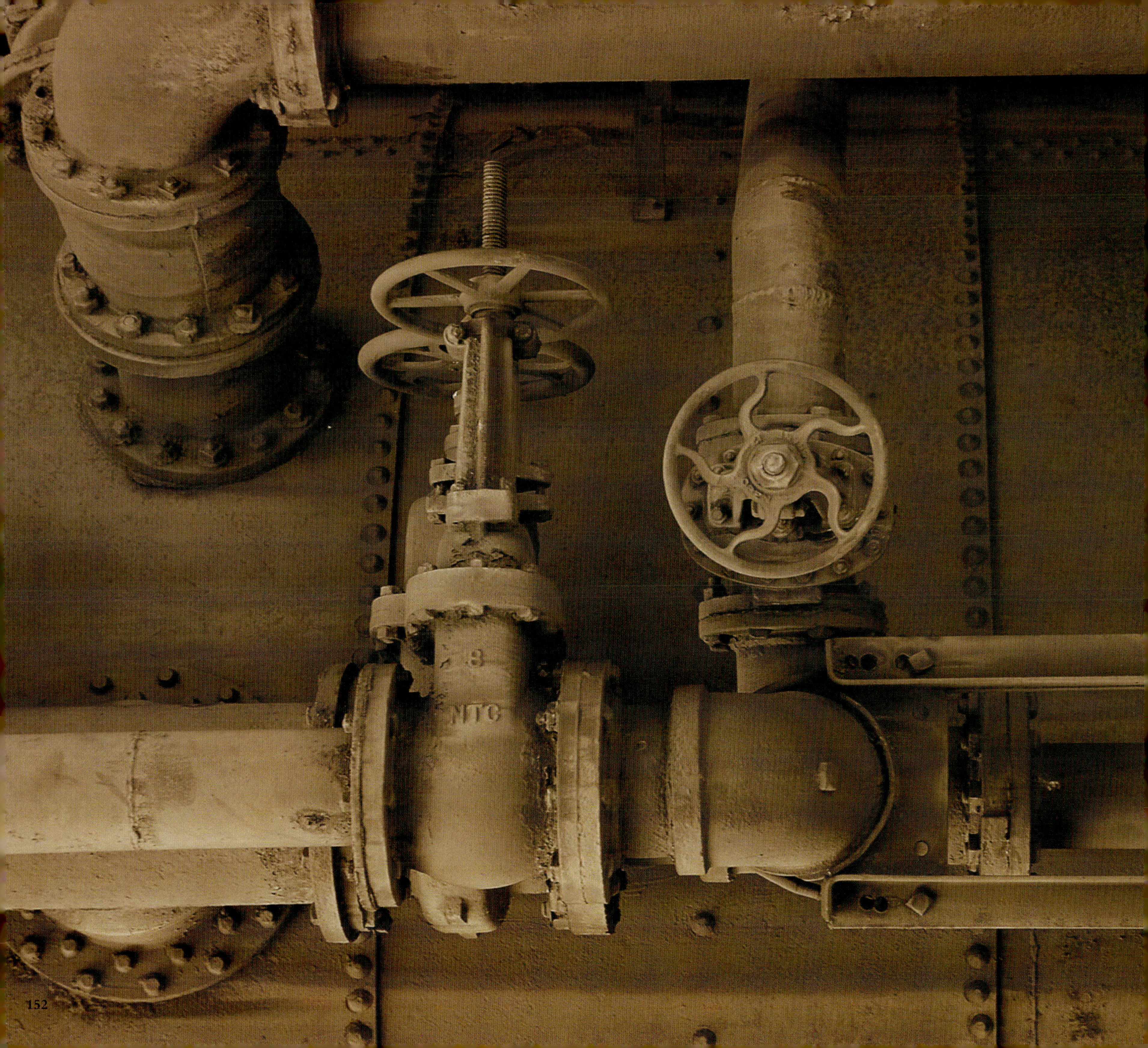
NTC

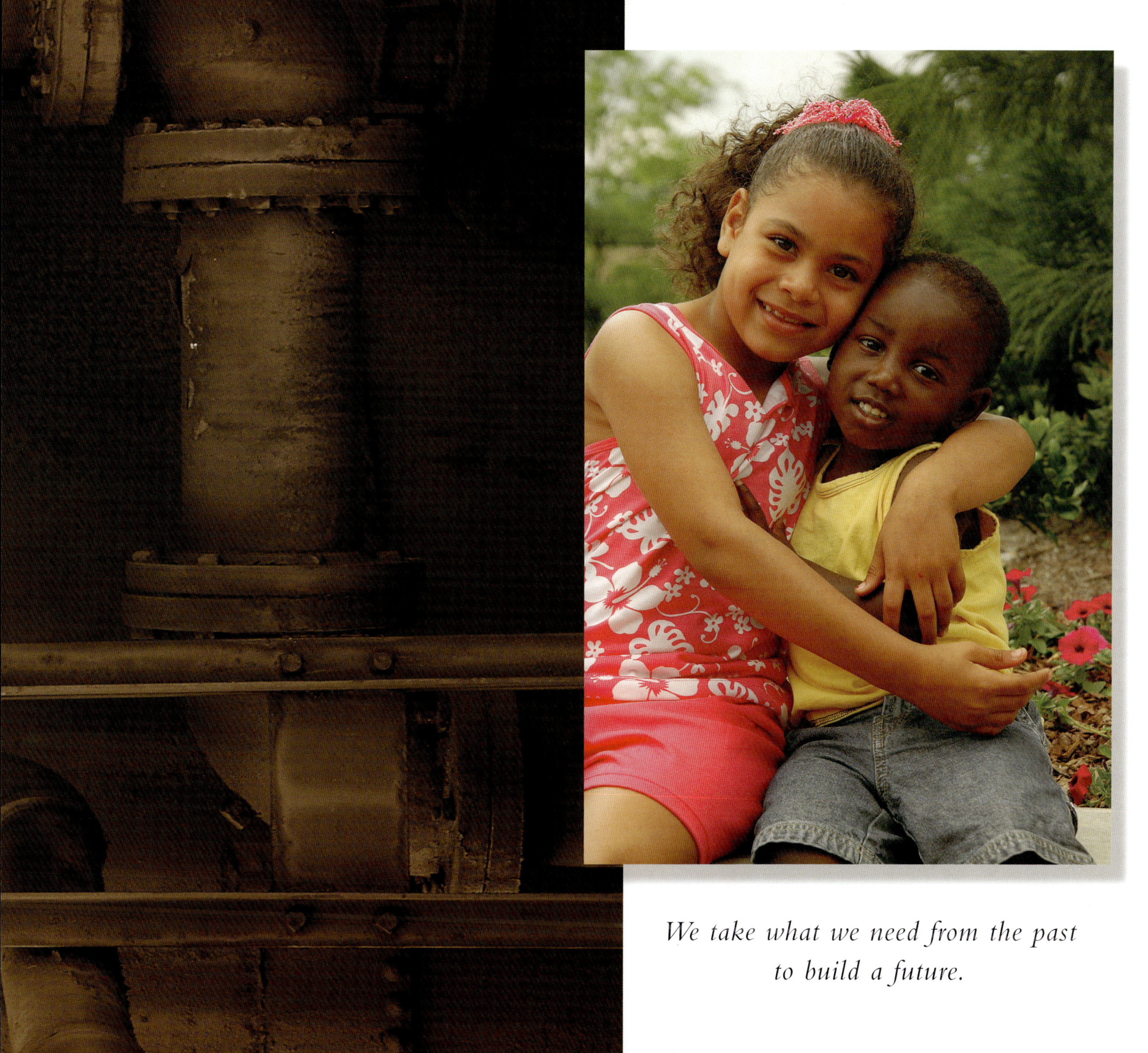

We take what we need from the past to build a future.

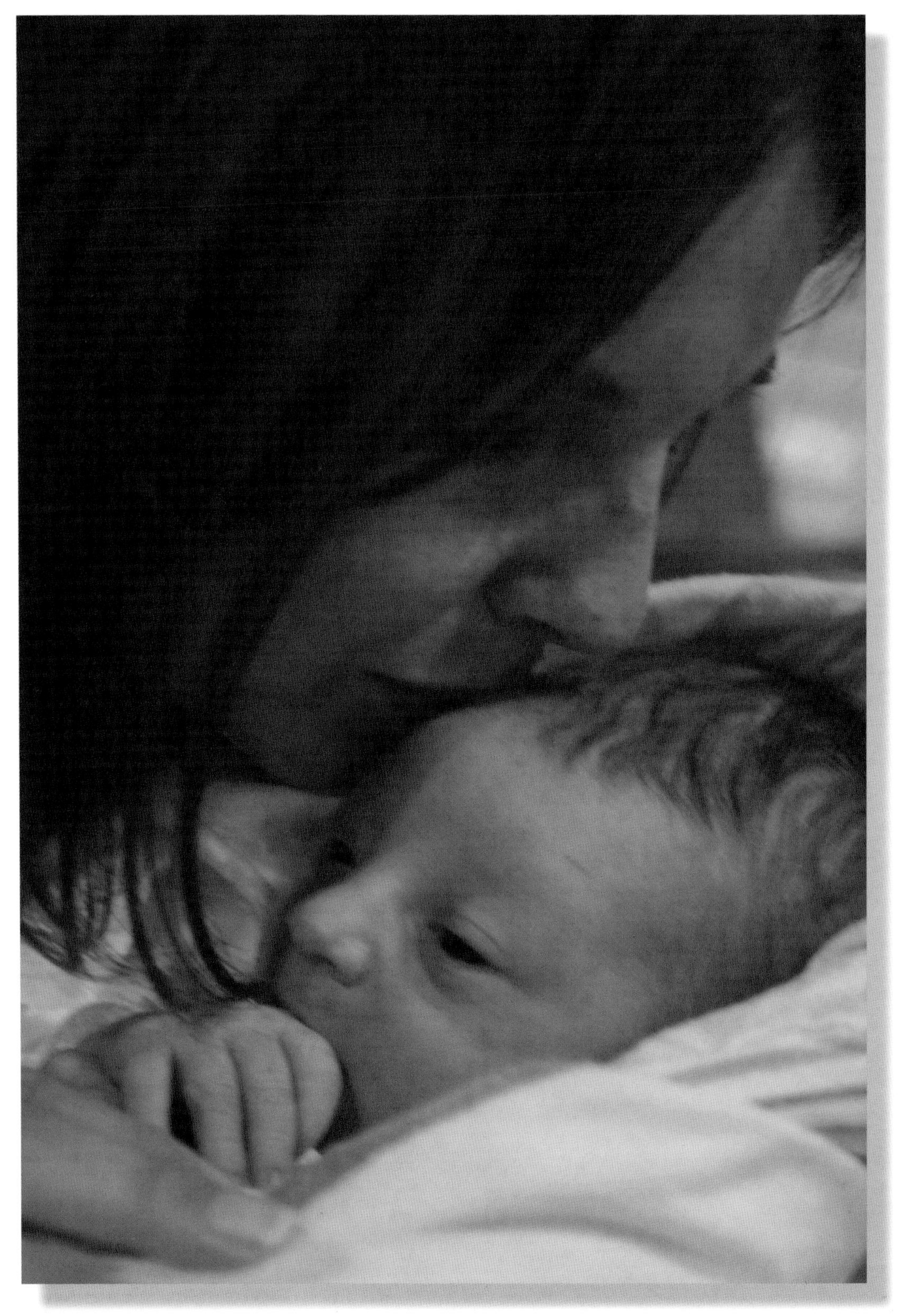

[CLAIRE AND BABY WILL
– ONE DAY OLD]

Alabama fits me like a warm, soft sweater on a cold day. Or maybe I should say it's like a cold glass of sweet tea on a sweltering day! This state is my comfort zone, which is why I've never moved away. I was born in Birmingham at St. Vincent's Hospital in 1966. My children were born there, as well. They help me see Alabama through their eyes and remind me why our state is so beloved. Mountains, sugar-white beaches, crystal clear lakes ... we couldn't ask for a better list of beautiful places in one state. Sitting atop Red Mountain, watching the sunset over Birmingham may well be one of my favorite views.

I adore Alabama because I've never been anywhere else where I felt such a great sense of "family" among neighbors and friends. Growing up here, I was a long way from both sets of grandparents, who lived in South Dakota and South Carolina. But I never lacked for family. The warmth, pride, and human spirit that reside in this state cannot be matched. That's the reason I believe so many people who move here planning to stay only a couple of years end up staying a lifetime. And that's despite the humidity!

Andrea Lindenberg Neal
[TELEVISION JOURNALIST]

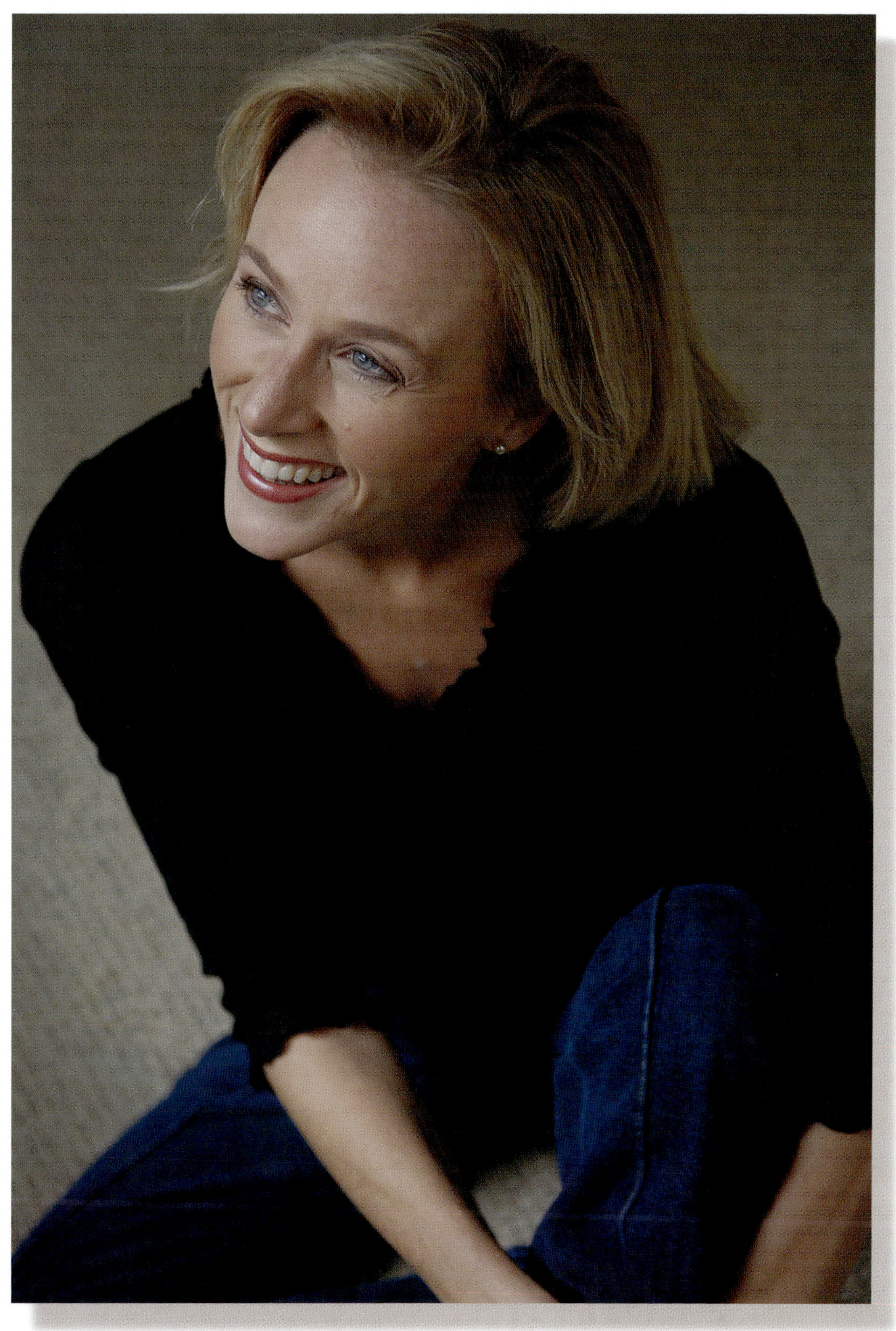

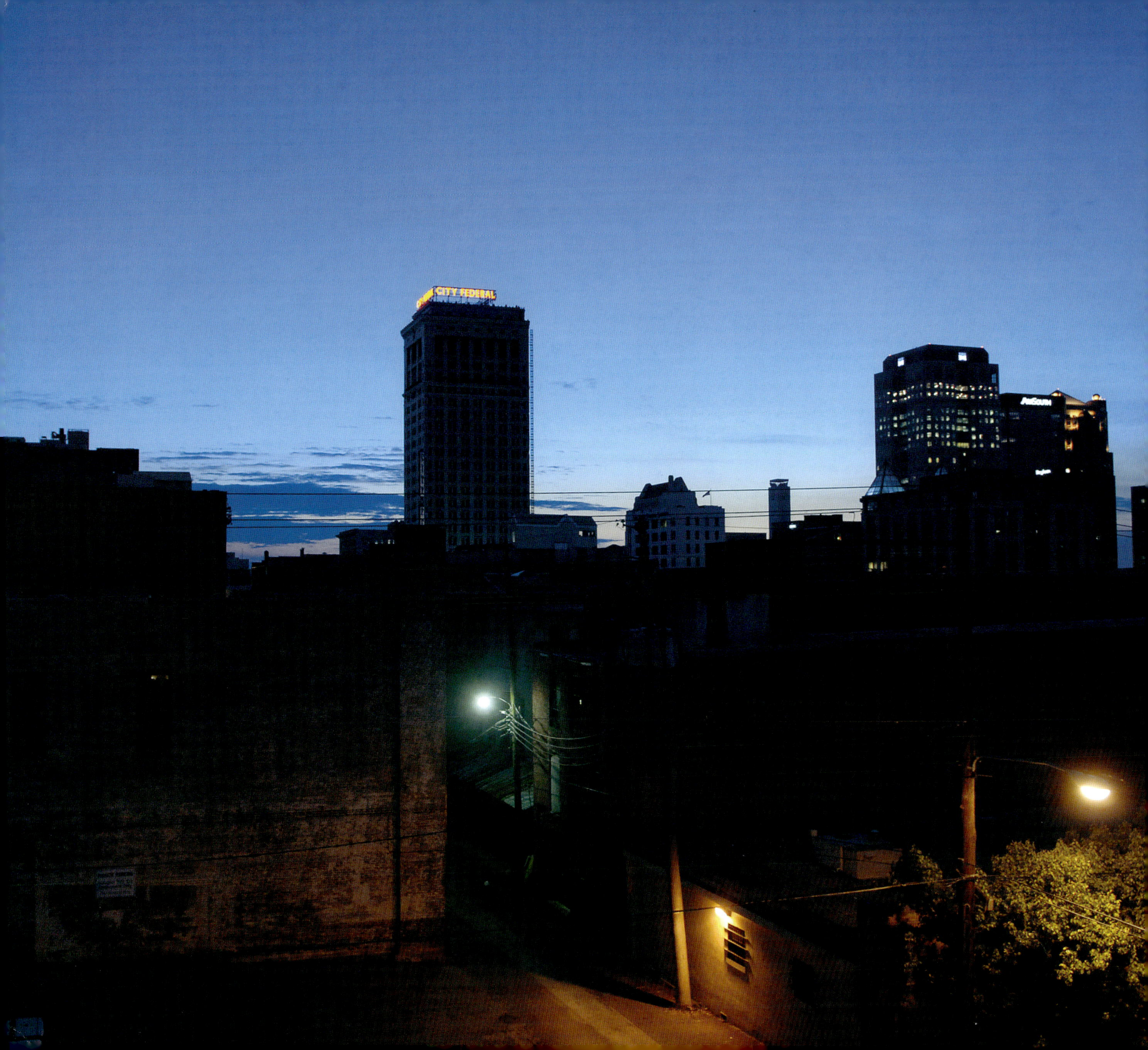
CITY FEDERAL

I came to Birmingham, Alabama, to be the cantor at Temple Emanu-El. I could never have imagined the warmth with which I was received. I still have that feeling today. The wonder of a place is what the people bring to it. Birmingham is a wonderful, beautiful place.

JESSICA ROSKIN
[CANTOR, TEMPLE EMANU-EL]

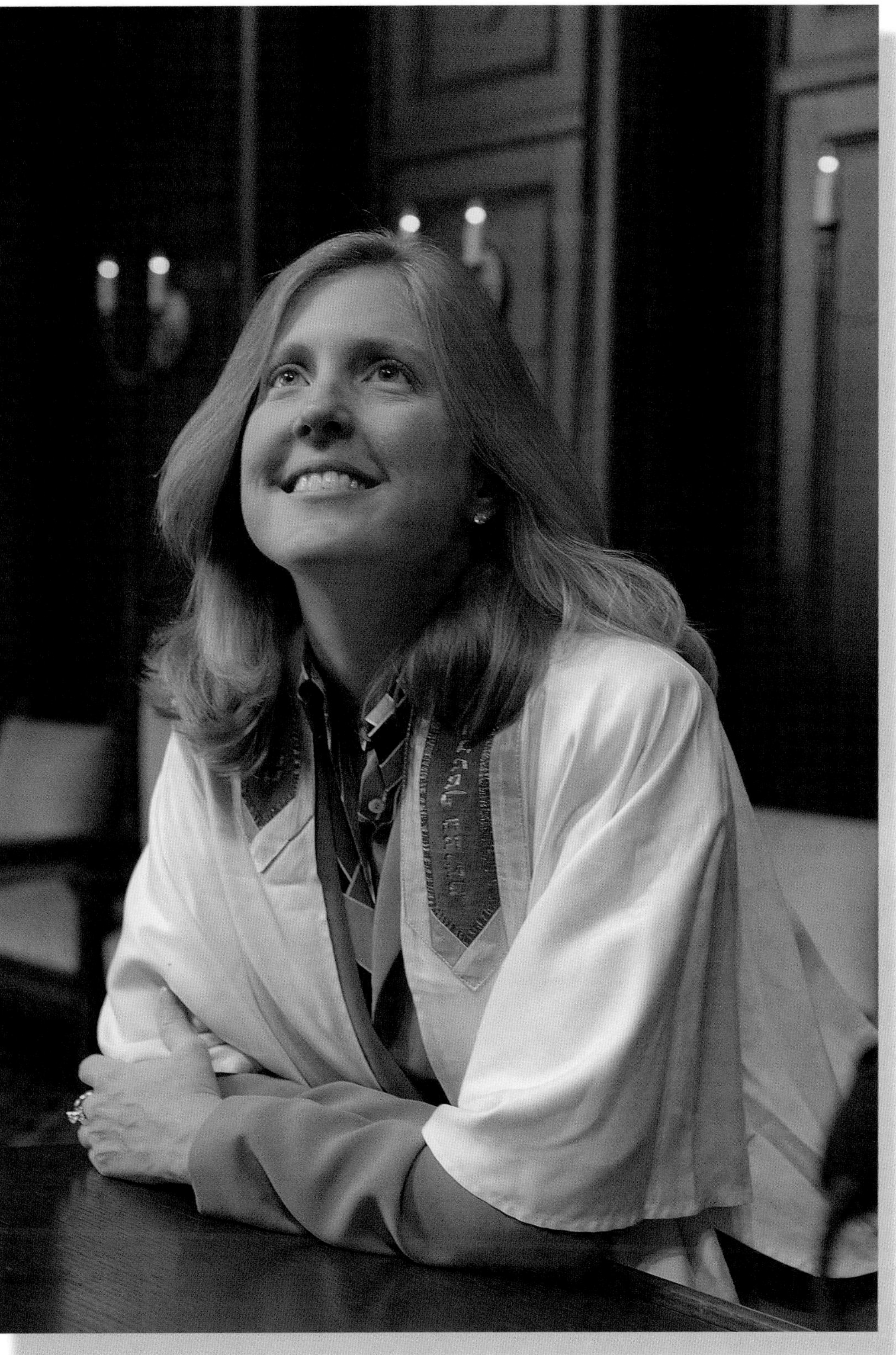

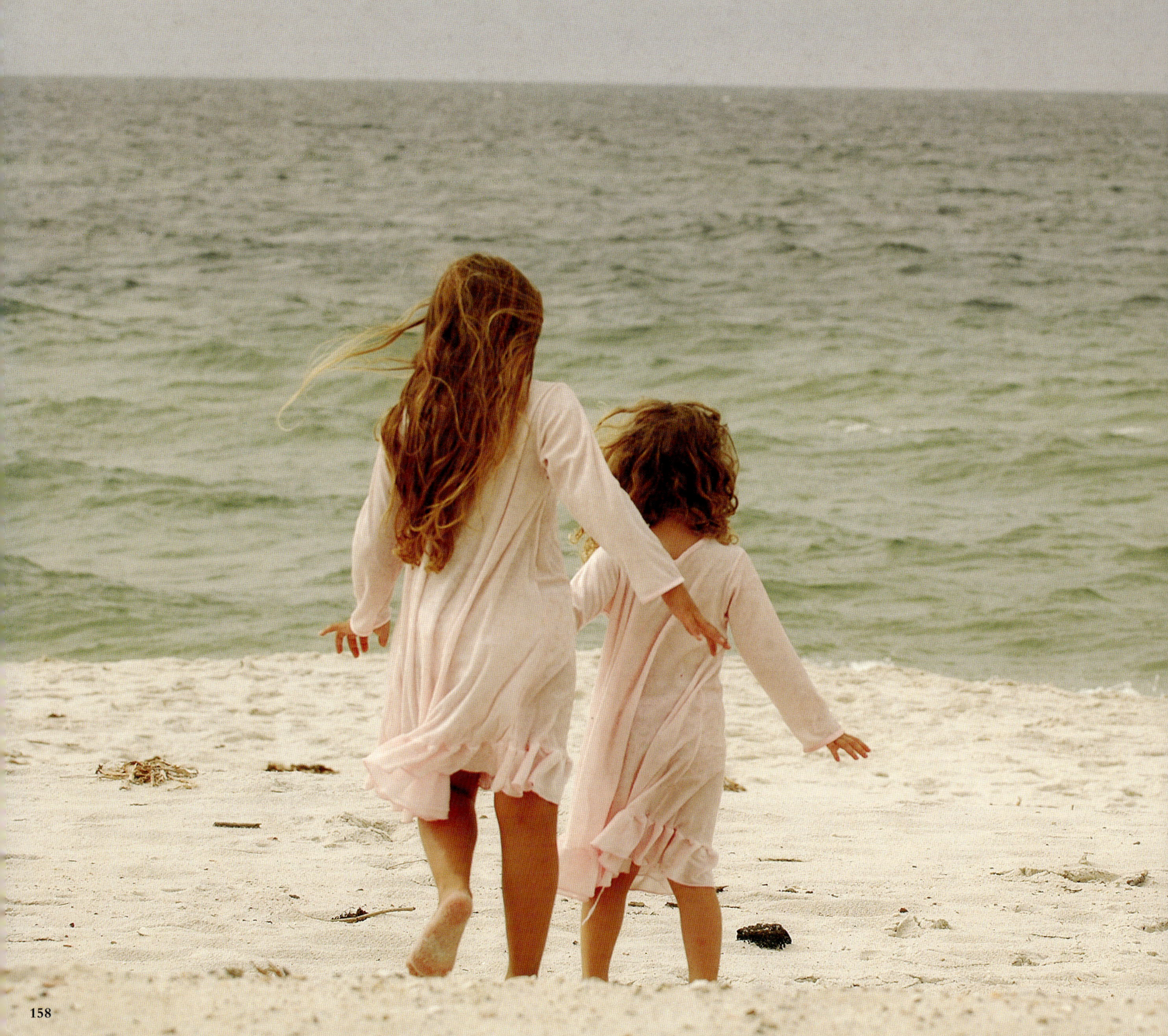

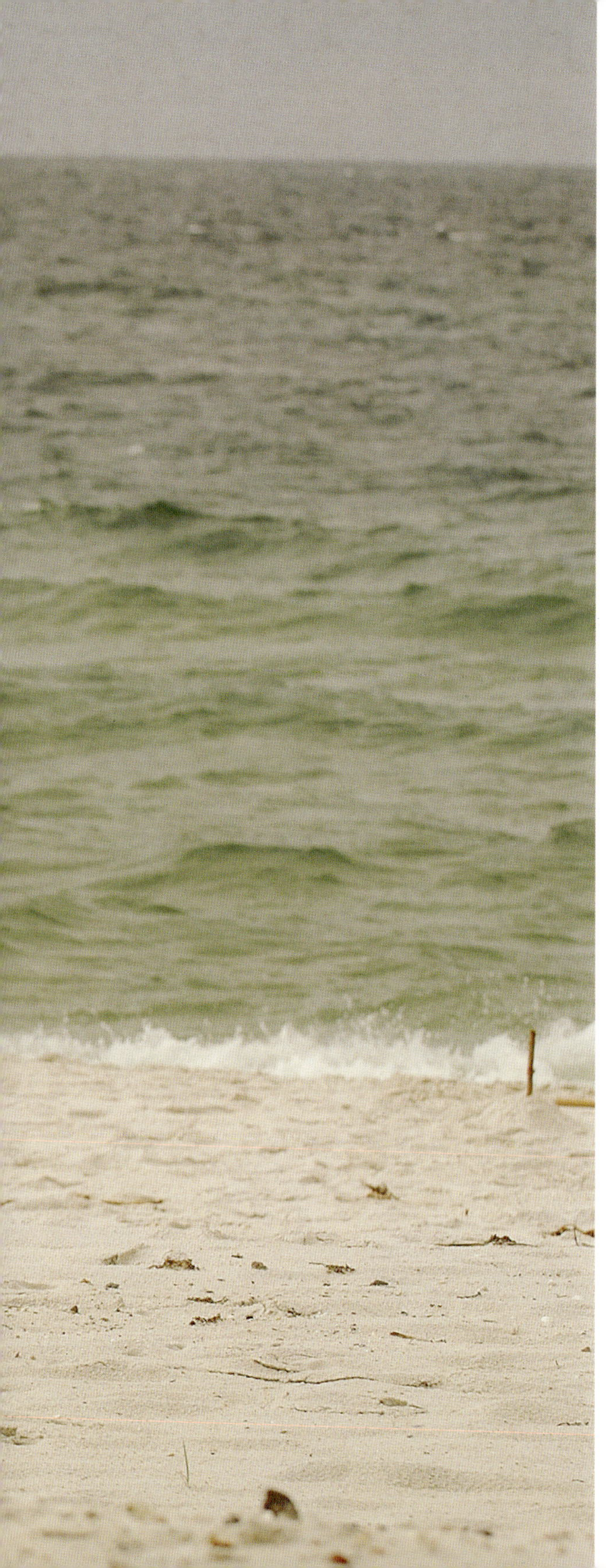

Why We Stay

This is home, in a way no place else could ever be. Alabama speaks deeply to our hearts and resonates in our souls. When we travel, no matter how exotic the destination, we carry Alabama with us; and when we return, it is with that satisfying feeling of completing ourselves. Of reaffirming our roots, our identities, our communities. Alabama will always be for us like a set of opening arms, welcoming. It is a real place where life is lived without apology, with kindness, charity, spirit, and passion, every day.

My love for Alabama comes from the stories of community that my father, Toofie Deep, told me about the people in this great state.

The Deep family, who operated the popular Sahara Restaurant, also ran the Blue & Gray Grill down on Church Street, across from what was the "new Post Office." In those days, pedestrians were constantly asked for food and

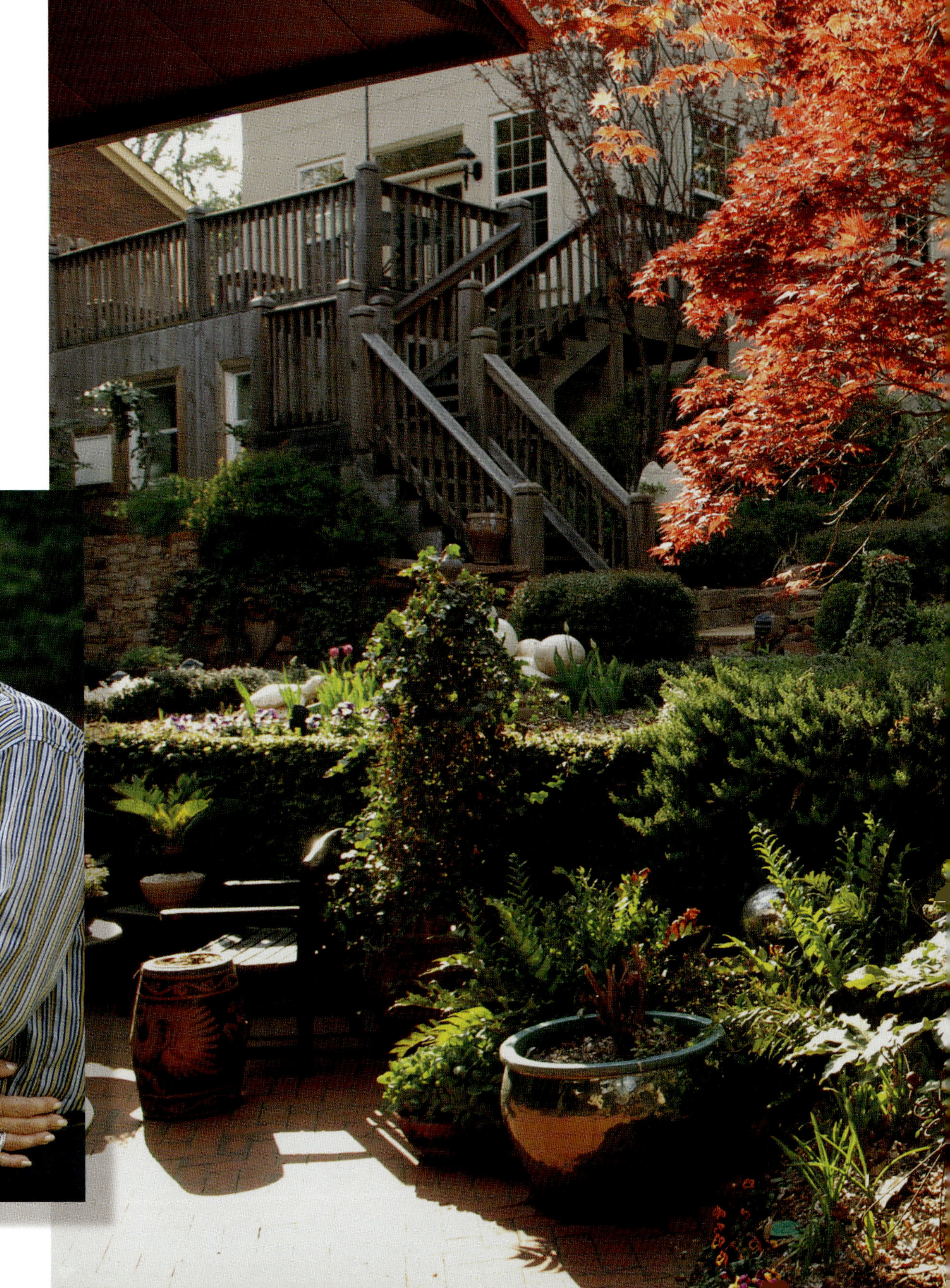

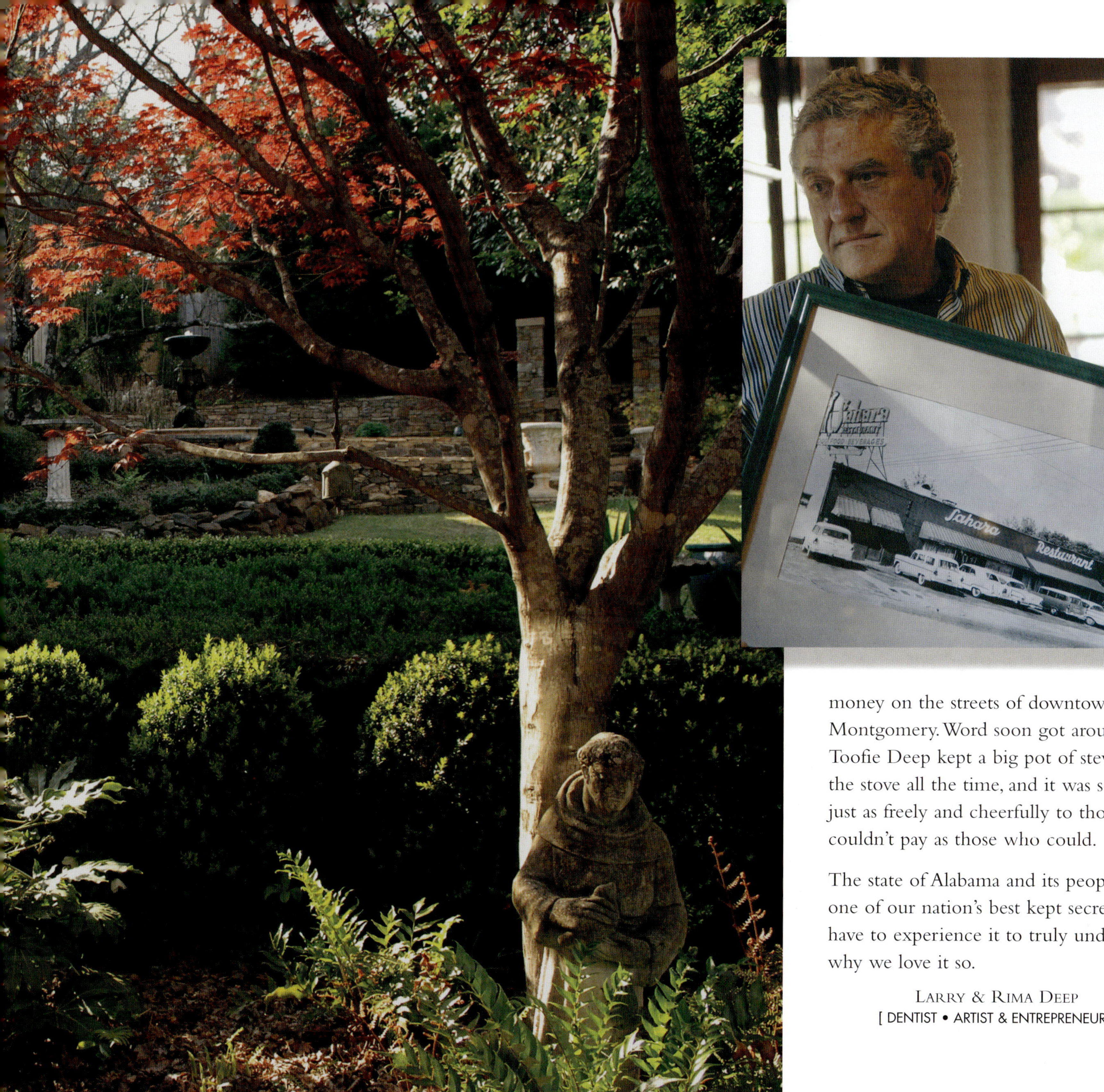

money on the streets of downtown Montgomery. Word soon got around that Toofie Deep kept a big pot of stew on the stove all the time, and it was served just as freely and cheerfully to those who couldn't pay as those who could.

The state of Alabama and its people are one of our nation's best kept secrets. You have to experience it to truly understand why we love it so.

LARRY & RIMA DEEP
[DENTIST • ARTIST & ENTREPRENEUR]

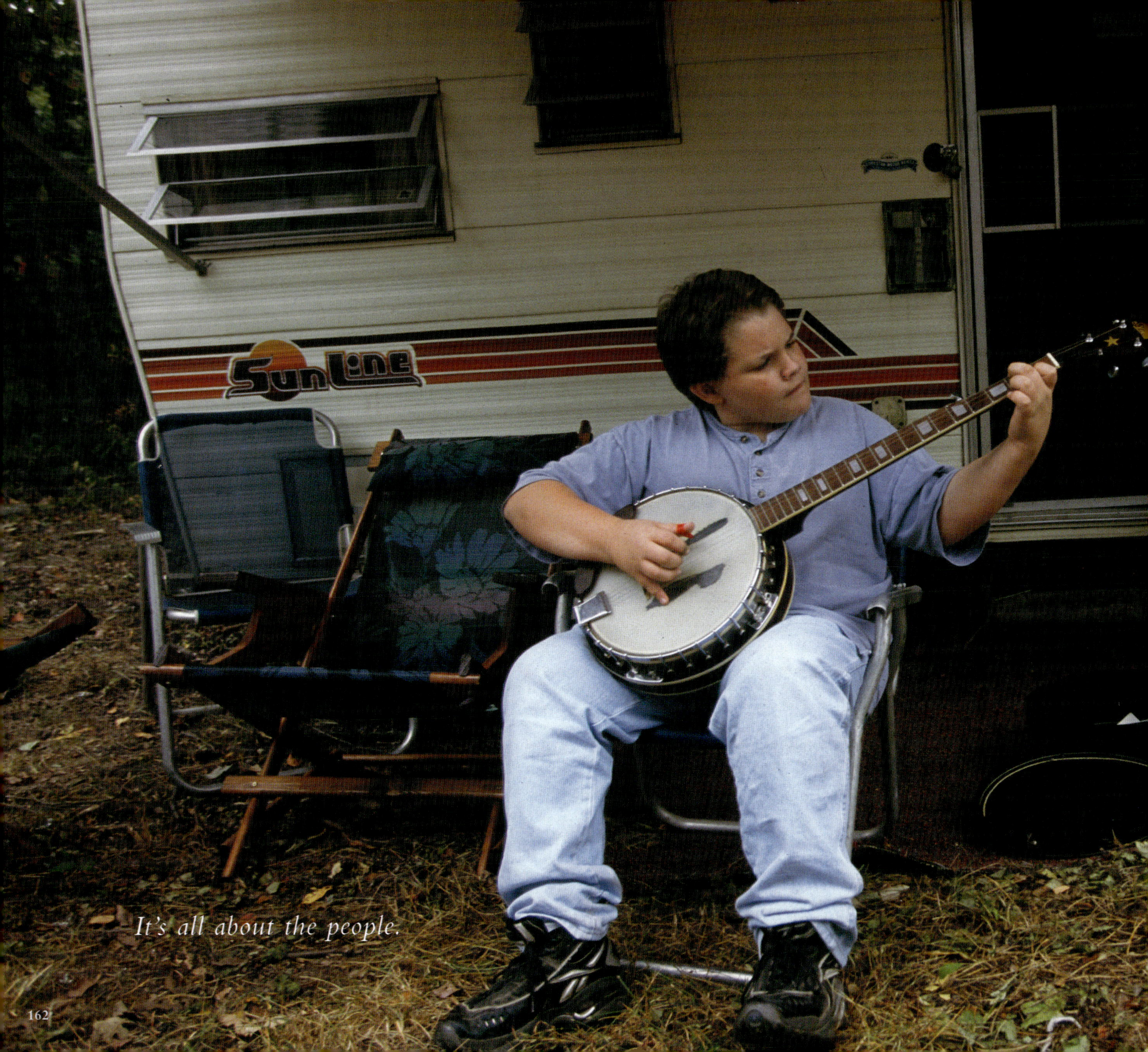

It's all about the people.

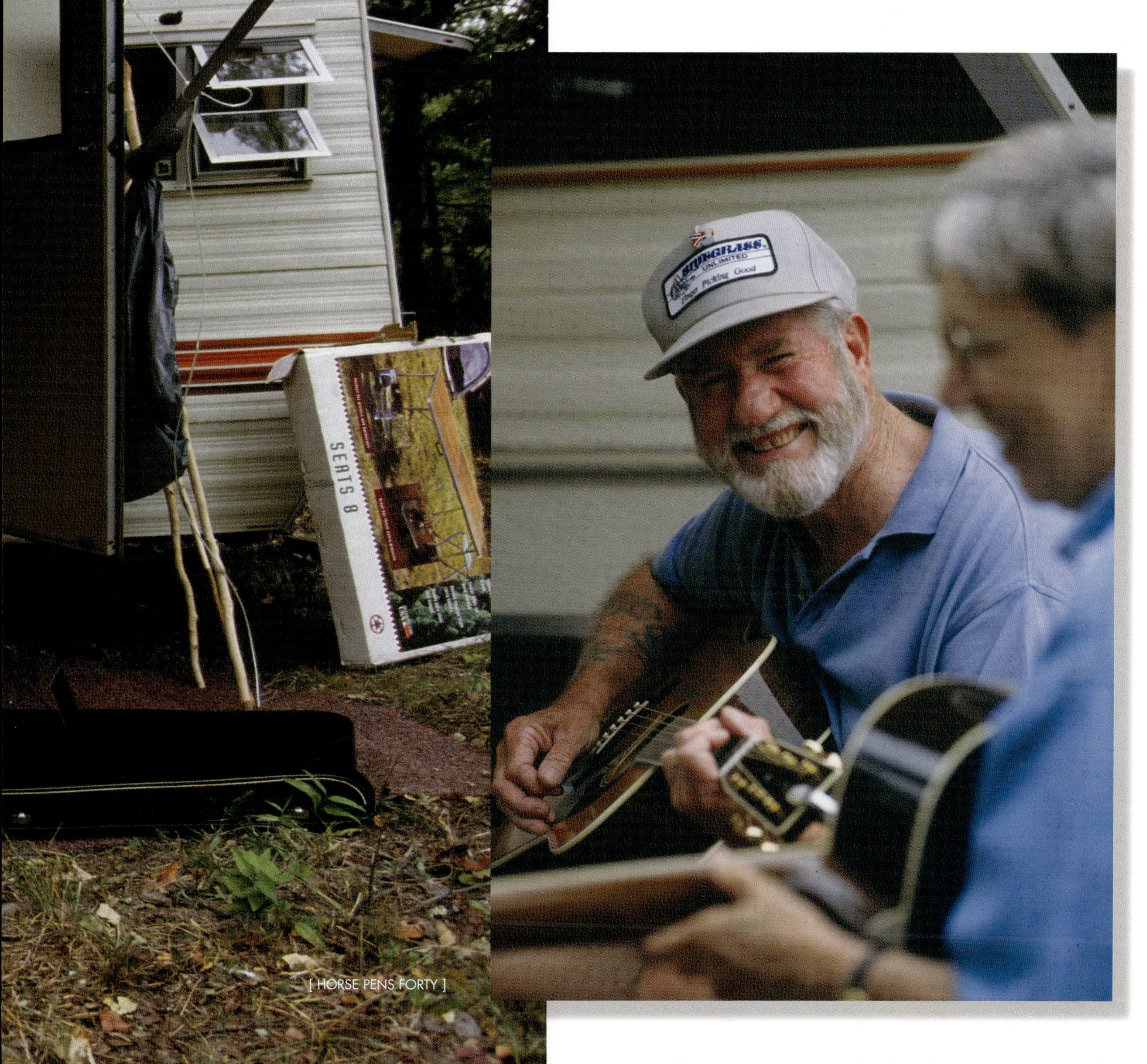
SEATS 8
UNLIMITED

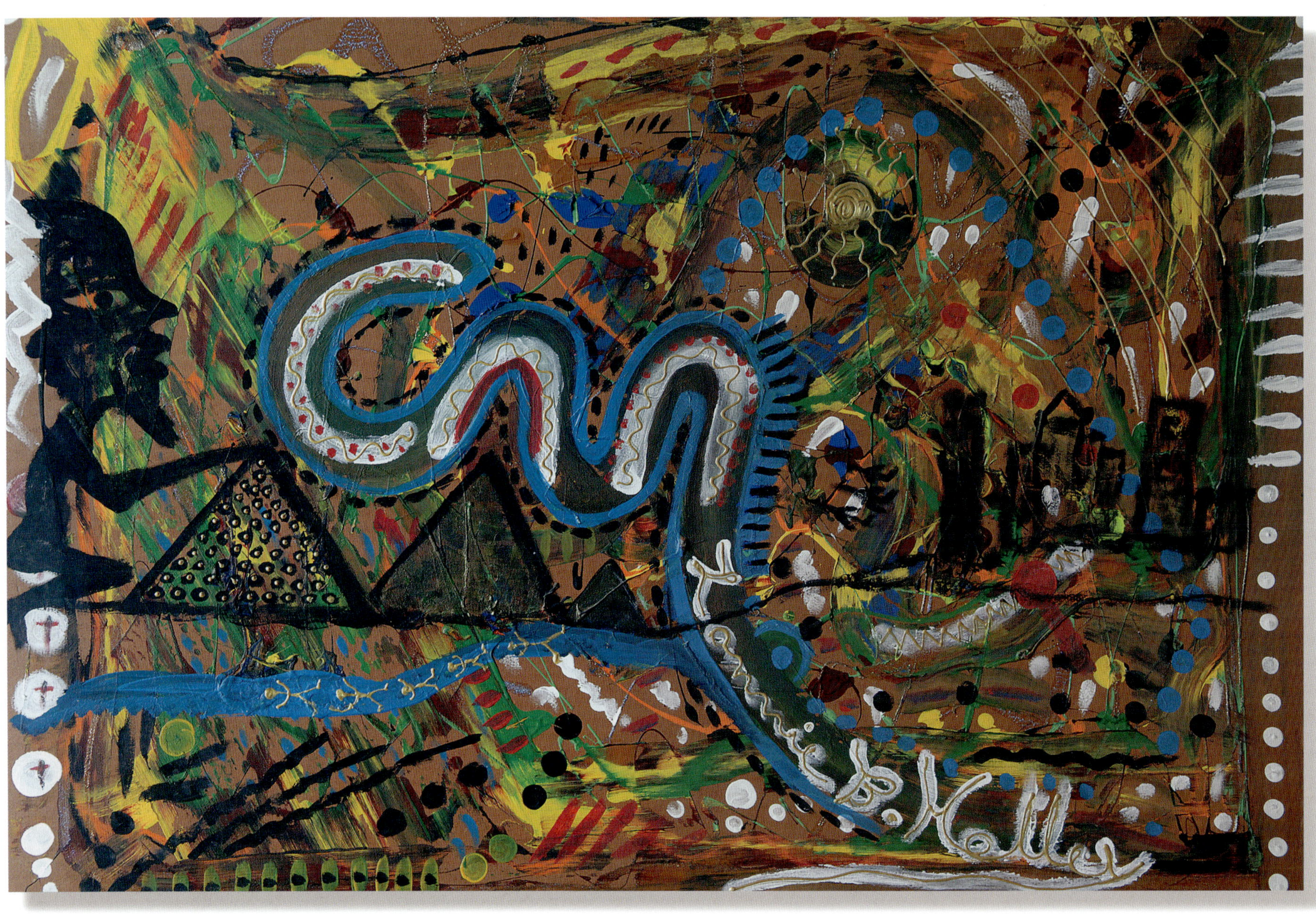

Through my work I hope that people can understand the ways of reclaiming something and adding new values for the sake of our future and others to use this universe.

LONNIE HOLLY
[FOLK ARTIST]

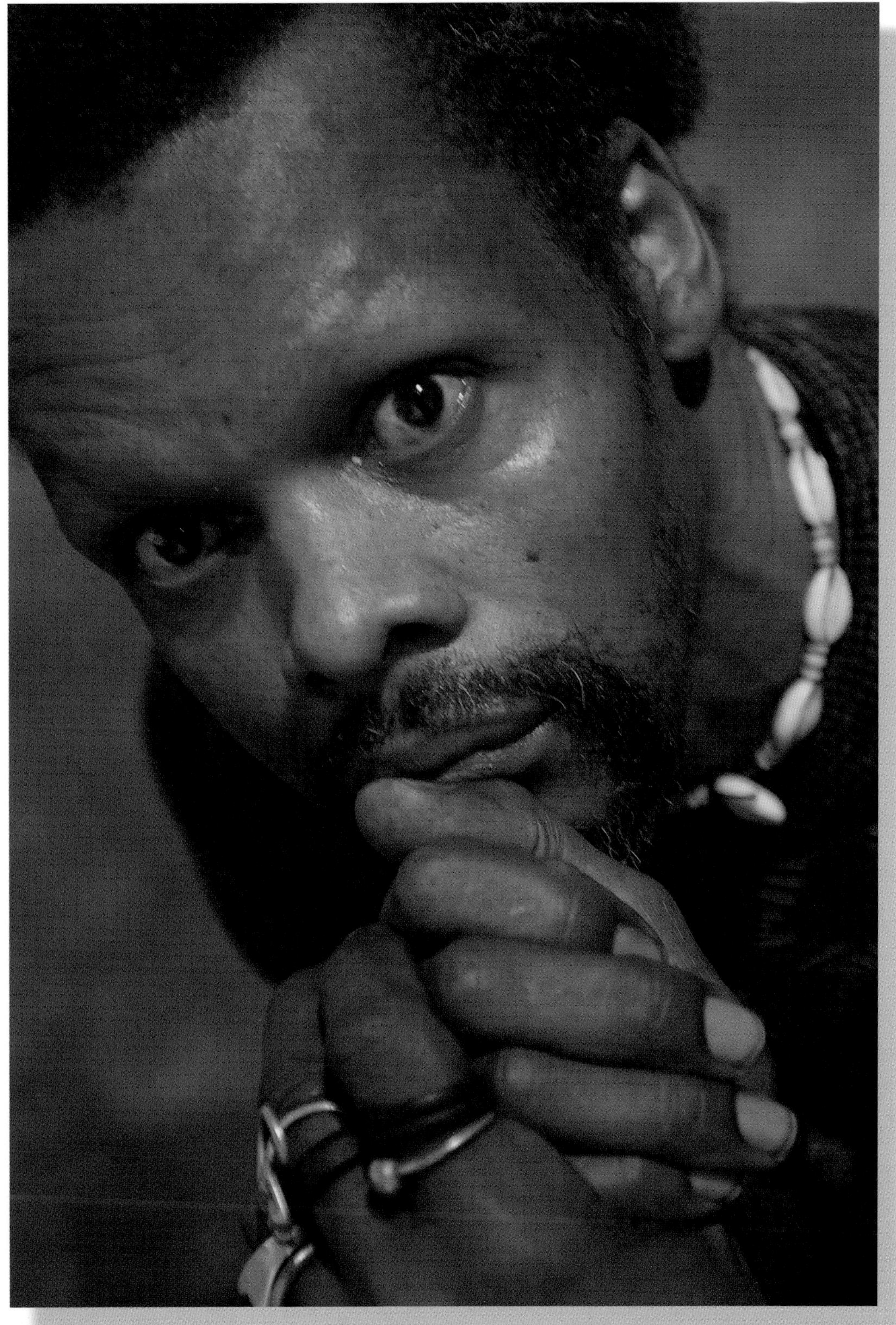

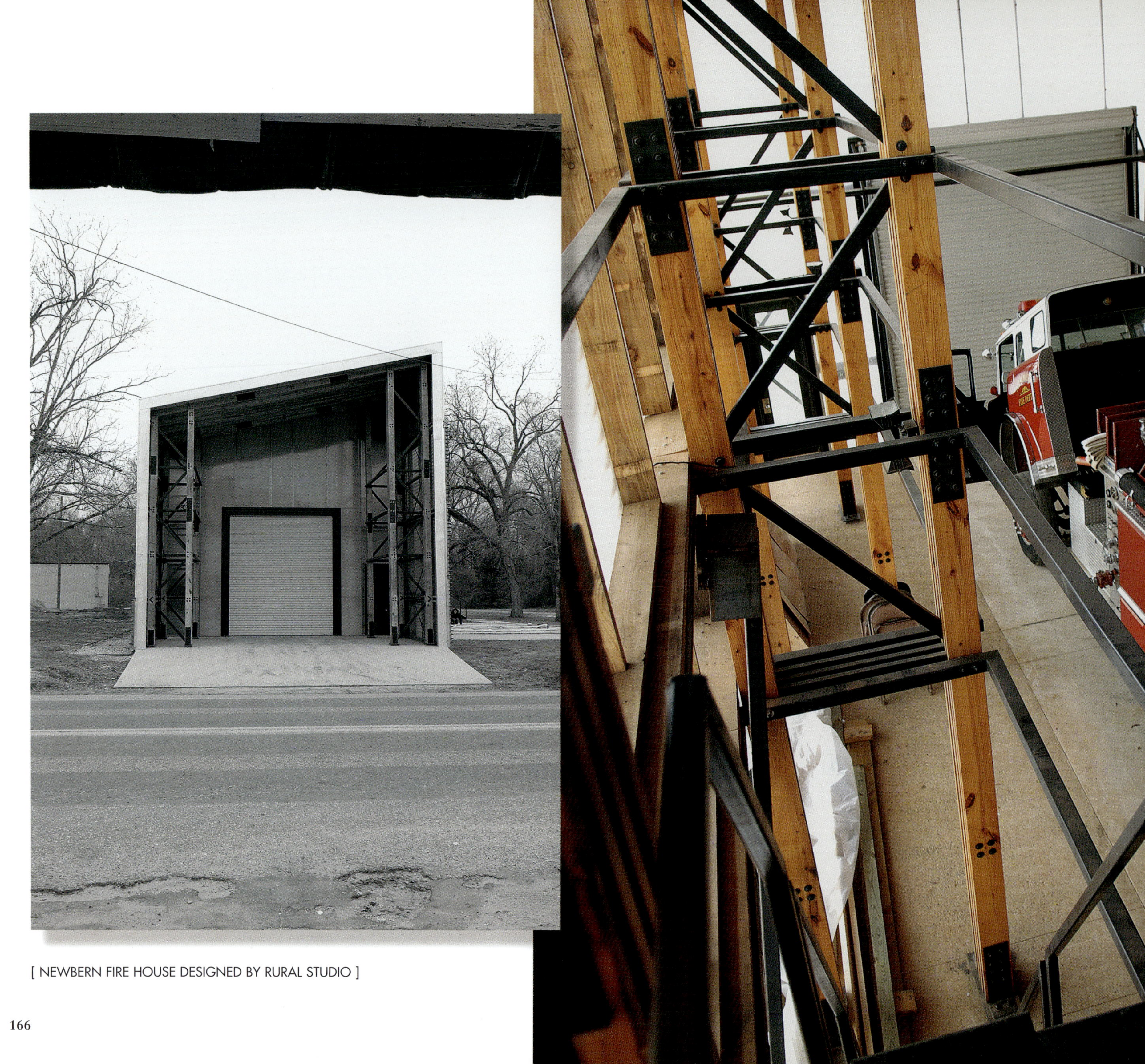

[NEWBERN FIRE HOUSE DESIGNED BY RURAL STUDIO]

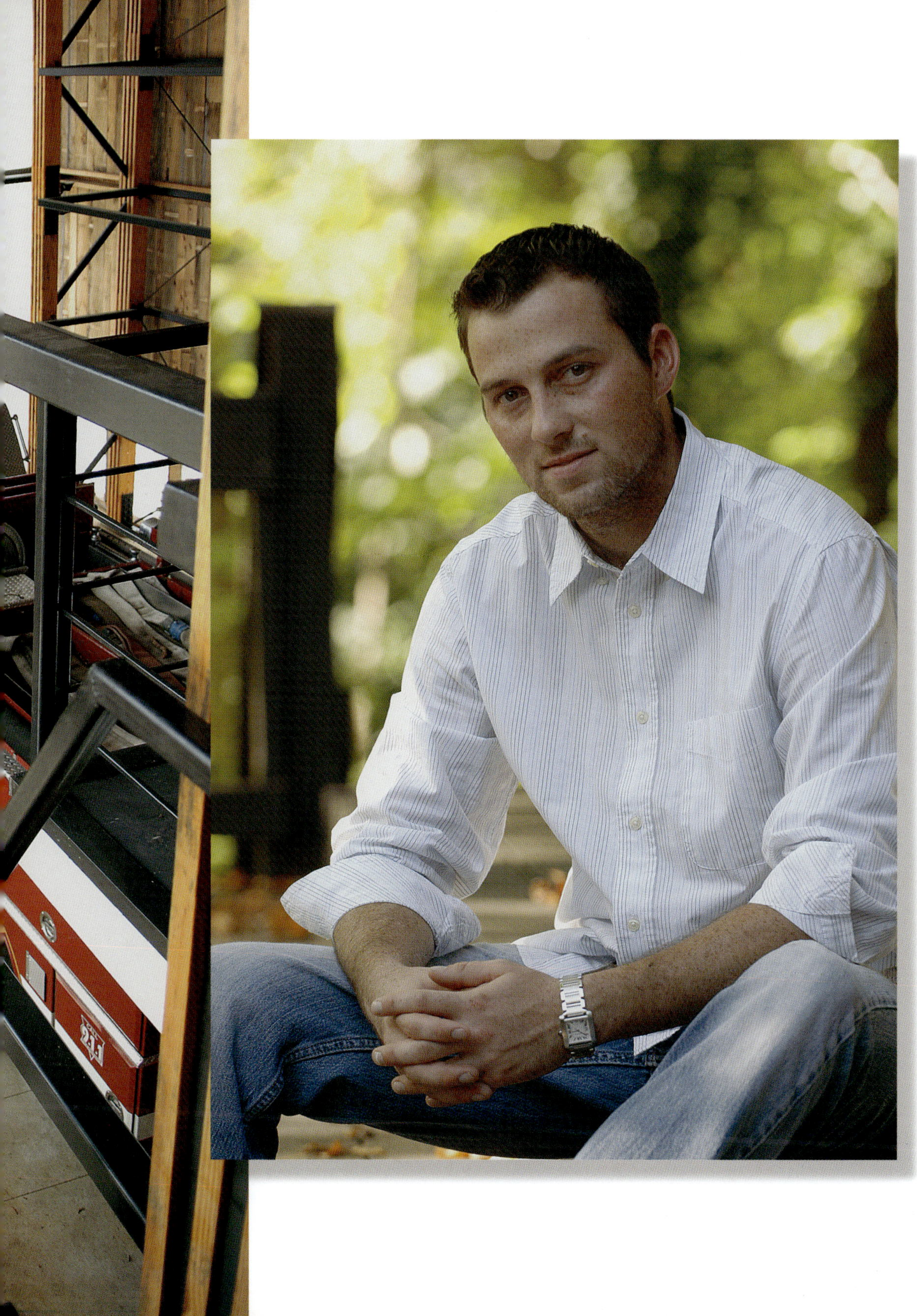

I have lived in Alabama for almost fifteen years. During that time, I have lived in Birmingham, graduated from Auburn University, and spent two years in Newbern. Having lived in Alabama's largest city and spent time in one of its smallest rural communities, I have gained an appreciation for, and better perspective of, what this state has to offer. The unique foods, arts, music, architecture, landscape, and people define each community. It is the mountains and beaches and other landmarks that bring people to Alabama, but it is the communities and people that make them want to stay. Fifteen years later, I am proud to call Alabama home.

Matthew Finley
[DESIGNER]

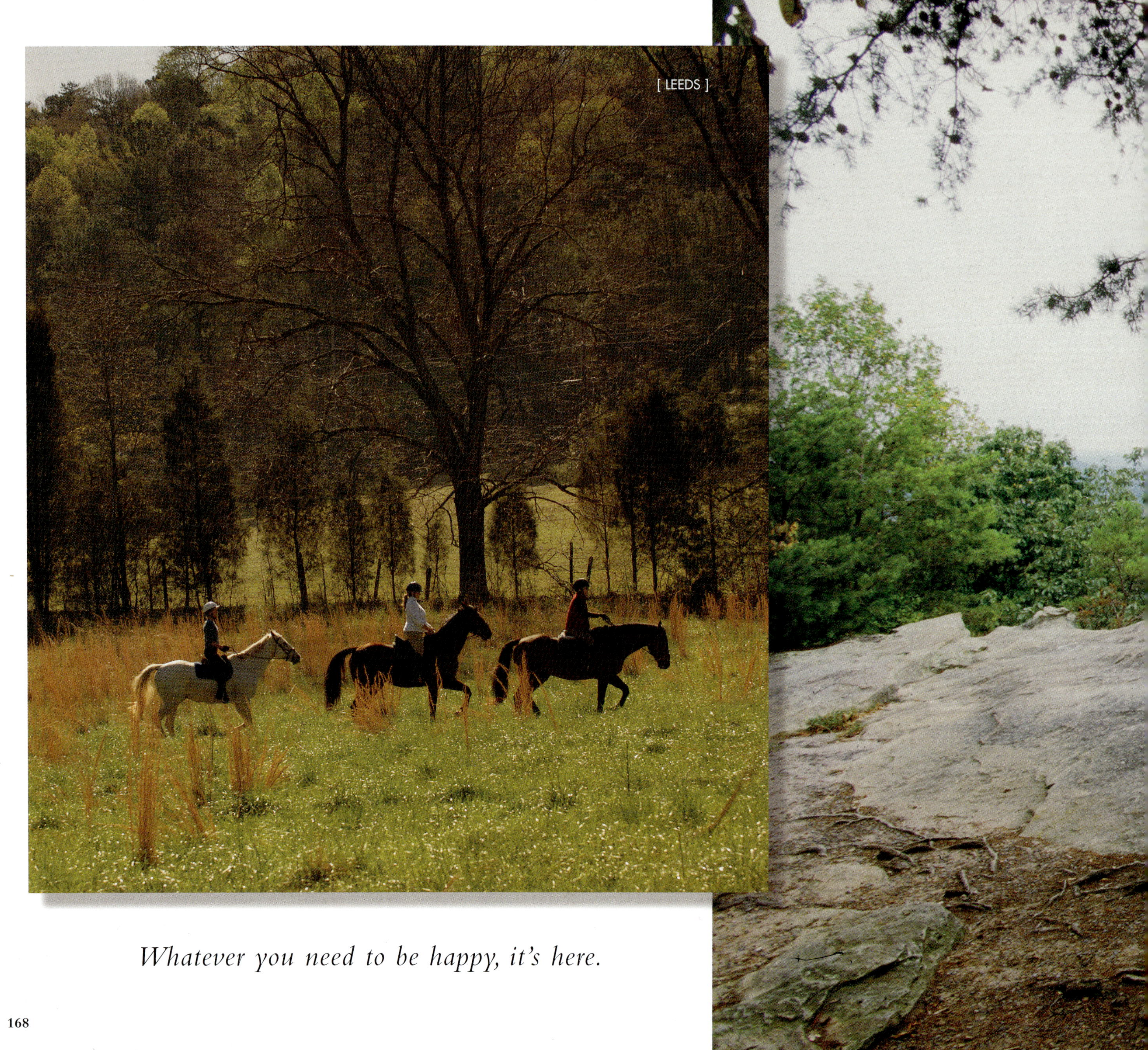

Whatever you need to be happy, it's here.

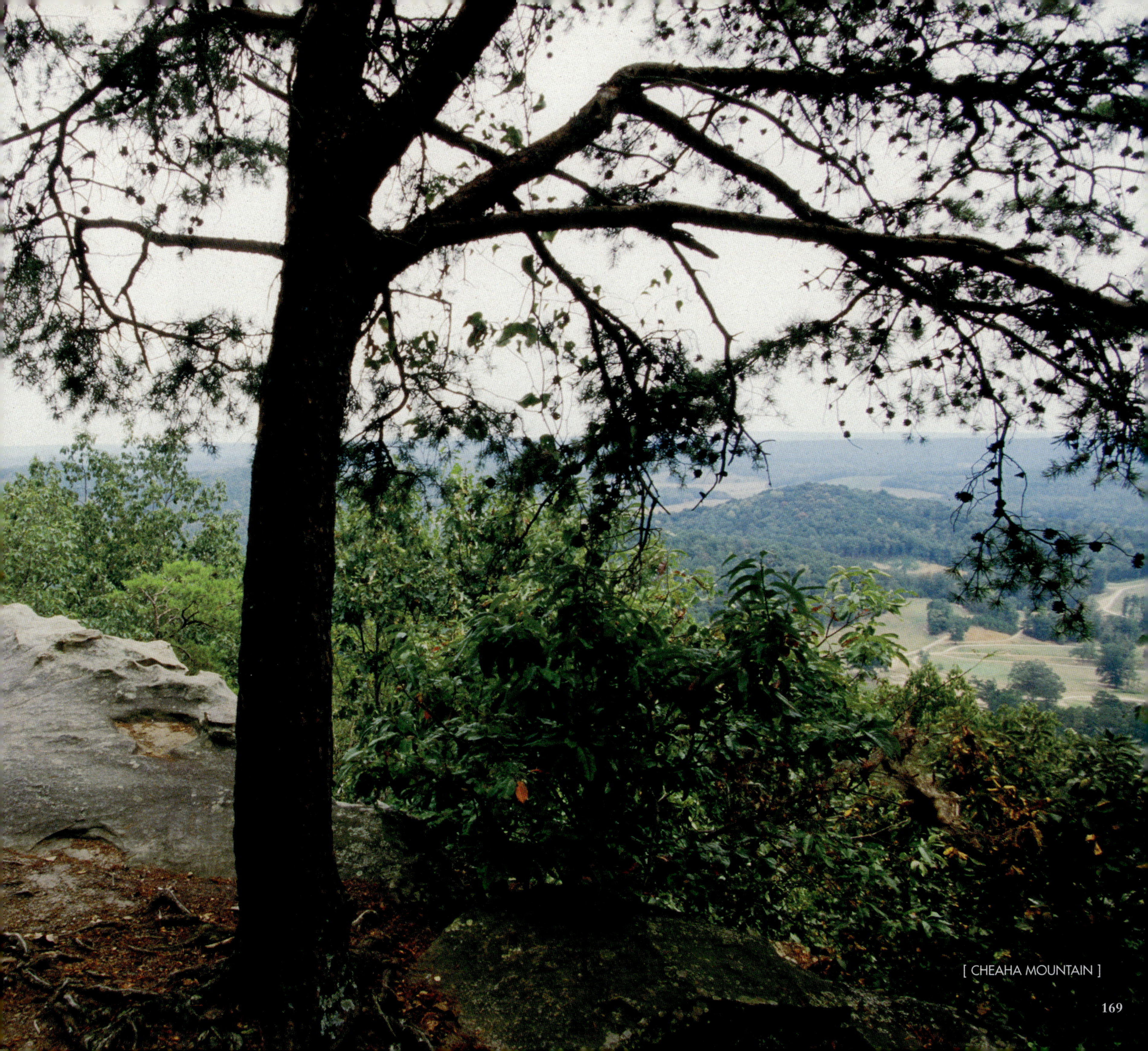
[CHEAHA MOUNTAIN]

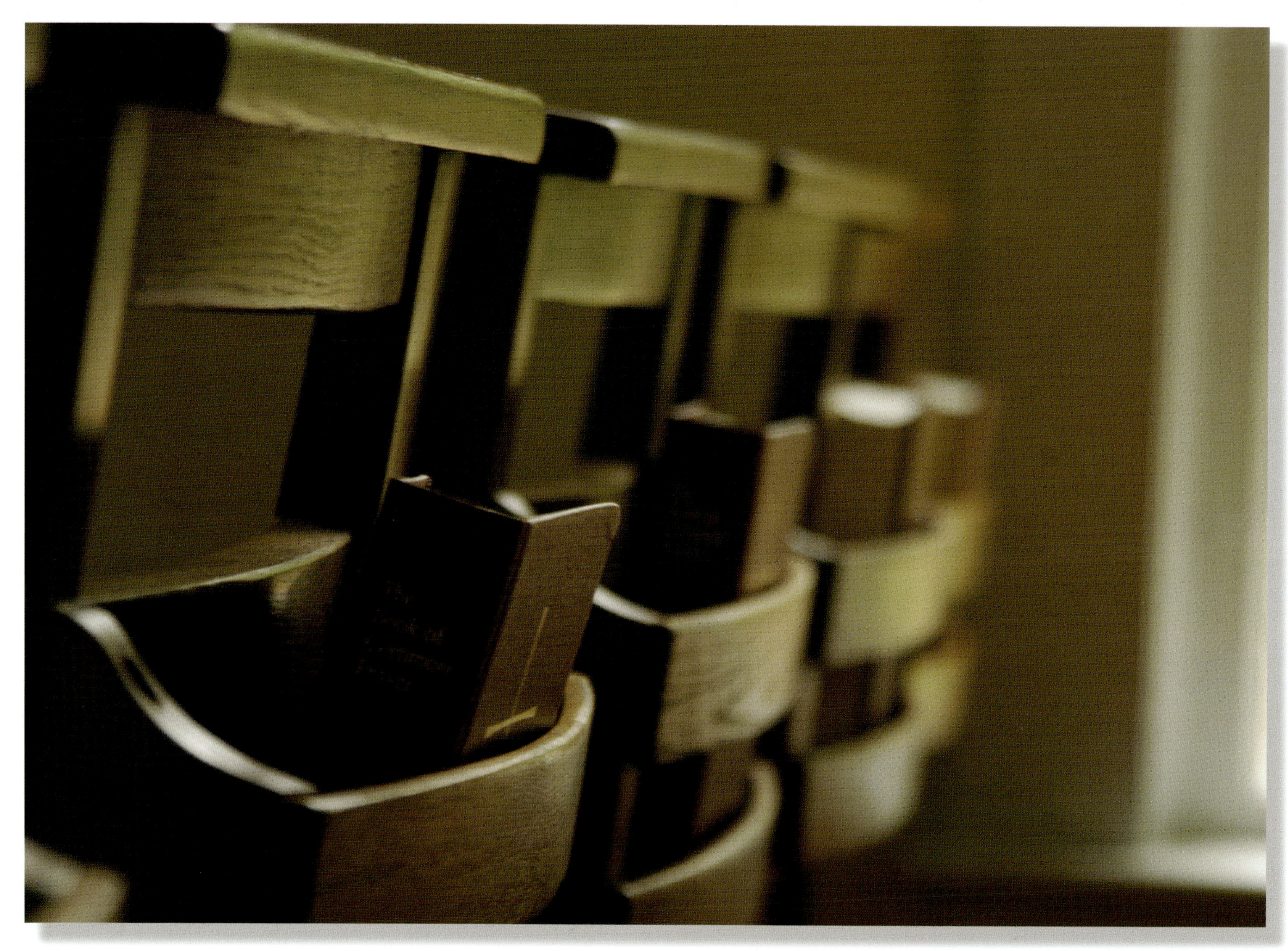

You can hear the music.

Home sweet home Alabama, to me, is chocolate and biscuits, worn church hymnals, funky Muscle Shoals soul and sweet gospel, beautiful rusty barn roofs, and tractors on two lanes.

MARK NARMORE
[SONGWRITER]

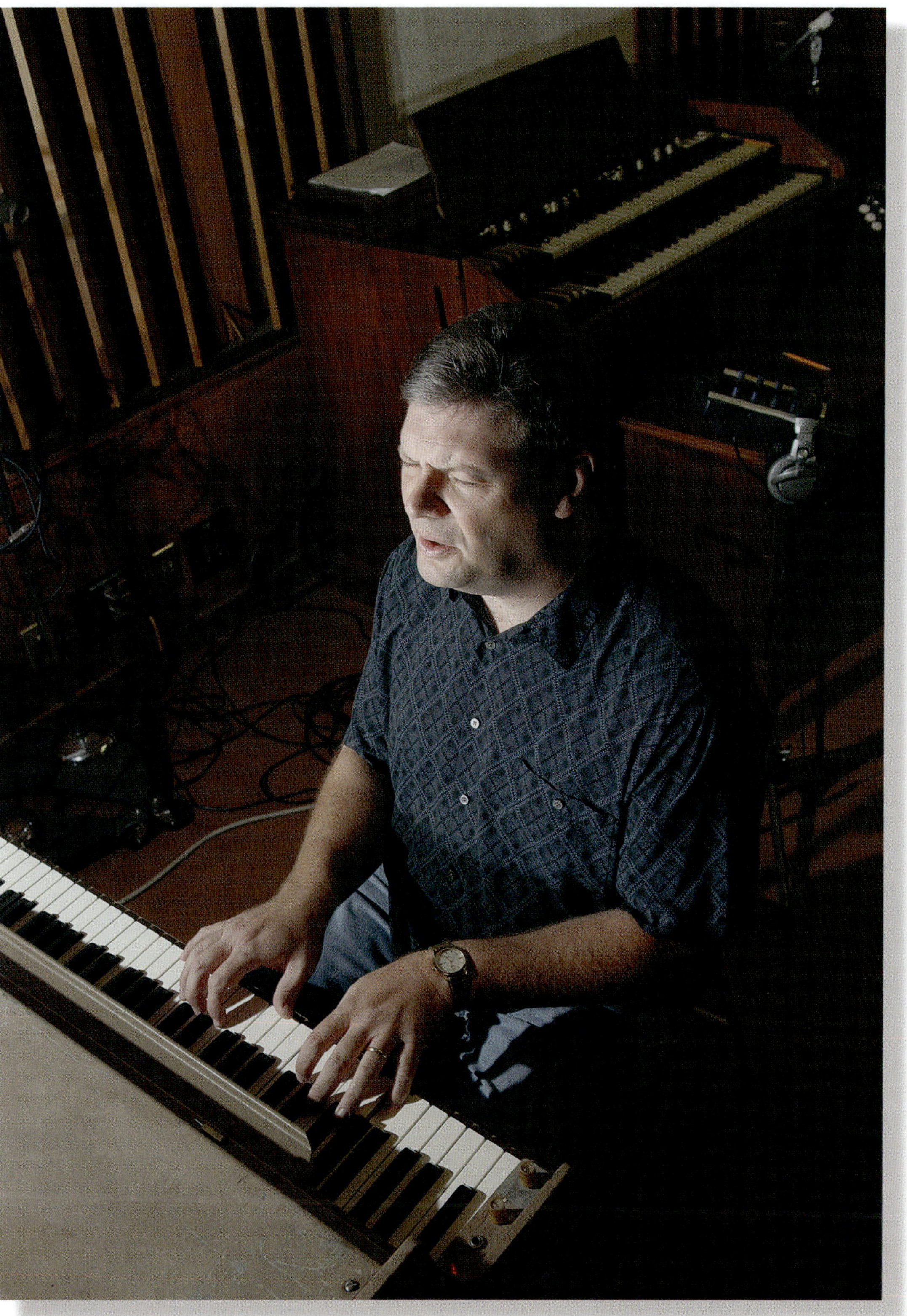

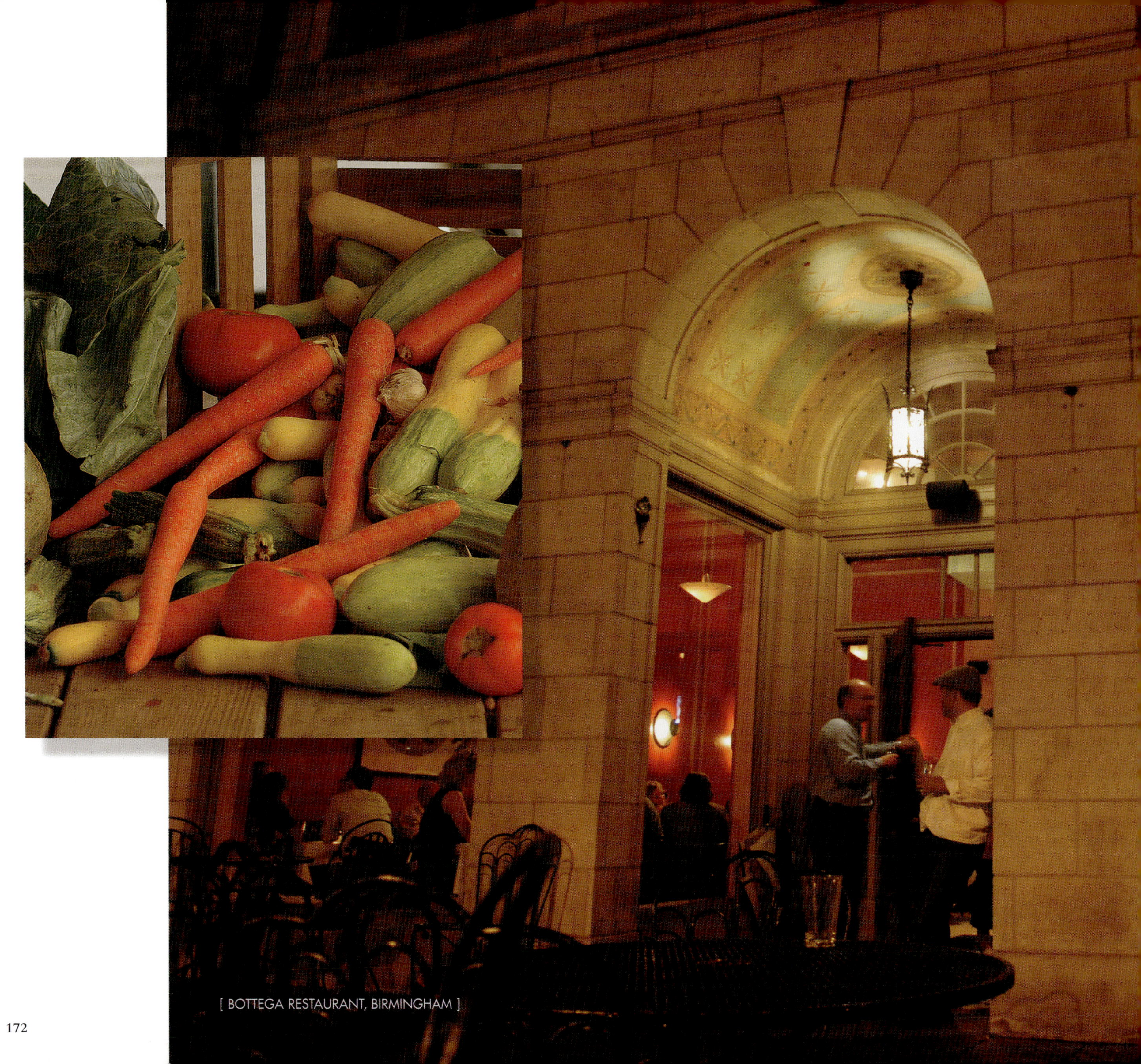

[BOTTEGA RESTAURANT, BIRMINGHAM]

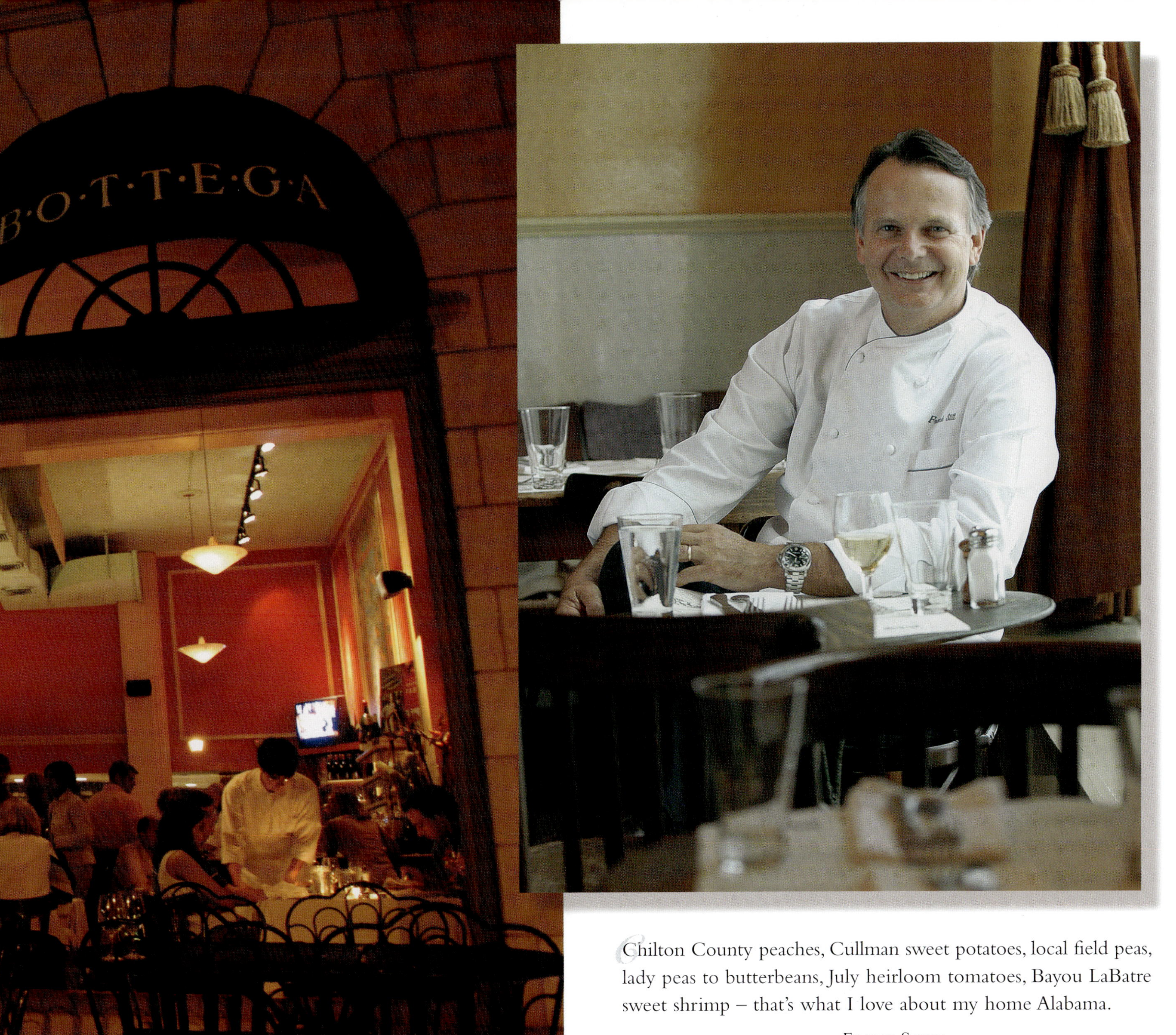

Chilton County peaches, Cullman sweet potatoes, local field peas, lady peas to butterbeans, July heirloom tomatoes, Bayou LaBatre sweet shrimp – that's what I love about my home Alabama.

FRANK STITT
[CHEF, AUTHOR]

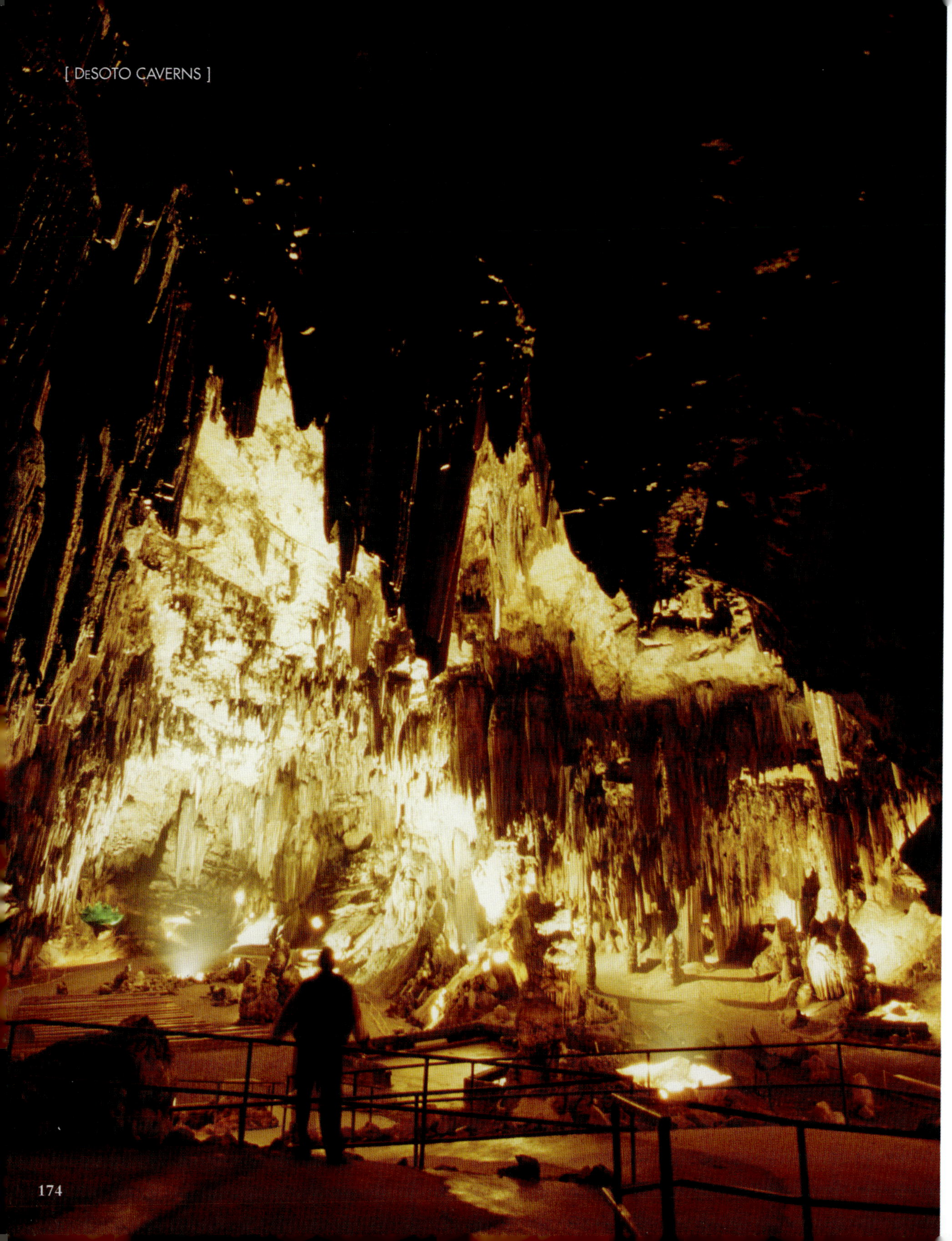

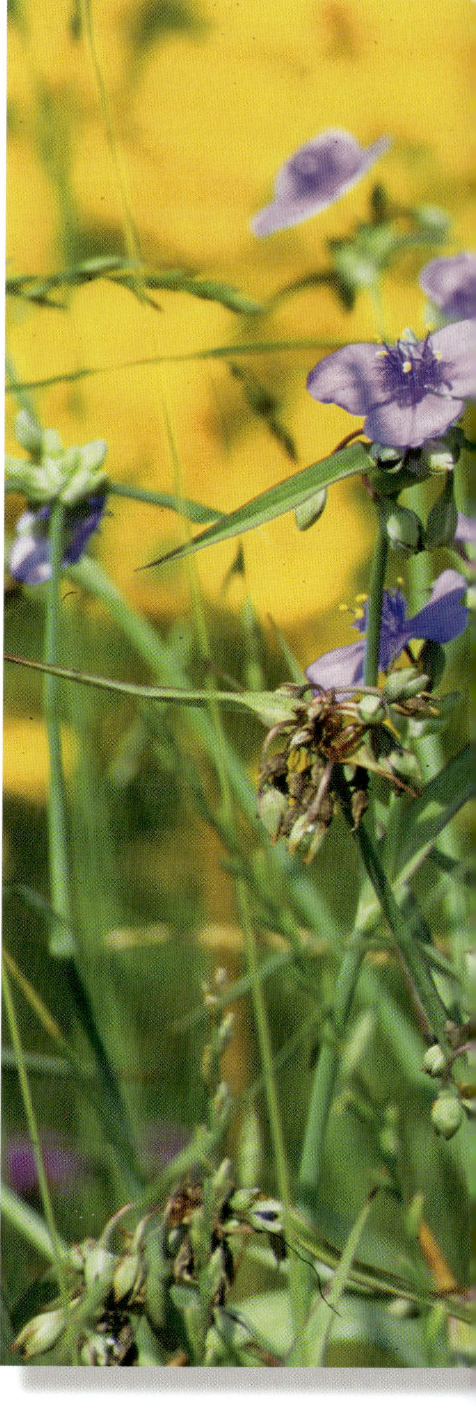

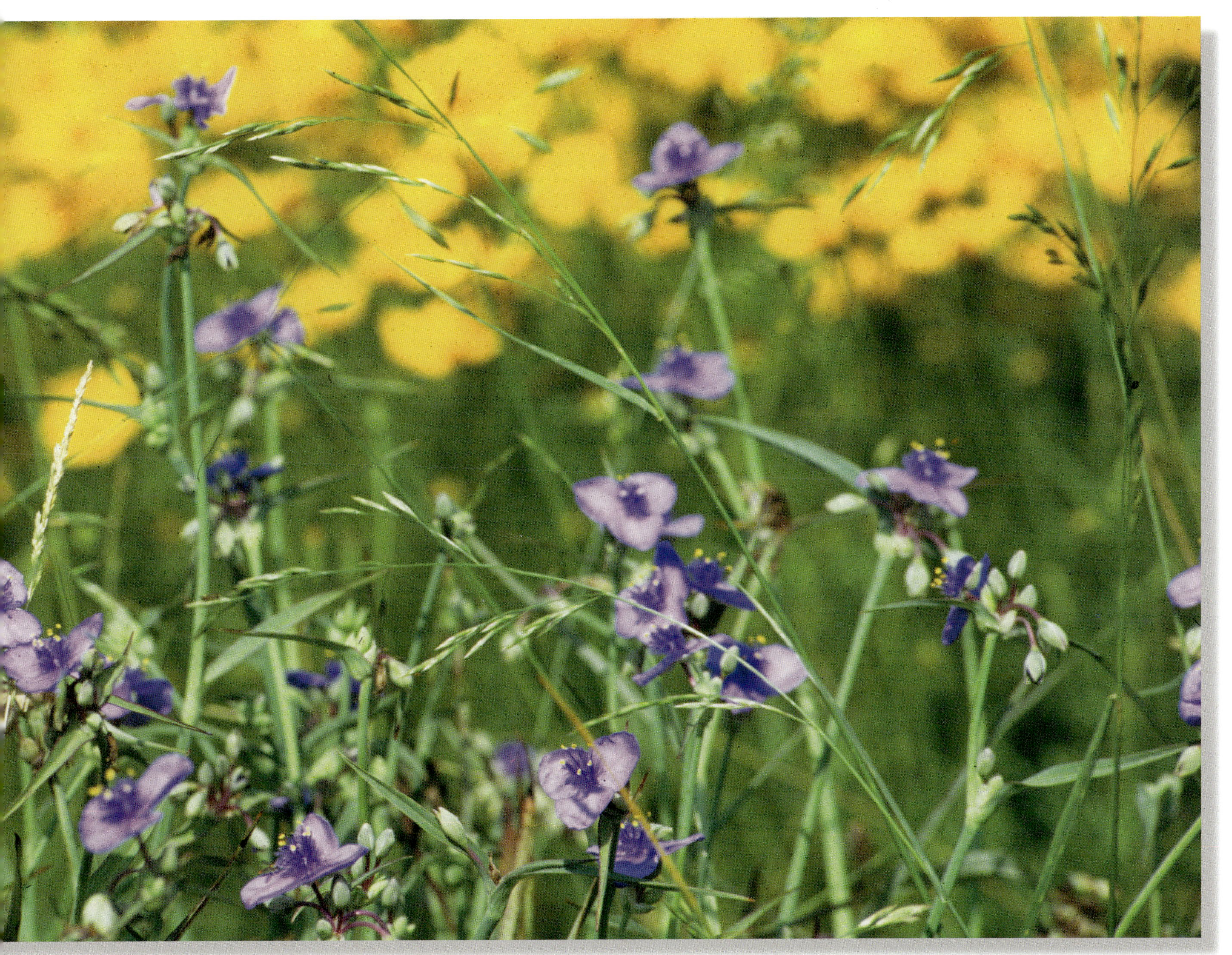

You can see the colors of the universe.

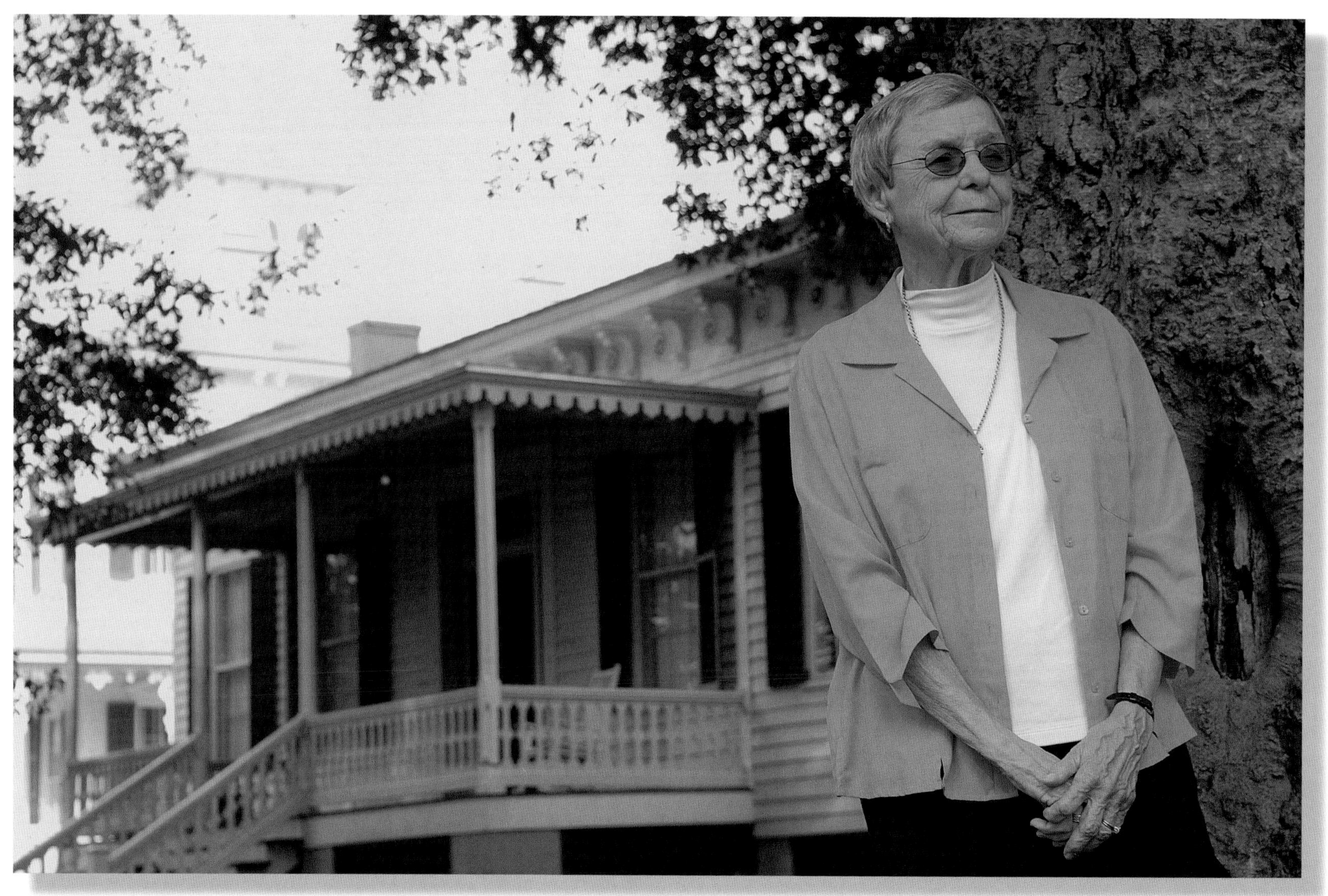

I love Alabama for its diversity: its beautiful lands and waters, its complex history, its regional crops, food, accents, stories, music, and interests, but above all, I love Alabama for extraordinary people. We have agreed, disagreed, understood and misunderstood, been tolerant and intolerant, and laughed and cried together and separately. Yet through it all, we have developed and maintained an interdependency based on mutual need and respect that has been, and will continue to be, the glue that makes us all fellow Alabamians.

Mary Ann Neeley
[HISTORIAN]

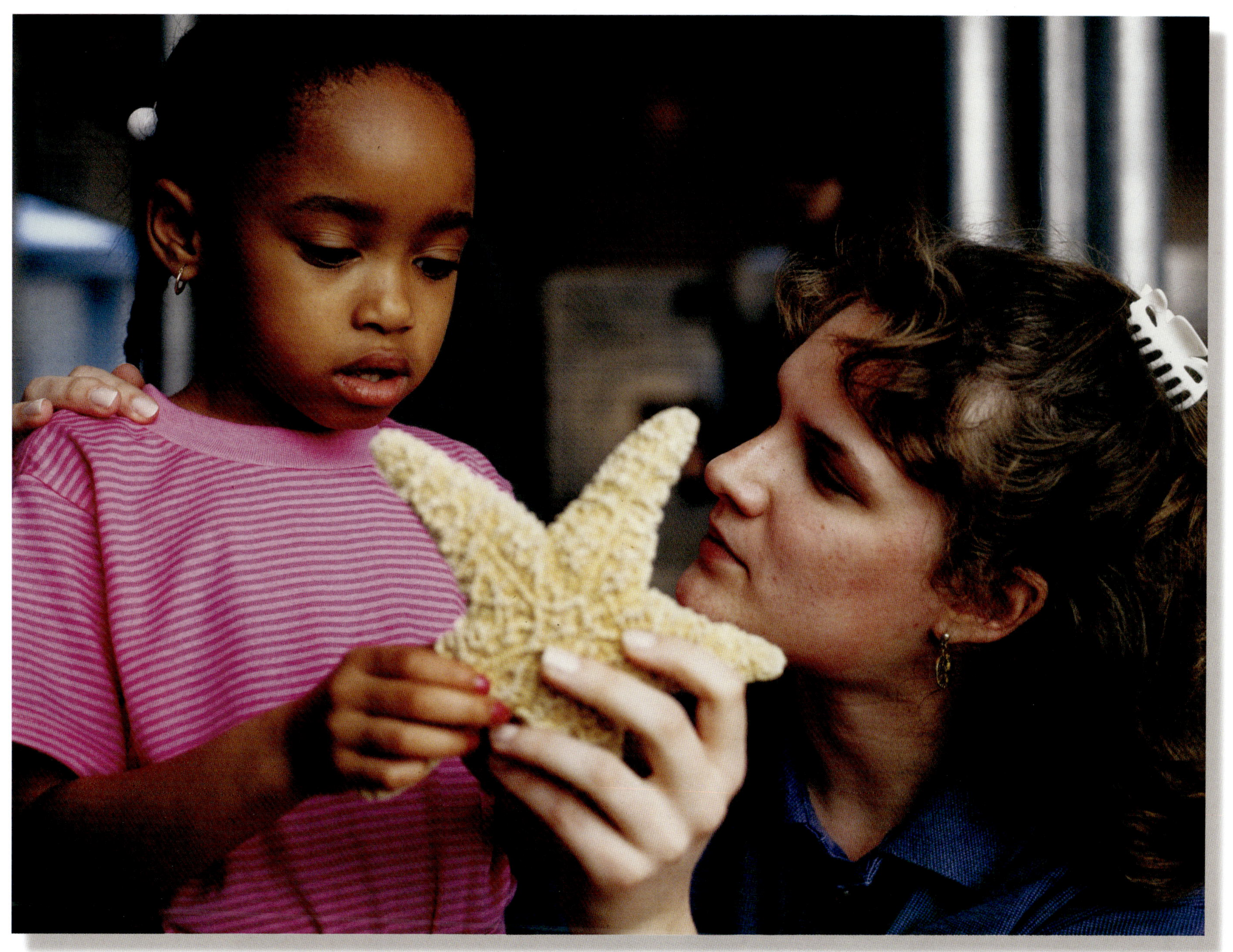

[GULF COAST EXPLOREUM, DAUPHIN ISLAND]

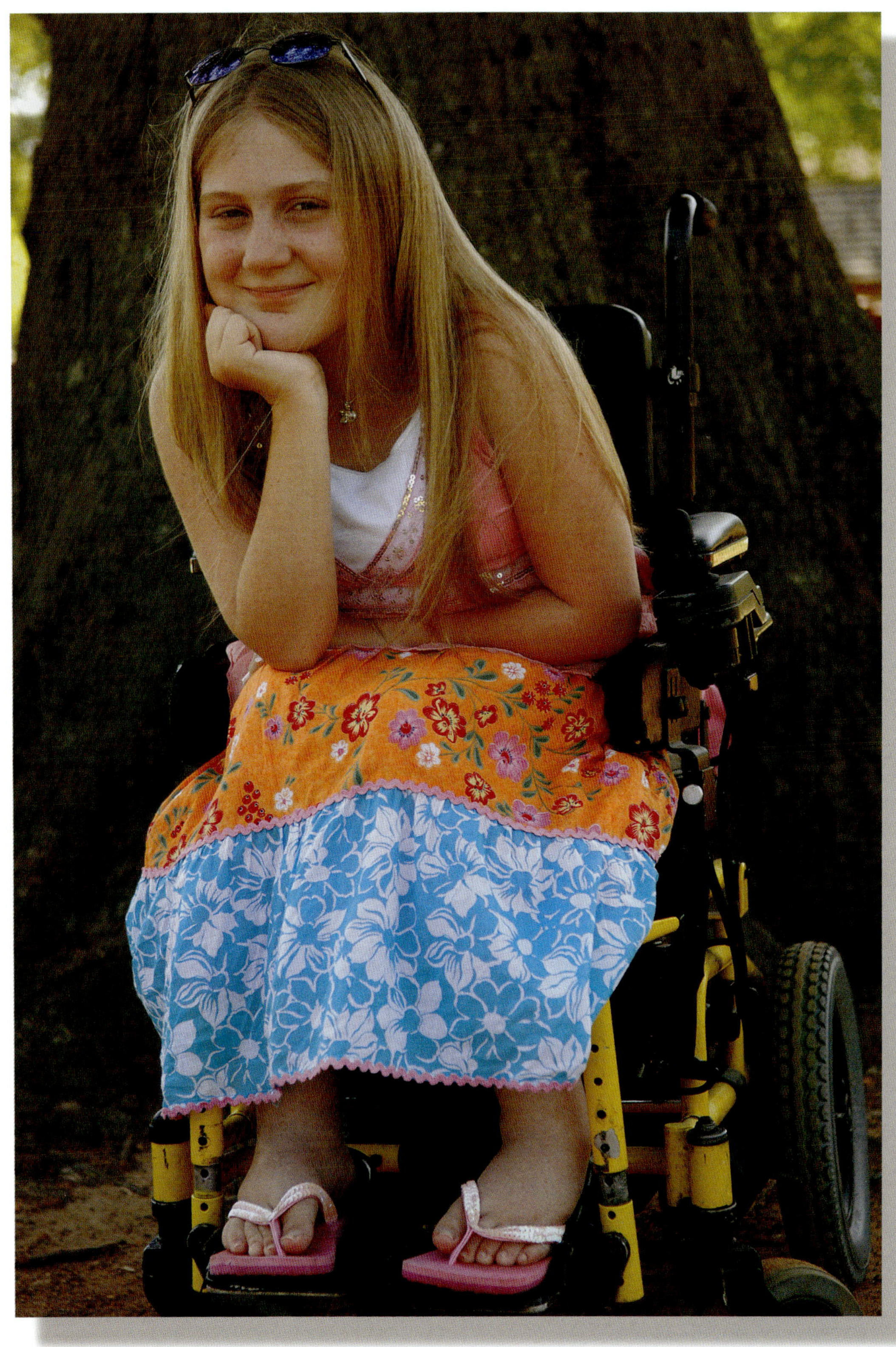

Nice parks, neighborhoods.
My whole family lives here.
I was born here.
All my friends are here.
It is beautiful.
And it is never too cold.

AMELIA O'HARE
[STUDENT]

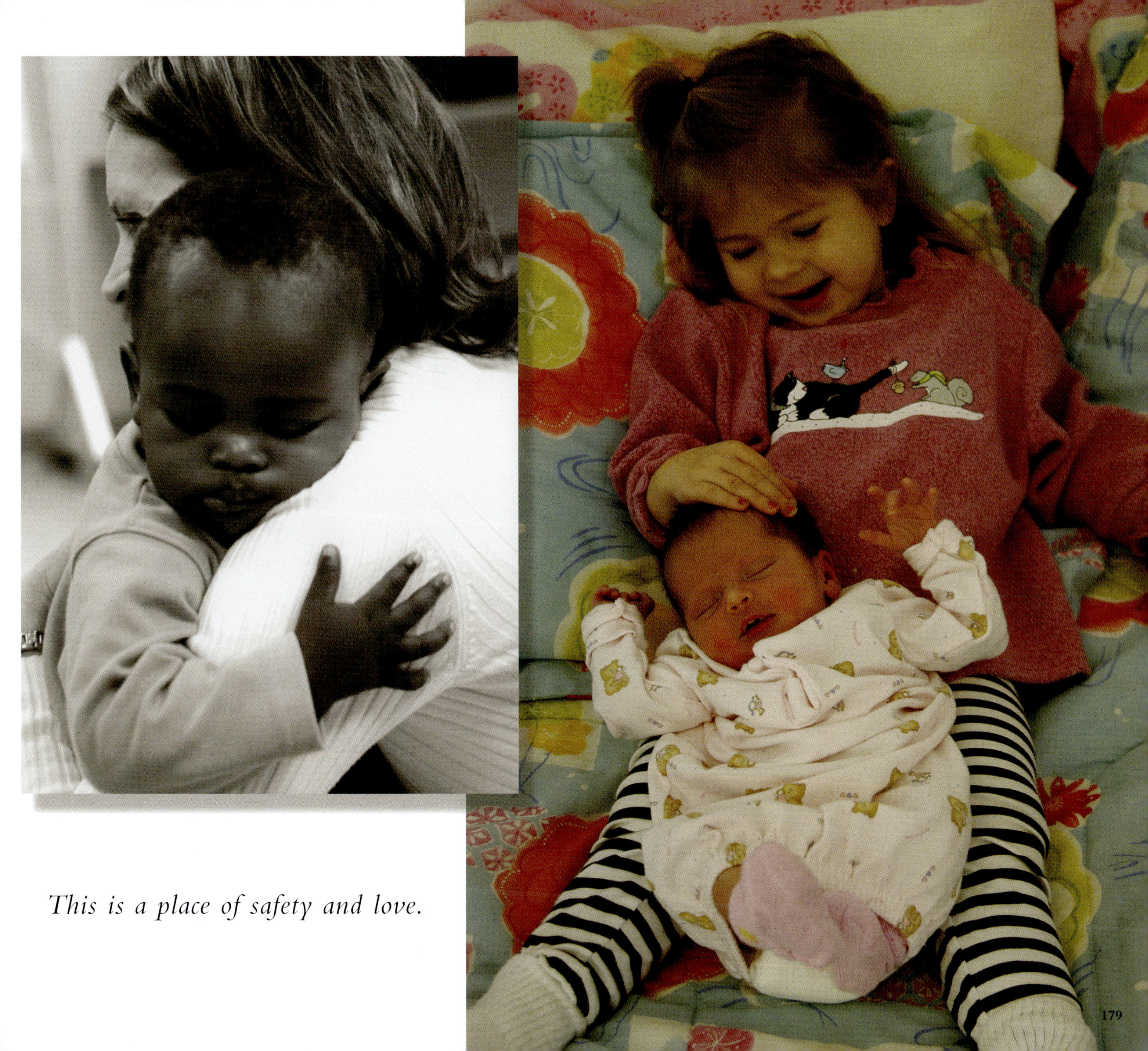

This is a place of safety and love.

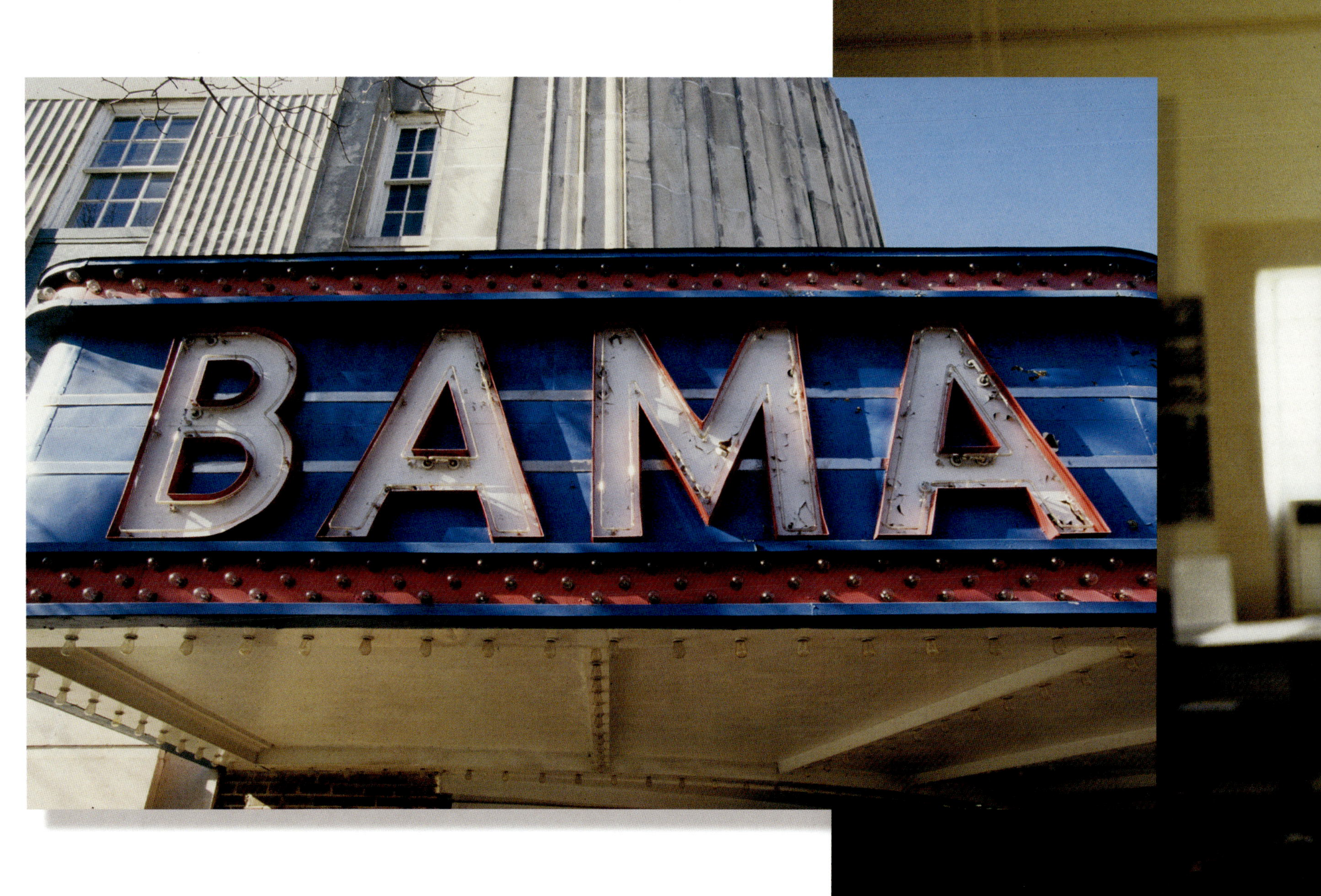

This is a place with a rich, never-ending story.

[GEORGIANA]

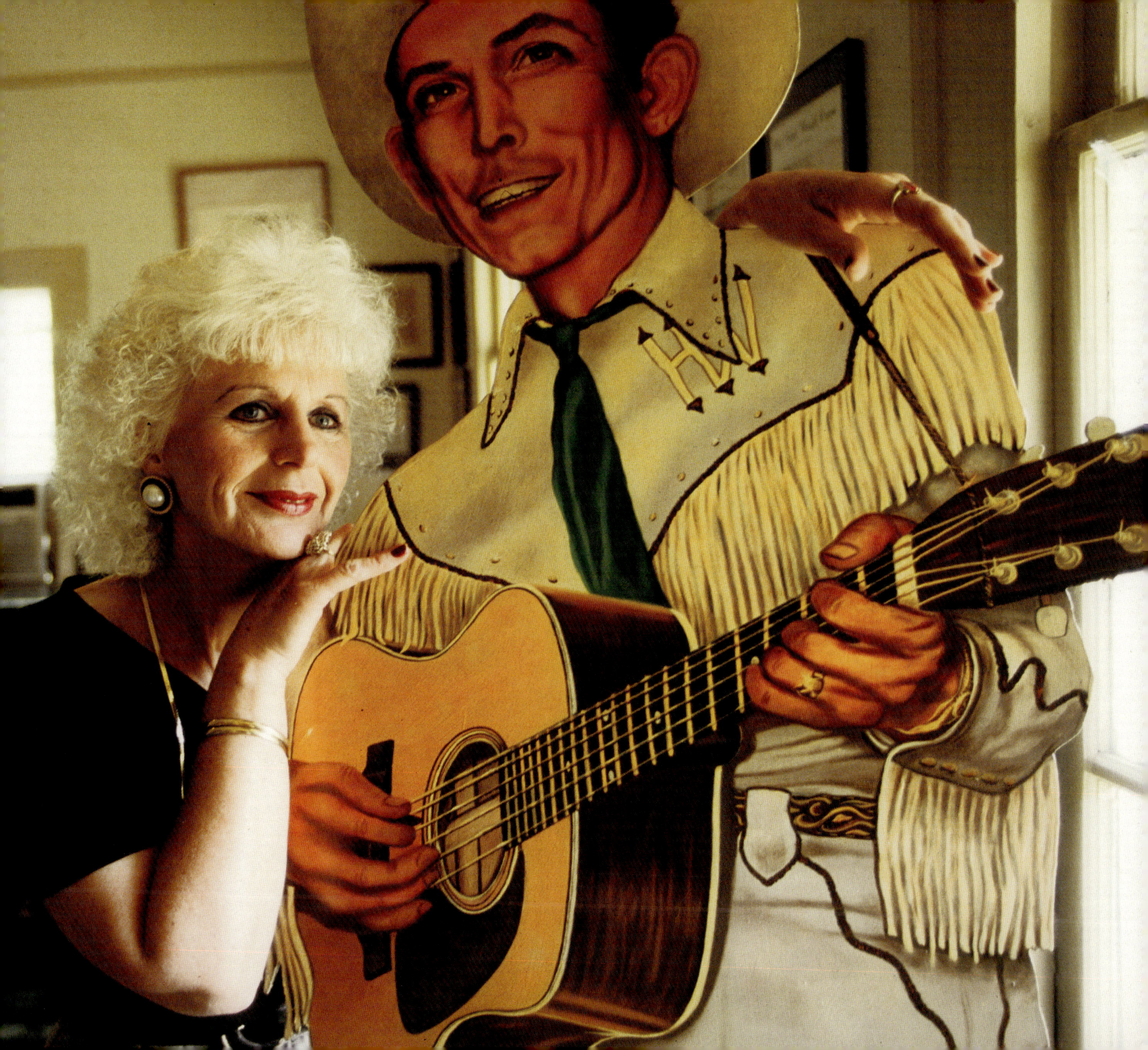
HW

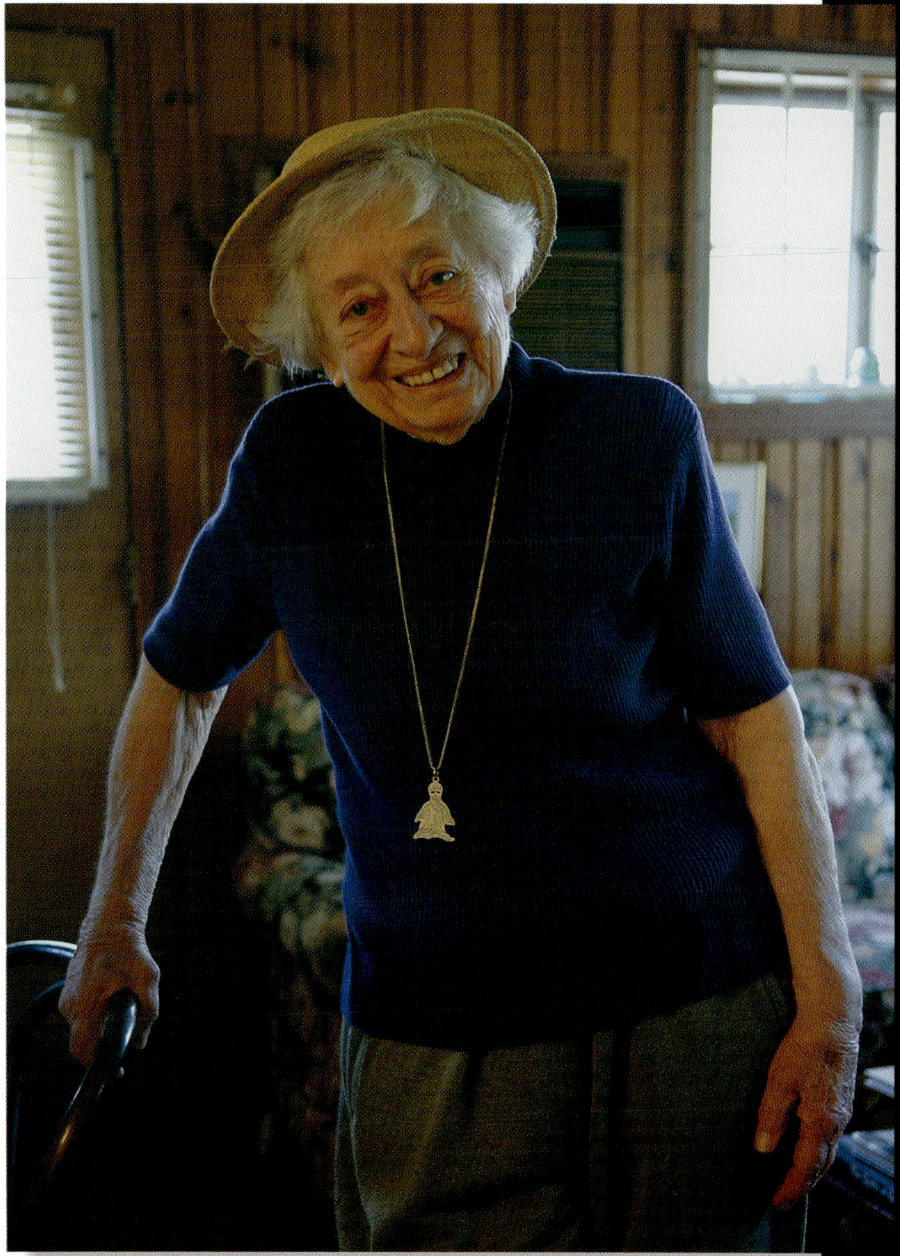

I love Alabama because its people are as varied as its natural beauty, a rare combination that fills my life with wonder and makes this blessed place a home.

KATHRYN TUCKER WINDHAM
[STORYTELLER/WRITER]

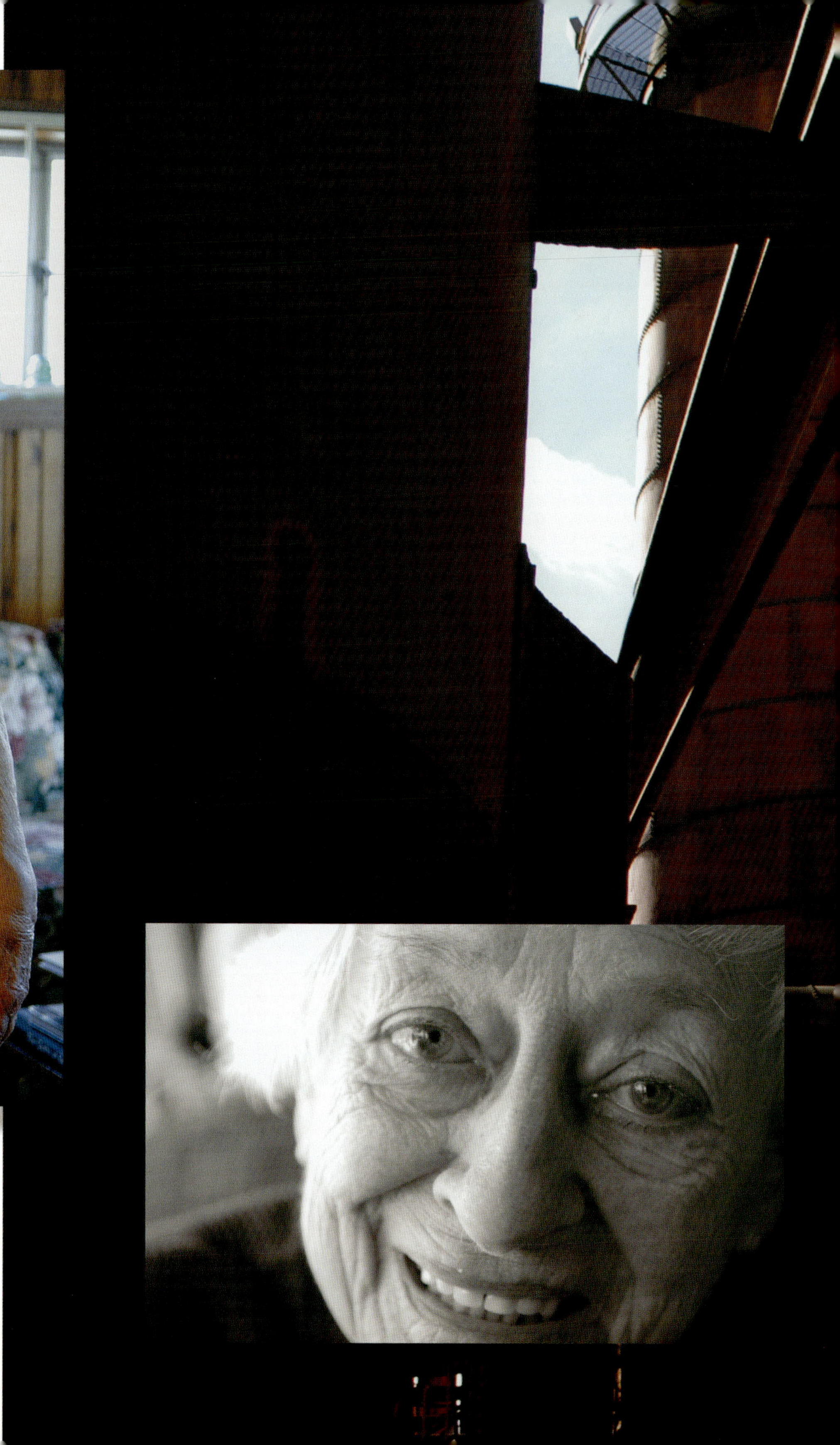

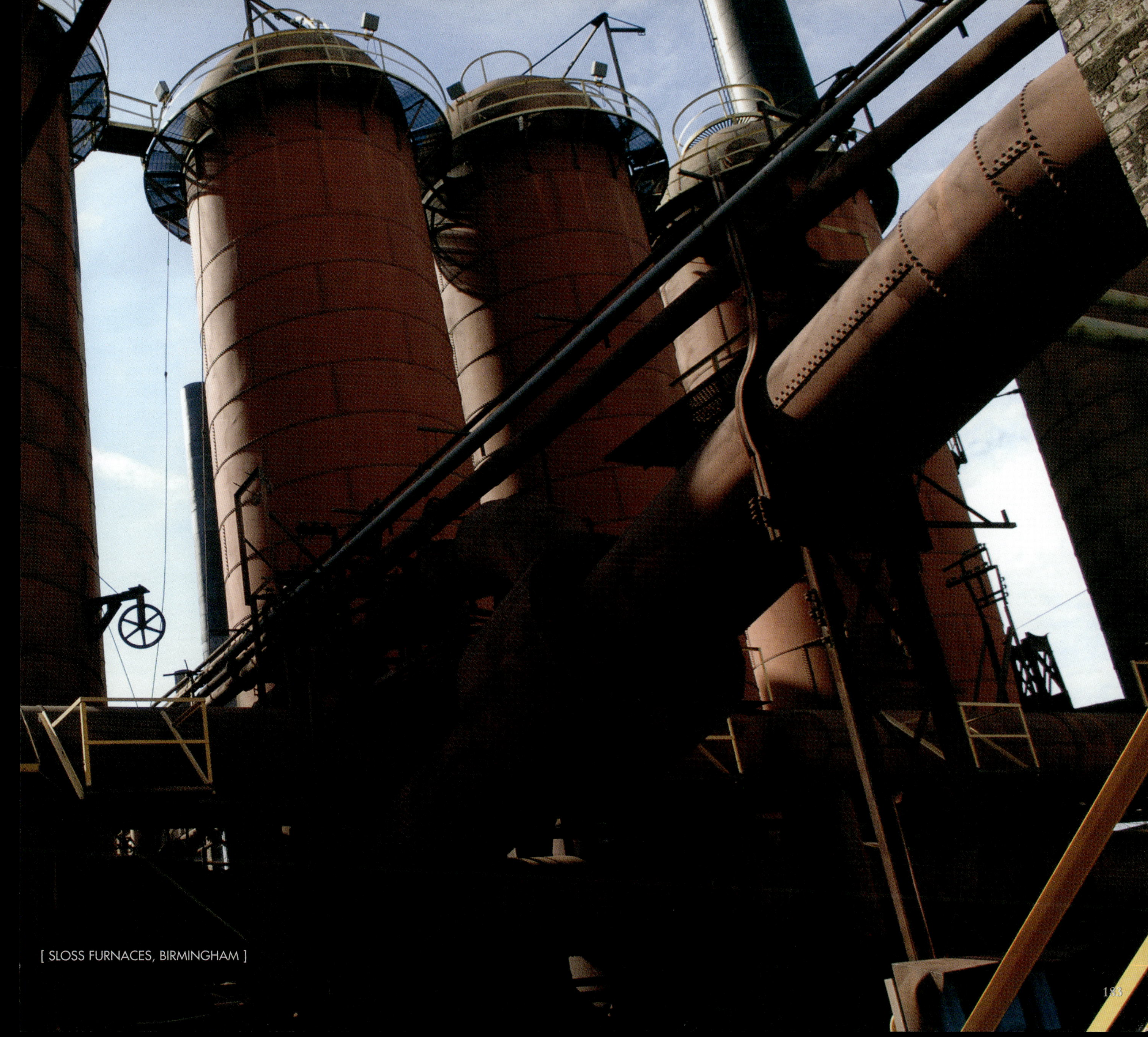

[SLOSS FURNACES, BIRMINGHAM]

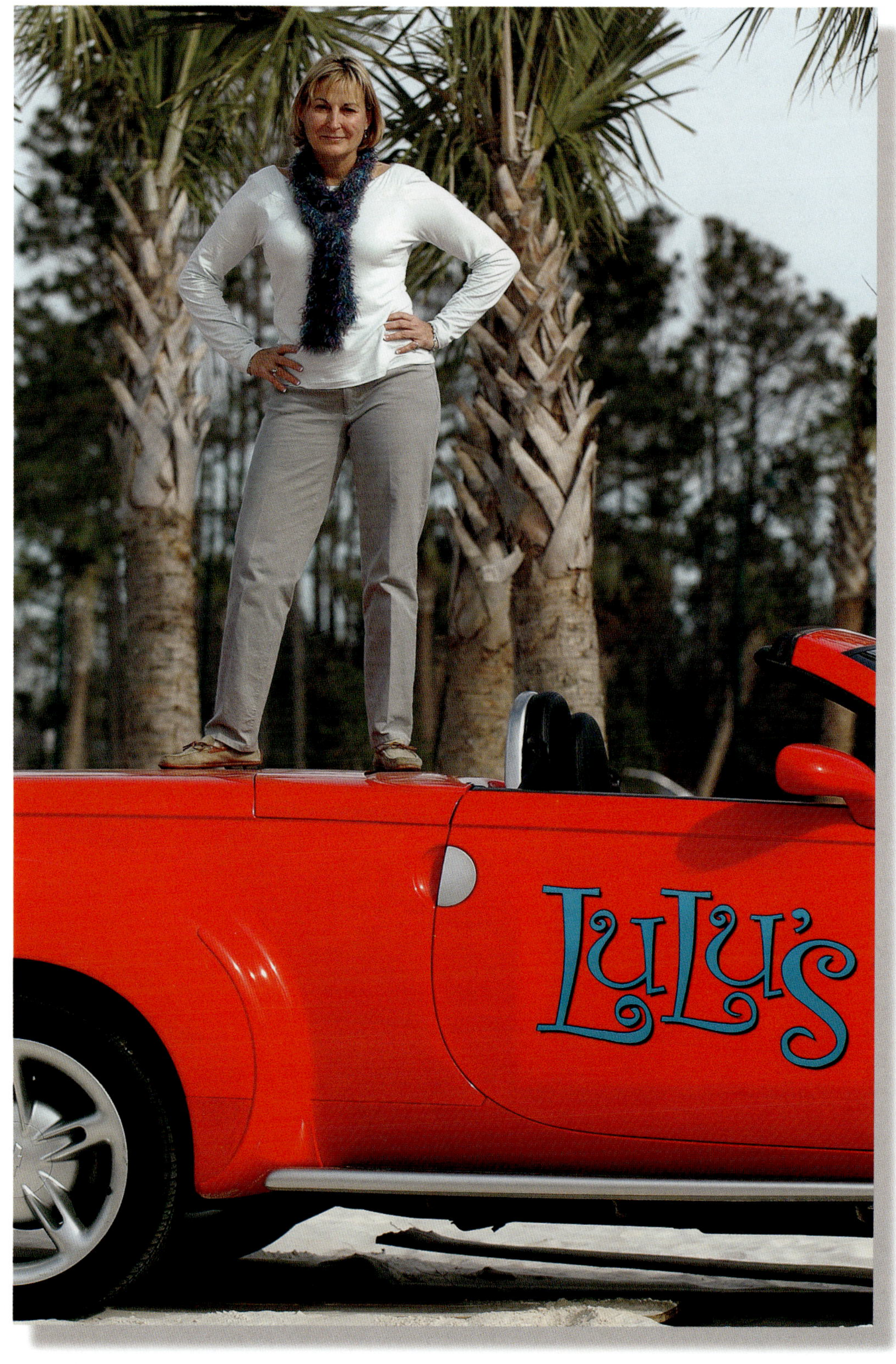
LuLu's

My perfect Alabama is filled with days that begin with coffee at my barn in Point Clear while I feed horses as the sun rises over the rolling pastures and giant oaks. I then drive to my restaurant in Gulf Shores, LuLu's, along two-lane county highways, through fields of silver queen corn. At LuLu's, I have fish tacos for lunch on the deck while barges breeze past on the Intra-Coastal Waterway and children play in the sand overlooking the marina. I head back to my home on Fish River: a boathouse, actually, designed by my husband, Mac. We pack a basket with saltines, pimento cheese, and red wine and jump into his boat for a leisurely cruise down this pristine river, waving at friends and stopping to chat with neighbors. When we reach the big bridge, we zoom across the shallows of Weeks Bay like teenagers in a hot rod, until we get to the pass, where we idle into Mobile Bay. Then we head to the channel marker about half a mile out, cut the engine, and drift, with only the sound of waves slapping the hull and the occasional "pop" of a cork. An amazing neon sun slides into the Bay, splashing the heavens with pink, purple, and crimson. On a perfect day, the "green flash" slices the horizon. Sailors say life is good when that happens. Alabama? What's not to love?

LUCY BUFFETT
[RESTAURATEUR]

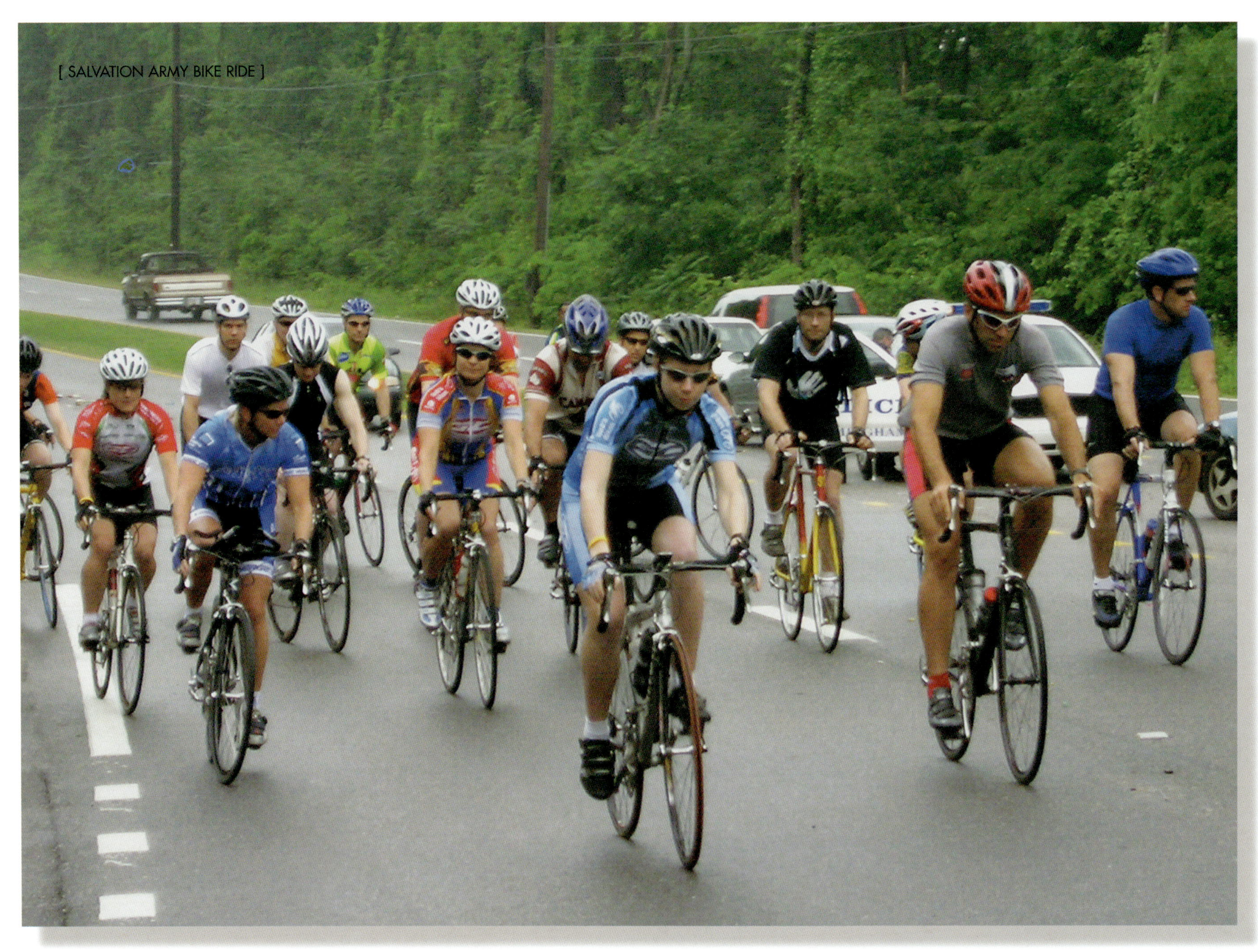

Alabama. Whatever the future holds, we're in it together.

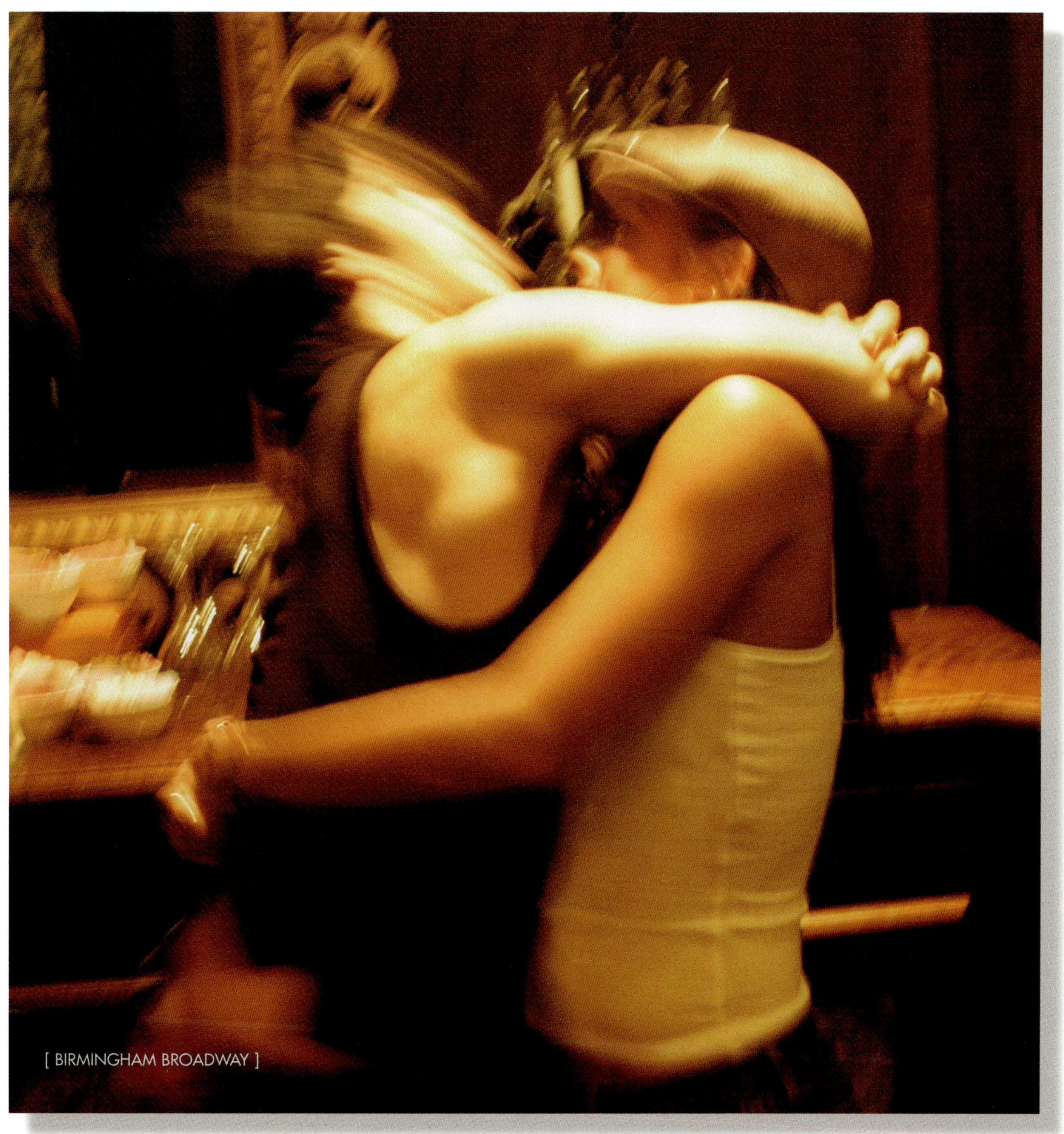

[BIRMINGHAM BROADWAY]

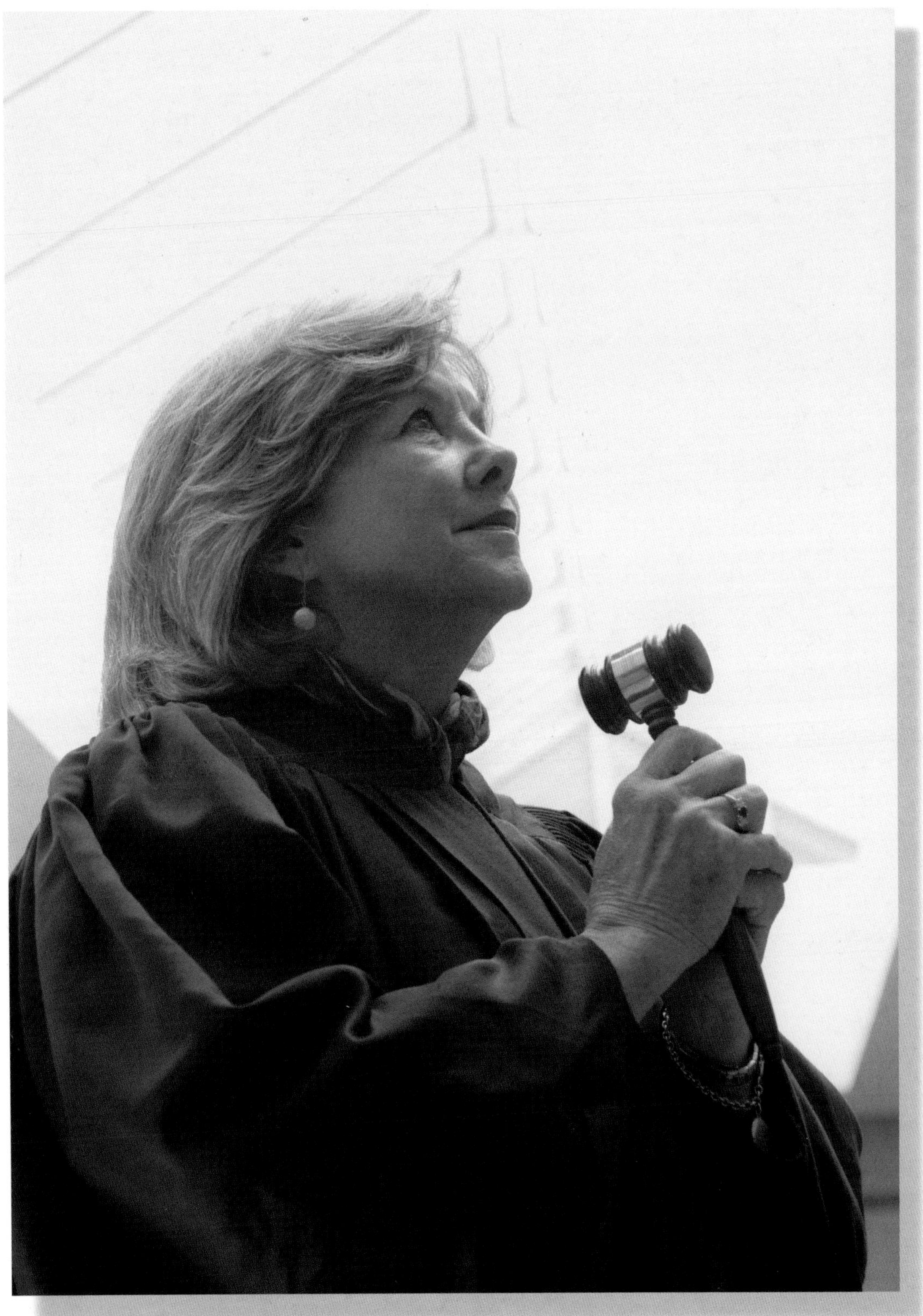

What I love about Alabama:

1. The hospitality and kindness of Alabama's people give great opportunity to those who come here. Alabama, especially Birmingham, is full of opportunity for its citizens. There are many open arms for newcomers and strangers. In my case, a girl who grew up going to six schools in Mississippi and Alabama came here to Birmingham-Southern College and was able to live here and build a career for myself because I was welcomed and encouraged by this community. There is room to make it here if a person wants to work hard.

2. I love the climate and the heat as I am a gardener and a cook. Summer vegetables, especially tomatoes, are beyond compare. And the best peaches in the world are here.

3. The green of everything. On returning from traveling, I am always overwhelmed by the green of our area. At first glance it is almost smothering and then it is embracing.

4. The beaches, may God bless them.

SANDRA STORM
[JUDGE/COMMUNITY VOLUNTEER]

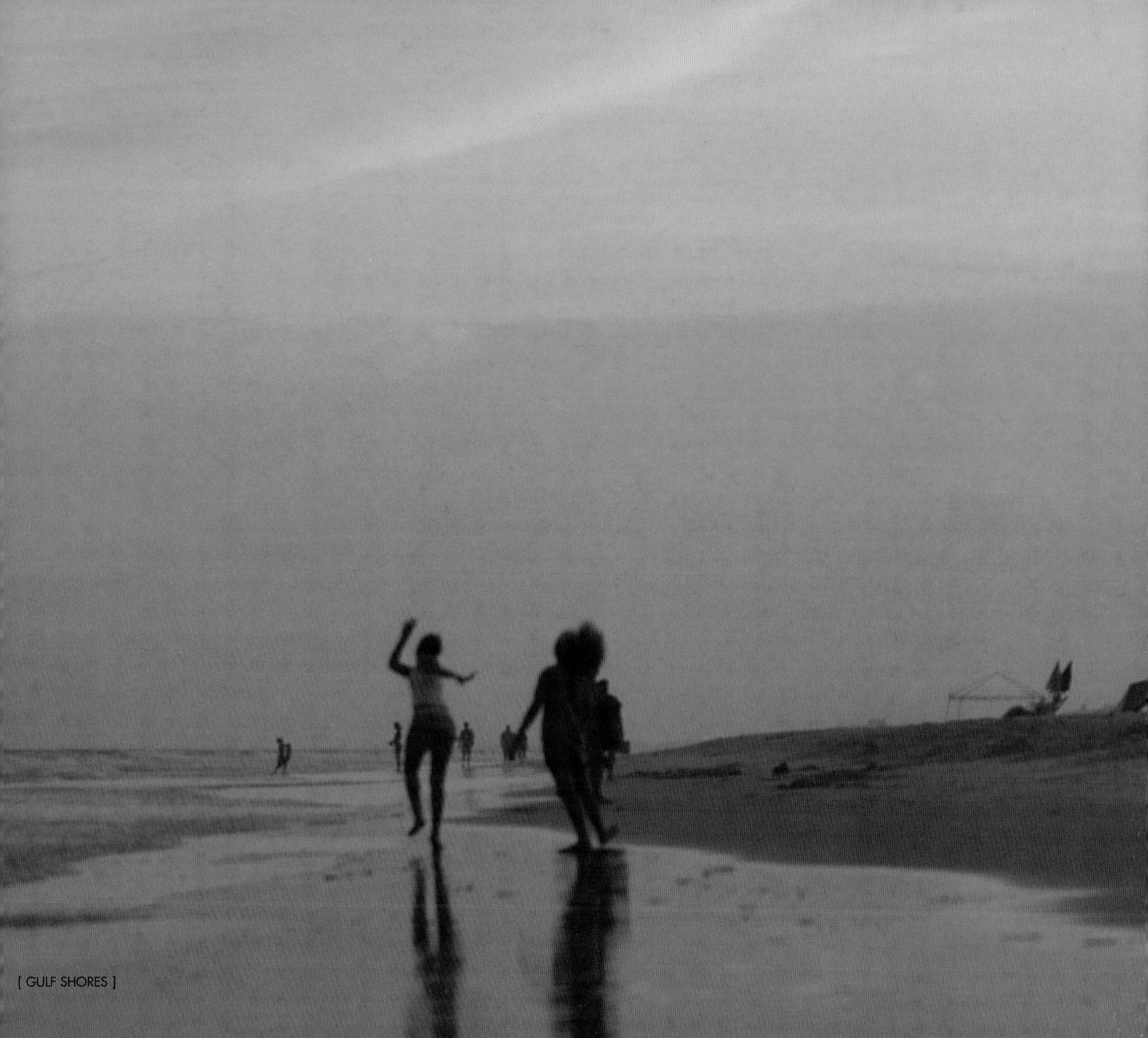

[GULF SHORES]

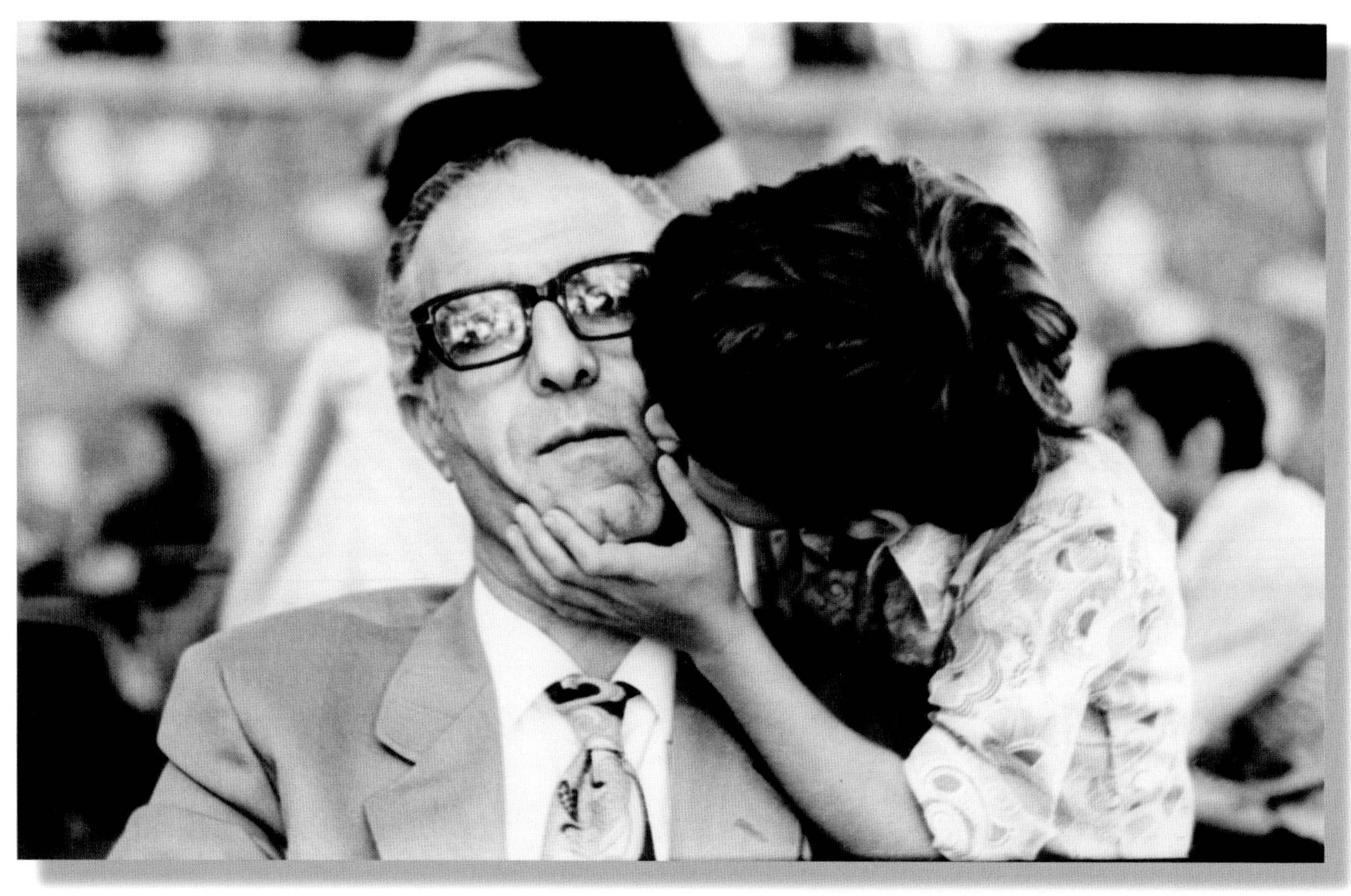

Dedication

To my father, Kerridean Shamsi-Basha

1917 - 2005

Now that Alabama is my home, I still remember those warm and tender moments of my life back in Syria, moments which shaped me into what I am today. The following explains my love for this place.

The hallway to Dad's library in our first-floor flat in Damascus seemed to go for miles as I dodged the furniture pieces, dashing into the room lined with book shelves in every direction. Mother was chasing me as fast as her little feet could carry her, screaming, "Come here you misbehaving little troublemaker." Sitting in the corner of the room was a familiar sight, my dad in his "Abaya," a camelhair house robe, reading. Never slowing down, I continued my run into him. Smiling, he opens the Abaya, and I jump onto his chest, which seemed to my seven-year-old body the size of a small oasis. He closes the Abaya and returns to reading. I lay there still as a rock listening to the rhythm of his heartbeat. From my dark and cozy cocoon, I could hear Mother entering the room and asking Dad my whereabouts. He acts innocent of seeing me. Mother sounds doubtful as he assures her that I might be hiding in another room. I hear her moving a chair, then departing. As her footsteps fade, Dad starts laughing. His chest starts vibrating in a defining, welcome noise as he opens the Abaya and looks at me with his loving eyes. "We did it again," he says as he kisses me and squeezes me so tight I could hardly breath.

This continued for over a year. I would misbehave, a daily occurrence in my youth, and he would hide me from Mother; who was the disciplinarian in the family. As I grew in size, our cover was finally blown when Mother noticed that Dad looked rather large one day.

Kerridean Shamsi-Basha passed away on February 3 in 2005, after eighty-eight years of protecting me and my three siblings from all threats. He was the Poet Laureate of Damascus and has written over fifteen several-volume books on Arabic literature and poetry. A few of his books are taught in Universities and literary Councils all over the Arab world. He spent fifteen years writing an encyclopedia on Arabic proverbs that is considered today the most comprehensive book on the subject. In 2004, he was honored by the Ministry of Culture and Education with Syria's most prestigious literature award, The Outstanding Life-Time Achievement Award, for his efforts in preserving the Arabic language.

I left Syria twenty-two years ago to enjoy education, work, family, and freedom in the United States. Now that Dad is gone, my one regret is that I missed being with him every second that I could. We had a connection that was rare between a father and son. We would talk for hours about matters that ranged from my school work to politics, religion, love, and my obsession in my teenage years: freedom. He managed to lean on his literary fame, but he aspired for me to go where I could literally fly. "You will actually fly with wings someday, and I will taste total freedom through you," he would tell me during my senior year in high school when I was planning my trip to the United States. He wanted me to live life, and live it abundantly.

He was also a master teacher in the department of "love." Like many Mediterranean men, he was extremely passionate about showing his love for Mother. He used to tell me, "Never forget to tell your future wife that she is the most beautiful creature on the planet...and do it every day." He was a believer in the man protecting his princess and making sure all of her wishes come true.

Now, I am raising my three children in Birmingham instead of Damascus. My father always wanted me to come back to Syria until he came and saw life here. "If you are going to live in America, I am happy you chose the South," he would say. A few years before his death, he gave me his blessing to stay in Alabama. He would always compare the traditions of the South to the ones back home, and he was fond of what "family" meant to people of the South.

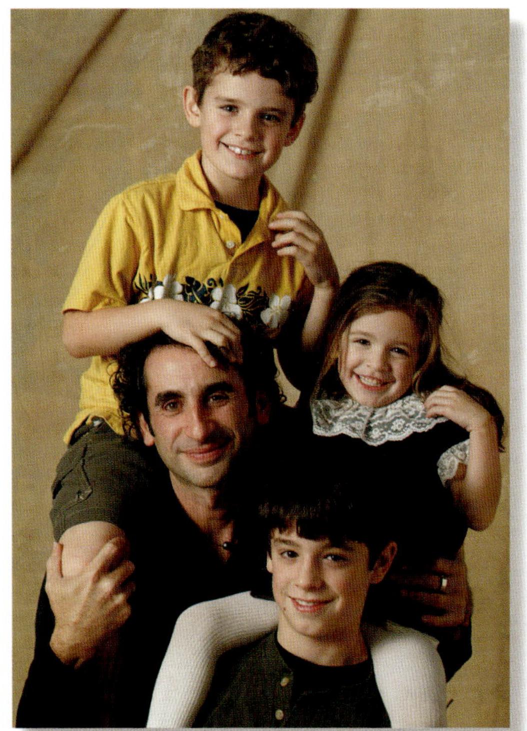

LIESA COLE

My father taught me many lessons, with one resonating the most: "Regardless of any circumstance, always do the right thing." While not being the most profound statement, it has been the hardest one to observe. "If you keep only one virtue in life, make it integrity. You will never regret it," he would always say.

Dad, you lived, and died, with integrity, and while knowing my own faults and limitations, I will always do my best to be as pure and virtuous as you wanted me to be.

I wear your Abaya now, and I shield my own children when they need a place to hide.

I dedicate this book to you; you would have been proud...maybe you *are*.

I love you.

Karim Shamsi-Basha